Victims of Violence

Victims of Violence
For the Record

First Edition

William S. Parkin and Peter A. Collins
Seattle University

cognella®
SAN DIEGO

Bassim Hamadeh, CEO and Publisher
Mary Jane Peluso, Senior Specialist Acquisitions Editor
Alisa Muñoz, Project Editor
Christian Berk, Associate Production Editor
Jess Estrella, Senior Graphic Designer
Sara Schennum, Licensing Associate
Natalie Piccotti, Senior Marketing Manager
Kassie Graves, Vice President of Editorial
Jamie Giganti, Director of Academic Publishing

cognella® | ACADEMIC PUBLISHING

3970 Sorrento Valley Blvd., Ste. 500, San Diego, CA 92121

Dedicated to

Claudia, Ariana and Mateo—W.S.P.

Sancheen, Kaiya and Lucas—P.A.C.

Brief Contents

Detailed Contents

Chapter 8: Victims of School Violence 239

Chapter 9: Victims of Virtual Violence 269

SECTION III   Violence Against the Other   301

Chapter 10: Victims of Hate Crime   303

Chapter 11: Victims of Terrorism   325

Foreword

Steven M. Chermak, School of Criminal Justice, Michigan State University

When I was a graduate student in Albany, New York, 30 years ago, I volunteered for an organization that helped crime victims. It was through this work that I met many survivors—parents, wives, husbands, sisters, brothers, friends, and other family members and friends who lost a loved one tragically to homicide. It is through their willingness to talk about their suffering that I started to better understand the pain caused by such senseless acts of violence. I learned about trauma and the extraordinary obstacles that survivors face following an event. I saw how an incident took a single life, but then how the impact of that event would seep into the existence of everyone who knew and loved the victim. It was difficult to understand how individuals who worked with victims every single day—police officers, prosecutors, defense attorneys, and judges—often exacerbated their pain and suffering because they were not kind, compassionate, or understanding. I do not want to overgeneralize as there were plenty of exceptions, but more often than not the victims I interacted with talked about how the people who were in a position to help them only added to their pain.

Homicide is an important news story. In many jurisdictions, where homicide is a relatively rare event, every single one will be reported in the news. Moreover, even in those jurisdictions where homicides occur much more frequently, a majority will be covered in the news but with different levels of emphasis. Imagine this: you have just learned that your daughter, on the way to school, was shot and killed by a bullet that was intended for another person. In the midst of the shock and sadness, a reporter knocks on your door and wants to put you on camera to give the public a victim's perspective of the homicide. You are part of the news cycle now. No matter how long you spend with that reporter, you will discover that only a small portion of what you say gets in the news, and you will feel that the reporter missed the mark describing who your daughter was and how you feel about the loss. It is not satisfying at all. The good news is that you are likely to get several other chances. If there is an arrest and the case progresses through the criminal justice system, it is likely that the reporter or reporters will contact you with more questions. The bad news is that your continued participation as a news source is not likely to be any more satisfying, and you are likely to feel further victimized by the process.

These experiences with crime victims and their friends and family led me to write a book about victims in the news media. In the book, I looked at how victims are presented in television and newspapers relative to defendants and other crime topics; I also observed how news gets created, and I tried to understand how and why reporters turn to specific news sources and ignore others. My book was published in 1995. There has been a lot of very insightful research published since 1995 examining crime coverage in general, and some work that has further developed our understanding of crime victims. Despite what is now a large body of research that has provided some significant advances into understanding of this important topic, significant gaps remain. This edited volume helps to fill many of these gaps.

Although there are many reasons to carefully read all chapters in this book, I want to highlight two themes that were particularly striking to me. First, it is extraordinarily important to think about the social construction of crime victims and how the labeling of victims will lead to judgments that increase or decrease the status of those victims. Who has the right to be called a victim? Why are some presented in the media as more deserving of this status and others' victim status is contested? This is a difficult issue because society does not view all victims similarly. That is, how a victim looks, their background, their living situation, and their social networks all significantly influence these decision-making processes.

Consider the impact of race on criminal justice and media decision-making. Some homicides will be presented on the front page with photographs and large amounts of description, and others are presented in a short paragraph. Many homicides are ignored. When researchers examine the characteristics of every single homicide that occurs within a jurisdiction for a specific period of time, we learn that a number of factors predict whether a homicide is covered at all and how much space or time it receives. One of the most significant predictors of this decision-making process is the race of the victim. When African Americans and Hispanics are murdered, the media socially constructs these events as being less important compared to when Whites are killed. These decisions may have real-life consequences as researchers have also documented that homicides with defendants who kill White victims are more likely to be arrested, prosecuted, and sentenced to longer periods of incarcerations compared to defendants who kill Blacks or Hispanics. I encourage you to think about these social construction processes as you think about the representation of each type of victim and how the representations are similar and different across victim types.

Second, I found this book to be intriguing because it provides such an in-depth coverage of the victims of so many different crimes, provides theoretical orientations to think about these victimizations, and contrasts with news coverage in *The New York Times*. It is not surprising that the authors find a distortion between research-based and media-constructed realities. This finding is common when content analysis studies compare what gets presented in the news to what is known about crime events. For example, serious violent crime is least likely to occur in every city compared to nonviolent crime, but these events are most likely to be presented in the news. Each chapter provides interesting insights in these processes of distortion. What is particularly troubling though, and should be kept in mind when reading these chapters, is that a distorted understanding of these victims has real consequences—it impacts how the public thinks about them, how the criminal justice system responds to them, and how policymakers legislate to respond to them.

Acknowledgment

We would like to first and foremost thank Mary Jane Peluso, Alisa Muñoz, and Christian Berk at Cognella for their support during this process. In addition, we would like to thank all of the contributors for their hard work and interest in being a part of this project. Their efforts and unique perspectives on violent victimization provide the heart and soul of this manuscript. We would also like to thank Steven Chermak, who is a pioneer in researching and understanding how the interplay between the media and the criminal justice system impacts the victims of crime. Finally, we would like to thank the faculty in the Criminal Justice Department at Seattle University, all of whom have supported and guided us in innumerable ways while we worked on this project.

Victims of Violence

William S. Parkin, Department of Criminal Justice, Seattle University;
Peter A. Collins, Department of Criminal Justice, Seattle University

INTRODUCTION

This edited volume examines violent victimization during the first decade and a half of the 21st century. Each chapter focuses on a specific type of victimization by presenting a literature review of each topic and then a content analysis of articles on that topic from *The New York Times*. As the "newspaper of record," *The New York Times* has been used across many disciplines to analyze what is of interest to society and why (see, e.g., Benoit, Stein, & Hansen, 2005; Clark & Illman, 2006; Golan, 2006; Kiousis, 2004; Kothari, 2010; Lule, 2002). These components, the literature review and the content analysis, allow us to examine how the victims that *The New York Times* chooses to cover may, or may not, represent the typical victim and typical victimization patterns that are reported in empirical research.

The introductory chapter serves as a topic primer, providing important background information on the intersection of violent victimization and the media. To start, we pose multiple questions about the media and its coverage of victims so that the audience can begin to think critically about the information they consume on a daily basis. The intent of many of these questions is to think about what makes a violent victimization newsworthy, that is, what makes it of interest and of value to the public and therefore to journalists (Chermak, 1995b; Moore, 2014; Surette, 1998). We also discuss the varying ways in which one can think about victims and violence. Next, we quickly review several theories on victimization that are part of the criminological literature. Violent victimization statistics for 2001 through 2015 are then presented so that the reader can approach the rest of the chapters with a broad understanding of the frequency and rates of violent crime in the United States. The literature on the intersection of crime victimization and the media is then discussed before reviewing the research methodology used in the following chapters. Finally, a brief overview of each chapter and its topic of focus is provided.

Consider the following crime news stories, all printed in *The New York Times*, somewhere between pages 12 and 20 of Section A. In Ohio, local prosecutors file charges against a 17-year-old suspected of killing three classmates in a school shooting. A picture of fellow students marching in tribute to the dead accompanies the article. The majority of the article discusses the shooter. The final three of the article's 18 paragraphs provides information about the victims and their families (Tavernise, 2012). With no image, another article reports on a Georgian jury verdict. The defendant, who murdered four people, is found guilty on all charges. The not guilty by reason of insanity defense his lawyers argued, failed. Although the defendant's race is not explicitly stated, it is implied that he is African American based on the language used in the article. In addition to the facts of the case, the cost, as well as the extreme likelihood that the defendant will be sentenced to death are discussed. In the second paragraph of the 11-paragraph article, only the names and professions of those murdered are provided, but no other victim information is listed (Brown, 2008). At the bottom of another page, an article details the history of a rape case beginning in Montana. The defendant, a former university football player, is charged with sexually assaulting an acquaintance. A small image of the accused is situated within the text of the article, most of which focuses on the larger issue of sexual assault in the community and how the university and the criminal justice system address sex crimes, especially allegations against student athletes. Two paragraphs of the 20-paragraph article are dedicated to discussing the incident and the actions of the victim. Two more paragraphs detail the allegations made by a separate female rape victim against other student athletes from the same university. In both cases, neither of the victims are named (Robbins, 2013).

A man is convicted of murder and a hate crime in Colorado, having killed an 18-year-old transgender woman. The article provides information about the victim and quotes from her family. In addition, the larger context of using hate crime statutes in cases where victims are targeted for being transgender is discussed. Three photos accompany the article, one in the courtroom of the victim's family, one of the defendant, and one of the victim (Frosch, 2009). In Alabama, a man who was sentenced to death is exonerated. A photograph of him with his supporters accompanies the article, which details the crime for which he was convicted, as well as the case history that led to his release. Claimsmakers, those quoted within the article, discuss the impact of race and poverty on his original conviction (Blinder, 2015). In Mississippi, a private prison is locked down after a riot resulted in the death of a prison guard. A small photo of the victim is placed halfway through the article, while a large photo of the facility at night, surrounded by law enforcement, is positioned above the article. No additional background information about the murdered guard is given (Brown 2012).

Now, consider what readers might infer about the victims of violence presented in these articles? Would they assume a victimization hierarchy, where some victims are more important than others? Could their perceptions be impacted by choices made by editors and journalists, such as who was quoted, what information was presented about the victims, whether the article was on the front page or not, positioned above or below the fold, or whether it contained an image? Based on how journalists write about violent acts, offenders, and victims, could readers be more likely to blame some individuals for their victimization or believe one victim's story is more worthy to tell? What unintended impact might editorial and legal policies, such as not naming victims or providing information about race, have on how the audience understands specific types of victimization? What if a victimization is chosen simply because it can highlight a broader societal issue, such as how the criminal justice system processes sexual assault cases? Does this provide the context users need to understand how one victim fits within a broader pattern, or does it skew our view of who is victimized and how victimization occurs? Each article tells the reader about one event, but what impact might dozens, if not hundreds, of articles over decades tell readers directly, and indirectly, about victims of violence?

These, as well as many others, are questions that we ask you to consider while reading this book. Why, however, is it important to think critically about how the news media covers crime victimization? For one, the "media is critical to public debates about policy issues. The public is overwhelmed with the amount of information available on various issues and is ill equipped to do the types of analysis that might lead to a critical understanding of these issues" (Gruenewald, Parkin, & Chermak, 2014, p. 1). Due to this, the tools we are provided to understand victimization and its relationship with the criminal justice system often come from the media. In addition, as with most pieces of the criminal justice system, what the public knows about victims of violence comes from two sources—either from media coverage or their own personal experience (including friends and family). In fact, the vast majority of people receive their information about the criminal justice system from the media (Graber, 1980; Surette, 1998). Most individuals in the United States have limited or no direct interaction with agents of the criminal justice system (Gruenewald et al., 2014). Even if we move a step away from direct victimization and count the likelihood of an individual knowing a victim of a violent crime, the reality is still that most people, throughout their lives, learn most of what they know about violent victimization through mediating sources, such as traditional news media, social media, and fictional media accounts (e.g., courtroom dramas or police procedurals on television or streaming content services). The types of media we consume drive our perceptions of who the typical victim of violence is, the circumstances in which they are victimized, and even the narratives around those victimizations. Fictionalized accounts can actually be associated with real-world perceptions of crime. For example, there is evidence that individuals that watch crime dramas on a regular basis are more fearful of crime (Dowler, 2003).

Local news services, as compared to national news or fictional programming, provide more information about violent victimization in one's community, but even that coverage is skewed. Lesser offenses, such as simple assault, receive little to no coverage, and more severe offenses, such as homicide, receive amounts of coverage disproportionate to their real-world frequency. That being said, even the amount of coverage that homicides receive is not constant. Whether a homicide is covered, and how much it is covered, can be impacted by the specific characteristics of the victim, the offender, the homicide event, the way the case moves through the criminal justice system, and even the relationships between reporters and their sources.

Take the examples of Casey Anthony and Jessica Rosado, two women suspected of filicide and charged with the deaths of their young daughters, Caylee Anthony in 2008 and Kiana Rosado in 2006. Through 2015, *The New York Times* published 68 articles referencing Casey Anthony's case and three articles referencing Jessica Rosado. All of the articles about Rosado were published in the newspaper's Metro section, signaling the editors viewed the murder as local, not national, news. What could explain such a large discrepancy in coverage? Both mothers were young and their daughters were close to the same age. Was it based on the race of the victims and the suspects? Casey and Caylee were White, non-Hispanic females, while Jessica and Kiana were Black, Hispanic females. Was it because of perceived socioeconomic status? The Anthonys lived in the suburbs of Orlando, Florida, while the Rosados lived in East New York, a neighborhood in Brooklyn known for its high levels of poverty and crime. What about differences in how the children were killed? In the case of Caylee Anthony, she disappeared more than a month before she was reported missing, her mother provided uncorroborated and inconsistent information as to what happened to her, and her body was not found until six months after she was last seen by anyone other than Casey. The medical examiner could not determine the cause of death, but did rule it a homicide. Kiana Rosado was found unconscious after being beaten by her mother and died in the hospital. *The New York Times* only published one additional article after the initial coverage of the death and charges, a 110-word update on the case, stating that Jessica had been deemed competent to stand trial. A person investigating the case would only know that Jessica was found guilty of first-degree manslaughter if they accessed public court and correctional records provided by New York State. Caylee Anthony's case proceeded with great interest by the national media, as well as *The New York Times*, ending with a verdict of not guilty on the murder charges.

The coverage of the case peaked in 2011 for *The New York Times*, and, in addition to focusing on the progress of the trial, articles were also printed on other media's coverage and commercialization of the trial.

Now, if we return to our original question—What drives the discrepancy in the coverage of what appear to be two similar cases of young mothers suspected of killing their daughters?—we are presented with no clear explanation. Side-by-side comparisons, although anecdotal, provide important examples for thinking critically about the media coverage of crime victims. The way that Casey Anthony's case moved through the criminal justice system appears to be qualitatively different from that of Jessica Rosado's. From what we can tell, the length of, and outside media exposure to, the Anthony trial provided multiple entry points from which *The New York Times* could report and reflect. In addition, Casey Anthony's demeanor and "obvious" guilt provided additional pathways for analysis and reporting. However, because *The New York Times* never printed anything about the conclusion to the Rosado case, we are left to guess about all of the possible similarities and differences between the two cases. Also to consider, there are systemic differences in how the criminal justice system engages with victims and offenders that can be connected to race, ethnicity, gender, age, and socioeconomic status. These differences can impact the trajectory of a criminal case, for example the likelihood of a defendant receiving bail, being able to afford their own lawyer, and/or pleading guilty. All of this is in addition to editorial decision-making processes that take into account the types of stories a newspaper's audience is interested in. Newspapers, like all media outlets, need a source of funding to operate, and therefore part of the decision-making process that determines what story to cover and how to cover it is based on potential audience interest as well as cost.

The initial articles from *The New York Times*, as well as the coverage of the murders of Kiana Rosado and Caylee Anthony, provide examples for you to consider what the media chooses to cover, why it chooses to cover it, and how it is then presented. Although, for all of the questions asked, there are no clear answers. We believe, however, that the following chapters in this book present a meaningful contribution to the study of violent victimization in the media and they will allow you to begin to answer these questions on your own. It is important for readers to be critical of the media they consume, to think about what is being presented—or not presented—to them, and why.

VICTIMS

The victims of violence covered in this text are impacted by a wide range of criminal and non-criminal behaviors and include law enforcement officers, the public, exonerees, correctional officers, inmates, juveniles, parents, intimate partners, co-workers, students, educators, virtual social networks, racial and ethnic minorities, and many others. As you will read, there is not always consistency between who these victims are and who is portrayed in the media as a victim. However, it is important to have a shared understanding of who a victim is or what constitutes victimization, as each chapter may introduce some individuals as "victims" that might not traditionally, or universally, be thought of as such.

According to the Oxford English Dictionary Online (2018), there are multiple definitions that can be used to describe a victim and provide avenues for understanding victimization. Even the straightforward definition—"A person who is put to death or subjected to torture by another; one who suffers severely in body or property through cruel or oppressive treatment"—might not be so clear when examined further. Across geographic and temporal locations, who we think of as a victim changes. For example, there are many who would agree that such acts in time of war do not create victims if they occur against enemy soldiers or combatants. Even the second definition—"One who is reduced or destined to suffer under some oppressive or destructive agency"—becomes difficult to universally apply. What constitutes such agency is arguably subjective in nature. Today, most people would acknowledge that indigenous peoples of the Americas were victims of violence by European nations colonizing the continents, murdering, enslaving, and forcibly relocating the peoples who already lived there. At the time, however, these were not seen as acts of victimization, but the will of a higher authority and not the oppressive or destructive agency of territorial expansion supported by the doctrine of Manifest Destiny. A more recent example could include immigration. Society does not universally accept the idea that immigrants might be victims of oppressive and destructive forces outside of their control who are seeking a better way of life for themselves and their families. In this worldview, it is acknowledged that immigrants, refugees, and asylum seekers can be victimized within the countries they emigrate from and the countries they immigrate to. However, the framing of immigrants as victims currently is juxtaposed with competing ideas of immigrants as offenders—seeking to victimize others.

The third and fourth definitions of victim are even more abstract and subjective in nature. What if we apply the idea that a victim is "One who perishes or suffers in health, etc., from some enterprise or pursuit voluntarily undertaken" to a person struggling with drug addiction? Some would unequivocally reject this notion, while others would wholeheartedly agree that individuals who are addicted to a drug and suffer from that addiction are victims. There are those who would argue that addiction is not voluntary, while some might believe that only those addicted to certain types of drugs are victims. Even others might believe that any drug use is voluntary and those who engage in it are in no way victims. The criminalization of drug use, evident in laws and policies that were (and continue to be) prevalent at the local, state, and national levels in the United States during the last half of the 20th century present evidence that those in the United States are more likely to agree with the last statement. However, as current policies shift toward drug addiction as a public health, not a criminal justice, issue, perhaps our society is beginning to accept the framing of drug addicts as victims.

The final definition of a victim is the broadest—"One who suffers some injury, hardship, or loss, is badly treated or taken advantage of." This framing of victimization opens up many more avenues for thinking about and discussing victims. Are individuals who are born into a lower socioeconomic status victims of a country's historic and current political and/or economic systems? What about a person injured on the job because of unsafe work conditions? What about a person who studies at a for-profit academic institution that goes out of business before they are able to graduate? What about a family that defaults on their mortgage and loses their home because of the predatory lending practices of unethical bankers? While these modern examples may not be illegal or violent, per se, they present a much broader interpretation for who might be victimized by individuals and institutions in our society.

Outside of these dictionary definitions, there are multiple ways to understand victimization in criminological and criminal justice research. The most clear-cut is a person who has been negatively and directly impacted by violent criminal behavior—the murder victim, the sexual assault victim, the robbery victim, the aggravated assault victim. There can also be secondary victims of criminal behavior—the daughter of the murder victim, the partner of the sexual assault victim, the friends of the robbery victim, the grandfather of the theft victim, the co-worker of the harassment victim. Communities can also be victimized. One of the central tenets of restorative justice practices is to heal the community or restore it to where it was before the crime or the victimization occurred. The chapters in this book use these more traditional criminal conceptualizations of victimization, but many also expand outside of them in important ways. For example, victimization does not solely have to be the outcome of a criminal event. Law enforcement officers are granted the authority and have legally and un/justly used deadly force against citizens. This, in a broader non-criminal sense, is an example of violent victimization that directly impacts the individual who was killed, but also their family, friends, and community. However, this also puts forth a difficult question that can be hard to discuss in a politically polarized society—If a violent act is legal and justifiable, can it still produce a victim who, along with their family, friends, and community, deserve empathy?

Another example could apply to those we incarcerate in our jails and prisons, where it is the legal obligation of the state to protect and keep inmates safe. Depending on the jurisdiction where a person is jailed or imprisoned, this obligation is met at varying degrees of satisfaction. If a person is violently assaulted in prison by another inmate, or even a guard, how do we discuss and frame this act? Is the inmate a victim of others or are they receiving their just deserts? As still another example, what about individuals who are victimized while engaging in illegal activity, for example, a sex worker who is raped or sexually assaulted? How, as a society, can we understand and support those who are violently victimized, even if this victimization occurs while they break society's codified norms? And how can we research and discuss these important issues surrounding victimization without blaming those that have been physically, emotionally, and psychologically injured?

These are important forms of victimization that also need to be examined and discussed by researchers and society as a whole. This text does not address all of these types of ideas of violent victimization. Instead, we lay a groundwork for the reader to think about how society and the media define and report on more traditional types of violent victimization. We also provide evidence for when the media's portrayals of victimization do not sync with the current research on the topic. Importantly, each chapter discusses what types of victimization are being examined and how they identify articles about these topics in *The New York Times*. One of the strengths of presenting this research as an edited volume is that the reader is presented with different viewpoints from each author, allowing for the consideration of multiple perspectives of victims and violence.

VIOLENCE

As with victimization, most of what is considered violence has a shared meaning within society. The Oxford English Dictionary Online (2018) defines violence in part as "The deliberate exercise of physical force against a person, property, etc.; physically violent behaviour or treatment" and "the unlawful exercise of physical force, intimidation by the exhibition of such force." With these definitions, the use of force is a necessity for violence to occur. The law would concur as inherent in the legal definitions of murder, sexual assault, robbery, and aggravated assaulted is the use of force. All of the chapters in this book include and, for the most part, primarily focus on violence from the socio-legal perspective. Part of this is pragmatic, needing to use near universally agreed upon terminology to search *The New York Times* for cases of such violence. Part of it is so that there is also research from the criminology and victimology literature on such topics to compare and contrast *The New York Times* coverage.

However, as with the definitions related to what makes and who is a victim, the additional definitions of violence open up further avenues to investigate the topic of violence. As stated, most chapters do not focus on these broader ideas of violence, however many authors touch on them to provide insight into the importance of expanding research outside of the traditional research foci of crime events and offender typologies. The Oxford English Dictionary Online continues in part with additional definitions, stating violence is

- great strength or power of a natural force or physical action, esp. when destructive or damaging; violent motion or effect.
- great intensity or severity, esp. of something destructive or undesirable.

In these definitions, violence can be broadly applied to non-human actions such as the weather. Individuals who lose their home, health, and/ or lives to hurricanes or tornados are victims, but they are also arguably victims of violence. Those killed in Hurricane Katrina were victims of an intense, destructive, and undesirable storm. They were also victims of the failures of local, state, and national governments. Also, these definitions do not preclude non-human organisms from befalling violence. Environmental extremists, such as those associated with the Earth Liberation Front and the Animal Liberation Front, groups still active in the first decade of the 21st century, believe that nature in all forms has been subjected to violence by industry, through such things as deforestation and pollution. At the same time, the argument can also be made that societies as a whole, and disproportionately those in developing countries and of lower socioeconomic statuses, are also victims of such violence through severe environmental and climatic changes.

The final definition of violence states that it is "Vehemence or intensity of emotion, behaviour, or language; extreme fervour; passion." This presents the idea that violence does not need to include force against an individual, but some interactions can be so fierce, whether because of how and what words are used, or one's body language, that they are inherently violent. In the criminal justice system, the legal definition of assault or threats would encompass such behavior, although components of these crimes would not define them as violence. It is not difficult to imagine a verbal assault between intimate partners or hate speech against a religious minority that could be perceived as violent within the final definition. Once again, although most chapters do not explicitly measure acts that fit within these non-legal definitions of violence, we challenge the readers to think of how the idea of violent victimization can encompass much more than severe, physical attacks as they read about more typical acts of violence.

THEORIES OF VICTIMIZATION

Criminological theory is often offender focused, asking not why a person is a victim, but why does the offender victimize. Many theorists traditionally shied away from theories of victimization because they did not want their research to be interpreted as victim blaming. That is to say, could the patterns and insights they gained by studying victims be used to blame the victims, or assign some culpability, for their victimization (Lauritsen, 2010; Meier & Miethe, 1993)? Although victimology has become more mainstream, the amount of research on the subject is still overshadowed by the research on offenders and crime events. That is not to say, however, that we have no theoretical explanations for why an individual or groups of individuals are at a higher risk of victimization than others. One of criminology's first theories of victimization, routine activities theory, posits that communities that have larger numbers of suitable targets or victims, lack of capable guardians, and have more motivated offenders, will have higher crime rates. In the original description of the theory, Cohen and Felson (1979) believed that populations of motivated offenders were constant and therefore researchers should focus on victim populations and measures of guardianship. For example, routine activities theory would expect that a community with a high rate of homes that were empty during the day (suitable targets), with few resources allocated to law enforcement or private security (lack of capable guardianship), would have higher rates of home burglaries. To decrease crime, communities would only need to increase guardianship or decrease target suitability. For example, on college campuses that might be concerned with the relatively rare crime of stranger sexual assault, administrators might increase the number of security or police patrols at night, offer safe ride programs from local bars, and provide students with access to self-defense training.

Similar to routine activities theory, lifestyle-exposure theory (Hindelang, Gottfredson, & Garofalo, 1978) would predict that one's risk of victimization, and the type of victimization, can be tied directly to their lifestyle. Individuals who regularly went out on the weekends drinking with friends would be more likely to be victims of a stranger assault, theft, or robbery. An older couple who is home every night of the week by 5 p.m. and rarely spends time in crowded public places has a very low chance of being victimized by strangers (although victimization by family and friends may be a different story). Intuitively, lifestyle theory makes sense and presents a reasonable explanation for the age-victimization curve seen in crime data that mirrors the offender age-crime curve. It also provides a partial explanation for the patterns of victim-offender overlap we see in criminological research, where the same characteristics that predict offending are very good at predicting victimization, and that many people who have offended have been victimized, and vice versa (see, e.g., Jennings, Higgins, Tewksbury, Gover, & Piquero, 2010; Lauritsen, Sampson & Laub, 1991; Wolfgang, 1958).

Two additional theories, which have not been researched as often nor received as much attention, include victim precipitation and deviant place theories. Victim precipitation examines whether there are certain types of victims whose behaviors incite, encourage, or place them in high-risk situations (see, e.g., Polk, 1997; Sobol, 1997; Wolfgang, 1957). For example, an individual who is a repeat victim of aggravated assault may engage in behaviors that antagonize others in social situations where alcohol and/ or drug use is prevalent. Deviant place theory, or the examination of crime hot spots, focuses on physical locations, such as bars, clubs, or check cashing stores, as generators of crime. These places increase the likelihood of victimization of individuals who frequent them based on the types of social interactions that occur there (see, e.g., Meier & Miethe, 1993; Stark, 1987; Weisburd, Groff, & Yang, 2012). Throughout the chapters, the authors may reference these and other criminological and victimization theories as appropriate for the topic they are researching.

VIOLENT VICTIMIZATION IN THE UNITED STATES, 2001–2015

Although each chapter presents data on the specific type of violent victimization discussed, we believe it is important to provide a general understanding of the level of violent victimization that occurred within the United States between 2001 and 2015. There are two data collection efforts in the United States that provide us with some idea about the frequency of violent victimization—The National Crime Victimization Survey (NCVS) (Bureau of Justice Statistics, 2018a) and the Federal Bureau of Investigation's Uniform Crime Report (UCR) (Federal Bureau of Investigation, 2018). The NCVS is a survey of households conducted by the United States Census Bureau in conjunction with the Department of Justice. A random sample of households is followed over multiple years and the residents are asked questions about crime victimization. From these results, researchers are able to extrapolate the estimated number of individuals and households that are victimized in a given year. The Uniform Crime Report is built from data collected by local and state law enforcement agencies that are then submitted to the FBI. The FBI releases the data yearly to the public. The UCR also provides supplementary data on homicides and other crimes, such as hate crimes and law enforcement officers killed in the line of duty.

However, there are limitations to each data collection effort. The NCVS data is only as reliable as its sampling methodology, as is all survey data. Also, the NCVS has changed its questionnaire multiple times over the life of the survey and, in some cases, this makes comparisons across years unreliable. Finally, the survey also relies on the individuals answering the questions to remember and be honest about victimization experiences. For the UCR, the main limitation is that reporting to the FBI is not mandatory and therefore there is missing data when agencies decide not to report their crime statistics. Also, the UCR only includes reported crimes, which means a very large percentage of crimes are not accounted for, as they were never reported. The UCR also changed their definition of rape/sexual assault in 2011, which in certain cases makes it difficult to compare data collected before this date to data collected after.

Using National Crime Victimization Survey data, Uniform Crime Report data, and U.S. Census population estimates, Tables 1.1 and 1.2 provide the frequencies and rates of violent crime victimization from 2001 to 2015. In Table 1.1, we see that the number of homicide victims reported in the SHR was lowest in 2013, with 14,319 homicides, and highest in 2006, with 17,309 homicide victims. During the entire period, there were 236,588 homicide victims in the United States and its territories. When compared across all violent crimes, homicide victims are the most infrequent victims of violence, followed by rape and sexual assault victims, then robbery victims and aggravated assault victims. Simple assault is the most frequent type of violent victimization, with the NCVS estimating that there were more than 65,000,000 victims of simple assault between 2001 and 2015.

Table 1.2, once again ranked from lowest to highest rates per 100,000 people, shows that all victimization rates have decreased from 2001 to 2015. The homicide, robbery, aggravated assault, and simple assault rates peaked in 2006, while the rape/sexual assault rates were highest in 2001. The lowest homicide victimization rates were in 2014 with 4.4 homicides per 100,000 people. Rape victimization was lowest in 2004 with 70 per 100,000 people. In 2011, robbery had its lowest victimization rate during the 15 years covered in this book with 179 robbery victims per 100,000 people. Aggravated assault and simple assault were at their lowest rate in 2015 with 254 and 990 victims for 100,000 people, respectively.

In Tables 1.3 through 1.5, characteristics of each victimization are presented for the different types of violent victimization. Using the UCR's Supplementary Homicide Report data, Table 1.3 provides basic

TABLE I.1 Estimated Frequency of Violent Victimization in the United States, 2001–2015

YEAR	HOMICIDE[a]	RAPE/SEXUAL ASSAULT[b]	ROBBERY[b]	AGGRAVATED ASSAULT[b]	SIMPLE ASSAULT[b]
2001	16,037	476,578	667,736	1,383,667	4,948,619
2002	16,229	349,805	624,391	1,332,518	5,117,836
2003	16,528	325,311	708,376	1,362,267	5,283,096
2004	16,148	255,769	616,419	1,418,657	4,435,215
2005	16,740	207,760	769,148	1,281,491	4,689,395
2006	17,309	463,598	932,397	1,753,819	5,280,616
2007	17,128	248,277	775,522	1,218,923	4,571,462
2008	16,465	349,691	679,789	969,216	4,394,774
2009	15,399	305,574	635,073	1,029,273	3,699,316
2010	14,722	268,574	568,510	857,751	3,241,148
2011	14,661	244,188	557,258	1,053,391	3,957,686
2012	14,856	346,830	741,756	996,106	4,757,902
2013	14,319	300,165	645,645	994,220	4,186,394
2014	14,164	284,345	664,211	1,092,091	3,318,923
2015	15,883	431,837	578,578	816,757	3,179,444
Total	236,588	4,858,302	10,164,809	17,560,147	65,061,826

[a]Contains data from National Center for Juvenile Justice (2018)
[b]Contains data from Bureau of Justice Statistics (2018b)

demographics for each victim, as well as their relationship with the primary offender and the weapon used in the homicide. For the variable of race, the more frequent characteristics for victims were Black (49%) and White (47.1%). It is important to acknowledge that the SHR data used for this chapter did not provide information on the victim ethnicity of Hispanic, a category which would, most likely, disproportionately lower the overall percentage of the victims in the White category. During the same time period, around three quarters of the homicide victims were male or

TABLE I.2 Estimated Rates of Violent Victimization in the United States, 2001–2015 (per 100,000 people)

YEAR	HOMICIDE[a,c]	RAPE/SEXUAL ASSAULT[b,c]	ROBBERY[b,c]	AGGRAVATED ASSAULT[b,c]	SIMPLE ASSAULT[b,c]
2001	5.6	167	235	486	1,738
2002	5.6	122	217	464	1,781
2003	5.7	112	244	470	1,823
2004	5.5	87	211	485	1,516
2005	5.7	70	260	434	1,588
2006	5.8	156	313	588	1,771
2007	5.7	82	258	405	1,519
2008	5.4	115	224	319	1,446
2009	5.0	100	207	336	1,207
2010	4.8	87	184	277	1,048
2011	4.7	78	179	338	1,270
2012	4.7	110	236	317	1,515
2013	4.5	95	204	314	1,324
2014	4.4	89	208	343	1,042
2015	4.9	135	180	254	990
Average	5.2	107	224	389	1,439

[a]Contains data from National Center for Juvenile Justice (2018)
[b]Contains data from Bureau of Justice Statistics (2018b)
[c]Contains data from United States Census Bureau (2016, 2018)

between the ages of 18 and 49. With homicide victims, often a suspect is never identified. This can be seen in the large number of unknown cases found in the relationship variable. However, where the offender and the relationship are known, homicide victims are more likely to be killed by someone they know, as only 11.7 percent of victims were killed by a stranger. Arguably, stranger victimization could be higher, if the number of unknown relationships were disproportionately stranger homicides. Finally, more than two thirds of homicide victims were killed by a firearm

TABLE I.3 Average Homicide Victimization Characteristics, 2001–2015[a]

VARIABLE	CHARACTERISTICS	%
Race	White	47.1
	Black	49.0
	Amer. Indian/Alaskan Native	0.8
	Asian/Native Hawaiian/Pacific Islander	1.8
	Unknown	1.3
Sex	Male	77.6
	Female	22.2
	Unknown	0.2
Age	0 to 5	3.9
	6 to 11	0.8
	12 to 14	0.8
	15 to 17	4.2
	18 to 24	25.1
	25 to 49	48.8
	50 & older	15.1
	Unknown	1.5
Relationship	Family	11.6
	Acquaintance	28.9
	Stranger	11.7
	Unknown	47.8
Weapon	Firearm	67.4
	Knife	12.7
	Blunt object	4.2
	Personal	6.0
	Other/unknown	9.8

[a]Contains data from National Center for Juvenile Justice (2018)

between 2001 and 2015. The second most frequent weapon used, accounting for only 12.7 percent of homicide victims, was a knife.

Tables I.4 and I.5 present data on the other violent victimizations that occurred between 2001 and 2015 and that were reported in the NCVS. For Table I.4, race and ethnicity were separated into three race categories that included non-Hispanics and a distinct Hispanic category. Comparing across type of violence, we see that Blacks, others, and Hispanics made up

TABLE I.4 Average Percent for Violent Crime Victim Characteristics, 2001–2015[a]

VARIABLE	CHARACTER-ISTICS	RAPE/SEXUAL ASSAULT	ROBBERY	AGGRAVATED ASSAULT	SIMPLE ASSAULT
Race/ Ethnicity	White	67.8	54.3	61.3	70.3
	Black	14.4	20.6	19.2	11.8
	Other	6.7	7.2	5.7	6.3
	Hispanic	11.5	17.9	13.8	11.6
Sex	Male	11.8	58.8	57.3	52.1
	Female	88.2	41.2	42.7	47.9
Age	12 to 14	7.9	7.5	6.8	11.7
	15 to 17	9.0	9.6	8.6	9.3
	18 to 20	12.6	10.2	11.3	8.4
	21 to 24	16.3	13.2	13.0	10.3
	25 to 34	17.8	21.0	19.9	20.6
	35 to 49	24.3	21.3	25.1	24.4
	50 to 64	9.7	13.5	13.4	13.2
	65 or older	2.3	3.7	1.9	2.3
Reported	Yes	36.9	60.9	60.6	42.3
	No	62.4	38.5	37.6	56.1
	Do not know	1.2	0.9	1.6	1.5

[a]Contains data from Bureau of Justice Statistics (2018b)

a larger percentage of the robbery victims than the other victimization types. Whites, on the other hand, made up a larger percentage of victims for rape/sexual assault and simple assault. For sex, victims were majority male for robbery, aggravated assault, and simple assault, while females represented nearly 90 percent of the victims of rape/sexual assault. For age, the largest percentage of violent crime victims across all types of violence fell within the 35 to 49 age range. Finally, we see that approximately 60 percent of all robberies and aggravated assaults were reported to the police. Unsurprisingly, this is in stark contrast to the 36.9 percent of rape and sexual assault victims who reported their victimization.

Table 1.5 provides information on the distribution of event level characteristics. For victims of rape and sexual assault, nearly half were victimized at their homes (49.4%). This trend was similar to aggravated and simple assault, as the plurality of victims for these crimes were also victimized at home (38% and 32.85%, respectively). For robbery victims, the differences between those victimized at or near their homes (42.1%) and the top location (commercial place, parking lot, or other public area; 42.3%) was minimal. For the victim-offender relationships, rape and sexual assault victims were attacked by a stranger less than a quarter of the time. Stranger victimization was much higher for robbery (50.9%), aggravated assault (43.4%), and simple assault (36.3%). Rape and sexual assault victims were also disproportionately victimized by those with whom they had an intimate relationship. For the final variable, weapon, no weapon was used in 81.6 percent of rape and sexual assault cases, 46 percent of robbery cases, and 91.4 percent of simple assaults. In these cases, a bodily weapon such as a hand or fist could have been used. Firearms were used 22.2 percent of the time against robbery victims and 25.7 percent of the time against aggravated assault victims. For aggravated assaults, knives and other weapons were used often (25.1% and 34.1%, respectively).

Millions of people in the United States are victims of some form of violence every year, although we may not ever know "exactly" how many people are affected, we can and do produce some trustworthy estimates. While both the NCVS and FBI UCR data have limitations, the findings reported here do provide a foundation upon which we can build

TABLE I.5 Average Violent Crime Victim Event Characteristics, 2001–2015[a]

VARIABLE	CHARACTERISTICS	RAPE/SEXUAL ASSAULT	ROBBERY	AGGRAVATED ASSAULT	SIMPLE ASSAULT
Location	At or near victim's home	49.4	42.1	38.0	32.8
	At or near friend, neighbor, or relative's home	14.0	6.0	11.2	7.0
	Commercial place/parking lot/other public area	18.9	42.3	36.7	30.8
	School	7.6	6.1	7.2	16.9
	Other location	10.1	3.5	6.9	12.5
Relationship	Intimates	27.2	13.9	13.4	13.7
	Other relatives	3.4	7.0	7.2	6.6
	Well-known/casual acquaintances	40.3	18.3	28.1	35.8
	Stranger	23.7	50.9	43.4	36.3
	Do not know relationship	2.7	7.0	5.0	4.6
	Do not know number of offenders	4.1	3.0	2.9	3.1
Weapon	No weapon	81.6	46.0	6.8	91.4
	Firearm	3.0	22.2	25.7	—
	Knife	4.4	12.8	25.1	—
	Other type weapon	1.5	7.2	34.1	—
	Type weapon unknown	1.9	2.1	7.6	—
	Do not know if offender had weapon	7.6	9.7	0.6	8.6

[a]Contains data from Bureau of Justice Statistics (2018b)

comparisons and gain some insight into the prevalence of victimization, as well as how the various categories of offenses and victims are represented in news stories.

THE MEDIA & VICTIMIZATION

As discussed, and as with other elements of crime events, not all victim types are covered equally by the news. All things considered, the most newsworthy are typically the most rare or sensational types of victimization. Sorenson, Peterson Manz, and Berk (1998) state this succinctly:

> If different kinds of homicides were covered in the news media in the proportion in which they occur, the general public might have an accurate sense of the scope and nature of the homicide that occurs in their communities. Some research suggests, however, that cases covered by the media are chosen for their deviance from the statistical norm. (p. 10)

Although there are many publications that discuss varying components for newsworthy stories (see, e.g., Cohen & Young, 1981; Jewkes, 2014; Moore, 2014), we would like to highlight Chermak (1995b), who identifies five characteristics that can impact the newsworthiness of a story—seriousness, incident participants, incident producers, uniqueness, and salience. All things considered, the more serious the crime, the more likely it will be covered. Murders are most likely to be covered, murders with more than one victim, even more so. Incident participants include the offenders and the victims. As discussed below, crimes victims and offenders with certain characteristics are more likely to be covered in the news. Depending on the characteristics, these may increase the likelihood that a low-level crime is covered—for example, an aggravated assault against a famous actor or a judge who is arrested for drunk driving. At a less obvious level, demographic characteristics such as age, sex, and race, will also impact the newsworthiness of a story. Incident producers, such as editors and journalists, may have a shared ideological perspective that systematically identifies specific types of stories as newsworthy, while excluding others. Also, if any component of the crime makes it unique, such as an act of domestic violence by a teenage grandson against their great-grand-father, or an arson at a fireworks factory, the crime's newsworthiness will increase. Finally, the more salient a story is, the more newsworthy it will be. The crime could be salient because it occurs where the audience of the news outlet lives or works, or it could be salient because it fits within a pattern of recent, similar cases that the media has been covering. One car prowl is not newsworthy, several dozen in the same neighborhood over a short period of time could be. All of these criteria should be taken into consideration when thinking about what makes a crime newsworthy enough to be covered by a news agency and, as important, why certain crimes and victims are not covered.

Additionally, in many introduction to the criminal justice system textbooks, how resources are allocated to preventing, investigating, and prosecuting crime are explained through the example of a wedding cake (Friedman & Percival, 1981). Murder, the rarest type of crime, uses up the largest amount of resources within the criminal justice system. Lower level offenses, such as misdemeanors, are the most frequent, yet, per offense, are allocated the fewest resources. This is similar with media coverage of victimization. All media outlets have a finite number of resources to cover the news. Even for *The New York Times*, which is one of the most well-funded newspapers in the world, what they can cover, and how, is limited by the number of reporters they have and the resources they can expend on any one story. Therefore, what is true for *The New York Times* is even truer for local news outlets. Murder victims are prioritized over robbery victims, who are prioritized over assault victims. And even within victim types, coverage is not equal. Race, gender, age, and socioeconomic status play a role in which victims are covered. It is more likely that a rich, elderly White woman beaten to death in her home by a stranger will appear in a newspaper than a poor, young Black man shot and killed by an acquaintance. Other factors can also play a role, such as whether the journalist can get a quote from a family member or law enforcement. Entman (1994) states that the literature on the news media shows that "professional culture, economic incentives, political pressure, and cognitive limitations among journalists and their audiences ensure that the news offer only partial, selective representations" (p. 516).

Evidence that crime victims are not represented in the media at the same rates that they are victimized is documented in the research. Specific to televisions news stories about homicide, Dixon and Linz (2000) found that Whites were overrepresented as victims, Blacks were neither over-represented nor underrepresented, and Latinos were underrepresented. Using multivariate statistical techniques, research has shown that other variables, such as the number of victims, can explain whether a crime story is covered and how prominent the coverage is (Chermak, 1998; Chermak & Chapman, 2007; Gruenewald, Pizarro, & Chermak, 2009). In fact, even a crime type such as murder, which has a high likelihood of being covered, may not be as important as the number of individuals victimized during the crime. Even crimes that the public assumes will be covered, such as acts of terrorism, do not always rise to the level of a newsworthy event. In a study of domestic terrorism coverage in *The New York Times*, Chermak and Gruenewald (2006) found that terrorism "incidents receive little or no coverage in the media. Almost all terrorism incidents, if covered by the media at all, are insignificant news events" (p. 455). The authors also found that relatively few incidents made up a large proportion of the domestic terrorism news.

Comparing official homicide data to whether or not the homicide was covered by the media in Newark, New Jersey, a majority-minority city, Gruenewald and colleagues (2009) found that specific to victims, the like-lihood of a homicide being covered at all increased with the number of people killed and whether the victim was murdered by a Hispanic male offender. However, the amount of coverage was explained by different variables. Increases in the number of articles were related to whether the victim was White, younger, engaged in a deviant lifestyle, and, once again, if there were multiple victims. The amount of coverage decreased if the offender and victim were both Black and of the opposite sex. The fact that the murders of minorities is covered less often by the media has been replicated in other research (see Weiss & Chermak, 1998). Although her sample of news media was outside of the United States, Gilchrist (2010), a

Canadian scholar, found that when matched to coverage of White women, the coverage of Aboriginal women who were missing or murdered was three and a half times less.

Although this book focuses on the print media, as already discussed, research on crime victims in the news has also been conducted for electronic media. This is important as there appear to be differences in how victims and offenders are presented across news mediums (Pollak & Kubrin, 2007). Bjornstrom, Kaufman, Peterson, and Slater (2010) found that in television news White victims were more likely than minorities to be represented, which supported their hypotheses that Whites are given a privileged status over minorities in American society, that owners of media outlets (who are predominantly White) are supportive of content that supports these societal structures, and that the reporting of White victims also supports the traditional idea that the news reports on events that are atypical. Additional research also found that newsworthy victims are those who are White, rich women, either very young or very old, and murdered by strangers (Sorenson et al., 1998).

Why does crime representation in the news matter? In one study, participants viewed a television news program with a story about a man killing his girlfriend (Dixon, 2008). The researchers randomized whether the respondents viewed a story where the victim and offender were White, Black, or unidentified. The study found that respondents were more punitive against future perpetrators when the offender was Black or unidentified and the victim was White, and least punitive against future offenders when both the victim and offender were Black. Such research not only informs us of inherent human biases against victims of violence based on their race, but also of the potential issues the media can cause related to punitiveness and victim blaming, especially when they disproportionately cover certain types of victims.

Other research has found that individuals who consume a lot of news were more likely to view a victim positively if the offender was Black (Dixon & Maddox, 2005). There is also an argument to be made that newsmakers should be cognizant of the impact of the media they produce. As Entman (1994) explains, although a single story on a single day may be an accurate representation of crime news in one's community, the impact of these stories every day over an extended period of time may result in the development of stereotypical views of groups in the minds of the audience. This is especially true when demographic details of both victims and offenders play toward negative stereotypes of minorities in the minds of majority audience members.

The production of crime news by the media is also an important process to understand when thinking about victims of violence in the news. Chermak (1994) discusses another underlying reason for why media coverage of the criminal justice system can result in disproportionate coverage—the reliance of reporters on criminal justice professionals to provide sources for news stories. The relationships that reporters build with actors within the system, such as law enforcement public affairs personnel, prosecuting attorneys, or judges, are symbiotic. Reporters need convenient and efficient access to information to write articles that their audience wants to read. Criminal justice professionals need reporters to tell the story in a way that garners public support for their organization, policies, and cases. Through these relationships, reporters must balance being the watchdogs of the criminal justice system with keeping agencies satisfied that they will cover them fairly, while agencies must balance attempts to frame the discourse and providing information that is valuable to reporters. This back and forth is based on a mutual understanding that at any point agencies can make it difficult to access information and reporters can write stories that are negative about the agencies (Chermak, 1997). Outside of these relationships, other claimsmakers are only used when it is beneficial economically to a media outlet. Chermak (1994) states that "unaffiliated sources, such as crime victims, defendants, experts, and citizens, typically are excluded from the news production process" (p. 579).

DATA, METHODS, & ANALYSIS

Each chapter of the book follows the same format. This systematic overview of each violent victimization type provides the reader with a summary of what the research tells us about each victim type, followed by a content analysis of what *The New York Times* covers. Each chapter ends with a critical discussion of how the differences between the coverage and the reality of such victimization might skew the public's perception of who and what constitutes a typical victimization experience, and how that can impact policy and support for victims within the criminal justice system. Unlike other edited volumes on crime and media, this volume focuses solely on one topic (victims of violence) and one media source (*The New York Times*) allowing for a uniform and in-depth experience for the reader to understand how media coverage can impact our views of crime and justice. One reason we focus almost exclusively on violent victimization is because research has found that almost 85 percent of the crimes they identified in their research were violent in nature (Pollak & Kubrin, 2007).

Although many criminal justice scholars have used *The New York Times* for research, this is the first edited volume that we know of that takes a uniform methodology and applies it to every chapter allowing for a focused examination of the impact that media coverage has on the public's understanding of multiple forms of victimization. Victimization is conceptualized as crime victims supported by the criminal justice system and in some cases those who are victimized by the criminal justice system. To our knowledge, no victimization research has explored this subject in a way that is rigorous and accessible to both academic and non-academic audiences.

Media research can be difficult, given today's ever-changing technological landscape. The focus on *The New York Times* is an attempt to provide a uniform source and method across topics. The newspaper was first referenced as the paper of record, at least within its own pages, in 1926 by Bernard Gimbel, in his commentary on the 75th anniversary of the paper, stating that "*The New York Times* has come to be regarded as the paper of record in every department of news which properly belongs in a modern newspaper." This status, however, is not without question, especially within the 21st century. The media landscape has become more splintered over the last 20 years and the advent of digital news and social media has weakened the status and the power of traditional news sources.

This manuscript presents only a tiny slice of understanding in the complex field of criminal justice and media research that exists today. Similarly, there are many victimization topics that are not addressed in this research that are as important as, if not more important than, the topics covered in this text. For example, how have hundreds of years of violence against Indigenous peoples in the United States, both government sanctioned and otherwise, been portrayed in the media? Are readers provided with a complex understanding of the economic, psychological, and social impacts of violence and the negative effects it has across generations? What about the psychological toll that engaging in military violence has on soldiers? For the individuals who have offended, as well as been victimized themselves, what narrative does the media piece together that allows society to understand and support their experiences?

In addition, articles published from the National Desk were specifically selected. The purpose of this was to keep a focus on violent victimization occurring within the United States. Admittedly, there will be non-U.S. victimizations reported from the National Desk, as well as U.S. victimizations reported from other sections of *The New York Times*. However, we believe this methodology allows us to identify the majority of violent victimization events on which the newspaper reported. The authors of each chapter also focus their analysis on the years 2001 through 2015. We limited the research to the first decade and a half of the new millennium for several reasons. First, our desire was to create a structured methodology within a manageable time period that was also relatively current and of interest to readers. Second, this time period also coincided with some of the largest technological shifts in history, as the propagation of the Internet, social media, personal computing, and smartphones not only impacted society as whole, but also shifted the media landscape. Also, in September 2001, terrorist attacks in New York, Virginia, and Pennsylvania had a significant impact not only on U.S. government priorities but also on media priorities. During this time period, *The New York Times* needed to make room in its pages to report on the War on Terror in Afghanistan and Iraq as well as domestic counterterrorism policies that were at the forefront of political and societal concerns. This meant that the amount of the news dedicated to other topics decreased.

Although the authors of each chapter reflect individually on the limitations of their research, there are a few that we would like to highlight from the onset. Most of the research only focuses on violent victimization events or the total number of violent victimizations mentioned, whether unique or not. Research that only counts events, regardless of how often that event is reported on, may be underestimating the impact that repetition of information has on the readers. Likewise, those reporting data on every time a victimization is discussed may be artificially increasing the newspaper's reporting rates.

A second limitation is that almost all of the authors removed policy articles and articles on research from their content analysis to focus solely on victimization events. These types of articles aggregate information and discuss the overall importance and trends of these types of violence and could have a disproportionate impact on a viewer's ideas of victims of violence, how these types of victimizations occur, as well as who are the typical victims and offenders. A third limitation is that our keyword searches rely on journalists and indexes using the same keywords we use. Although each chapter's authors used an array of keywords in an attempt to capture as many articles that discuss the type of victimization under study as possible, there could be victims reported on in *The New York Times* where different terms are used or, in some cases, the journalists do not even discuss the individual as a victim. However, we believe that if certain terminology is not used in the article, then there is an argument to be made that the readers of the article will not universally view the event as a violent victimization. For example, if the term rape or sexual assault is not used in an article in connection to an incident, perhaps not all readers will, from their point of view, identify the act as a violent victimization.

Also, as previously discussed, we only focus on articles published by the National Desk. The articles that discuss international violent crimes, such as genocide, terrorism, and human trafficking, could be different yet still impact our views on violence occurring in the United States. This limitation could also expand to individuals in areas of the country that receive the New York Regional coverage, who would be exposed to articles that were not part of our National Desk articles, but domestic nonetheless. The final limitation is that our search of National Desk articles, as well as keywords and terms, relies on the indexing provided by the search service and content provider that we used, ProQuest. Often, these services change their search protocols, as well as the key terms and metadata they attach to articles, making it difficult to replicate the studies over extended periods of time. Please keep these limitations in mind as you read through the text.

BOOK OUTLINE & CHAPTER OVERVIEWS

What follows is a brief overview of each chapter so that you will have a general understanding of what the authors are researching and how their work fits within the larger theme of the book. The chapters in this volume are arranged into three sections, the first section, *Violence in the Criminal Justice System*, focuses on violent victimization that occurs during the criminal justice process. Chapter 1, *Victims of Policing*, partially focuses on the unlawful police use of force, currently one of the most salient issues in policing. It is, however, not the only issue within the "victims of policing" focus area worthy of rigorous discourse. The authors briefly outline what American policing is and some of its history and development over the last few centuries. They then turn their focus on the how and why of policing-related victimization. The authors explain why the unlawful targeting of individuals based on race, for example, increases distrust, fear, and negative perceptions of police by the community and how this exacerbates community-police relations. Additionally, the authors argue that police officers can also be victims of policing; as violence towards police and the stress of police work can have both a direct and vicarious negative impact on police, their families, and their communities. As communities experience violence from various points of view (e.g., police, community members, etc.), buttressed by the media's portrayal of crime and victimization, the effects can and do have a lasting effect on public perceptions and fear of crime and the police, which ultimately impacts trust. Important questions follow as we examine the media's portrayal of "newsworthy" crime, victimization, and explore ideas about how to improve community-police relations and, ultimately, decrease policing-related victimization.

In Chapter 2, *Victims of Wrongful Convictions*, the authors take on the important task of providing some insight into how violence is perpetrated by the state through wrongful convictions, along with an analysis of the factors that contribute to false conviction. The authors conclude with some suggested policy changes that target the prevention of wrongful conviction. To varying degrees, wrongful conviction has always been a concern for folks toiling within the criminal justice system, as it, in a very general sense, undermines the overarching goal of justice and the system's legitimacy in segments of the population. Over the last few decades, however, practitioner and public interest in wrongful conviction have increased alongside technological advances in forensic science, such as DNA testing, and the related implications in death penalty and other types of cases. To meet the needs of those believed wrongfully convicted and, in part, to meet the public's growing demand for accountability within the criminal justice system, organizations that focus entirely on wrongful conviction became established. Indeed, the work completed by folks in these "innocence projects" and similar organizations, their partners, advocates, and practitioners have resulted in over 2,300 exonerations nationwide (recorded since 1989; see The National Registry of Exonerations website: http://www.law.umich.edu/special/exoneration/). As the authors note, however, there are many other considerations to be made when thinking critically about wrongful convictions, one such example is how to implement pre-conviction policy changes that decrease wrongful outcomes.

Well over two million individuals are incarcerated within the U.S. correctional systems at any given moment—the second highest rate of imprisonment in the world. In Chapter 3, *Victims of the Correctional System*, the authors open with these staggering details, followed by an observation that most of the general public, especially those who do not know anyone directly affected by incarceration, do not know or understand that people within correctional settings (both the keepers and the kept) can also be victims of violence. In their review, the authors show that our conceptual understanding of victimization within correctional settings is not separate from nor less complex than our understanding of victimization outside of correctional settings. Demystifying this is important, as approaches to our understanding of, and our efforts at reducing, violent victimization in correctional settings can be drawn from a long line of theoretical and applied research. Moreover, since the turn of the century, more rigorous data collection and research efforts have been made within correctional settings, spurred on by legislation. The authors then turn to a content analysis of news articles and delve into the questions surrounding perceptions of violent victimization in jails and prisons and how the media portrays victims within these unique correctional settings.

The second section, *Violence in Everyday Life*, looks at victims of violence who are injured or killed in common, routine settings as they move through their lives. In the first chapter of this section, the authors examine a subset of homicides, those involving youth offenders. Chapter 4, *Victims of Youth Homicide Offenders*, examines both the offenders, murderers under the age of 18, and their victims. From the turn of the 20th century child savers, to fear in the 1980s surrounding so-called juvenile super predators, to a modern understanding of brain development, our approach to managing young offenders is shaped by the paradigm or era within which a particular case is situated. Media coverage of juvenile homicide offenders and victims also influences how the general public thinks and feels about them. In many cases, these offenders are also victims, both of family members and society. Using the Federal Bureau of Investigation's Supplementary Homicide Report, the authors present data on youth homicide offenders and victims, comparing and contrasting empirical data and facts with characteristics of the cases reported on in *The New York Times*. Given the rich data presented in this chapter, readers should think about the reported patterns and what they reveal about our perceptions of children and teenagers who kill.

Intimate partner violence (IPV) affects over 10 million people in the United States every year. The pervasive nature of IPV, defined into four main types—physical violence, sexual violence, stalking, and psychological aggression—has spurred a great deal of new policy and research. As the authors state in Chapter 5, *Victims of Intimate Partner Violence*, IPV can impact anyone's life, but some populations are at a higher risk than others and much of the research has focused on defining its victims. However, there are differences in patterns of incidence and prevalence, which vary based on the type of IPV and other factors, such as sex, age, race/ethnicity, disability, sexual orientation, and gender identity. Beyond understanding risk among different populations, many researchers focus on the ramifications of IPV, from direct physical violence to psychological violence, and the harm that can and does have negative and long-lasting impacts on both the victims and their families, friends, and community. After establishing our current understanding of risk and offense patterns, the authors provide insight into how *The New York Times* reports on IPV, how this reporting likely shapes the public's perception of IPV, and how these perceptions do not necessarily reflect reality.

As the authors note in Chapter 6, *Victims of Sexual Violence,* a very large number of people experience sexual assault or violence in their lifetime, including an estimated one in five women. Understanding the true prevalence of sexual assault and violence, however, is difficult because of high levels of underreporting. Recent social movements, such as the #MeToo social media tag/movement and the Time's Up organization, have brought more attention to sexual assault and victimization. The elevation of sexual harassment, violence, and assault into a national sociopolitical discourse brings with it issues surrounding how the media influences the public's perceptions of survivors/victims, offenders, their various cases, and, ultimately, public opinion. In this chapter, the authors shed some light on these and other issues, beginning with a discussion about the common attributes, or risk factors, shared among many victims of sexual violence, as well as offenders. Next, the authors provide evidence regarding how the media tends to perpetuate myths about offenders and victims of sexual assault, followed by an analysis of how *The New York Times* portrays acts of sexual violence, and then conclude with some general observations about the patterns they uncovered.

In Chapter 7, *Victims of Workplace Violence,* the authors focus on the broad category of workplace violence. As they describe, workplace violence can take many forms, from acts occurring within a work space by unknown members of the public (such as a robbery), to those committed by a person or persons known to the employee, business, or organization, such as an aggrieved customer, a current or ex-employee, or those in a personal or domestic relationship with an employee. Violence can be borne from actions such as denial of promotion, bullying, and sexual harassment. They can result in simple threats all the way to homicide. Furthermore, the negative consequences of workplace violence span from personal injury and death to lost productivity and damage to the organization and community. Whatever the act, combination of victim-offender relationship, or outcome, workplace violence affects an estimated two million Americans every year, including hundreds of homicides per year on average. Are some employees more likely to experience workplace violence than others? Why? The authors provide a rich description of official statistics, followed by an introduction to explaining why workplace violence occurs using popular criminological theory. They then turn to an analysis of how the media reports on workplace violence and whether and to what degree reporting matches the patterns found in the extant research literature.

Thoughts and prayers, gun control, mental health, bullying, and school safety are among the most salient contemporary terms used in discussions surrounding school shootings. In fact, discussions focused on school shootings in relation to school violence are so ubiquitous that it is probably the most common form of violence that people associate with schools, beyond (or directly linked to) the focus on topics such as bullying, sexual harassment, and assault. Indeed, examples such as Parkland, Newtown, and Virginia Tech garnered international media attention, and these and other examples continue to influence much debate on social media platforms, in political discourse at the national and local levels, as well as influence policy change regarding school safety. The focus of Chapter 8, *Victims of School Violence*, goes beyond school shootings and presents empirical information regarding the prevalence of various types of school violence as well as a discussion of risk factors. The authors then turn to a content analysis and provide insight into how *The New York Times* portrays school violence and how the patterns found in the news articles compare to official rates of victimization, as well as some concluding thoughts.

Computer technology and the Internet have changed the way that people interact with each other on a global scale. In the early 1990s, few would have imagined the terms virtual and violence being combined to explain a new set of deviant, harmful, and criminal acts. The pace at which the justice system must keep up with technological advances is crippling. However, as new cases or incidents arise and our collective experiences change, new policies and laws are put into place. To make matters more complicated, the Internet does not have the same geographical boundaries as a nation or state, for example, and one's identity can be easily masked, among many other considerations. This makes prosecuting offenders very difficult and sometimes impossible. Although there are many types of online or virtual crimes, in Chapter 9, *Victims of Virtual Violence,* the authors focus on cyberbullying and cyberstalking. They begin with an overview of the current trends for both victims and offenders, addressing issues with reporting and describing why some people are at a higher risk of victimization, becoming an offender, or both. Next, the authors use criminological theories to help explain virtual violence as well as a discussion as to why it is difficult to identify risk factors. The authors conclude this chapter by comparing and contrasting contemporary empirical research to how these virtual crimes are depicted in *The New York Times.*

In the final section of this book, *Violence Against the Other,* the authors examine violence that is often targeted against victims who are perceived or treated as individuals from society's outgroups—because of attributes such as their race, ethnicity, gender, sexual orientation, gender identity, religion, nationality, or immigration status. In Chapter 10, *Victims of Hate Crime,* the authors begin by discussing the source of hate crime statistics in the United States and many of its limitations. One limitation that is worth noting here is that a hate crime will only be recorded in federal hate crime data if it is identified as such, and reported, by local and state law enforcement agencies. In effect, if an agency and the community that it serves do not value the importance of hate crime statutes, they are less likely to report and charge such crimes. Although the number of states that have hate crime statutes and when they were codified varies, the federal *Matthew Shepard and James Byrd Jr. Hate Crimes Prevention Act* was not passed into law until 2009. The recency of such legislation at the national level speaks volumes about how difficult it has been for victims of hate crime to be adequately protected under the law, even in the 21st century. Therefore, it is not surprising when parts of the content analysis of *The New York Times* articles in this chapter demonstrate that the media coverage of hate crime distorts what is known about the phenomenon from the current empirical data.

The victims of violence in Chapter 11, *Victims of Terrorism*, are researched and discussed infrequently because of an assumption by researchers and policymakers that they are random. To determine whether there are indeed patterns to terrorism victimization, as well as media coverage, the authors of this chapter approach the content analysis using a different methodology. Instead of searching *The New York Times* for articles about terrorism, they use a known population of acts of terrorism and systematically search the newspaper for articles about each event. This method, which was impossible for other chapters to utilize as there were no known lists of victims or events, allows the authors to not only know the characteristics of the acts of terrorism that are covered, but also the characteristics of the acts not covered. Through this analysis, the authors are able to present the results to one of the only pieces of empirical research to date that examines the coverage of terrorism in the media from a victimization perspective.

The final chapter in the book, Chapter 12, *Victims of Human Trafficking*, focuses on a topic that is very difficult for academics to research and for journalists to report on. In many cases, and for myriad reasons, the victims of human trafficking, either for sex or labor purposes, are a difficult population to access. In addition, men and women who may be engaged in illegal activity, such as sex work or being undocumented migrants, could very well be victims of human trafficking. However, law enforcement and the media might focus solely on the criminal behavior that brought them to their attention. First, the authors of this chapter provide a thorough overview of the current state of theoretical and policy-level research on human trafficking and its subcategories of sex trafficking and labor trafficking. Next, they present their content analysis of *The New York Times* articles that are connected to the topic, before comparing their results to the research. Importantly, this chapter also highlights some of the limitations of the study as well as next steps. As this is the last chapter of the book, these are important points to keep in mind not only for this chapter, but also for the research presented in the rest of the book.

CONCLUSION

We invite you to delve into each chapter with enthusiasm and several things in mind. First, there are a lot of comparisons where official or empirical patterns differ significantly from those found in the media analyses. We do not claim, nor do our authors, that *The New York Times* stories or reporters are purposefully misleading, providing false information, or approaching a topic from an overly biased perspective. We believe that the news stories are indeed trustworthy accounts, but when these stories are aggregated over time, they portray people and events in a way that does not necessarily represent official patterns of victimization. Second, we urge you to keep our original set of guiding questions in mind while reading, and we hope that you critically consider why differences between patterns of reporting and empirical data exist. Moreover, we hope that you can focus reflexively on your own thoughts and perceptions of victimization and ask how your perceptions have been, and continue to be, influenced by the media. Finally, at the end of each chapter the authors provide the reader with a list of key terms and their definitions, references to articles from *The New York Times* that are representative of those analyzed for each topic, and questions to focus critical discussion. We hope you find these resources useful as you explore victims of violence and their representation in *The New York Times*.

REFERENCES

Benoit, W. L., Stein, K. A., & Hansen, G. J. (2005). *New York Times* coverage of presidential campaigns. *Journalism & Mass Communication Quarterly, 82*(2), 356–376.

Bjornstrom, E. E. S., Kaufman, R. L., Peterson, R. D., & Slater, M. D. (2010). Race and ethnic representations of lawbreakers and victims in crime news: A national study of television coverage. *Social Problems, 57*(2), 269–293.

Blinder, A. (2015, April 3). Alabama man on death row for three decades is freed as state's case erodes. *The New York Times,* A11.

Brown, R. (2008, November 8). Man guilty in murders at Atlanta courthouse. *The New York Times,* A15.

Brown, R. (2012, May 23). Mississippi prison on lockdown after guard dies. *The New York Times,* A12.

Bureau of Justice Statistics. (2018a). *Data collection: National Crime Victimization Survey (NCVS).* Retrieved from https://www.bjs.gov/index.cfm?ty=dcdetail&iid=245

Bureau of Justice Statistics. (2018b). *NCVS Victimization Analysis Tool (NVAT)* [Online data analysis and documentation]. Available from the Bureau of Justice Statistics website: https://www.bjs.gov/index.cfm?ty=nvat

Chermak, S. M. (1994). Body count news: How crime is presented in the news media. *Justice Quarterly, 11,* 561–582.

Chermak, S. M. (1995b). *Victims in the news: Crime and the American news media.* Boulder, CO: Westview Press.

Chermak, S. M. (1997). The presentation of drugs in the news media: The news sources involved in the construction of social problems. *Justice Quarterly, 14*(4), 687–718.

Chermak, S. M. (1998). Predicting crime story salience: The effects of crime, victim, and defendant characteristics. *Journal of Criminal Justice, 26*(1), 61–70.

Chermak, S. M., & Chapman, N. M. (2007). Predicting crime story salience: A replication. *Journal of Criminal Justice, 35,* 351–363.

Chermak, S. M., & Gruenewald, J. (2006). The media's coverage of domestic terrorism. *Justice Quarterly, 23*(4), 428–461.

Clark, F., & Illman, D. L. (2006). A longitudinal study of *The New York Times* Science Times section. *Science Communication, 27*(4), 496–513.

Cohen, L., & Felson, M. (1979). Social change and crime rate trends: A routine activities approach. *American Sociological Review, 44,* 588–608.

Cohen, S., & Young, J. (Eds.). (1981). *The manufacture of news: Deviance, social problems, and the mass media.* London: Constable.

Dixon, T. L. (2008). Who is the victim here? The psychological effects of overrepresenting White victims and Black perpetrators on television news. *Journalism, 9*(5), 582–605.

Dixon, T. L., & Linz, D. (2000). Race and the misrepresentation of victimization of local television news. *Communication Research, 27,* 547–573.

Dixon, T. L., & Maddox, K. B. (2005). Skin tone, crime news, and social reality judgments: Priming the stereotype of the dark and dangerous Black criminal. *Journal of Applied Social Psychology, 35*(8), 1555–1570.

Dowler, K. (2003). Media consumption and public attitudes toward crime and justice: The relationship between fear of crime, punitive attitudes, and perceived police effectiveness. *Journal of Criminal Justice and Popular Culture, 10*(2), 109–126.

Entman, R. M. (1994). Representation and reality in the portrayal of Blacks on network television news. *Journalism Quarterly, 71*(3), 509–520.

Federal Bureau of Investigation. (2018). *Uniform crime report program*. Retrieved from https:// www.fbi.gov/services/cjis/ucr

Friedman, L. M., & Percival, R. V. (1981). *The Roots of Justice: Crime and Punishment in Alameda County, California, 1870-1910*. UNC Press Books.

Frosch, D. (2009, April 23). Murder and hate verdict in transgender case. *The New York Times*, A20.

Gilchrist, K. (2010). "Newsworthy" victims?: Exploring differences in Canadian local press coverage of missing/murdered Aboriginal and White women. *Feminist Media Studies, 10*(4), 373-390.

Golan, G. (2006). Inter-media agenda setting and global news coverage: Assessing the influence of *The New York Times* on three network television evening news programs. *Journalism Studies, 7*(2), 323-333.

Graber, D. A. (1980). *Crime news and the public*. Westport, CT: Praeger Publishers.

Gruenewald, J., Parkin, W. S., & Chermak, S. M. (2014). Quantitative studies on media and crime research. In G. Bruinsma and D. Weisburd (Eds.), *Encyclopedia of criminology and criminal justice* (pp. 4428-4235). New York: Springer.

Gruenewald, J., Pizarro, J., & Chermak, S. M. (2009). Race, gender, and the newsworthiness of homicide incidents. *Journal of Criminal Justice, 37*, 262-272.

Hindelang, M., Gottfredson, M., & J. Garofalo. (1978). *Victims of personal crime: An empirical foundation for a theory of personal victimization*. Cambridge, MA: Ballinger.

Jennings, W. G., Higgins, G. E., Tewksbury, R., Gover, A. R., & Piquero, A. R. (2010). A longitudinal assessment of the victim-offender overlap. *Journal of Interpersonal Violence, 25*(12), 2147-2174.

Jewkes, Y. (2014). *Media and crime: Key approaches to criminology* (3rd ed.). Thousand Oaks, CA: SAGE.

Kiousis, S. (2004). Explicating media salience: A factor analysis of *New York Times* issue coverage during the 2000 US presidential election. *Journal of Communication, 54*(1), 71-87.

Kothari, A. (2010). The framing of the Darfur conflict in *The New York Times*: 2003-2006. *Journalism Studies, 11*(2), 209-224.

Lauritsen, J. L. (2010). Advances and challenges in empirical studies of victimization. *Journal of Quantitative Criminology, 26*, 501-508.

Lauritsen, J. L., Sampson, R. J., & Laub, J. H. (1991). The link between offending and victimization among adolescents. *Criminology, 29*(2), 265-292.

Lule, J. (2002). Myth and terror on the editorial page: *The New York Times* responds to September 11, 2001. *Journalism & Mass Communication Quarterly, 79*(2), 275-293.

Meier, R. F., & Miethe, T. D. (1993). Understanding theories of criminal victimization. *Crime and Justice, 17*, 459-499.

Moore, S. E. H. (2014). *Crime and the media*. New York: Palgrave Macmillan.

National Center for Juvenile Justice. (2018). *EZASHR: Easy access to the FBI's supplementary homicide reports: 1980-2016* [Online data analysis and documentation]. Available from the Office of Juvenile Justice and Delinquency Prevention website: https://www.ojjdp.gov/ojstatbb/ezashr/

Polk, K. (1997). A reexamination of the concept of the victim-precipitated homicide. *Homicide Studies, 1*(2), 141-168.

Pollak, J. M., & Kubrin, C. E. (2007). Crime in the news: How crimes, offenders and victims are portrayed in the media. *Journal of Criminal Justice and Popular Culture, 14*(1), 59–83.

Robbins, J. (2013, February 7). Trial of former college quarterback accused of rape starts Friday in Montana. *The New York Times,* A18.

Sobol, J. (1997). Behavioral characteristics and level of involvement for victims of homicide. *Homicide Studies, 1*(4), 359–376.

Sorenson, S. B., Peterson Manz, J. G., & Berk, R. A. (1998). News media coverage and the epidemiology of homicide. *American Journal of Public Health, 88*(10), 1510–1514.

Stark, R. (1987). Deviant places. *Criminology, 25,* 893–908.

Surette, R. (1998). *Media, crime, and criminal justice* (2nd ed.). Belmont, CA: Wadsworth Publishing.

Tavernise, S. (2012, March 2). Teenager is charged in killing of 3 at a school. *The New York Times,* A12.

U.S. Census Bureau. (2016). *National intercensal tables: 2000–2010* [Data and methodology]. Available from the U.S. Census Bureau website: https://www.census.gov/data/tables/time-series/demo/popest/intercensal-2000-2010-national.html

U.S. Census Bureau. (2018). *National population totals and components of change: 2010–2018* [Data and methodology]. Available from the U.S. Census Bureau website: https://www.census.gov/data/tables/time-series/demo/popest/2010s-national-total.html

Victim. (2018). In *Oxford English dictionary online.* Retrieved January 2019.

Violence. (2018). In *Oxford English dictionary online.* Retrieved January 2019.

Weisburd, D. E., Groff, E., & Yang, S. (2012). *The criminology of place: Street segments and our understanding of the crime problem.* Oxford, England: Oxford University Press.

Weiss, A., & Chermak, S. M. (1998). The news value of African-American victims: An examination of the media's presentations of homicide. *Journal of Crime and Justice, 21*(2), 71–88.

Wolfgang, M. (1957). Victim precipitated criminal homicide. *Journal of Criminal Law, Criminology, and Police Science, 48,* 1–11.

Wolfgang, M. (1958). *Patterns in criminal homicide.* Philadelphia, PA: University of Pennsylvania Press.

SECTION I

Violence in the Criminal Justice System

CHAPTER 1

Victims of Policing

Gloria Lara, Department of Criminal Justice, Seattle University;
Matthew Hickman, Department of Criminal Justice, Seattle University

INTRODUCTION

When thinking about victims of policing, it is natural for one to envision the most extreme or high-profile forms of police-citizen interaction. For example, the **police use of deadly force** against Walter Scott in North Carolina, the death of Freddie Gray in Baltimore, Maryland, or perhaps the use of excessive force on Rodney King in Los Angeles. While the issue of police violence is a primary concern for the field of policing, several other types of victims of policing are often unidentified. This chapter examines the research literature on violence and victimization that occurs while police engage in their law enforcement duties and how this type of victimization is portrayed by one major news outlet, *The New York Times*. Throughout this review, an emphasis will be placed on victims of violent incidents related to policing, focusing specifically on those who are disadvantaged, minorities, police officers, and overall community relationships. Examining how these victims are affected by police violence, and policing in general, is critical to understanding citizen trust and confidence in the criminal justice system. Importantly, the public victims of policing were often not, until recently, a major focus of the media. This chapter examines how victims of policing are represented in the media, in contrast to other available data.

LITERATURE REVIEW

Prior to determining what defines a victim of policing, it is important to briefly outline a general review of what policing is, its history, and its development. First, to identify victims of policing, one must understand what is meant by policing. There are several functions of the police, but a primary function is law enforcement. According to Davis (1970) "police are among the most important policymakers of our entire society. And they make far more discretionary determinations in individual cases than any other class of administrators; I know of no close second" (p. 61). Due to the amount of discretion police officers have in enforcing the law, it is important to see how, at times, enforcement creates victims. Victimization in this case refers not only to the public in general, but to the officers themselves. In addition, several factors, such as officer characteristics or department policies, can affect both desirable and undesirable outcomes and are also discussed below.

HISTORY OF POLICING

In the United States, policing has evolved to improve safety and performance and to address citizen concerns. When examining the history of policing in the United States, it becomes clear that some of these changes have resulted in higher levels of victimization for particular groups when compared to others. While policing strategies have changed over time, the literature shows that those groups who are victimized remained static.

Kelling and Moore (1988) state that during the political era of policing in the 1800s, the police function consisted of crime prevention and order achieved through foot patrols and a strong collaboration with politicians. Officers responded to citizens directly when there was a safety concern, or they would comply with demands set forth by politicians. Politicians during this era played a significant role and had a lot of power in the organization and operations of policing (Archbold, 2013). Many police officers and chiefs were selected by politicians, leading to numerous problems. While politicians and power had a strong influence in law enforcement, policing tactics still allowed officers to have close ties with the community. These ties increased the relationships between community members and the police, but police received the most support from citizens in neighborhoods with stronger political ties (Kelling & Moore, 1988). Although this policing strategy made some citizens feel safe, the lack of oversight made it easy for corruption to grow (Kelling & Moore, 1988). The strategies used by officers were not systematically observed or evaluated during this time, which raised concerns about the discretion given to line-level officers. The lack of oversight also resulted in victimization, especially with those labeled as outsiders in these communities. Citizens in these neighborhoods felt safe, but there was increasing marginalization of those who violated neighborhood norms (Kelling & Moore, 1998). Minority and ethnic groups were largely victimized because of bribes by individuals in affluent neighborhoods and disproportionate enforcement of laws in immigrant neighborhoods (Fogelson, 1978).

The reform era of policing during the late 19th and early 20th centuries consisted of both internal and external pushes to reform policing strategies. These pushes came with several changes in police tactics. The updated tactics included the use of automobiles and telephone systems (Kelling & Moore, 1998). According to Sherman (2013), over time the goal of law enforcement agencies was to respond to calls for service rapidly and then leave as quickly as possible. After previous issues with gaining legitimacy and removing the power from political leaders, there was a renewed effort to improve policing. Reforms became focused on the enforcement of criminal law to increase legitimacy in the field and to narrow crime control strategies. Although policing was changing, the needs of citizens were still not being met.

The change in police strategy meant a change in how citizens could directly interact with police. The number of arrests dictated whether a crime control strategy was effective or not, as police efforts targeted the apprehension of criminals and, as a result, purportedly prevented crime. The use of technology in this era focused on number of arrests and service or emergency call response time. Although the police function was narrowed, within communities, fear of crime increased. Skogan and Frydl (2004) explain the use of police perception surveys during the 1960s to measure society's increasing fear of crime. While crime rates may drop in certain neighborhoods, community perception and fear of crime impact the way the community feels about policing. Along with a rise in fear of crime, there was an increase in feelings of victimization by minority communities due to police mistreatment and overall insufficient services.

Indeed, during the 1960s and 1970s, research showed that the rapid response to calls for service was not improving crime control (Kelling & Moore, 1988).

As each law enforcement agency has its goals, so does every community and their culture. Every culture has its own set of problems and demands to which the police should be sensitive. Tifft and Bordua (1969) argued that knowledge of the community and neighborhood is essential to the police function because it allows law enforcement to be more effective in terms of crime control. Unfortunately, policing practices used during this era led to an increase in violence and victimization. Minority communities rioted against the police, and women, who also felt victimized, protested because they wanted to be represented by law enforcement and to be given adequate and equal treatment (Kelling & Moore, 1988). However, minorities and society were not the only victims during this period—officers also experienced acts of violence from the community.

According to Kelling and Moore (1988), the reform era was unable to adjust to growing civil unrest around societal issues during the 1960s and 1970s. Several movements during this era, most notably the Civil Rights and Prisoners' Rights Movements, and an increase in immigration, challenged policing policies. Those who connected to these movements were further marginalized through policing tactics due to the type of violence employed by law enforcement officers. To recover from these difficulties, the problem-solving era was dominated by new methods of management and supervision of policing on all levels within a department (Maguire & Shin, 2003). New programs were developed, such as the Safe and Clean Neighborhoods Program, and community policing methods were funded for some jurisdictions. The focus of this policing paradigm was to increase police-public relations through **community-oriented policing** (Kelling & Moore, 1988). It is important to note that, although policing strategies took the public's concerns into account and used tactics favored by the public, not everyone benefitted from such changes. Disadvantaged groups suffered because of a lack of resources and representation within the community. As law enforcement restructured its relationships within communities, there was doubt as to whether such strategies would work

(Kelling & Moore, 1988). Skogan and Frydl (2004) note that, during this time, researchers found that police could not successfully prevent crime without the help and partnership of the community.

Policing has yet again evolved since the problem-oriented and community-oriented eras. There has been a push towards the use of data-driven tactics and technology to address crime. One goal of this modern paradigm is to avoid problems and violence seen during the political era. In increasing the use of data for crime fighting, departments are trying to remove the emotional undercurrent of the criminal justice system and replace it with science (Garland, 2001). Such strategies can include the use of technology and partnerships with researchers. "Actuarial methods in criminal law use statistical predictions about the criminality of groups or group traits to determine criminal justice outcomes for particular individuals in that group" (Harcourt, 2007, p. 17). However, these actuarial methods can sometimes increase the risk of victimization by law enforcement for those who are disadvantaged. For example, crime data shows there is an increase in crime in a particular community, but that community is disproportionately poor and/or minority. The increase in crime then increases police activity in that community, which in turn increases the risk of negative interactions with police and leads to increased risk of violent victimization by police. Despite the good intentions of such policing strategies, this type of policing can increase the victimization risk for such communities.

Alton Sterling, an African American man, was shot and killed by police in Baton Rouge, Louisiana, on July 5, 2016. Partial video of this incident was captured by the community and went viral. The following day in Falcon Heights, Minnesota, Philando Castile's girlfriend captured the aftermath of Castile's deadly shooting after being stopped by police. While the context for both of these police shootings was unknown at the time, the public reacted and protested nationwide. The implementation of police body-worn cameras has become more common in part due to incidents such as these. Body-worn cameras are thought to decrease police use of force and public complaints against the police while improving police-citizen relations (Drover & Barak, 2015). But Lum (2015) explains that while these initiatives are common in the criminal justice field, the rapid adoption of technology can be found to have adverse effects. It is possible that there are some unintended consequences of this relatively new technology, including the possibility of increasing negative attitudes towards officers or departments (McClure, La Vigne, Lynch, Golian, Lawrence, & Malm, 2017). Videos, whether they are from the public or police body-worn cameras, offer limited information following an incident, but are not thought of as that by the public. Many videos lack context to the events that occurred prior to a shooting and events that occur outside the video frame.

Although these videos are an important record and provide needed transparency, they are not the full record. Cases that include a partial record of an incident, which may or may not be evidence of police wrongdoing, increase the risk of victimization to the public and the police. For example, on July 7, 2016, protestors gathered on the streets of Dallas to protest police brutality following Sterling and Castile's deaths. During these protests, Micah Johnson ambushed and opened fire on groups of police officers present. Johnson killed five police officers and injured nine other officers and two civilians. Johnson was said to have been angry about the recent police shootings of African American men and wanted to kill White police officers. Videos from police body cameras and the public are important pieces of evidence in any incident, but they are often not the entire record. The use of these videos needs to be combined with more incident information in order to get a full accounting of an event. As a society, we need to think about this evidence and how to react to it responsibly in order to decrease the risk of victimization and its overall societal implications (e.g., anti-police sentiment, which has increased due to several incidents like these).

TYPES OF VICTIMS AND VICTIMIZATION

When examining the literature on victims of policing, the number of empirical articles that contain information about minority victims is much higher than those focused on police officers as victims and the broader societal repercussions. Because of this, it is important to address all three types identified in this review: disadvantaged groups and minorities, law enforcement, and societal implications such as anti-police sentiment.

Disadvantaged Groups & Minorities

The major focuses of victims of policing in the media are disadvantaged groups and minorities. This includes victimization of the mentally ill, homeless, neighborhoods with low socioeconomic status, and the LGBTQIA+ communities. When examining the role an individual's race/ethnicity, gender, sexual orientation, or socioeconomic status plays in their risk of victimization by police, the literature is plentiful. Chamlin (1989) explains that minorities often have disproportionately more frequent contact with the police. There are many competing theories for this pattern. While some theorize that disproportionate minority contact with the police is a result of racism, corruption, and law enforcement prejudice, others argue that it stems from the disproportionate amount of crime certain groups commit compared to others (Werling & Cardner, 2011). Despite what the cause may be, the fact is that victims of crime are more likely to be a part of disadvantaged groups. This does not mean that all victims of law enforcement violence are victims of criminal activity, but when there is law enforcement violence, it often occurs within the bounds of the law. The literature examined tended to focus on the use of physical force and discrimination based on racial/ethnic minority status.

Generally, neighborhoods with low socioeconomic status and a high proportion of minority residents tend to have negative feelings towards the police (low trust and legitimacy) because of the perception (and reality) of the use of excessive force (Collins, 1998). Smith (2003) explains that officers who police minority neighborhoods are often feared and mistrusted. Such problems contribute to the use of force because of the lack of legitimacy and perceived fear of police. For example, an increase in fear and lack of trust may affect a citizen's attitude or response to an officer, which could lead to unwillingness to comply, resistance to commands, and a greater likelihood of withholding information during an interaction.

Public perception of police officers and use of force varies geographically and by amount of crime in that community (Chapman, 2012). It is often believed that more victims of policing come from disadvantaged communities. Anecdotal examples of this include cases such as force used against Rodney King and the shooting of Michael Brown in Ferguson, Missouri. The U.S. Department of Justice Civil Rights Division (2015) conducted an investigation into the Ferguson Police Department's use of force and biased policing statistics. The report found the department had a substantial amount of racial bias in their daily operations (USDOJ, 2015). Reports such as these not only exemplify the unlawful targeting of individuals based on race, but also promote distrust, fear, and negative perceptions of police in the community, as clearly evidenced in the many organized protests and marches following incidents of police use of excessive or deadly force. Some measures have been taken to mitigate such problems, such as the increase in the adoption of police oversight or review boards; however, the victimization of these disadvantaged groups continues. Understanding the whole story of who these victims of policing are and how they became victims is important. The entire incident needs to be known in order for the media and community to respond appropriately and avoid a response that will only lead to more victimization. Therefore, the U.S. Department of Justice, Bureau of Justice Statistics, has produced several police-public contact surveys to collect data on the type of contact and will soon be implementing a government database from which analysts can review police killings to illuminate the whole story in an incident (Bureau of Justice Statistics, 2002).

Law enforcement agencies have also implemented new ways to report victimization like **biased policing** by creating general professional accountability oversight mechanisms. This type of reporting is important because victims can more easily come forward by reporting these issues online or by phone. The more victims come forward, the more these issues can be addressed in each community or department. Rather than have victims from particular neighborhoods continue to be victimized, information about violence or victimization stemming from police or policing can help to identify and address any problems.

Law Enforcement

Another group of victims of policing who are often overlooked by the media are law enforcement officers. While officers **killed in the line of duty** are often reported in the media, they are rarely seen as victims of policing. From 2001 through 2015, on average, 52 law enforcement officers were killed feloniously each year, not including the 72 who were killed on 9/11/01 (U.S. Department of Justice, Federal Bureau of Investigation, 2018). These incidents may be increasing nationwide as evidenced by the latest FBI Law Enforcement Killed in the Line of Duty (LEOKA) report. As of May 2018, 27 law enforcement officers had been feloniously killed compared to 14 at the same time the previous year (U.S. Department of Justice, Federal Bureau of Investigation, 2018). The majority of these incidents have been through enforcement/investigation (11) and ambush (9) (U.S. Department of Justice, Federal Bureau of Investigation, 2018). Recent ambush shootings, like those in Dallas, have drawn attention to the idea of officers as victims. How are law enforcement officers victims? Due to their authority, some may be skeptical about officers being considered victims; however, police officers can become victims of policing in various ways: being placed in high stress situations, responding to unruly and dangerous citizens, and using physical force. The act of policing and enforcing specific laws in growing and varying cultures can also adversely affect some officers. Many individual and organizational factors influence the likelihood of these types of victimization, such as education, temperament, department culture, and training.

There are several data sources dedicated to law enforcement officers who have died in the line of duty, such as the Officer Down Memorial page (www.odmp.org). The Federal Bureau of Investigation also maintains statistics on the number of federal law enforcement officers killed or assaulted (LEOKA) by state. In 2015, approximately 50,212 officers were assaulted and 41 feloniously killed while 1,336 federal law enforcement officers were assaulted and one was killed (U.S. Department of Justice, Federal Bureau of Investigation, 2018). In addition, several studies have investigated the causes of police victimization. Wilson and Zhao (2008) provide an overview of police victimization and the types of calls, such as domestic disturbance, robbery, and burglary calls, which result in higher rates of victimization. Uchida, Brooks, and Kopers' (1987) study explained that legal intervention calls like domestic disturbance frequently resulted in greater numbers of assaults compared to other calls. While the research conducted is dated, it does portray how victimization of police is related to policing tactics and hazards to which they are exposed.

The amount and type of policing law enforcement agencies choose to employ are often based on the demands and issues of the community served. While some agencies are more responsive than others, the act of policing does cause some officers to become victims of violence; examples range from the mundane, to rare situations such as riots. Brandl (1996) explains that police work as a whole becomes dangerous depending on the situation to which the police are responding, and this affects whether the officer will become a victim of policing.

Specific to use of force, officers can become victims by having to exert force in order to control the situation with which they are faced, resulting in psychological effects from using force or injury from operations. The victimization of police officers is not always due to physical violence. Several studies have been conducted on police stress levels when responding to calls for service or performing other duties (see Hickman, Fricas, Strom, & Pope 2011, for a review). Hickman et al. (2011) explain that both the physical and mental well-being of the officer is affected due to the long-term impacts of policing in general. Stress associated with lethal violence by and against police is typically identified as a greater stressor for officers, but some studies show that administrative stressors (such as one's supervisor) are an equal or greater source. The authors further explain that policing exposes officers to random violence, injuries, or even death in addition to negative effects on officer health and safety.

Family members of police officers are also victims of policing due to the death, injury, or stress experienced by their loved ones. Research on how police families are victims of policing is very limited. Research usually consists of police-involved intimate partner violence. While this is an important effect of policing and police stress, there are several others effects that have yet to be identified. Police families may suffer from policing through vicarious strain or the direct strain caused by violence or death of an officer in the line of duty. Stress can be passed on to close family members because of what the officer is experiencing or through the officer's death. Literature on police family homicide-suicide shows that domestic violence and divorce are significant factors in police homicide-suicide (Klinoff, Van Hasselt, & Black, 2015). Not only can the act of policing affect the officer, but the actions taken in a particular situation can later victimize the officer's family. Police families can also be victimized if the officer engages in any mistreatment of individuals they encounter on the job and this is brought to the attention of the general public. While research in these areas is limited, it is important to identify these issues as being related to victimization of law enforcement or their families.

As noted by the FBI (U.S. Department of Justice, Federal Bureau of Investigation, 2018), most officers are assaulted or killed in the line of duty during investigative/enforcement situations. Law enforcement officers can also become victims of policing due to organizational inadequacies such as poor training. The policies, practices, and training in a department are crucial to an officer's well-being. When thinking about use-of-force victims, keep in mind that most victims of police violence are not subjects of illegal use of force. In the majority of incidents, force falls within the boundaries set by department guidelines and applicable laws. However, there is an argument to be made that those policies and laws still result in the disproportionate victimization of certain societal groups, and those communities should evaluate whether these policies and laws are within the standards they deem appropriate in their communities. These policies and laws still leave officers exposed to victimization by their communities and their departments.

The role of the media is one that is often overlooked in police perceptions (Callanan & Rosenberger, 2011). The ways in which some media outlets report police activity can change the perceptions of those within the community and also affect police perception. This perception is crucial to the response from the community when approached by law enforcement. All of these issues can increase the risk of police victimization.

Community Relationships

Communities can also be victimized by citizen responses to policing tactics (e.g., riots) and police-public perceptions at the national level that may have local implications. Although not everyone is directly affected by police victimization, society as a whole can be indirectly affected. While some communities may not have been directly affected by victimization, the media's exposure of certain law enforcement interactions has societal implications such as anti-police sentiment. This not only increases the risk of victimization on police, like potential ambush killings, but it also has the potential to increase victimization in a community. For example, some communities may not want to report incidents to the police due to anti-police sentiment, or if they do, community members may become afraid due to moral panic caused by media coverage and may intensify interactions with police. Fear of crime and fear of police are important to consider when attempting to understand community victimization.

A number of factors can influence citizen perception of police, including their interactions with police as well as the media's portrayal and coverage of certain events in their communities and elsewhere. Studies show that this perception and fear is affected by the quality of police contacts (Dowler & Sparks, 2008). Additionally, an individual's perception and the community they are in when police contact occurs can shape the outcome of the police-citizen interaction.

Dowler and Sparks (2008) explain that race and ethnicity significantly influence levels of support for law enforcement. Neighborhood disorder is also a contributing factor to negative police perceptions. Dowler and Sparks (2008) examined the attitudes of African Americans and Hispanics towards the police through a survey across 12 cities in the United States. The researchers found that race was related to police satisfaction because, compared to their White counterparts, their level of satisfaction was much lower (Dowler & Sparks, 2008). Despite this, the individual's quality of life was a much higher factor in satisfaction with police than race. Along with these variables, the media's coverage of certain police-public interactions can impact the perception of police. This same coverage helps shape a community's perception of police even if an incident has not occurred in their community. The national media can have local impacts which may increase victimization of those in the community who maintain a neutral stance.

The history of policing shows that there have been several attempts to improve the quality of policing in the hopes of producing better crime control outcomes and a reduction in the rate of victimization by police. Policing strategies have evolved to address the community's concerns and to keep up with changing society. Programs that aim to reduce racial profiling and bias in policing have been implemented across the United States to reduce the amount of victims of policing within disadvantaged groups. The **President's Task Force on 21st Century Policing** (2015) focused in part on training and education in a number of areas such as bias awareness and crisis intervention, as well as de-escalation training and officer safety and wellness.

There is greater awareness of the need to address victimization of policing for all types of victims. Despite this, further research is needed in order to provide some empirical basis for improvement. Each group discussed above is a potential victim of policing based on different factors. Understanding what those factors are and how they are reported in the media is important. This is especially true when trying to address such factors as officer bias, inadequate training, unruly suspects, and misinformed community response. There may be a combination of factors, but comparing and contrasting what we "know" about victimization to what is being reported in the media is important. The next section explains the methodology for the content analysis of news articles. Keywords used to gather the data will be explained along with how the total sample was derived. The types of victims and victimization previously explained will be further analyzed and explained in the discussion portion based on the analysis conducted.

METHODS

In order to identify articles for content analysis, a query was developed to examine victims of policing in *The New York Times* National Desk. The initial query contained the following terms: "officer involved shooting"

OR "officer shooting" OR "line of duty" OR "police abuse" OR "police mistreatment" OR "officer injured" OR "officer arrested" OR "police corruption" OR "use of force" OR (off-duty AND officer) OR (police AND "civil right*" AND violat*) OR ("officer involved" AND (homicide OR murder OR killed)) OR "killed on duty" OR "injured on duty". The query was restricted to the period January 1, 2001, through December 31, 2015. The query resulted in a total of 1,244 articles.

Articles that were not specifically incident based were removed. For example, articles that were not based on a particular incident, but rather on policy changes such as increased arrests for alcohol-related crimes, were not included in this analysis. The largest exclusion of articles were related to the 9/11 terrorist attacks. Several articles in the initial data extraction discussed unrelated court proceedings and the Iraq War. After these exclusions, the final sample included 265 articles.

A total of 10 variables were coded from each article, including *Publication Year, Article Start Page, Victim Mentioned, Victim Focus, Article Theme, Victim Type, Victim Race, Victim Sex, Type of Incident*, and *Victim Precipitation*. All variables are nominal, coded in either binary or categorical format. *Victim Mentioned* indicates whether the victim in the incident was specifically mentioned by name, and *Victim Focus* indicates whether the victim was the primary focus of the article. This is because sometimes articles shift in focus from the victim to something else like the investigation, community response, or the officer(s) involved. The *Article Theme* variable was created in order to capture those shifts. These were developed throughout the analysis process and the most common themes were identified and grouped. The themes include investigation, court process, community response, victim, victim's family, political, and other. *Victim Type* refers to the groups explained in the types of victims section, and *Victim Race* and *Victim Sex* were gathered to provide more information on victim demographics. *Type of Incident* was included to gain more information on the types of incidents covered for victims of policing. The final variable, *Victim Precipitation*, asks "was there any act by the victim, prior to their victimization, which could be seen as precipitating the event?" This was included in order to gain more information on the incident and a possible explanation as to why this victim was a victim of policing and whether precipitation makes a difference in the outcomes of such incidents.

RESULTS

The historical context of the data is an important initial consideration. While victims of policing have received some degree of media coverage across time, police use of force has received increased attention in more recent years. *Publication Years* were grouped into five periods: 2001–2003, 2004–2006, 2007–2009, 2010–2012, and 2013–2015. Table 1.1 lists the article frequencies during each period and demonstrates a sharp increase in published articles during the period of 2013–2015. During this period there were 154 articles, compared to a range of 21 to 38 articles during prior periods. The *Article Start Page* was also an important initial consideration as an indicator of the importance attributed to these incidents. Most articles in the sample came from the front page, A.1 (n = 40). When looking at the *Article Start Page* and *Publication Year* groups together, we see that the majority of articles on the front page were from the years 2013–2015 (n = 33) (Figure 1.1).

TABLE 1.1 Number of Articles by Year

PERIOD	# OF ARTICLES
2001–2003	25
2004–2006	21
2007–2009	27
2010–2012	38
2013–2015	154
Total	265

Table 1.2 presents descriptive statistics for the remaining eight variables. The first two are *Victim Mentioned* and *Victim Focus*. Ninety-seven percent of the articles examined mentioned the victim(s) specifically by

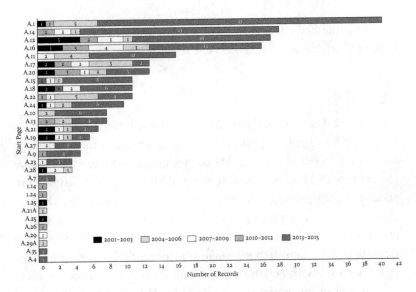

FIGURE 1.1   Article Start Page by Year

TABLE 1.2   Descriptive Statistics for Study Variables

VARIABLE	RESPONSES	FREQUENCY	PERCENT
Victim Mentioned	Yes	258	97.4
	No	7	2.6
	Total	265	100.0
Victim Focus	Yes	163	61.5
	No	102	38.5
	Total	254	100.0
Article Theme	Victim	26	9.8
	Victim Family	10	3.8
	Investigation	84	31.7
	Adjudicative Process	71	26.8
	Community Response	52	19.6
	Political	3	1.1
	Other	19	7.2
	Total	265	100.0

TABLE 1.2 (*Continued*)

VARIABLE	RESPONSES	FREQUENCY	PERCENT
Victim Type	Law Enforcement	55	20.8
	Disadvantaged Group	148	55.8
	LGBTQ	2	0.8
	Family	3	1.1
	Society	23	8.7
	Not Mentioned/Other	34	12.8
	Total	265	100.0
Victim Sex	Male	185	69.8
	Female	12	4.5
	Transgender	1	0.4
	Multiple	41	15.5
	Not Mentioned	26	9.8
	Total	265	100.0
Victim Race	Asian	1	0.4
	Black	107	40.4
	White (not Hispanic or Latino)	8	3.0
	Hispanic or Latino	13	4.9
	Other	17	6.4
	Not Mentioned	119	44.9
	Total	265	100.0
Type of Incident	Assault	36	16.6
	Death	211	79.6
	Assault & Death	10	3.8
	Other Violence	8	3.0
	Total	265	100.0
Victim Precipitation	Yes	62	23.4
	No	203	76.6
	Total	265	100.0

TABLE 1.3   Victim Focus and Article Theme Crosstabulation

ARTICLE THEME	YES	NO	TOTAL
Victim	26	0	26
Victim Family	9	1	10
Investigation	59	25	84
Adjudicative Process	28	43	71
Community Response	35	17	52
Political	0	3	3
Other	6	13	19
Total	163	102	265

name and 3 percent did not. Of the total sample, 62 percent of articles focused on the victim in the incident while 39 percent did not.

The variable *Article Theme* identifies whether an article's main theme is the victim, victim's family, investigation, adjudicative process, the community's response, political issues, or other. Most articles focused on details of the incident and phases of the investigation rather than the victim's background. From the articles analyzed, about one third (32%) focused on the investigation, followed by the adjudicative process (27%) and community responses (20%). Further analysis (Table 1.3) demonstrated that articles in which the victim was the focus were centered on the investigation (36%) followed by the community's response (21%).

Looking at *Victim Type* group, just over one half (56%) of *The New York Times* National Desk articles on victims of policing reported about victims from disadvantaged groups. For example, Kelly Thomas, a homeless individual suffering from mental illnesses, succumbed to his injuries following police use of force in Fullerton, California, in 2011. The next most frequently covered group was law enforcement officers killed or injured in the line of duty (21%)—for example, the fatal shooting of two Mississippi officers and a K-9 officer in 2015, and the killing of a New Mexico officer by a known gang member following a traffic stop in 2015. Thirteen percent of the articles did not mention any information about whether the victim was homeless or was from any particular community or group.

In terms of victim demographics, 70 percent of the victims identified were male and only 4.5 percent were female. These victims included Suzie Marie Pena, a toddler who was killed by a stray bullet from police in 2012; Tamir Rice who was shot and killed in 2014; and Freddie Gray who was killed in 2015. In nearly half (45%) of the articles, the victim's race was not mentioned, while 40 percent were cited as Black.

The *Type of Incident* was recorded using the following categories: death, assault, other violence, and both assault and death in one incident. Eight in 10 articles reported a death (80%), and another 17 percent reported an assault.

Victim Precipitation was recorded when an article reported any act by the victim, prior to their victimization, which could be seen as precipitating the event. As previously mentioned, factors such as community perceptions and fear of crime gathered from the media's coverage of incidents can affect how citizens respond when being contacted by police. About one quarter (23%) of the articles mentioned some form of victim precipitation. For example, an article may indicate that the citizen had a weapon and would not comply with the officer's instruction or that the officer was assaulted by the citizen which led the officer to use force.

A cross-tabulation between *Victim Type* and *Type of Incident* shows that *The New York Times* reported the most on victims of policing who were from disadvantaged groups and died (49%), followed by law enforcement officers who were killed (16%) (Table 1.4). Together, these two groups compose about two thirds of the articles studied.

DISCUSSION

This analysis of 265 *The New York Times* articles reporting on victims of policing over a 15-year period gives some insight into the types of victims and incidents that are deemed "newsworthy." The focus of this review was to raise some awareness about victims of policing and how they are being reported through *The New York Times*. Although 97 percent of the articles

TABLE 1.4 Victim Type and Incident Type Crosstabulation

VICTIM TYPE	DEATH	ASSAULT	OTHER	BOTH	TOTAL
Law Enforcement	43	5	2	5	55
Disadvantaged	130	14	1	3	148
LGTBQ	1	1	0	0	2
Family	3	0	0	0	3
Society	9	8	4	2	23
Not Mentioned/Other	25	8	1	0	34
Total	211	36	8	10	265

reviewed mentioned the victim by name, 32 percent focused on the investigation and 27 percent on the adjudicative process, rather than focusing on the victim. There were relatively few articles that only focused on the victims (10%) or their family (4%). This is somewhat disappointing, since, as discussed in the literature review, the victim's family can also be victimized, both physically and psychologically.

In addition, not all articles mentioned the type of victim or any victim characteristics. For example, many failed to list the victim's background or related information. In terms of the victim's race, most of the articles mentioned the victim's race if he or she was Black (40%); if the victim was not Black, race was not mentioned (45%). For example, most of the articles examined discussed the cases of Eric Garner, Michael Brown, and Freddie Gray. Several of the articles reporting on any incident that occurred after the Michael Brown incident mentioned Ferguson, Missouri, in some way or another. The authors often focused on the details of the Brown incident rather than the incident on which they were reporting.

While the incidents reported by *The New York Times* are likely not representative of all victims of policing, the articles that are published reflect current police-community tension nationwide (as seen, for example, in the spike of coverage during the period of 2013–2015). The ability to identify the population of victims of policing has also been limited until recently. Data dashboards and databases created by *The Washington Post* and *The Guardian* have begun tracking the number of citizens killed by police nationwide. The problem with these databases is the lack of clarity or context provided. Not all the deaths listed in these interactive digital databases resulted from use of excessive force; some were justified or within the policy of the department. This information is not presented, which has the potential to negatively impact police-community relations.

The types of victims that appear most frequently in the articles are those from disadvantaged populations, as well as law enforcement officers, and the incidents reported most often resulted in death and/or assault. Although these issues are currently being reported on by multiple media outlets, not all victims of policing are comprehensively represented by *The New York Times*. For example, only one article mentioned any victims from the LGBTQIA+ community, yet there were six such incidents in 2015 that stemmed from police violence (Waters, Jindasurat, & Wolfe, 2016). Families of the victims are also underrepresented in reporting.

Policing can also result in the victimization of police due to the high level of danger associated with the work, but *The New York Times* articles tend to focus on citizens involved as the victims. Both the physical and psychological effects on officers are rarely seen as victimization unless there is targeted violence against officers, such as ambush killings.

If this analysis is compared against actual numbers of victims of policing from 2001–2015, one can see the difference. Sixty-six law enforcement officers were killed in 2015 alone, and *The New York Times* only reported on 55 from 2001–2015. The incidents covered tended to be those involving some degree of controversy. For example, an incident that was well covered involved the two officers in Ferguson, Missouri, who were shot following protests related to the Michael Brown incident.

The investigations and adjudicative processes are important to the general public, especially when it comes to high-profile cases, but there is still a lack of attention given to the victims themselves. Several more recent articles have focused on community responses to victimization, which are usually related to the lack of attention given to victims. Controversial police-citizen interactions are difficult for all parties involved, but when victimization occurs, the media is a major contributor to how the public and police react. Stories that are reported more frequently are more likely to gain attention and more likely to be addressed by politicians and law enforcement agencies. Media reporting can influence the overall relationship between police and communities. A person's trust in the police or fear of crime may be altered due to current events involving victims of police use of force. While it is important to cover these issues to bring attention to any problematic policies and practices, it is also important to have as much information as possible. As a society, learning how to respond to such incidents and what questions to ask is key to getting justice for the victims involved. Victimization that stems from policing is a difficult subject to analyze and understand. The number of victims associated with policing is a "fuzzy" number to begin with, and these victims are likely underrepresented in the media. Community responses are often fueled by the lack of awareness for those who have been victimized in particular neighborhoods and, based on the results of this study, the victims who are acknowledged tend to be from controversial incidents. The important factor in all of these incidents is the victim; it is important to identify them and acknowledge factors contributing to these victimizations.

CONCLUSION

The results of this analysis indicate that *The New York Times* National Desk covered several types of incidents, but controversial cases were more often covered which may have led to the observed spike during the period of 2013–2015, and 2015 in particular. Although victims were mentioned in most of the articles, it is rare that the victim is the focus of the article. It is even rarer to find any demographic information about the victim, until more recent years. *The Guardian's* "The Counted" website lists a total of 1,146 individuals killed by police nationwide in 2015. Most of *The New York Times* articles in 2015 listed the victim's race if they were male and African American, while "The Counted" (*The Guardian*, 2015) lists 584 White victims compared to 307 Black victims. While there is currently a spotlight on law enforcement throughout the nation and related movements such as Black Lives Matter, it is important to give equal coverage to all victims.

The goal should be to decrease victimization for all, regardless of whether they are citizens from a disadvantaged group or law enforcement officers.

Fear-based media typically focuses on articles that create a moral panic and drive community reactions. "If it bleeds, it leads" is a common motto for journalism of this kind. The problem with this practice is that it greatly misrepresents the reality of victimization, which in turn negatively affects policy formation and also works to misdirect resources for services and awareness for all victims. Future research should focus on nonviolent forms of victimization caused by policing for all groups. In addition, it would be important to compare these findings with other newspapers such as *The Los Angeles Times* to examine any differences in the "newsworthiness" of victims. We encourage interested scholars to undertake this important research on the victims of policing.

REFERENCES

Archbold, C. A. (2013). *Policing: A text/reader*. Thousand Oaks, CA: SAGE Publications.

Brandl, S. G. (1996). In the line of duty: A descriptive analysis of police assaults and accidents. *Journal of Criminal Justice, 24*(3), 255–264.

Callanan, V. J., & Rosenberger, J. S. (2011). Media and public perceptions of the police: Examining the impact of race and personal experience. *Policing & Society, 21*(2), 167–189.

Chamlin, M. B. (1989) as cited in: Wilson, S., & Zhao, J. (2008). Determining the correlates of police victimization: An analysis of organizational level factors on injurious assaults. *Journal of Criminal Justice, 36*, 461–468.

Chapman, C. (2012). Use of force in minority communities is related to police education, age, experience, and ethnicity. *Police Practice & Research, 13*(5), 421–436.

Collins, A. (1998). *Shielded from justice: Police brutality and accountability in the United States*. New York: Human Rights Watch.

Davis, K. (1970). Discretionary justice. *Journal of Legal Education, 23*(1), 56–62.

Dowler, K., & Sparks, R. (2008). Victimization, contact with police, and neighborhood conditions: Reconsidering African American and Hispanic attitudes toward the police. *Police Practice & Research, 9*(5), 395–415.

Drover, P., & Barak, A. (2015). Leading an experiment in police body-worn video cameras. *International Criminal Justice Review, 25*(1), 80–97.

Fogelson, R. M. (1978) as cited in: Reiner, R. (1978). Big-city police. *Sociological Review, 26*(2), 411–412.

Garland, D. (2001). *The culture of control: Crime and social order in contemporary society*. Chicago: University of Chicago Press.

Harcourt, B. E. (2007). *Against prediction: Profiling, policing, and punishing in actuarial age*. Chicago: University of Chicago Press.

Hickman, M. J., Fricas, J., Strom, K. J., & Pope, M. W. (2011). Mapping police stress. *Police Quarterly, 14*(3), 227–250.

Kelling, G. L., & Moore, M. H. (1998). The evolving strategy of policing. *National Institute of Justice, 4*(1), 1–16.

Klinoff, V. A., Van Hasselt, V. B., & Black, R. A. (2015). Homicide-suicide in police families: An analysis of cases from 2007–2014. *Journal of Forensic Practice, 17*(2), 101–116.

Lum, C. (2015). Body-worn cameras: Rapid adoption in low-information environment? *Center for Evidence-based Crime Policy, Translational Criminology.* Retrieved from http://cebcp.org/wp-content/TCmagazine/TC8-Spring2015

Maguire, E. R., & Shin, Y. (2003). Structural change in large police agencies during the 1990s. *Policing: An International Journal of Police Strategies & Management, 26*(2), 251–275.

McClure, D., La Vigne, N., Lynch, M., Golian, L., Lawrence, D., & Malm, A. (2017). *How body cameras affect community members' perceptions of the police.* Washington, DC: Urban Institute.

President's Task Force on 21st Century Policing. (2015). *Final report of the President's Task Force on 21st Century Policing.* Washington, DC: Office of Community Oriented Policing Services.

Sherman, L.W. (2013). *The rise of evidence-based policing: Targeting, testing, and tracking.* Chicago, IL: The University of Chicago.

Skogan, W., & Frydl, K. (2004). *Fairness and effectiveness in policing: The evidence.* Washington, DC: National Academies Press.

Smith, G. (2003). Actions for damages against the police and attitudes of claimants. *Policing & Society, 13*(4), 413–422.

The Guardian. (2015). The counted. Retrieved from https://www.theguardian.com/us-news/ng-interactive/2015/jun/01/the-counted-police-killings-us-database

Tifft, L. L., & Bordua, D. J. (1969). Police organization and future research. *Journal of Research in Crime & Delinquency, 6*(2), 167–176.

Uchida, C. D., Brooks, L. W., & Kopers, C. S. (1987) as cited in: Wilson, S., & Zhao, J. (2008). Determining the correlates of police victimization: An analysis of organizational level factors on injurious assaults. *Journal of Criminal Justice, 36,* 461–468.

U.S. Department of Justice, Bureau of Justice Statistics. (2002). *Police-public contact survey.* Ann Arbor, MI: Inter-university Consortium for Political and Social Research.

U.S. Department of Justice, Civil Rights Division. (2015, March). *Investigation of Ferguson Police Department.* Retrieved from http://www.justice.gov/sites/default/files/opa/pressreleases/attachments/2015/03/04/ferguson_police_department_report.pdf

U.S. Department of Justice, Federal Bureau of Investigation. (2018). *Law enforcement officers killed and assaulted (LEOKA) Program.* Retrieved from https://www.fbi.gov/services/cjis/ucr/leoka

Waters, E., Jindasurat, C., & Wolfe, C. (2016). *Lesbian, Gay, Bisexual, Transgender, Queer, and HIV-Affected Hate Violence in 2015.* New York: National Coalition of Anti-Violence Programs.

Werling, R. L., & Cardner, P. A. (2011). Disproportionate minority/police contact: A social service perspective. *Applied Psychology in Criminal Justice, 7*(1), 47–58.

Wilson, S., & Zhao, J. (2008). Determining the correlates of police victimization: An analysis of organizational level factors on injurious assaults. *Journal of Criminal Justice, 36,* 461–468.

KEY TERMS

- *Biased Policing:* When law enforcement unintentionally or intentionally polices minority communities disproportionately because of their minority status.

- *Community-Oriented Policing:* A method of policing that emphasizes building and strengthening relationships between law enforcement agencies and the communities in which they work.

- *Killed in the Line of Duty:* When a law enforcement officer is fatally injured in the course of their job duties.

- *Police Use of Deadly Force:* When a law enforcement officer engages in the use of force to the degree that a member of the public is fatally injured.

- *President's Task Force on 21st Century Policing:* Convened through executive order under President Barack Obama in 2014, this task force examined the current state of policing in the United States and produced a final report that provided recommendations for best policing practices.

THE NEW YORK TIMES ARTICLES

Baker, A., Goodman, J. D., & Mueller, B. (2015). Beyond the chokehold: The unexplored path to Eric Garner's death. *The New York Times.* Retrieved from https://www.nytimes.com/2015/06/14/nyregion/eric-garner-police-chokehold-staten-island.html

Eligon, J., Dewan, S., & Perez-Pena, R. (2015). Manhunt is underway after police officers are shot in Ferguson. *The New York Times.* Retrieved from https://www.nytimes.com/2015/03/13/us/ferguson-police.html

Hurdle, J. (2008). Police beating of suspects is taped by TV station in Philadelphia. *The New York Times.* Retrieved from https://www.nytimes.com/2008/05/08/us/08philadelphia.html

Kirk, S. (2007). Police chase ends in death of 2 officers. *The New York Times.* Retrieved from https://www.nytimes.com/2007/11/29/us/29deputies.html

Robles, F., & Blinder, A. (2015). Pastor denounces racism at Walter Scott's funeral one week after police shooting. *The New York Times.* Retrieved from https://www.nytimes.com/2015/04/12/us/walter-scott-funeral-police-shooting.html

DISCUSSION QUESTIONS

1. How might high-profile events, such as the 2016 shooting in Dallas that resulted in the deaths of five officers or the 2016 shooting of Philando Castile, a minority who was killed by a law enforcement officer when he was pulled over, impact the media narratives related to deadly police-public interactions?

2. What are the different groups of victims the chapter discusses that can result from policing in the United States? Are there any other ways in which people may be victimized by policing that were not discussed?

3. Why might law enforcement agencies be slow to adapt the recommendations put forth by the President's Task Force on 21st Century Policing? What are some recommendations you would provide to reduce the number of victims of policing?

CHAPTER 2

Victims of Wrongful Convictions

Karmen Schuur, Department of Criminal Justice, Seattle University; Amy Shlosberg, Department of Social Sciences and History, Fairleigh Dickinson University

INTRODUCTION

Criminal justice organizations have a powerful hand in steering the policy pendulum toward the interests of **due process** or crime control. This chapter conceptualizes wrongful conviction under the lens of the latter approach, insofar as the efficiency of incarceration is a means to the end of controlling crime (Kraska & Brent, 2011). Meanwhile, the pursuit of such goals exercised under the guise of crime control have been said to undercut the constitutional rights of American citizens (Kauzlarich, Mullins, & Matthews, 2003; Kraska & Brent, 2011; Stratton, 2015). In providing context for this understanding of exonerees as victims of the criminal justice system, Kauzlarich et al. (2003) have a helpful framework that defines and classifies violent actions of the state. Part of their definition of state violence is that which "generates harm to individuals, groups and property," and thus produces victims (Kauzlarich et al., 2003, p. 244). On the part of the state however, it is argued that violence meet several requirements. First, it must be the product of action or inaction. For example, state legislatures where there are currently moratoria on capital punishment can actively pass legislation meant to reinstate the death penalty, killing the innocent among the guilty (action), or they can simply continue their state moratorium without formal abolition and continue to allow convicted innocents to die while waiting on death row (inaction). Second, the violence itself is entailed in the duties of the state that provide the basis for community trust (an example of this is the trust placed in police to enforce laws or defense attorneys to adequately protect their defendant from a prosecutor's charges, but failure due to negligence or malfeasance is possible). As a result, state violence will reflect the self-interest of government organizations because violent acts by the state, it is argued, are engaged in for the sustainment of government systems (as an example, the credibility of state prosecutors and judges who have a stake in securing convictions and winning re-election can be maintained, prisons and jails that stand to benefit from the increase in the prison population continue to profit financially) (Kauzlarich et al., 2003). In this manner, the criminal justice system and its constituent parts are responsible for bringing about charges, using their authority to imprison someone with some degree of malicious intent for the purpose of maintaining order, and the stately authority of law. It is in this spirit that this chapter considers wrongful conviction as a violent act against factually and legally innocent individuals.

For the purposes of this chapter, it is important to distinguish between factual/actual and legal/procedural innocence. The former means that someone else committed the crime, whereas the latter involves the overturning of a conviction on the basis of a procedural error by the police and/or the courts. In law, a wrongful conviction is often considered "legal" innocence and often results from an appellate court reversal based on procedural error (Zalman, Smith, & Kiger, 2008). However, many researchers focus on the idea of "actual" innocence, a situation in which an individual did not commit the acts underlying the conviction. It is possible for an **exoneration** to fall into both categories (for example, perhaps a there was a DNA match to another person and there was also a procedural error).

The current chapter examines the popular discourse and news coverage of wrongful conviction and exoneration to determine whether news media coverage reflects the findings of empirical research on the contributing causes of wrongful conviction and the characteristics of victims in each case. By the end of the chapter, the reader will be able to provide meaningful answers to the following questions: "how is violence (in the form of wrongful conviction) perpetrated by the state?" and "what are the constituent elements of court cases that lead to wrongful conviction?" The chapter begins with a review of the current literature on contributing factors to false conviction and takes a special look at **innocence projects** as remediation for state violence. Next, the results from a content analysis will be reported. The content analysis provides a rich review of the thematic elements of past cases and various demographics associated with victims of the criminal justice system as framed by news articles within *The New York Times* from 2001 to 2015. This exercise serves to inform a more practical understanding of the popular discourse on wrongful conviction. Finally, the chapter concludes with policy suggestions that target the prevention of wrongful convictions.

VIOLENCE BY THE STATE

Wrongful conviction can be conceived of through broader frameworks within sociology and criminal justice. The classic crime control ideology constructed by Herbert Packer (1968) is appropriate for describing the goals of crime control ideologues. Those goals are most often efficiency and the retributive repression of crime (Packer, 1968). Wrongful conviction can be thought of as an extension of such goal-oriented behavior on the grounds that imprisonment, and especially the death penalty, is intended to provide a general and specific deterrent effect, thus maximizing its impact upon crime in society (Radelet & Akers, 1996). Secondly, rather than letting a criminal go free to commit more crime and take up more law enforcement and correctional resources associated with a life sentence, a conviction is meant to incapacitate offenders and prevent crime (Packer, 1968). However, such decisions are generally made under the presumption by the state that the defendant is guilty of a crime, an error that is often at the root of wrongful conviction. In this way, it is apt to apply crime control as a scheme for understanding how wrongful convictions proceed (i.e., the efficiency-driven input and output of offenders into a system that keeps them from absorbing criminal justice system resources, all while serving a sentence doled out by the state as 'just deserts'). However, this framework for understanding wrongful conviction lacks an explicit understanding for *why* a social institution would make an error; that is, is this intentional oppression or an unforeseen consequence of state control? By taking a closer look at the correlates of wrongful conviction and exoneration as well as the thematic elements that inform popular conscience of wrongful conviction, this question can be further explored.

Another useful criminal justice framework that brings further nuance to the understanding of wrongful conviction as state violence as already discussed is provided by Kauzlarich et al. (2003). For Kauzlarich et al. (2003), there are two key dimensions, each with two extremes, along which violence can be committed, leaving four possible ideal types of state violence. The first dimension is that of action or inaction (what they call "commission" and "omission," or C and O respectively) by the state. Second, whether the violence committed was explicitly or implicitly (E or I) beneficial to the state (Kauzlarich et al., 2003). To this effect, wrongful state violence is conceived of as a crime by a government enacted actively or through negligence and provides either an indirect or direct benefit to that system. Because the criminal justice system is fragmented into roughly three different processing junctions (policing, courts, and corrections), this framework can be observed at each level of processing, exposing each of the four types. For example, in our courts there is a great deal of implicit omission (OI) violence. This can be observed where structural inequalities to legal resources (such as poverty) can result in an absent or incompetent defense and, later, a wrongful conviction. An example of explicit omission (OE) in court could be exemplified by a forensic scientist who specializes in hair sample analysis, who knows such techniques to be scientifically questionable and still *knowingly* uses the results of a hair sample analysis to provide evidence that convicts an innocent person. As Kauzlarich et al. (2003) explain, "[t]he major distinction between OE and OI is the degree of negligence or facilitation and whether the state has a responsibility to act to reduce the likelihood of harm" (p. 247). At the far end of both dimensions is explicit commission (CE), which could arguably describe the very work of the carceral state and its creation and proliferation of systems (for-profit prisons, surveillance technology) that profit directly from the deprivation and internment of its own citizens.

While there can be arguments made that wrongful conviction can fall into all four types at various points within the criminal justice system, for the purposes of this writing, it can be aptly categorized as implicit commission, where "states or state agencies tacitly support reactions which result in social injury but their connection is more distal than proximal" (Kauzlarich et al., 2003, p. 248). The adversarial process by which would-be offenders are convicted prevents this from being explicit insofar as there is a legal presumption of innocence and the process of fact-finding is built into the adversarial process. These are all tools incorporated into the state's system (implied) and function as part of that system. In practice, however, these tools work in favor of the state by way of various evidentiary exclusions, evidence mishandling, the biased selection of witnesses and jurors, and through witness cross-examination that overwhelmingly favors the case made by the prosecution (Spohn & Hemmens, 2012). Ultimately, "what distinguishes this form of state crime from CE (explicit commission) is the directness of action—the degree to which the state is actively involved in actions that would cause harm" (Kauzlarich et al., 2003, p. 248). In the case of implicit commission, the government implicitly facilitates harm by fashioning few resources for innocent defendants, while securing convictions, lending credibility to courtroom actors, and maintaining the ideology that the criminal justice system works, meanwhile diffusing the benefits of that conviction across the criminal justice system to its various actors.

In contrast, the subsequent gamut of challenges offenders face upon reentering society after being successfully exonerated represents a swing towards the opposite side of the continuum and is more or less an explicit act of omission (OE in Figure 2.1) by the criminal justice system (Kauzlarich et al., 2003). Victims of wrongful conviction have been known to suffer from a broad array of mental and physical ailments after their release due to sustained pressures of the prison environment, and they have very few resources to rely upon after being exonerated (Thomas, 2015; Westervelt & Cook, 2010). Additionally, access to financial security, jobs, housing, and spousal support is strikingly limited in comparison to those who are released from prison after serving a full sentence (Westervelt & Cook, 2010). Looking at the spectrum of omission versus commission in this case, the criminal justice apparatus as well as other welfare agencies are ill-equipped and often reluctant to provide the resources necessary for former "convicts" to rectify their position in society, representing a bureaucratic failure that spans across state agencies and renders the needs of victims invisible and unserved (Kauzlarich et al., 2003). Looking to the wrongful conviction process as well as the post-release period, victims of state violence, in this case, are actually doubly victimized.

WHY INNOCENTS ARE CONVICTED

It may be difficult to believe that a system with many legal safeguards and bureaucratic regulations would be subject to such egregious errors. Nevertheless, the implicit violence of the criminal justice apparatus is well known and now well documented; recent estimates indicate that approximately 1 percent of all convictions are wrongful convictions (Alexander, 2012; Kauzlarich et al., 2003; Krieger, 2011; Olney & Bonn, 2015; Stratton, 2015). The most commonly cited factor in wrongful conviction is faulty witness identification (Garrett, 2011; Krieger, 2011; Medwed, 2006). Witnesses are often used by the prosecution and the defense in cross-examination and later accepted by juries as gospel (usually under the pretense that the witness was at or near the crime scene at the time of the offense), and yet the use of eyewitness testimony has the potential to distort reality and foster confirmatory biases, or **confirmation bias**, among that same jury (Findley & Scott, 2006; Krieger, 2011; Loftus, 1980). A striking example of this dynamic at work is the case of Kirk Bloodsworth, a Maryland man who was convicted of the rape and murder of a 9-year-old girl. The most damning evidence in this case came from witness testimony from two children who confirmed the accuracy of a composite sketch as well as law enforcement tactics that suggestively framed Bloodsworth as having knowledge of the murder weapon (Junkin, 2004). Despite having an alibi, no prior violent felony charges, and multiple appeals for his death sentence and filing a writ of habeas corpus, Bloodsworth was only exonerated after exclusionary DNA evidence was found on some of the victims' only remaining clothing that had been stored in a closet for nearly a decade (Junkin, 2004).

Eyewitness testimony has the potential to be damaging to defendants chiefly because instances of wrongful witness identification have been found to stem from the routine practices of law enforcement and lawyers (Findley & Scott, 2006; Loftus, 1980). One estimate from Medwed (2006) indicates that roughly 80 percent of cases in which retroactive exonerations have taken place had secured their original convictions with the help of eyewitnesses. While this does not single out eyewitness testimony as the only problematic factor, it certainly lends credibility to the contention that eyewitness testimony is not fit for presentation in court (Loftus, 1980). What has come to be known about eyewitness errors indicates that not only can such testimony be susceptible to alteration during recall, but it can be shaped by a multitude of subtle factors. These factors include both the presentation of questions and information as well as the order in which that information is presented (Lindsay & Wells, 1985). The literature regarding the impact of faulty eyewitness recall is among some of the most well-established and corroborated applications of cognitive psychology tested within the court systems (Lindsay & Wells, 1985; Loftus & Zanni, 1975; Krieger, 2011). A meta-analysis of studies that assessed the relationship between the confidence and the accuracy of eyewitness identification finds that the relationship between these variables is, at best, partially supported (Sporer, Penrod, Read, & Cutler, 1995). Results also indicated that there are a host of other factors such as lineup structure, age of the identifier, and exposure to the opinions of other witnesses that need to be considered *in addition to* witness confidence when assessing the accuracy of witness testimony (Sporer et al., 1995).

Applying this research to court cases, one of the most compelling findings comes from studies regarding suspect lineup structures. Lindsay and Wells (1985), for instance, found that sequential lineups are more effective in producing higher ratios of accurate identifications because such processes eliminate the need for relative judgments that often take place during more commonplace simultaneous lineups. On a more granular level, even phrasing has been demonstrated as impactful in shaping perceptions of past events. In one study, Loftus and Zanni (1975) demonstrated that a simple change in grammatical presentation of an article such as a substitution of "a" versus "the" was enough to sway study participants into confirming the existence of otherwise nonexistent stimuli ("did you see *a* broken headlight?" or "did you see *the* broken headlight?"). Similar to framing and suggestion, actual manipulation of evidence may prevent eyewitnesses from producing accurate statements. Wade, Green, and Nash (2010) manipulated whether witnesses saw doctored video evidence of a person cheating or whether witnesses were told that there was evidence of another person cheating. Subjects in the former condition were more likely to express confidence in their assessment that they had witnessed cheating than those who were simply told by a confederate that the other person had cheated. In short, presentation of questions and information within the court is not an inherently objective process and does have the potential to alter the perception of witness testimony.

Findley and Scott (2006) describe another phenomenon contributive to wrongful conviction known as "tunnel vision," in which evidence is selected and interpreted in a manner that is centric to a suspect and that confirms existing biases against them. Due in part to already-warped perceptions of the event upon recall, the cross-examination and police lineup presentation add additional layers of distortion through the biased presentation of suspects and the framing of probing questions (Findley & Scott, 2006; Krieger, 2011). Bandes (2006) claims that a great deal of tunnel vision can be attributed to the actions of prosecutors who act as the legal spearheads that culminate investigatory evidence to convict suspects. According to Bandes (2006), the competition between institutional pressures to zealously and impartially uphold the letter of the law and the more informal requirement to secure convictions serves to create cognitive dissonance. Such dissonance is, ironically enough, resolved through conviction which acts as a measure of success for both the individual prosecutor taking satisfaction in a job well done and for the criminal justice system, where the state has been able to uphold the sanctity of the law (Bandes, 2006). Later on, and because juries and judges are ultimately the ones to officially render convictions, prosecutors are able to justify their cognitive biases against the defendant if their guilt is ever questioned in the post-conviction phase by reasoning quite simply that the judge and jury founded "the truth" (Bandes, 2006).

Another factor contributing to wrongful convictions related to tunnel vision is lawyerly misconduct or incompetence. While the majority of prosecutorial assessments of suspect guilt are rooted in legal factors, a prosecuting attorney's charging decisions are also known to be influenced by "perceptual shorthands" that often inhere stereotypes about the suspect on the basis of their characteristics (race, gender, class, etc.) (Spohn & Hemmens, 2012). Furthermore, political pressures (such as prosecutorial re-election) as well as the professional integrity of the prosecutor play an important role in incentivizing a larger number of and more repressive charges (Spohn & Hemmens, 2012). This results in a "downstream orientation" in which the "prosecutor's concerns about the practical consequences of charging decisions focus on the likelihood of conviction rather than the social costs of punishment" (Spohn & Hemmens, 2012, p. 114). More tangibly, such a mindset can lead to the misrepresentation of evidence, exclusion of evidence that favors the defendant, and overcharging for minor offenses (Krieger, 2011). Acting on behalf of the state, prosecutors wield a great deal of power in potentially victimizing an otherwise innocent person merely through the channels of their supposed duties (if in this case their duties entail securing convictions), and without more willful consideration of the possibility that the justice system can perpetrate *in*justice, wrongful conviction is likely to continue.

Another channel through which wrongful convictions are reached is the use or misuse of DNA and other forensic evidence. Although DNA evidence is typically only found in a small minority of cases, with the advent of new technology and greater public awareness of forensic methodology, scientific evidence is rapidly becoming a requisite for conviction (Olney & Bonn, 2015). Also adding to the timeliness of this issue is the fact that in recent years the veracity of forensic science has come into question due to the seemingly overwhelming lack of uniform training, standards, and resources among most laboratories (Collins & Jarvis, 2009; Krieger, 2011; Thomas, 2015). The so-called **CSI effect** is pertinent to this discussion, both providing the standard against which evidence and expert witness testimony in court is evaluated by juries and raising the standard against which appellate juries compare new evidence in favor of wrongfully convicted victims (Thomas, 2015). Rightfully so, this latter scenario describes what has been called the "reverse CSI effect" in that it works against the defendant to keep him or her imprisoned rather than allowing scientific merit to grant greater validity to their innocence (Thomas, 2015). In the conviction phase, DNA evidence that may be improperly collected at the crime scene or is tested using outdated or ill-supported methods provides greater legitimacy. After sentencing and after the victim appeals the charges leveraged by the state, juries of laypeople have by and large come to expect scientific evidence as the only evidence able to eliminate reasonable doubt (Thomas, 2015). This paradox is extremely problematic for the defendant fighting a system that permits a limited range of appellate actions (Mandery, Shlosberg, West, & Callaghan, 2013; Thomas, 2015). In short, victims of wrongful conviction are victims along several axes: perceptual inaccuracies, political factors, prosecutorial misconduct, shifting standards of scientific evidence, and even the presentation of evidence. As long as these various practices continue to flow in the "downstream" direction (towards conviction) mentioned previously, and unless courtroom actors take a reflective look at the social consequences of their actions, innocents will continue to be victimized.

Speaking to the ways in which science intervenes to lend credibility to claims of prosecution and defense, there is very little agreement both on what is empirically valid in the context of court and how this information should be used. Scientific evidence that is presented to juries carries weight not only because of the widespread interpretation that science is fact, but also because of the subject experts that represent such evidence. This is also because "scientists frequently find themselves in a competitive environment where strong emotional commitment to their views and sensitivity to finance and funding are essential to career progression—even academic and institutional survival" (Edmond & Mercer, 1998, p. 9). Caudill and Redding (2000) similarly point to the ineffectiveness of current standards in capturing the nuanced definitions of what constitutes valid scientific evidence. Stated quite simply, while there are important implications behind verdicts upheld by such scientific evidence, more important is the debate about how to differentiate between junk science and "real" science when the scientific community itself has so many disagreements on this issue (Caudill & Redding, 2000). For the purposes of this chapter, junk science can be understood as findings and methods that appear on their face to be scientific but stem from un-validated methodology (Thomas, 2015). Among prior investigative examples of un-validated scientific evidence are hair and fiber analysis, bite mark analysis, and dog-sniff lineups, all of which were at one time or another believed to be both useful and accurate methods of suspect identification (Thomas, 2015).

In addition to the informal court dynamics that shape the interpretation of so-called scientific evidence, existing legal statutes have lowered the threshold of what is considered admissible evidence. For many years, the case of *Frye v. United States* (1923) dictated such admissibility by holding that expert testimony was only acceptable if it was generally accepted by the larger scientific community (Huber, 1991). Beginning in the 1960s however, *Frye* was questioned in both tort and criminal courts and was later replaced in many jurisdictions through the decision rendered in *Daubert v. Merrell Dow Pharmaceuticals* (1993). The *Daubert* standard is decidedly broader than that of *Frye*, permitting the admissibility of scientific evidence based upon relevance rather than general acceptance (Black, Ayala, & Saffran-Brinks, 1994; Huber, 1991). Furthermore, *Daubert* recognizes an expert witnesses' opinion as valid, a decision predicated on the assumption that the expert's opinion will be informed by his or her experience within the scientific field at hand (Black et al., 1994). This becomes problematic without proper scrutiny employed by judges and juries, allowing pseudoscience and other un-validated forms of study to make their way into criminal courts (Black et al., 1994).

The lack of consistency in the application of *Daubert*, coupled with shifting standards of forensic science that do not always keep pace with common and judiciary knowledge and the use of science in legal contexts, has the potential to be more harmful than helpful. A study by

Garrett and Neufeld (2009) reviewed 137 separate trial transcripts from the cases of defendants that had since been successfully exonerated with newly discovered DNA evidence. In this study, 60 percent (n = 82) of the cases had relied upon faulty evidence called by the prosecution; within these cases, evidence from serology (examination of blood serum), hair and fiber analysis, bite mark analysis, footprint matching as well as fingerprint analyses were used to convict the defendant (Garrett & Neufeld, 2009). These results, as well as the current debate surrounding whether legal professionals should be the gatekeepers of what is "relevant" science, call for a more uniform standard of what constitutes scientific evidence as well as further study of how and why innocent defendants are ultimately betrayed by scientific evidence (Black et al., 1994; Garrett & Neufeld, 2009; Huber, 1991). The next section will continue the discussion of wrongful conviction by considering the costs borne by the victims of wrongful conviction.

THE COST OF WRONGFUL CONVICTION

The social cost of wrongful conviction and imprisonment has also been well documented, and many exonerees are often treated akin to guilty defendants upon release (Mandery et al., 2013). While the stressors faced inside prison environments are formidable, there is little in the way of remediation for a former prisoner's troubles outside of prison which may include but are certainly not limited to post-traumatic stress disorder, anxiety, depression, loss of financial security, poverty, addiction, and loss of familial and spousal support (Mandery et al., 2013; Naughton, 2014). What's more, fewer than 30 states have legislation that allows exonerees to seek compensation from the state after their release (Thomas, 2015). This figure is further limited by the fact that the process of seeking financial **reparations** is long and difficult; the wrongfully convicted may seek a private bill, a preexisting state statute that demonstrates wrongdoing by the state, or they may file a civil suit (Mandery et al., 2013). In one of the first studies of its kind, Mandery et al. (2013) examined post-release compensation data from the Center for Wrongful Conviction maintained by Northwestern University and found that the amount of money paid to exonerees post-release did impact the potential for post-release offending. More specifically, those who received more than $500,000 post-release demonstrated higher rates of success demonstrated by no convictions within the three-year follow-up period (Mandery et al., 2013). Provisions of resources for those exiting incarceration, guilty or not, is grossly underfunded and often leads to what can be considered as secondary victimization in the form of deprivation by the state (Mandery et al., 2013; Naughton, 2014). Thus, unfortunately for the wrongfully convicted, both ends of the justice system leave them without resources or viable options for preventing imprisonment and or rebuilding their livelihoods after being processed. Luckily, one area in which there is evidence of promise for post-conviction outcomes is the foundation of innocence projects. The next section will consider the current literature on innocence projects and weigh the merit of these institutions as a viable solution to wrongful imprisonment.

INNOCENCE PROJECTS AS A RETROACTIVE SOLUTION TO WRONGFUL CONVICTION

Innocence projects have played an integral role in shaping new sentencing paradigms, especially for capital cases. Individualized innocence projects typically operate through law schools and consist of several interested law students and their clinical legal instructor who then collectively select cases based on criteria specific to each project (Schehr & Sears, 2005; Zalman, 2006). While the work of innocence projects has brought to light multiple egregious cases of wrongful conviction, the value of such projects to the larger efforts of criminal justice reform have been questioned by various legal scholars who perceive such work to be a proverbial drop in the bucket or simply regarded as a distraction to larger reform efforts to be made within pre-conviction and pre-sentencing (Raymond, 2001; Smith, 2009). Nevertheless, the emergence of innocence projects speaks to their utility and need within a largely imperfect system. Both the history and the future of innocence projects are as important to revisit as the theoretical frameworks that give them context. According to Stratton (2015), wrongful conviction is not a representation per se of negligence, nor a built-in regularity of the criminal justice apparatus, but is more of an organizational failure. Reconciling this perspective with that of Kauzlarich et al. (2003), it may be time to reconsider the position of the justice system along their continua—perhaps placing it firmly in the middle as neither committed or omitted.

Innocence projects have their early roots in the so-called reform era of the 1970s. The verdict in *Furman v. Georgia* (1972) placed a nationwide moratorium on the death penalty and brought national attention to the plight of abolition. In later decades, innocence projects were to be granted greater legitimacy by the advent of DNA testing and admissibility in the 1980s and early 1990s (Gross & O'Brien, 2008). At the same time, in 1992, the MacCrate report was issued by the American Bar Association, drawing attention to the widespread need in American law schools for practical programs such as clinical legal courses (Schehr & Sears, 2005). Although the first innocence project proper had been developed in the early 1980s in New Jersey under the guise of the Centurion Ministries (at Rutgers University in Newark), innocence projects did not gain the necessary traction throughout the United States until the successes of Peter Nuefeld and Barry Scheck in establishing the Innocence Project at the Cardozo Law School in New York (Zalman, 2006). Additionally, throughout much of the 20th century, the majority of the American lay public as well as prosecutors and judges assumed that the criminal justice system *worked*; quite simply, they believed that wrongful convictions were rare or a very small price to pay for a more efficient justice apparatus (Godsey & Pulley, 2004; Risinger, 2007; Zalman, 2006). This, in combination with the highly visible trial and execution of prolific serial killer Ted Bundy in 1989, served to galvanize the moral rectitude of the death penalty as a just punishment for criminals (Collins & Jarvis, 2009; Radelet & Akers, 1996). Such social and pedagogical changes have set the stage for what has led to the re-reemergence of the innocence movement as well as greater public scrutiny of court proceedings and forensic evidence (Collins & Jarvis, 2009; Zalman, 2006).

EXPLORING THE CURRENT LITERATURE ON INNOCENCE PROJECTS

Existing literature that takes a purely empirical stance to investigating the structure and function of innocence projects is largely lacking (Krieger, 2011). Much of what can be found on this subject is limited to law or policy review papers, with only limited empirical data from additive inquiries sought by the authors (Leo & Gould, 2009; Krieger, 2011). Furthermore, most of these articles tend to focus upon the outcomes of capital cases, chasing estimates of how many wrongly convicted persons are in prison and/or currently sitting on death row (Gross & O'Brien, 2008; Huff, 2004). One critique by Leo and Gould (2009) suggests that research endeavors exploring the impact of innocence projects have yet to partner with those of social science research, rendering the body of literature somewhat one-dimensional. There remains debate as to the metrics with which project outcomes should be measured, as some academics see the true number of wrongfully convicted as the best gauge, while still others claim that the number itself pales in comparison to the evidence that wrongful convictions, especially in the context of capital cases, take place at all (Leo & Gould, 2009; Risinger, 2007; Steiker & Steiker, 2005).

With respect to structure, most studies to date take a comparative approach, often pitting the newly formed, independent innocence projects against similar bodies in the United Kingdom or Australia (Huff, 2004; Norris, Bonventre, Redlich, & Acker, 2011). Academic reviews that describe how these projects came about, their history, scholarship, and best practices can be useful to the topics discussed hereafter because these works often provide a window to the origins of innocence projects, their current standing and successes, as well as their possible futures (Carey, 2002; Stiglitz, Brooks, & Shulman., 2001). That said, any qualitative research that would otherwise contribute to understanding individual projects and how they structure themselves and influence the practices of the courtroom workgroup are almost wholly absent (Spohn & Hemmens, 2012).

INNOCENCE PROJECTS & ORGANIZATIONAL CULTURAL CHANGE

Much of the literature related to the paradigm shift embodied by the innocence movement includes an explication of just how defendants are wrongfully convicted (Gross & O'Brien, 2008). Some of these factors have already been discussed, but other sources of false conviction point outside the courts as well as within, with law enforcement engaging in interrogations, testimony from jailhouse snitches being deemed admissible as evidence, and junk forensic science making its way into expert witness testimony (Krieger, 2011; Steiker & Steiker, 2005; Thomas, 2015; Zalman, 2006). Essentially, large-scale misconduct continues to pervade the criminal justice system in such a manner that allows the courtroom workgroup to remain complicit in the wrongful conviction of factually and actually innocent persons.

Edgar Schein (2004), in outlining the definition of organizational culture reliant upon structural stability, states that the depth and breadth of a culture is evident within the long-standing crime control–based culture of conviction (Risinger, 2007). With the larger justice system as the level of analysis, it follows that the culture surrounding capital cases has been deep, broad, and had structural support insofar as it was institutionalized in the very perceptions of the United States Supreme Court justices who ruled in favor of removing legal barriers to capital punishment. Innocence projects themselves have ushered in a cultural change whose permanence has yet to be decided, but whose challenges to the normativity of crime control can already be felt at several levels of the criminal justice system (Krieger, 2011; Zalman, 2006). Leo and Gould (2009) explain that "innocentrism" has come to constitute the new norm in capital convictions. As an example of this, Zalman (2006) indicates that reforms after these and other sociopolitical events has included a cadre of police agencies falling in line with more ethical interrogation practices as well as the building of multidisciplinary innocence movement communities that include cognitive psychologists, writers, nonprofit organizations, and lawyers.

All progress aside however, Raymond (2001) as well as Steiker and Steiker (2005) contend that any rate of false conviction is unimportant in the face of the evidence that points to larger miscarriages of justice by prosecutors and inability to systematically reform the justice system both beyond the courts and within them. Furthermore, the focus upon innocence as a necessary cultural change may be detrimental to the integrity of future cases insofar as it reassigns the burden of proof to the defendant (Raymond, 2001; Smith, 2009). Along with the scientific validation of DNA testing, the expectation that a high standard of factual proof be available and made ready by the defendant in court will fundamentally change the way in which the court understands presumed innocence as a privilege of the American citizen (Raymond, 2001). Similarly, Huff (2004) and later Zalman (2006) have argued that the scope of the research on innocence communities has largely overlooked the courtroom as a microcosm possessing its own culture and tradition of being adversarial. This failure represents the inability by the scholarly and legal community to acknowledge what Blau and Scott (as cited in Shafritz, Ott, & Jang, 2013) would call the informal organizational practice running parallel to the formal operations of lawyers in the courtroom. Therefore, the reform agenda that innocence projects operate under, while idealistic, has yet to reconcile itself with the conflicting goals that will inevitably emerge between defense and prosecution (Zalman, 2006).

Law schools, and the institutions they partner with to create formal organizations, have an interest in creating good lawyers—those who will practice in the name of due process and who will be as skeptical as they are zealous in their work (Carey, 2002). However, when students who have participated in innocence projects graduate to become public defenders, private practice lawyers, or state prosecutors, will the norms and practices imparted by these projects impart the behaviors necessary to change the problematic culture of the courtroom workgroup? These and other questions have yet to be answered due to the paucity of research that closely examines the adversarial process and presumptions of innocence. In the meantime, it appears that the disruptive arguments of innocence movements will need to be made with greater continuity in order to truly change the informal culture both within and outside of the courtroom (Krieger, 2011). This chapter will now turn to a content analysis of publicly available data to further explore popular discourse on wrongful conviction and exoneration.

CONTENT ANALYSIS METHODOLOGY

The content analysis that follows will seek to fill existing research gaps by qualitatively examining themes related to courtroom dynamics that are associated with wrongful conviction and whether innocence projects contributed in subsequent exoneration. This qualitative review seeks to answer firstly, how is violence (in the form of wrongful conviction) perpetrated by the state? And secondly, what are the constituent elements of court cases that lead to wrongful conviction? A search for articles published in *The New York Times* from years 2001 to 2015 included terms "national desk" AND "exoner" OR "Innocence Project" OR "wrongful conviction" OR "wrongfully convicted." This search returned 472 articles, and each article was coded using binary variables for thematic elements including whether or not there was an explicit mention of those elements. Articles were first parsed on the condition that there was, in fact, a successful exoneration in the story itself. This was done to both ensure the relevance of the article content (i.e., articles searched only on the basis of keywords may not cover anything pertaining to the subject matter at hand) and to make the sample size more manageable for the purpose of in-depth qualitative analyses.

Afterward, and in reading the articles that remained from this selection, if a theme of interest was explicitly mentioned and present as the primary topic of the article, it received a 1 for that category (all others received a "0"). Themes included DNA exoneration, innocence projects, reparations by the state, new legislation, and/or policy and criminal justice misconduct or incompetence. These variables were chosen on the basis that DNA exonerations, in tandem with innocence projects, have entered the fore in recent decades as DNA testing becomes more available and as popular conscience about wrongful conviction increases (Gross & O'Brien, 2008; Medwed, 2006; Zalman, 2006). Reparations was selected as a theme on the grounds that many exonerees often receive little to nothing (in terms of money or otherwise) from the state that initially prosecuted them (Mandery et al., 2013; Thomas, 2015). New legislation and/or policy was another theme selected in light of the recent moratoria upon the death penalty (Lanier & Acker, 2004). Politicians and members of the public (some of whom have been vocal in years prior about their staunch support for capital punishment) continue to shift their gaze towards the appeal of due process in light of more recent evidence that the system may not work as effectively as once thought and that it can, in fact, contribute to loss of life (Collins & Jarvis, 2009; Norris et al., 2011). Ideally then, popular news media should be reflective of these more recent events and their consequences. Finally, misconduct on the part of criminal justice actors was selected due to the evidence (cited previously) that prosecutorial as well as defense misconduct and negligence often work against the victim to produce a guilty verdict and is typically only discovered retroactively (Bandes, 2006; Findley & Scott, 2006; Huff, 2004; Krieger, 2011; Medwed, 2006; Zalman, 2006).

Victim profile was also examined among the studies that identified a successful exoneration. If mentioned, demographics were coded using basic categories of age, race, and gender (age included 20–29, 30–39, 40+; race included African American, Hispanic, White, Asian categories; gender included male or female). These factors were of interest because of the large discrepancy in the demographic breakdown of those who have been retroactively exonerated (with males and especially African American males being more frequent) (Gross & O'Brien, 2008; Johnson, Griffith, & Barnaby, 2013). From this point, the articles vetted in the first stage of the coding were also filtered so as to determine whether there was an identified reason for wrongful conviction. Next, mentions of some of the variables already discussed (use of evidence, forensic lab misconduct, prosecutorial and defense misconduct) were coded again, using 1 to denote a "yes" and 0, "no." Additional attributed causes for wrongful conviction included the use of jailhouse snitches, existing courtroom policies, law enforcement misconduct, expert witness testimony, testimony of crime victim, testimony of exoneree, as well as whether or not a combination of these factors were attributed to wrongful conviction (Krieger, 2011). These were considered as non–mutually exclusive categories on the basis that often "causes," as they are identified by popular press, are better thought of as contributing factors (Collins & Jarvis, 2009; Gould & Leo, 2010).

RESULTS

Only a portion of the original 472 articles made mention of a successful exoneration (n = 92) and were used for subsequent analyses (remaining articles were excluded). After screening each article for predominant themes, results from this general thematic coding revealed several themes that included DNA evidence, changes in policy or legislation related to the death penalty and/or admissibility of new evidence to a case, innocence projects, and reparations paid by the state. For obvious reasons, many of these themes overlapped within each article and were not distinct, leading to totals and percentages that will exceed the total sample size of 92 (Table 2.1). The most common theme was the presence or use of DNA evidence either during conviction, exoneration, or both (n = 38; 41%). This is likely owed to growing visibility of cases handled by innocence projects over the past 15 years alongside advances in DNA processing as well as the fact that most innocence projects will only agree to take a case if there is a possibility that DNA can be retroactively analyzed (Gross, Jacoby, Matheson, Montgomery, & Patil, 2005). DNA evidence as a theme was followed by themes of misconduct or negligence by criminal justice system actors (prosecutors, defense attorneys, witnesses, forensics teams, law enforcement, judges, and politicians) (n = 21; 23%). This result is not surprising provided that DNA evidence is so highly trusted by juries for reasons related to the "CSI effect" as well as findings from Garrett and Neufeld (2009) that indicate that the misrepresentation of forensic evidence by prosecutors is rampant among wrongful conviction cases that have since been resolved with the aid of innocence projects (Krieger, 2011; Thomas, 2015). The next most-prevalent themes were that of new legislation or policy leading to exoneration (n = 15; 16%), discussions of innocence projects (n = 11; 9%), and reparations paid by the state to exonerees and their families (n = 8; 9%). There were several articles (n = 16) in which there was no prominent theme associated with the article and only factual information about a specific case of exoneration was provided.

TABLE 2.1 Frequency and Confluence of Article Themes Across the Sample of 92 Coded Articles

	DNA Evidence	Misconduct/ Negligence	Policy/ Legislation	Innocence Projects	Reparations
DNA Evidence	24	6	3	3	2
Misconduct/ Negligence	6	14	1	1	0
Policy/Legislation	3	0	13	0	0
Innocence Projects	3	1	0	6	0
Reparations	2	0	0	0	6

Within the 92 thematically coded articles, much of the discourse surrounding new legislation and policy was related to recent moratoria on the death penalty, namely the moratorium in Illinois that was put in place just two years prior to Governor George Ryan granting clemency to 156 death row inmates (Lanier & Acker, 2004). Since this declaration, states nationwide (including but not limited to Oregon, Washington, Maryland, Nebraska, Arizona, Kansas, Oklahoma, and New Jersey) have either removed the death penalty completely, placed moratoria on it, or at least reviewed the conditions of punishment statutes under the scrutiny of state attorney generals and/or policy review commissions (Collins, Boruchowitz, Hickman, & Larrañaga, 2016; Lanier & Acker, 2004). Thus, as the national climate continues to progress towards a less favorable view of the death penalty and as state leaders question its necessity, exonerations in the wake of policy change could become more frequent. The relatively sparse mention of state-paid reparations is not surprising provided the number of legal obstacles exonerees must overcome in order to even qualify, let alone succeed in collecting money (Mandery et al., 2013). However, the Innocence Project has begun to advocate a $50,000 annual (per year spent on death row) reparation for those wrongly convicted, providing greater legal clout to defendants who would otherwise be unwilling to seek financial reparations from the state (Mandery et al., 2013).

Within the same sample of 92 articles, a portion (n = 29) revealed the specific cause or attributed a cause for wrongful conviction of the victim. Within these 29 articles, there were cases in which multiple causes were identified (the sum of thematic occurrences listed in Table 2.2 exceeds 29). Within the articles that did cite the cause for wrongful conviction, the most commonly cited reason (in number of mentions) for that conviction was the manner and context in which evidence was presented in court, with the two least-common categories being existing policies and testimony of the exoneree (Table 2.2).

TABLE 2.2   Thematic Attributions for Wrongful Convictions Across 29 Articles

CAUSE OF WRONGFUL CONVICTION	FREQUENCY
Use of Evidence in Court	18
Combination of 1+ Factors	13
Legal Misconduct	8
Forensic Labs/Med Examiner	8
Forensic Analysis of Evidence	8
Actions of Law Enforcement	7
Testimony of Crime Victim	6
Jailhouse Snitch	2
Use of expert or Additional Witnesses	2
Existing Policy	1
Testimony of Exonoree	0

VICTIM DEMOGRAPHICS

Among articles that enumerated the victims of wrongful conviction (n = 1,382 victims), the most commonly cited demographic category was victim gender (n = 498 victims). The demographics for those exonerated (where specified) overrepresented male victims (n = 494) as compared to female victims (n = 4) (Table 2.3). This is likely reflective of the disproportionate number of violent male offenders in general (Helfgott, 2008). Most victims mentioned in these cases were African American (n = 14); the second most specified racial background was White (n = 4), with no other racial backgrounds explicitly mentioned (Table 2.4). This echoes the findings by Smith and Hattery (2011) as well as West and Meterko (2015) that African American males also account for the majority of those later exonerated, even after controlling for their overrepresentation among the incarcerated population. Interestingly, this result was juxtaposed with the finding that African American men perpetrate just 16 percent of the rapes against White females, but such crimes accounted for 78 percent of the exonerations with demographic mentions in this study. This and other research demonstrates that status as an African American male is likely a risk factor for conviction and even wrongful conviction especially when the victim is White (Smith & Hattery, 2011).

TABLE 2.3 Frequency of Victim Gender Across 92 Articles

GENDER	FREQUENCY (BY VICTIM)
Male	494
Female	4

TABLE 2.4 Frequency of Victim Race Across 92 Articles

RACE	FREQUENCY (BY VICTIM)
Black	14
White	4

With respect to age, and among the articles where age was mentioned, most exonerees were above the age of 40 (n = 9) at the time of their release from prison (Table 2.5). While there is little empirical evidence to support this exact pattern, it would make sense that the majority of exonerees are 40 and older provided that the average length of incarceration before exoneration is about 10 years and that violent offenses tend to be committed by young men (Gross & O'Brien, 2008; Helfgott, 2008; West & Meterko, 2015). Additionally, and considering once more the legal obstacles that include overburdened appeals courts and the subjective speed at which evidence can be retroactively analyzed, adult offenders are apt to remain in prison for some time even after the appeals process has been initiated.

TABLE 2.5   Frequency of Victim Age Across 92 Articles

AGE	FREQUENCY (BY VICTIM)
20–29	2
30–39	2
40–49	6
50–59	3

ANALYSIS OF VICTIMS OF WRONGFUL CONVICTIONS

From the above results, it is clear that the majority of the cases that reported demographic information involved African American males, supporting the research by Johnson et al. (2013) that this segment of the population is more frequently the subject of wrongful conviction. The lower base rate for women within the criminal justice system more generally is likely another contributing factor for why there are fewer women represented in this study. The results of the age category revealed that victims were likely to be older (40+), perhaps reflective of their sentence at the time of conviction. Most cases involving innocence projects and other forms of retroactive exoneration are typically capital rape/murder cases where resulting sentences are lengthier and the average amount of time between conviction and exoneration for capital cases is around 10 years (Gross & O'Brien, 2008). The number of cases mentioned is not surprising provided that, most often, exoneration cases are highly visible and relatively few and far between and are thus framed as anomalies. However, one example worth mentioning is the media coverage of Texas

Governor Rick Perry, in which 167 sentences were commuted at once. In reading each article, it was common to find larger numbers such as this one mentioned in conjunction with new or existing policies (moratoria on the death penalty, greater admissibility of DNA evidence), while for the smaller numbers, each case was highlighted more individually and pointed to how the person was exonerated, typically via DNA evidence.

Worth noting in this review is that the most prominent cause, other than the use of evidence in court, was lawyerly or forensic misconduct/negligence. This result is similar to those of a recent review of cases (between 1989 and 2014) taken on by innocence projects wherein the individual was exonerated with the aid of post-conviction DNA testing (West & Meterko, 2015). Here, the misapplication of forensic evidence, coupled with misidentification by eyewitnesses, accounted for the largest portion of wrongful convictions (West & Meterko, 2015). While there are likely many causes for criminal justice actors' malfeasance or simple negligence, this speaks somewhat to the validity of Stratton's (2015) argument that state violence is not always intentional but is an organization-wide phenomenon that spans bureaucratic lines of the justice system, affecting witnesses, lawyers, and forensic scientists together and in different ways to produce injustice. Because this study did not delve deeper into the courtroom-level factors impacting the verdict and sentence in a given case, it is almost impossible to effectively parse the true reason for conviction. Finally, and in support of the growing public interest in forensic evidence and the use of DNA, DNA exoneration was the most common theme evinced in the articles reviewed. This again is likely owed to not only popular media's love affair with science-as-crime-fighting, but also the growing standard of proof juries and the public at-large seek in criminal and appellate cases (Boorsma, 2017; Thomas, 2015).

While innocence projects have brought much-needed attention to cases of wrongful conviction, news as well as popular media representations of noteworthy cases may be overstating their frequency as well as the availability of exoneration to all innocents. It is important to understand that not all criminal offenses are treated equally. Friedman and Percival's (1981) "wedding cake theory" of criminal justice is relevant to consider when thinking about why cases are treated differently both by the criminal justice system and in public discourse (Walker, 1983). The theory places the majority of offenses (misdemeanors) at the bottom tier and more rare, sensationalized, and violent offenses near the top (Walker, 1983). Because the rare cases are sensationalized (either due to their celebrity or heinousness, or both), these cases become seminal frameworks through which the public understands subsequent and less serious ones that are processed more quickly and with less scrutiny (Walker, 1983). Indeed, studies of popular media such as true crime television and legal dramas demonstrate that such media contributes a great deal to the public's understanding of legal and procedural concepts (Boorsma, 2017). This is a fact that becomes more troubling when those retellings often misrepresent or exaggerate the legal process and standards of evidence and, even moreso, when one considers who is selected for jury duty in American court systems (Boorsma, 2017).

Selectivity in media coverage can have concrete implications when it is enacted within this context. For example, the increasing awareness of and preference for scientific evidence to exonerate may prove problematic for the majority of wrongfully convicted victims who likely do not possess the means to acquire DNA evidence due to a confluence of constraints. While the majority of the crimes that incur capital punishment are more likely to produce (induce the collection of) DNA evidence (e.g., rape or homicide), it is important to remember that often the legal and financial resources available to victims are slim to nonexistent, especially if they are indigent or are continually denied an appeal. As of this publication, only 18 states have legislations that mandate payment of reparations to the wrongly convicted, and often the resources provided to innocence projects are woefully limited (Klick & Mungan, 2017). Until there are financial means for victims of wrongful conviction to access such expensive techniques, victims may be unable to successfully appeal their cases and be successfully exonerated. In addition to these obstacles, recent estimates of the false conviction rate are pulled from data gathered from exonerations of victims using DNA evidence, leading to a sizeable underestimation of the total number of those wrongly convicted. This fact is staggering in the face of raw numbers; the previously cited 1 percent estimated wrongful conviction rate translates to over 20,000 individuals who are currently incarcerated in federal and state prisons (Olney & Bonn, 2015). In light of the "wedding cake" analogy then, the lower tiers are, in actuality, much bigger than most scientific methodologies could ever count for a cake that should have never been baked in the first place (if the system truly works, that is). In short, while there are many more wrongly convicted who have been charged with high "tier" crimes, not all appellants are endowed equally, and the social hierarchies that limit victims' realities are often reinforced by our existing systems. Between the lacking public awareness, increasing standards of evidence, and negligible legislative support, those seeking exoneration are unlikely to achieve it.

There are several limitations within the current study. Crime type was not a variable considered in this study, but future research should continue to examine the nexus of crime type and extralegal factors such as race within cases of wrongful conviction to better clarify this relationship. Additionally, greater attention should also be directed towards exploring the social movement discourse and its application to innocence projects (Zalman, 2006). Zalman (2006) makes the claim that in order to truly gather an understanding of wrongful convictions, there needs to be greater involvement by sociologists, organizational psychologists, and criminal justice academics in this field since their scope is much better suited to assess how systems interact with and generate social movements. In terms of policy and practice, the lack of existing databases containing data related to innocence projects has been cited as problematic (Krieger, 2011; Zalman, 2006). To this point, amicus briefs of all selected cases are typically held on file by law school–based projects and thus can serve as a starting point for legal scholars and criminal justice researchers who are trying to understand the case selection process within these projects and their case outcomes (Krieger, 2011; Medwed, 2002). Cases of wrongful conviction serve as a painstaking reminder to law students and practitioners of criminal justice of the importance of due process of law and the weighty power associated with the justice system in creating lasting and sometimes negative outcomes for defendants. Ideally, discussions of how the justice system can become more procedurally fair in the courtroom and within investigations will aid in providing more just outcomes for those who are legally and factually innocent.

REFERENCES

Alexander, M. (2012). *The new Jim Crow: Mass incarceration in the age of colorblindness.* New York: New Press.

Bandes, S. (2006). Repression and denial in criminal lawyering. *Buffalo Criminal Law Review, 9*(2), 339–389.

Black, B., Ayala, F. J., & Saffran-Brinks, C. (1994). Science and the law in the wake of Daubert: A new search for scientific knowledge. *Texas Law Review, 72*, 715.

Boorsma, M. (2017). The whole truth: The implications of America's true crime obsession. *Elon Law Review, 9*, 209.

Carey, S. V. (2002). An essay on the evolution of clinical legal education and its impact on student trial practice. *University of Kansas Law Review, 51*, 509.

Caudill, D. S., & Redding, R. E. (2000). Junk philosophy of science: The paradox of expertise and interdisciplinarity in federal court. *Washington and Lee Law Review, 57*, 685.

Collins, J. M., & Jarvis, J. (2009). The wrongful conviction of forensic science. *Forensic Science Policy and Management, 1*(1), 17–31.

Collins, P. A., Boruchowitz, R., Hickman, M., & Larrañaga, M. (2016). An analysis of the economic costs of seeking the death penalty in Washington State. *The Seattle Journal for Social Justice, 14*(3), 727–779.

Daubert v. Merrell Dow Pharmaceuticals. 509 U.S. 579 (1993).

Edmond, G., & Mercer, D. (1998). Trashing junk science. *Stanford Technology Law Review, 3.*

Findley, K. A., & Scott, M. S. (2006). The multiple dimensions of tunnel vision in criminal cases. *Wisconsin Law Review, 2.*

Friedman, L. M., & Percival, R. V. (1981). *The Roots of Justice: Crime and Punishment in Alameda County, California, 1870–1910.* UNC Press Books.

Frye v. United States. 293 F. 1013 (D.C. Cir. 1923).

Furman v. Georgia. 408 U.S. 238 (1972).

Garrett, B. L. (2011). *Convicting the innocent.* Boston, MA: Harvard University Press.

Garrett, B. L., & Neufeld, P. J. (2009). Invalid forensic science testimony and wrongful convictions. *Virginia Law Review,* 1–97.

Godsey, M., & Pulley, T. (2004). The innocence revolution and our evolving standards of decency in death penalty jurisprudence. *University of Daytona Law Review, 29*, 265.

Gould, J. B., & Leo, R. A. (2010). One hundred years later: Wrongful convictions after a century of research. *Journal of Criminal Law and Criminology, 100*(3).

Gross, S. R., Jacoby, K., Matheson, D. J., Montgomery, N., & Patil, S. (2005). Exonerations in the United States 1989 through 2003. *The Journal of Criminal Law and Criminology, 95*(2), 523–560.

Gross, S. R., & O'Brien, B. (2008). Frequency and predictors of false conviction: Why we know so little, and new data on capital cases. *Journal of Empirical Legal Studies, 5*(4), 927–962.

Helfgott, J. B. (2008). *Criminal behavior: Theories, typologies and criminal justice.* Thousand Oaks, CA: SAGE Publications.

Huber, P. (1991). Junk science in the courtroom. *Valparaiso University Law Review, 26*, 723.

Huff, C. (2004). Wrongful convictions: The American experience. *Canadian Journal of Criminology and Criminal Justice, 46*(2), 107–120.

Johnson, M. B., Griffith, S., & Barnaby, C. Y. (2013). African Americans wrongly convicted of sexual assault against Whites: Eyewitness error and other case features. *Journal of Ethnicity in Criminal Justice, 11*(4), 277–294.

Junkin, T. (2004). *Bloodsworth.* Chapel Hill, NC: Algonquin Books of Chapel Hill.

Kauzlarich, D., Mullins, C. W., & Matthews, R. A. (2003). A complicity continuum of state crime. *Contemporary Justice Review, 6*(3), 241–254.

Klick, J., & Mungan, M. (2017). A price for injustice. *Regulation, 40*(12), 12–15.

Kraska, P. B., & Brent, J. J. (2011). *Theorizing criminal justice.* Long Grove, IL: Waveland Press.

Krieger, S. A. (2011). Why our justice system convicts innocent people, and the challenges faced by innocence projects trying to exonerate them. *New Criminal Law Review: An International and Interdisciplinary Journal, 14*(3), 333–402.

Lanier, C. S., & Acker, J. R. (2004). Capital punishment, the moratorium movement, and empirical questions: Looking beyond innocence, race, and bad lawyering in death penalty cases. *Psychology, Public Policy, and Law, 10*(4), 577.

Leo, R. A., & Gould, J. B. (2009). Studying wrongful convictions: Learning from social science. *Ohio State Journal of Criminal Law, 7*, 2010–2011.

Lindsay, R. C., & Wells, G. L. (1985). Improving eyewitness identifications from lineups: Simultaneous versus sequential lineup presentation. *Journal of Applied Psychology, 70*(3), 556.

Loftus, E. F. (1980). Impact of expert psychological testimony on the unreliability of eyewitness identification. *Journal of Applied Psychology, 65*(1), 9.

Loftus, E. F., & Zanni, G. (1975). Eyewitness testimony: The influence of the wording of a question. *Bulletin of the Psychonomic Society, 5*(1), 86–88.

Mandery, E. J., Shlosberg, A., West, V., & Callaghan, B. (2013). Compensation statutes and post-exoneration offending. *Journal of Criminal Law & Criminology, 103*, 553.

Medwed, D. S. (2002). Actual innocents: Considerations in selecting cases for a new innocence project. *Nebraska Law Review, 81*, 1097.

Medwed, D. S. (2006). Anatomy of a wrongful conviction: Theoretical implications and practical solutions. *Villanova Law Review, 51*, 05–37.

Naughton, M. (2014). Criminologizing wrongful convictions. *British Journal of Criminology, 54*(6), 1148–1166.

Norris, R. J., Bonventre, C. L., Redlich, A. D., & Acker, J. R. (2011). Than that one innocent suffer: Evaluating state safeguards against wrongful convictions. *Albany Law Review*, 74(3), 1301–1364.

Olney, M., & Bonn, S. (2015). An exploratory study of the legal and non-legal factors associated with exoneration for wrongful conviction: The power of DNA evidence. *Criminal Justice Policy Review*, 26(4), 400–420.

Packer, H. L. (1968). Two models of the criminal process. In P. B. Kraska & J. J. Brent, (Eds.), (2011), *Theorizing criminal justice* (pp. 101–116). Long Grove, IL: Waveland Press.

Radelet, M. L., & Akers, R. L. (1996). Deterrence and the death penalty: The views of the experts. *The Journal of Criminal Law and Criminology*, 87(1), 1–16.

Raymond, M. (2001). The problem with innocence. *Cleveland State Law Review*, 49, 449.

Risinger, D. M. (2007). Innocents convicted: An empirically justified factual wrongful conviction rate. *The Journal of Criminal Law and Criminology*, 97(3), 761–806.

Schehr, R., & Sears, J. (2005). Innocence commissions: Due process remedies and protection for the innocent. *Critical Criminology*, 13(2).

Schein, E. (2004). The Concept of Organizational Culture: Why Bother? In E. Schein, *Organizational Culture and Leadership 3rd. ed.* (pp. 3–23). San Francisco: Jossey-Bass.

Shafritz, J. M., Ott, J. S., & Jang, Y. S. (2013). *Classics of organization theory*. Boston, MA: Cengage Learning.

Smith, A. (2009). In praise of the guilty project: A criminal defense lawyer's growing anxiety about innocence projects. *University of Pennsylvania Journal of Law & Social Change*, 13, 315.

Smith, E., & Hattery, A. J. (2011). Race, wrongful conviction & exoneration. *Journal of African American Studies*, 15(1), 74–94.

Spohn, C., & Hemmens, C. (2012). *Courts: A text/reader* (2nd ed.). Los Angeles, CA: Sage Press.

Sporer, S. L., Penrod, S., Read, D., & Cutler, B. (1995). Choosing, confidence, and accuracy: A meta-analysis of the confidence-accuracy relation in eyewitness identification studies. *Psychological Bulletin*, 118(3), 315.

Steiker, C. S., & Steiker, J. M. (2005). The seduction of innocence: The attraction and limitations of the focus on innocence in capital punishment law and advocacy. *The Journal of Criminal Law and Criminology*, 95(2), 587–624.

Stiglitz, J., Brooks, J., & Shulman, T. (2001). Hurricane meets the paper chase: Innocence projects new emerging role in clinical legal education. *California Western Law Review*, 38, 413.

Stratton, G. (2015). Wrongfully convicting the innocent: A state crime? *Critical Criminology*, 23(1), 21–37.

Thomas, S. (2015). Addressing wrongful convictions: An examination of Texas' new junk science writ and other measures for protecting the innocent. *Houston Law Review*, 52(3), 1037–1066.

Wade, K. A., Green, S. L., & Nash, R. A. (2010). Can fabricated evidence induce false eyewitness testimony? *Applied Cognitive Psychology*, 24(7), 899–908.

Walker, S. (1983). *Social Science History*, 7(4), 487–489. doi:10.2307/1171071

West, E., & Meterko, V. (2015). Innocence project: DNA exonerations, 1989–2014: Review of data and findings from the first 25 years. *Albany Law Review*, 79, 717.

Westervelt, S. D., & Cook, K. J. (2010). Framing innocents: The wrongly convicted as victims of state harm. *Crime, Law and Social Change, 53*(3), 259–275.

Zalman, M. (2006). Criminal justice system reform and wrongful conviction: A research agenda. In C. Spohn & C. Hemmens (Eds.), (2012). *Courts: A text/reader* (pp. 521–538). Los Angeles, CA: Sage Press.

Zalman, M., Smith, B., & Kiger, A. (2008). Officials' estimates of the incidence of "actual innocence" convictions. *Justice Quarterly, 25*(1), 72–100.

KEY TERMS

- *Confirmation Bias:* A perceptual flaw that causes people to seek evidence in support of their preexisting beliefs or opinions at the exclusion of other, contrary evidence.

- *CSI Effect:* A phenomenon among laypeople where a higher quality of forensic evidence is expected in criminal cases.

- *Due Process:* Procedural rights afforded to defendants as they move through the criminal justice system.

- *Exoneration:* The absolution of criminal charges levelled against a defendant.

- *Innocence Projects:* Nonprofit advocacy networks consisting of lawyers, law students, and current and former defendants who collaborate to establish the legal innocence of prisoners.

- *Reparations*: (Financial) Aid provided by the government (i.e., the state) to exonerated defendants as repayment for wages and/or assets lost during their imprisonment.

THE NEW YORK TIMES ARTICLES

Associated Press. (2008). Confession revealed, freeing prisoner of 26 years. *The New York Times.* Retrieved from https://www.nytimes.com/2008/04/20/us/20chicago.html

Blinder, A. (2015). Alabama man on death row for three decades is freed as state's case erodes. *The New York Times.* Retrieved from https://www.nytimes.com/2015/04/04/us/anthony-ray-hinton-alabama-prison-freed-murder.html

Grissom, B. (2011). Exonerated of crimes, but compensated differently. *The New York Times.* Retrieved from https://www.nytimes.com/2011/09/23/us/exonerated-of-crimes-but-compensated-differently.html

Hall, M. (2012). Released from prison, but never exonerated, a man fights for true freedom. *The New York Times.* Retrieved from https://www.nytimes.com/2012/04/01/us/released-but-not-exonerated-kerry-max-cook-fights-for-true-freedom.html

Healy, J. (2013). Wrongfully convicted often find their record, unexpunged, haunts them. *The New York Times.* Retrieved from https://www.nytimes.com/2013/05/06/us/wrongfully-convicted-find-their-record-haunts-them.html

Schwartz, J., & Grissom, B. (2011). Exonerated of murder, Texan seeks inquiry on prosecutor. *The New York Times.* Retrieved from https://www.nytimes.com/2011/12/19/us/texas-man-seeks-inquiry-after-exoneration-in-murder.html

DISCUSSION QUESTIONS

1. List one example of each of the four ideal types of state violence as per Kauzlarich et al. (2003) within the context of wrongful conviction.

2. Discuss the significance of *Daubert v. Merrell Dow Pharmaceuticals* in changing the standard for scientific evidence.

3. All defendants are innocent until proven guilty. How is this legal presumption challenged by our current court systems and their existing faults? List some examples.

4. How could investigative techniques be altered to be fairer to potential defendants?

5. Discuss the lasting impact of wrongful conviction in capital cases. What is known about the current state of reparations paid to innocent defendants after they have been exonerated?

6. Provided the findings of the content analysis, would you argue that wrongful conviction can be attributed to multiple actors or, instead, to a broader systemic failing? Where do these failings lie?

7. How can the wedding cake theory be applied to explain why exoneration might be misrepresented in the media?

CHAPTER 3

Victims Within the Correctional System

Elisabeth Walls, Department of Criminal Justice, Seattle University; Kevin Wright, School of Criminology & Criminal Justice, Arizona State University

INTRODUCTION

According to the World Prison Brief, in 2017, the number of individuals incarcerated in the United States totaled 2,145,100 or 666 per 100,000 people, the highest total prison population and second highest rate of imprisonment in the world. Fueled by an emphasis on "get tough" policies and incapacitation and deterrence based corrections, rates of imprisonment in the United States have steadily increased since the 1980s, only beginning to slow in the last decade and a half (Wilson, 2017). In addition, as prison populations have increased, so has research and data collection on victimization within U.S. **correctional facilities**, including violent assaults between prisoners and against correctional staff and, more recently, sexual assault and other sexual victimization.

In addition to injuries directly caused by in-prison violence, prisoner victimization has been found to be significantly related to emotional distress, aggressive and antisocial behavior, and increased chance of recidivism post-release (Boxer, Middlemass, & Delorenzo, 2009; Daquin, Daigle, & Listwan, 2016; Zweig, Yahner, Visher, & Lattimore, 2014). In the case of correctional officers, violent conditions and altercations with prisoners have been linked to stress, depression, burnout, post-traumatic stress disorder (PTSD), and strain on relationships (Boudoukha, Altintas, Rusinek, Fantini-Hauwel, & Hautekeete, 2013; Obidoa, Reeves, Warren, Reisine, & Cherniack, 2011). However, despite its impact on those directly affected, for most Americans without a personal connection to anyone incarcerated or working in prison, such victimization is out of sight and out of mind.

In light of increasing scholarship on violent victimization in correctional facilities, the impact of such victimization, and ongoing debates about correctional theory and policy, it is valuable to look at how such victimization is portrayed in official datasets, scholarly research, and the media. To do so, we begin this chapter by briefly exploring what has come to be defined as victimization within the correctional system and the different frameworks that have developed to explain its occurrence. Next, we review recent data and empirical research on victimization in correctional facilities—focused primarily on physical assault, sexual assault, and homicide- or suicide-related deaths in jails and prisons—to ascertain the prominence of such victimization as well as characteristics related to its nature, victims, and causes. We then share the findings of an original content analysis of 317 articles on victimization in correctional facilities published by *The New York Times* between 2001 and 2015. Lastly, we discuss the implications of both similarities and differences between empirical findings and media depictions, noting limitations of our analysis as well as recommendations for future research.

DEFINING & UNDERSTANDING VICTIMIZATION WITHIN THE CORRECTIONAL SYSTEM

While the range of what might be defined as victimization within the correctional system is vast and dependent on one's beliefs regarding criminality, corrections, and prisoner rights, the majority of research and these authors take the stance that incarceration is not victimizing in and of itself, but that certain conditions and/or occurrences inside of prison walls can be. In the study of victimization within the correctional system, official data and empirical literature predominantly focus on occurrences of physical and sexual violence in jails and prisons. An almost stereotypical attribute of prison life, specific acts considered to be victimizing include prisoner-on-prisoner, prisoner-on-officer, and officer-on-prisoner assaults as well as sexual assault, nonconsensual sex acts, and sexual harassment. During the first decade and a half of the 21st century, increased data collection and attempts to conduct representative studies have sought to construct an accurate picture of the extent and nature of victimization in correctional facilities. The goal of this data collection is to create prisons and jails that are safer for both prisoners and the staff who work there (Steiner, Ellison, Butler, & Cain, 2017; Wolff, Blitz, Shi, Siegel, & Bachman, 2007).

To achieve that goal, studies of victimization within the correctional system have attempted to identify contributing factors and theoretical frameworks that can both explain higher victimization rates inside prison (compared to outside) and predict patterns of non-random victimization within prisons and jails (Wooldredge & Steiner, 2014). Similar to research on victimization outside of prison, studies of in-prison victimization based on **importation theory** examine the influence of relatively static, preexisting individual traits on victimization risk (Steiner et al., 2017). Alternately, studies based on **deprivation theory** look at characteristics of the prison environment and how different individuals adapt to them for clues into both victimization prevalence and risk (Steiner et al., 2017). While recognizing the interaction of many influential factors, most researchers today have broadened their attempts to explain in-prison victimization through more general, multilevel explanations of its causes and predictors. Such factors include individual characteristics like age and sexuality, individual activities and associations like daily routines and gang membership, elements of prison culture like inmate code and unequal distribution of power, structural attributes such as facility characteristics, and systematic features such as correctional practices and policies (Steiner et al., 2017).

For example, an investigation of victimization within the correctional system through the lens of **lifestyle/opportunity theory** examines the roles of prisoner routines, target vulnerability and **victim/offender overlap**, and individual or institutional guardianship in shaping opportunities for victimization to occur (Pérez, Gover, Tennyson, & Santos, 2010; Wolff, Shi, & Siegel, 2009; Wooldredge & Steiner, 2014). As researchers continue to examine and identify various predictors of victimization within the correctional system, what has become clear is that victimization in the correctional system, and the study of it and how it is perceived, is no less complex than victimization outside of it. Some aspects of victimization within the correction system are the same as those related to victimization outside of prison, some are the same as those outside of prison but lead to increased risk of victimization for different reasons, and some are unique to victimization within correctional facilities (Wolff et al., 2009).

PRISONER ASSAULTS & DEATHS: OFFICIAL DATA & INDEPENDENT RESEARCH

According to the most recent data collected in the Census of State and Federal Correctional Facilities, the prevalence of prisoner-on-prisoner assaults (physical and sexual) in such facilities ranged from 34,355 in 2000 to 26,396 in 2005 (Bureau of Justice Statistics, 2017; Stephan & Karberg, 2003). Such datasets, however, are limited by the fact that victimization figures are almost never analyzed or presented in official reports, do not differentiate between physical and sexual assaults, and do not consistently contain figures on staff-on-prisoner assaults to which prisoner-on-prisoner assaults might be compared.[1] Data drawn from official disciplinary records, and published on the Bureau of Prisons (BOP) website, show that while counts and rates of physical assaults in federal facilities varied from month to month between May 2004 and December 2015, less serious assaults occurred at a higher rate (1,680–2,880 per year) than serious assaults (240–600 per year) (Bureau of Prisons, 2017). And broken down by security level, the BOP (2017) data also shows that the largest proportion of the incidents reported in federal facilities occurred at high security institutions.

In some cases, serious assaults lead to prisoner deaths and are reported as unnatural deaths by the Bureau of Justice Statistics (BJS) Death in Custody Reporting Program. In BJS reports authored by Noonan (2016) and Noonan, Rohloff, and Ginder (2015), deaths categorized as unnatural include homicide, suicide, and accidents. Between 2001 and 2014, for example, 130 federal prisoners died of homicide (3% of total deaths), 222 of suicide (4%), and 51 from accidents (1%). In state prisons, 845 prisoners died of homicide (2%), 2,826 died of suicide (6%), and 450 died from

---

[1] In studies comparing prisoner-on-prisoner assault to officer-on-prisoner assault, rates of prisoner-on-prisoner assault tend to be higher than officer-on-prisoner assault, though not necessarily at a statistically significant level (Pérez et al., 2010; Wolff et al., 2007).

accidents (1%). In local jails, suicide was the leading cause of death every year between 2000 and 2013—accounting for 4,134 (30%) deaths—while only 271 (2.7%) deaths were ruled accidents and 302 (2.2%) homicides.

Fueled by the increased attention about violence within prisons and jails, empirical research on victimization within correctional facilities grew into a more robust area of study during the first decade and half of the 21st century. This researched aimed to both obtain a more comprehensive and accurate picture of prison violence and understand factors contributing to increased victimization risk (Gibbons & Katzenbach, 2006; Wolff et al., 2007; Wolff, Shi, & Bachman, 2008). One way researchers set out to improve measures of in-prison victimization was by utilizing confidential, self-report surveys to overcome underreporting due to threats of retaliation, a difference that some scholars argue could result in a prevalence of in-prison assault as much as 11 times greater than officially reported (Wolff et al., 2007). In an attempt to correct for methodological issues of earlier studies, which yielded widely varying measures of the prevalence of prison violence (ranging from 10 to 25% for physical victimization and from less than one to 40% for sexual victimization) researchers have surveyed more generalizable samples and utilized more comprehensive, well-defined concepts of victimization, such as including both prisoner-on-prisoner and staff-on-prisoner assaults and adding questions about more specific incidents that individuals might not initially categorize as assault (Wolff et al., 2007; Wolff et al., 2008). In one of the first full-population, self-report studies of an entire state prison system, Wolff et al. (2007) found rates of prisoner assault (by prisoners and staff) to be 206 per 1,000 for women and 205 per 1,000 for men over the course of six months. In contrast, official figures on in-prison assaults reported rates of only 40 per 1,000 prisoners (in federal, state, and private prisons) per year (Stephan & Karberg, 2003).

Going beyond simply quantifying and describing incidents of prisoner assault, however, most researchers have sought to identify factors contributing to victimization risk in order to build practical and theoretical frameworks through which to reduce that risk (Bottoms, 1999; Wooldredge & Steiner, 2013). Drawing on importation theory, findings from a number of early studies of victim characteristics showed increased risk of victimization among younger, male prisoners with a history of mental health issues, prior abuse, violent criminal backgrounds, gang membership, and, in some cases, shorter imprisonment length (Blitz, Wolff, & Shi, 2008; Pérez et al., 2010; Wolff et al., 2009).

For a number of characteristics (such as race, age, and education), however, their influence on victimization risk was inconsistent or shown to vary depending on other individual traits (such as gender) or situational factors (such as type of confinement) (Blitz et al., 2008; Lahm, 2015; Wolff et al., 2009; Wooldredge & Steiner, 2012). While most studies found that younger prisoners were at an increased risk of assault by other prisoners, surveys of prisoners over the age of 65 found that they frequently experienced psychological or property victimization at the hands of younger prisoners (Kerbs & Jolley, 2007). Studies that differentiated between prisoner-on-prisoner and staff-on-prisoner victimization also found differences in risk for the two different types of victimization. While some individual characteristics increasing victimization risk were shared, younger, White prisoners with convictions related to sexual crimes were at increased risk of prisoner-on-prisoner victimization, while non-White prisoners convicted of violent crimes were at greater risk of victimization by staff (Wolff et al., 2009).

As studies have increasingly shown the influence of many different factors on victimization in correctional facilities, most researchers today look to a broader range of interacting predictors in their attempts to explain prison violence and victimization (Steiner et al., 2017). Based on a critical review of 16 studies on prisoner victimization between 1980 and 2014, Steiner et al. (2017) found 25 of 48 different variables to be significant predictors of violent or property victimization in prison. Among individual characteristics, younger age, introversion, employment prior to incarceration, prior physical or sexual abuse, higher security risk, and not fighting back were all positively associated with higher rates of victimization. Among characteristics related to prisoners' routines, housing in the general population, positive perception of prison safety, and favorable attitudes towards staff correlated with lower rates of victimization, while higher involvement in recreational activities and a history of misconduct correlated with higher rates of victimization. At the prison level, higher rates of victimization were associated with large populations, higher security levels, linear architectural designs, and institutions in which correctional officers perceived rules to be under-enforced.

Less common than non-lethal assaults, prison homicides—averaging four per 100,000 prisoners per year between 2000 and 2010—and suicides occupy only a small body of the research on in-prison victimization (Cunningham, Sorensen, Vigen, & Woods, 2010). In a study of 35 prison homicides in Texas, common attributes included occurrence in prisoners' cells, a single assailant, and beating as the cause (Cunningham et al., 2010). Both victim and offender were likely to be a gang-affiliated male with a history of violent arrests or problematic prison adjustments. Compared to perpetrators, victims of homicide were generally older.

In the latest of three nationwide studies on suicide among adult prisoners across 15,978 U.S. correctional facilities, Hayes (2012) found that individuals who committed suicide while in jail or prison were predominately White, male, charged with a personal and/or violent offense, and had a history of mental illness. Examining prison suicide at the institutional level, Dye (2010) found higher rates of suicide to be associated with supermax or maximum security facilities, overcrowding and violence problems, and a large proportion of prisoners receiving mental health services. In a study of prisoners who attempted suicide, subject characteristics included depressive symptoms, relationship problems, lower involvement in structured activities, and recent in-prison moves—especially to a disciplinary segregation unit (Suto & Arnaut, 2010).

PRISONER SEXUAL ASSAULT: PREA & ITS DATA BOOM

Following the passage of the **Prison Rape Elimination Act (PREA)** in 2003, government mandated national data collection on sexual violence within U.S. correctional facilities resulted in a significant growth of data on sexual victimization in prisons and jails (Beck & Hughes, 2005). In 2004, the Survey of Sexual Victimization (SSV) (formerly the Survey of Sexual Violence) began reporting annual data on incidents of sexual victimization[2] based on administrative records from a nationally representative sample of adult and juvenile prisons and jails (Beck & Hughes, 2005). Conducted less frequently, the National Prisoner Survey (NIS) and the National Survey of Youth in Custody (NSYC) reported on incidents of sexual victimization based on self-report surveys completed by prisoners (Beck, Berzofsky, Caspar, & Krebs, 2013; Beck, 2014a).

Based on administrative data from 2,730 facilities in the first SSV, Beck and Hughes (2005) reported 8,210 allegations of sexual violence (3.15 allegations per 1,000 prisoners) in 2004. Of those allegations, 42 percent involved sexual misconduct by staff, 37 percent nonconsensual acts between prisoners, 11 percent sexual harassment by staff, and 10 percent abusive sexual conduct between prisoners. Among different types of facilities surveyed, state juvenile facilities had the highest rate of sexual misconduct (11.34 allegations per 1,000 youth), though the higher rate may have been influenced by legal requirements already in place for recording and reporting such incidents. Overall, victim and perpetrator characteristics of prisoner-on-prisoner sexual violence matched prisoner population characteristics, with males composing the majority of victims and perpetrators. However, in relation to their representation

---

[2] Under PREA, sexual victimization is defined as "prisoner-on-prisoner sexual acts (including nonconsensual sexual acts and abusive sexual contact) and staff-on-prisoner sexual victimization (including staff sexual misconduct and staff sexual harassment)." A nonconsensual act is defined as "contact of any person without his or her consent, or of a person who is unable to consent or refuse; and contact between the penis and the vagina or the penis and the anus including penetration, however slight; or contact between the mouth and the penis, vagina, or anus; or penetration of the anal or genital opening of another person by a hand, finger, or other object." Abusive sexual contact is defined as "contact of any person without his or her consent, or of a person who is unable to consent or refuse; and intentional touching, either directly or through the clothing, of the genitalia, anus, groin, breast, inner thigh, or buttocks of any person." Staff sexual misconduct is defined as "any behavior or act of a sexual nature directed toward a prisoner by an employee, volunteer, official visitor, or agency representative. Romantic relationships between staff and prisoners are included. Consensual or nonconsensual sexual acts include intentional touching of the genitalia, anus, groin, breast, inner thigh, or buttocks with the intent to abuse, arouse, or gratify sexual desire; or completed, attempted, threatened, or requested sexual acts; or occurrences of indecent exposure, invasion of privacy, or staff voyeurism for sexual gratification." Staff sexual harassment is defined as "repeated verbal statements or comments of a sexual nature to a prisoner by employee, volunteer, official visitor, or agency representative, including demeaning references to gender or derogatory comments about body or clothing; or profane or obscene language or gestures." (Beck & Hughes, 2005, p. 3)

in the general prison population, women/girls were overrepresented as victims of abusive sexual contact and youth-on-youth nonconsensual sexual acts.

Tracking data collected over the next 11 years, SSV reports by Beck, Rantala, and Rexroat (2014) show a drop in the number of allegations of sexual violence in 2005, followed by statistically significant increases to 8,404 allegations in 2011. During this time, however, only a small percentage of allegations were substantiated. Based on their study of sexual victimization in Texas state prisons, Austin, Fabelo, Gunter, and McGinnis (2006) proposed that low rates of substantiation may be attributable to the implementation of programs encouraging the reporting of sexual assaults without equal resources for investigation, as well as significant delays in the reporting of most incidents.

Based on NIS survey data for 12 months in 2011 and 2012, Beck et al. (2013) reported 57,900 incidents of sexual victimization in state and federal prisons and 22,700 incidents of victimization in jails. Patterns in prisoner-on-prisoner victimization (reported by just over 50% of prisoners) included higher rates of female victimization (although a higher frequency of males were victimized), White victimization (compared to Black victimization), and victimization of older prisoners. Patterns in staff-on-prisoner victimizations (reported by nearly 60% of prisoners) included higher rates of victimization among males (compared to females) in jails, Blacks (compared to Whites) in prisons and jails, and prisoners aged 24 and under (Beck et al., 2013; Beck et al., 2014).

Among several especially vulnerable populations, Beck et al. (2013) found that those incarcerated for violent sexual offenses reported higher rates of prisoner-on-prisoner sexual victimization than other prisoners. Transgender prisoners reported one of the highest rates of victimization, with 35 percent of those in prisons and 34 percent in jails reporting sexual victimization by a prisoner or staff member in the past year (Beck, 2014b). Similarly, Beck et al. (2013) found that prisoners reporting their sexual orientation as gay, lesbian, bisexual, or other had a prisoner-on-prisoner victimization rate of 12.2 percent in prison (8.5% in jail) and a staff-on-prisoner victimization rate of 5.4 percent (4.3% in jail). Among prisoners suffering from psychological problems in state and federal prisons, about 6 percent reported being sexually victimized by another prisoner. And while special studies examining unique victimization risks of imprisoned juveniles reported 9,500 allegations of youth sexual victimization in juvenile facilities between 2007 and 2012, percentages of juveniles reporting sexual victimization in juvenile detention centers (1.7%–2.3%) and adult facilities (1.8%–2.3%) were not statistically different from percentages of adult reports (1.6%–2.4%) (Beck et al., 2013; Beck & Rantala, 2016).

Pointing to the problematic nature of sexual victimization as a form of ongoing victimization, 60 percent of sexual assault victims in Wolff and Shi's (2009) survey study of 6,964 male prisoners reported that the worst-case incident was not the first time they had been sexually assaulted by the same individual. However, comparing rates of sexual victimization to rates of physical assault, Wolff and Shi (2009) also noted that significantly more prisoners reported being physically assaulted (21%) than sexually victimized (2%–5%). This calls attention to the potential error of funneling so many resources towards the problem of sexual victimization in prison without an equal or greater allotment of resources devoted to the issue of physical assault.

CORRECTIONAL OFFICER VICTIMIZATION

While the majority of research and data on victimization within the correctional system focuses on prisoners, prison violence also affects correctional officers and other prison staff. In a report by the National Institute of Justice, Ferdik and Smith (2017) drew from existing literature to highlight the dangers and risks facing correctional officers. In addition to the commonly recognized threats of violent prisoner behavior, riots, and gang conflicts, other physical, institutional, and psychological dangers identified included infectious diseases, dangerous contraband, co-worker conflicts, and understaffing or inadequate resources. As a result, officers suffered from stress, burnout, serious injury, and even death.

Utilizing data from the Bureau of Labor Statistics Census of Fatal Occupational Injuries (CFOI) and National Electronic Injury Surveillance

System occupational injury supplement (NEISS-Work), Konda, Tiesman, Reichard, and Hartley (2013) reported 113 fatalities and 125,200 nonfatal injuries among correctional officers between 1999 and 2008, with the number and percentage of officers sustaining injuries reaching their highest level in 2006 (17,300, 14%). In 38 percent of nonfatal injury cases, assaults or violent acts were listed as the cause, with 37 percent occurring while restraining or interacting with a disruptive prisoner. Among fatal injuries, assaults or violent acts were indicated as the cause in 40 percent of cases, planned homicides in 25 percent, and suicides in 15 percent. In an examination of 79 serious assaults on prison staff in 2007 and 2008, however, Sorensen, Cunningham, Vigen, and Woods (2011) also point out that serious assault incidents are actually quite rare (only 284 per 100,000 staff or 53 per 100,000 prisoners).

Adhering to similar logic as studies on prisoner-on-prisoner victimization, research on assaults on prison staff also offers insight into the contexts of such assaults and potential predictors of non-random victimization risk. Most cases involved a single assailant and victim (88.6%), the use of the body (43%) or a knife/shank (21%) as a weapon, and took place in a corridor (32%) or cell (26%) (Sorensen et al., 2011). The most commonly cited reasons for attacks on correctional officers were a random act of violence (26%), a response to an officer's command (13%), and a protest to perceived injustice or unfairness (11%) (Lahm, 2009).

Taking into account both individual and institutional characteristics, Lahm (2009) found that correctional facilities with fewer staff per prisoner and larger proportions of non-White prisoners had an increased risk of officer assault. Utilizing a model based on officer routines, target vulnerability/antagonism, and guardianship, Steiner and Wooldredge (2017) found that younger male officers who were White, higher in rank, and/or had more years of service were at higher risk for victimization. Additionally, facilities with linear architectural designs, a large percentage of officers who felt rules were under-enforced, and higher rates of prisoner-on-prisoner assault put officers at higher risk of assault.

VICTIMS OF INCARCERATION: A CONTENT ANALYSIS

While studies on the evolution of correctional theory and policy shed some light on how incarcerated individuals may or may not be perceived as victims, little research has been done on how the media represents victims of incarceration. To better understand media representations of victimization related to incarceration, the extent of its coverage, the types of victimization represented, and the portrayal of its victims, we conducted a study examining 317 articles published by the National Desk section of *The New York Times* referencing victimization related within the correctional system between 2001 and 2015.[3]

ARTICLE ATTRIBUTES

For our initial analysis of *The New York Times* coverage of victimization related to incarceration, we examined several characteristics of the

---

[3] After limiting the focus by source and date, the initial sample of articles for the study was downloaded from an online news index by using the following search string: "National Desk" AND (prison* OR jail* OR "correctional facili*" OR "department of corrections") AND ((inmate* OR prisoner* OR guard* OR "correction* officer*") AND (kill* OR murder* OR assault* OR injur* OR violence)) NOT (death row). The * at the end of search terms allowed for different derivations of words, so kill* would return results that contained kill, kills, killed, or killing.

From the articles downloaded, we then systematically identified those containing some reference to victimization within or during incarceration at a U.S. correctional facility, specifically articles recounting incidents or patterns of violence/victimization, court hearings and/or legislation regarding alleged victimization, articles related to particular correctional system practices or policies deemed to be victimizing, profiles of victims, and articles relaying the findings of research or reports on in-prison victimization.

Articles about death row prisoners were systematically excluded due to our assessment of the discussion of the death penalty as a form of victimization as a separate, albeit extremely important, topic from that of general victimization within correctional facilities. Articles detailing victimization primarily occurring before individuals were incarcerated, such as while being arrested, were excluded as such victimization would be better categorized as victimization by police. Articles detailing abuses in non–U.S. based military prisons, such as Abu Ghraib and Guantanamo Bay detention camp, were also excluded due to their existence outside the U.S. corrections system. And incidents reported at immigrant detention centers were excluded as not all detainees are held on criminal charges and such detention represents a specialized form of incarceration not representative of the correctional system in general.

Out of a total of 2,061 articles initially identified, 317 articles were selected based on our inclusion criteria. An analysis of the sample based on victimization characteristics and risk factors identified in the literature and initial article analysis resulted in the following findings.

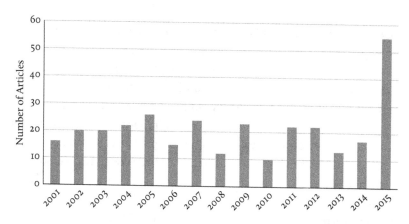

FIGURE 3.1   Number of *New York Times* Articles by Year

articles themselves. The first was the prevalence of coverage on the subject over time. As Figure 3.1 shows, between 2001 and 2015, the number of articles concerned with victimization within the correctional system ranged between 10 and 55 articles per year, with an average of 21 articles per year. The only year with a significantly increased amount of coverage (55 articles) is 2015. Rather than arising from a single high-profile incident, this elevation appears to be a culmination of coverage of a number of different incidents or areas of victimization, including 17 articles reporting on alleged abuse of prisoners by correctional officers, eight articles about the victimization of transgender prisoners and related court cases, eight articles related to sentencing reform, and six articles detailing specific outbreaks of violence in prisons.

Other article attributes examined as a reflection of the type of coverage given to prisoner or correctional officer victims were article type, placement, word count, and authorship. Out of all 317 articles—with some articles fitting into more than one category—164 (51%) primarily reported the details of one or more specific incidents of victimization, 138 (44%) reported on legal action or a court ruling related to an incident or practice of victimization, 93 (29%) examined a widespread practice or policy considered to be victimizing, 38 (12%) reported on recently issued research or reports, and 27 (9%) were profiles of specific victims or facilities (though many more articles contained brief descriptions of individual victims as examples).

In contrast with most reporting on victimization outside of prison, criminal justice system practices and policies, such as mandatory sentencing laws or the use of solitary confinement, are often presented as victimizing in themselves. Also unique to reporting on victimization within the correctional system is a larger percentage of articles that prominently feature recent research. Among those articles, sources include government bodies (e.g., the U.S. Justice Department), academic institutions, other newspapers, think tanks (e.g., The Pew Center), advocacy groups (e.g., The Sentencing Project), and rights advocates (e.g., The ACLU, Human Rights Watch). Topics include the effects of solitary confinement, the treatment of mentally ill prisoners, conditions in specific jails/prison systems, and general prison statistics.

The majority of the articles (238, 75%) were written by staff authors—reflecting an allocation of company time and resources—while only 79 (25%) were obtained from wire services (e.g., Associated Press, Reuters). Thirty-seven articles (12%) ran on the front page of a section—a placement reflecting a higher level of importance and visibility. Among those articles given front page placement, the type of victimization most referenced was excessive sentencing (17), followed by physical assault (15), sexual assault (10), and some sort of discriminatory treatment (10). The only type of incident/victimization never referenced in a front-page article was injury or death due to an accident (e.g., a vehicle accident or prison fire). Due to the variety of article types included in the analysis, article length varied greatly with a minimum of 52 words, a maximum of 5,250 words, and average length of 775 words. In general, the shortest articles were news briefs with minimal details on recent incidents of violence or announcements of charges, lawsuits, or sentencing decisions in court cases related to incidents of violence. Articles with the highest word counts (2,000 words and above) all had front page placement and dealt with topics including civil commitment, sentencing reform, ongoing abuse at Rikers Island in New York City, medical neglect of HIV-positive prisoners, special units for individuals convicted of terrorist acts, and a profile of a transgender prisoner who filed a lawsuit to obtain safe housing and hormone therapy.

VICTIMIZATION/INCIDENT CHARACTERISTICS

Next, we examined characteristics of victimization covered in *The New York Times* articles—including type of victimization, length of victimization, number of victims affected, and other contextual factors. It should be noted that many articles dealt with incidents involving multiple victims and/or addressed different incidents or types of victimization, therefore categories are not mutually exclusive.

As indicated in Table 3.1, the most represented type of victimization, appearing in 49 percent of the articles, was physical assault, followed by medical neglect (24%), excess sentencing (21%), and the

TABLE 3.1   Victimization Characteristics (*n* = 317)

VARIABLES	MEASURES	*n*	% OF TOTAL	% W/ INMATE VICTIM	% W/ C.O. VICTIM
Victimization Type	Physical Assault	156	49	78	33
	Property	17	5	88	47
	Sexual Assault	47	15	87	22
	Coerced Sex	18	6	100	16
	Sexual Harassment	17	5	94	6
	Self-Harm	44	14	98	11
	Basic Needs	62	20	98	21
	Medical Neglect	75	24	99	13
	No Rehab	21	7	100	29
	Solitary Confinement	37	12	100	14
	Excess Sentence	65	21	98	9
	Other Rights Violation	25	8	100	0
	Accident	8	3	88	63

(*continued*)

TABLE 3.1 Victimization Characteristics (*n* = 317) (*Continued*)

VARIABLES	MEASURES	n	% OF TOTAL	% W/ INMATE VICTIM	% W/ C.O. VICTIM
Injuries	Physical	164	52	83	30
	Death	111	35	83	31
	Psychological	38	12	95	13
	Financial	6	2	83	17
	Job Loss	16	5	81	38
	Other	14	4	93	21
	Not Mentioned	143	45	88	13
Number of Victims	Single	95	30	83	12
	>1 (different incident)	156	49	97	17
	>1 (same incident)	80	25	74	44
Victimization Length	Single Incident	121	38	73	45
	Multiple/Ongoing	197	62	96	14
Context	Riot	28	9	89	46
	Escape	28	9	18	71
	Overcrowding	49	15	98	27
	Understaffing	30	9	87	30
	Understaffing	30	9	87	30

denial of basic needs (20%). Examples of such victimization coverage included articles about poor care for HIV-positive prisoners and transgender individuals being denied hormone therapy, juveniles serving life sentences for murder, individuals serving long sentences under three-strikes laws, and prisoners sleeping on floors, surrounded by filth and/or in excessively hot or cold conditions. Incidents of self-harm (usually resulting in suicide) appeared in 14 percent of the articles. And sexual assault appeared in 15 percent of the articles, with coerced sexual acts and sexual harassment only appearing in 6 and 5 percent respectively.

In over half of the articles (62%), the victimization mentioned involved multiple incidents or ongoing victimization. Examples of such articles include indictments of harsh conditions and failures to reform in New York's Rikers Island Prison and Orleans Parish Prison in New Orleans, and an article reporting multiple stories of prisoner victims of sexual assault. In contrast, only 38 percent of articles address a solitary incident. Reflective of a higher proportion of articles detailing multiple occurrences of victimization, 49 percent of articles introduce multiple victims of different incidents while only 30 percent portray a single victim. In 25 percent of articles, however, a single incident with multiple victims (such as a riot) is described. Generally involving physical assaults resulting in multiple injuries or deaths, victimization within the context of a riot or escape is mentioned in 18 percent of the articles.

For nearly all victimization forms/incident types, prisoners are represented as the victims in much higher proportions than correctional officers. The one type of incident in which correctional officers are represented more than prisoners is escape attempts, frequently including a direct attack on one or more correctional officers by a prisoner. Additionally, correctional officers are represented almost equally to prisoners in accidental victimization, such as vehicle accidents or fires in which both officers and prisoners are injured. Because multiple types of victimization are mentioned in a large proportion of the articles, however, indications of association between specific victim groups and types of victimization were at times flawed (such as the representation of correctional officers as victims of solitary confinement).

Regarding other contextual factors related to victimization within the correctional system, such as type of facility or security level, the articles tend to provide fewer details. However, several trends are worth noting. Out of all 317 articles, 114 articles (36%) make no mention of the type of facility (federal, state, local) in which the victimization took place. In some instances, this is due to the use of facility names that contain no indication of facility type. In other cases, it is due to the article's reference to victimization as more system-wide than occurring at any specific facility. When type of facility or correctional system are indicated, however, the most mentioned are state prisons (121, 38%), followed by county jails (68, 21%), federal facilities (20, 6%), and juvenile detention centers (15, 5%). The private management of a facility is specifically mentioned in only 23 articles (7%). And while the security level of institutions is rarely included, when it is, maximum security is the most mentioned (28, 8%). References to the specific times or locations of incidents are also rare—in many cases due to a focus on ongoing practices of victimization rather than specific incidents. Regarding other facility characteristics, the most mentioned jail/prison characteristics related to various types of victimization are overcrowding (49, 15%) and understaffing (30, 9%).

VICTIM PORTRAYALS

Moving on from characteristics of victimization, our next area of examination was the portrayal of victims of incarceration. In our analysis, we looked at who the victims are, what is shared about them, and any patterns in their portrayals. As shown in Table 3.1 and Table 3.2, prisoner victims are portrayed significantly more than any other victim type. Prisoners are

TABLE 3.2. Victim Characteristics (n = 317)

VARIABLES	MEASURES	n	%
Victim Type	Inmate	276	87
	C.O.	66	21
	Other Staff	17	5
	Outside Person	13	5
Name	Named	182	57
	Not Named	136	43
Photo	Victim	80	25
	Perpetrator	17	5
Victim Blame	Yes	43	14
Age	Under 19	48	15
	19–24	33	10

TABLE 3.2. (*Continued*)

VARIABLES	MEASURES	n	%
	25–29	16	5
	30–34	13	4
	35–39	21	7
	40–44	10	3
	Over 44	65	20
	No Mention	170	54
Race	White	9	3
	Non-White	51	16
	No Mention	260	82
Gender	Male	180	57
	Female	59	19
	Transgender	13	4
	No Mention	102	32
Sexuality	Heterosexual	7	2
	Homosexual	7	2
	No Mention	305	96
Mental Health	Issues	60	19
	No Mention	257	81
Criminal Background	Violent	82	26
	Non-Violent	71	22
	Drugs	38	12
	Sex	39	12
	Terrorism	4	1
	No Mention	185	58

listed as the victims in 276 (87%) articles, while correctional officers are listed as the victims in only 66 (21%), other staff in 17 (5%), and an outside individual in 13 (4%). Beyond identification of victim type, however, further details identifying victims as unique persons are less consistent; especially with many articles on broad patterns of victimization or breaking news stories referring to victims as only prisoners or correctional officers.

When victims are further identified, several demographic variables representative of different victim groups or individual risk factors—such as age, race, gender, and sexuality—are sometimes included. Able to be conveyed simply through the use of gendered pronouns, victim gender is identifiable in 215 (68%) of the articles. Not surprisingly, males (a larger proportion of the prison population) are represented much more than females (Stephan, 2008). Going beyond simply using gender-specific pronouns, 13 articles (4%) specifically state victims' gender identity as transgender. Transgender (women) victims are primarily featured in articles related to lawsuits over safe housing in prison, rights to express their gender identity, and the provision of hormone therapy. The next most mentioned demographic characteristic of victims is their age. While over half (54%) of articles do not state victims' ages, when ages of victims are listed, the largest categories of victim ages are the youngest (juveniles and adults under 25) and the oldest (individuals over 44), both categories of victims are considered vulnerable and thus "worthy" within crime story scripts (Pritchard & Hughes, 1997). Articles mentioning young victims include a number about juveniles serving life sentences (presented as excessive). Juveniles also represent 30 percent of prisoner victims who are presented as suffering from/being victimized because of mental health issues. Articles mentioning older victims often frame their long sentences as excessive. Additionally, the association of older victims with younger attackers validates their status as more vulnerable, and thus newsworthy, victims.

Victims' race or ethnicity is also occasionally stated (or possible to infer from gang associations) in 18 percent of the articles. When race/ethnicity is mentioned, non-White victims (predominantly African American or Latino) are mentioned nearly six times more than White victims, reflecting both the larger non-White population in prisons and their status as the more vulnerable category of victims due to their minority status (Stephan & Karberg, 2003). Examples of articles that mention victims' minority racial status include articles on incidents of violence attributed to racial conflict as well as examinations of three-strikes laws and mandatory sentencing for drug crimes which disproportionally affect racial/ ethnic minorities. Victims with mental health issues are featured in 60 articles (19%), also representing a category of victims perceived as especially vulnerable. Several articles specifically mention a victim's mental health issues as an unaddressed risk preceding their suicide, while others more generally reference the lack of adequate treatment for prisoners with mental health issues. Victim sexuality is mentioned even more rarely (in only 4% of the articles). However, while victim heterosexuality is only ever inferred through the mention of a victim's relationship, victim homosexuality (when mentioned) is specifically called out by victims who attribute their victimization to their sexuality. When considering specific attributes of victims more frequently mentioned, it is valuable to note that authors not only chose to report certain characteristics about the victims mentioned, but chose certain victims to portray in more detail, potentially based on their characterization as more "worthy."

Beyond the handful of personal/demographic characteristics mentioned, *The New York Times'* portrayal of victims is also shaped by several choices regarding how such victims and their victimization are presented. Reflecting both the editorial decision to personify a victim and the ability to find a victim willing to have their name put in print, 182 articles (57%) use the name of at least one victim, even if other victims in the same article remain unnamed. The use of photos of victims in 80 articles (25%) also indicates an effort to humanize victims. Examples of victim photos that accompanied articles include those of juveniles serving life sentences and a transgender prisoner whose story is featured in multiple articles.

Related to the concept of prisoners as both victims of violence as well as criminals, another victim characteristic mentioned in 42 percent of the articles is the criminal charge(s) for which individuals were imprisoned. When prisoners' criminal backgrounds were mentioned, violent crimes were listed in 82 articles (26% of the total sample), nonviolent crimes in 71 (22%), drug crimes in 38 (12%), sex crimes in (12%), and terrorism in four (1%). What is interesting is that the presentation of individuals' criminal histories is not always done in a way that diminishes their worthiness as a victim by emphasizing their deviance. In the case of victims sentenced for violent offenses (frequently committed as juveniles), such offenses are often explained in detail and the prisoner's culpability in them brought into question. Nonviolent and drug offenses are frequently mentioned as a "third-strike" or minor crime resulting in what is presented as an excessive, victimizing sentence. Perhaps the only crime routinely mentioned in a way that villainizes the victim are sex offenses, such as in the 14 articles related to the murder of defrocked priest John Geoghan. Even in that instance, however, his crimes are also presented as a factor that put him at increased risk of victimization, and for which he should have been provided better protection.

While the concept of **victim blaming** is most commonly associated with victims of rape, in our analysis, we examined articles for blame placed on any type of victim. While not a common occurrence or the primary perspective taken by any article, 43 of the articles (14%) contain at least one statement conveying that the victim is somehow responsible for or deserving of their victimization. In most cases, that blame is inserted through a quote from an individual connected to the story. For example, one article cites two officers claiming that the victim of their attack attacked them first. An article about the suicide of convicted kidnapper and rapist Ariel Castro quotes the county prosecutor as saying, "This man couldn't take, for even a month, a small portion of what he had dished out for more than a decade" (Williams & Schwirtz, 2013, para. 16). In one case, a message of self-blame is echoed by a transgender prisoner even as she seeks the court's help in protecting her from sexual assault, saying, "If I wasn't so feminine, maybe if I didn't talk the way I talked or move the way I moved, I would be less of a victim that way" (Sontag, 2015, para. 2).

REASON, RESPONSIBILITY, & RESPONSE

Although our study is primarily concerned with victims (rather than their victimizers), several observations regarding offender motivations and the articles' portrayal of responsibility are worth noting (Table 3.3). Although not always stated, 36 percent of the articles made some reference to a reason for victimization related to a personal characteristic of the victim

TABLE 3.3 Motives/Responsibility for Victimization (*n* = 317)

VARIABLES	MEASURES	*n*	%
Interpersonal Motivation	Racial	43	14
	Gang	32	10
	Religion	15	5
	Criminal Background	29	9
	Sexual Orientation	14	4
	Gender Identity	13	4
	Retaliation	21	7
Facility Characteristics	Overcrowded	49	15
	Understaffed	30	9
Perpetrator(s)	Inmate	121	38
	Correctional Officer	95	30
	Other Staff	24	8
	Outside Individual	10	3
	Not Stated	112	35
Responsibility	Individual	63	20
	Group	126	40
	System	207	65

or interpersonal conflict/difference between the victim and offender. Among the most stated interpersonal motivations for victimization are race or gang conflicts (often interrelated), followed by attacks based on a victim's criminal background (usually sex crimes) and retaliation (such as for talking back to an officer or snitching). Other motivations mentioned less frequently include religious discrimination or victimization targeting individuals based on their gender identity or sexuality.

As noted earlier, however, environmental factors are also frequently mentioned as a cause or even a source of victimization. In fact, overcrowding was cited as a contributor to victimization more frequently (in 15% of the articles) than any category of interpersonal motivation.

Moving on to an examination of perpetrators of victimization, such a portrayal of systematic over individual responsibility is even more apparent. Out of all 317 articles, 63 (20%) identify individual perpetrators, while 126 (40%) identify a group. Among those individuals or groups, the types of perpetrators are identified as prisoners in 121 articles (38%), correctional officers in 95 (30%), other staff in 24 (8%), and an outside individual in 10 (3%). However, in 112 articles (35%), no specific individual/groups are identified at all. And in over half of all of the articles sampled (207, 65%), the broader correctional and/or criminal justice system is identified as either solely or partially responsible. Portrayal of the system as the primary perpetrator/responsible party is most common in articles about the victimizing nature of wider-reaching policies, practices, or issues—such as mandatory sentencing, solitary confinement, or overcrowding. Even in incident-focused articles, however, the system is often implicated in creating conditions in which prisoners were able to escape, harm officers or one another, or kill themselves.

Because many articles present victimization in the context of lawsuits, court proceedings, and/or legislation and policy debates, such portrayals sometimes include actions taken in response to victimization. One hundred and twelve articles (35%) referenced some sort of investigation that had been launched in response to a particular incident or pattern of victimization. A smaller percentage referenced punishment (45, 14%) and/or the arrest/charging (66, 20%) of responsible parties. Even fewer articles (18, 6%) made note of perpetrators being convicted. Coming back to a systematic focus on responsibility, however, 66 articles (21%) referred to a single ruling passed to remedy an incident of victimization, while 60 articles (19%) noted court orders or legislation mandating broader policy changes.

DISCUSSION: MEDIA PORTRAYALS VS. EMPIRICAL RESEARCH

Comparing victimization portrayed in *The New York Times* articles to research on victimization within correctional facilities, we find both similarities and differences. On the incident level, the types of victimization most often portrayed in articles both contrast with and resemble those most studied in empirical literature. Among the most mentioned forms of victimization in *The New York Times* articles, medical neglect, excess sentencing, and denial of basic needs are rarely the subject of empirical studies of in-prison victimization. In contrast, physical assault, the subject of much research, is the most mentioned form of victimization in *The New York Times* articles, and sexual victimization, homicide, and suicide (all subjects of some amount of study) are mentioned in a fair number of articles as well. Though the difference between the prevalence of physical (21% of inmates) versus sexual victimization (2%–5% of inmates) is greater in Wolff and Shi's (2009) study than in *The New York Times* articles, more articles still deal with physical assault (49%) than sexual assault (15%). However, in contrast to empirical findings that most assaults only result in minor injuries, a near equal number of articles (25%) report assault-related deaths as nonfatal injuries. Additionally, the balance of articles that mention suicide (8%) and homicide (25%) fail to represent the significantly higher frequency of suicides (33.8% in jails, 5.5% in prisons) compared with homicides (2.9% in jails, 2.6% in prisons) in official data (Noonan et al., 2015).

As expected, articles dealing with sexual assault in prison increased for several years following the 2003 passage of PREA. However, there are no articles on the topic in 2006 and 2010 and a drop in coverage after 2009, indicating lower media attention on sexual victimization in prison compared to the amount of empirical research on the subject.[4] While not prolific, 56 articles situate violence within the course of riots and escape attempts, a context rarely reported in research. Also interesting is the association of over half of correctional officer injuries with coverage of riots or escapes rather than the daily risk, danger, and/or injuries caused by single prisoner assaults reported in most studies on correctional officer victimization (Sorensen et al., 2011).

---

[4] It's important to consider that the lower numbers of articles on sexual assaults in prisons could be a feature of our search for articles containing the words "sexual assault" and not "rape" rather than of the coverage itself. A significant rise in articles dealing with sexual assault in prison in 2015—made up primarily of articles about transgender prisoners and featuring two articles about the failure to curb prison rapes since the passage of PREA—however, indicates that media attention on the topic may have been on the rise in recent years.

As found in a number of studies on violence in prison, victims rarely endure single incidents of victimization, a characteristic also reflected in articles that primarily depict ongoing rather than single incidents of victimization (Wolff et al., 2007; Wolff & Shi, 2009). Another common theme in studies of in-prison victimization is underreporting or failure to substantiate (prove) that such incidents occurred—perpetuating the belief that far more incidents of assault and sexual assault occur than are officially recorded. While underreporting and substantiation are never directly addressed in any of the articles studied, several characteristics of the articles and their presentation of victimization allude to both scenarios. With 43 percent of articles associated with court actions or rulings related to incidents/practices of victimization, nearly half of the coverage deals only with victimization/victims who have come forward and also had the resources to gain the attention of the courts. In many instances, those same cases (and individuals) are mentioned as examples in multiple articles, with other victims of similar incidents going unmentioned. A comparison of the number of articles which mention court cases (138, 44%) to the number of articles mentioning punishment (45, 14%), criminal charges (66, 21%), convictions (18, 6%) and/or legislative action (66, 21%) taken to remedy an act of victimization could also be interpreted as a representation of the stark difference between the number of victimization incidents reported and those that are substantiated (much less) (Beck et al., 2014).

Regarding victim portrayals, a number of the victim traits mentioned in articles correlate with individual risk factors identified in research. As in the research, considerably more articles mention prisoner victims than correctional officer victims. Victims who are younger or older than the average prison population were more frequently mentioned, both age groups which research has identified as at increased risk of victimization (Kerbs & Jolley, 2007; Steiner et al., 2017). Just as male prisoners are the subject of most research on prisoner victimization, most articles portray male (rather than female) prisoners as victims; only one article—detailing ongoing sexual coercion and rape of female prisoners by officers in a specific facility—specifically mentions the victimization of female prisoners.

Identified as particularly at risk of sexual victimization in government reports and empirical research, LGBTQ individuals are featured in a number of articles detailing not only their sexual victimization, but physical assault and medical neglect (Beck et al., 2013). Additionally, the increased victimization risk and/or neglect of mentally ill individuals identified in research is portrayed in nearly 20 percent of the articles.

In line with conflicting empirical findings regarding the role of race in prisoner victimization, few articles directly reference victim race. When they do, it is often associated with race-based gang conflict or gang membership, another individual characteristic identified as increasing individual victimization risk in prison (Wolff et al., 2009). In contrast, other victim characteristics examined in research literature, such as prior abuse, employment, or relationship issues, are never or only rarely mentioned in articles (Suto & Arnaut, 2010; Wolff et al., 2009). When such details are shared, they are only provided in longer, more investigative articles or profiles, both of which are less common than briefer descriptions of incidents or related legislative action. While victims' criminal background is often mentioned, the relatively equal mention of victims with both violent and nonviolent criminal histories runs counter to research showing that individuals with violent criminal backgrounds are at greater risk for victimization (victim/offender overlap). One explanation for such an occurrence may be that a significant proportion of articles depict individuals as victims of policies such as excessive sentencing, in the context of which prisoner's less severe crimes are a defining aspect of their victim status. Possibly due to the same focus on system-wide abuses, even fewer personal details are provided on perpetrators of victimization, especially in a context within which relationships between victim and offender characteristics can be ascertained and their individual characteristics compared (as done in most empirical studies).

Perhaps the most notable difference between research on victimization related to incarceration and *The New York Times* coverage of victims of incarceration, however, is the frequent depiction of victimization as perpetrated by a broader system rather than an individual offender. Throughout *The New York Times* articles, victimization due to medical neglect, the failure to meet basic needs, and excessive sentencing is presented alongside other forms of victimization and as the sole focus of a number of articles. However, in research on victimization, such factors are more likely to be studied as only a potential environmental or individual risk factor. While empirical research looks to individual characteristics as well as broader contexts to explain in-prison victimization, *The New York Times* articles' placement of responsibility on the system puts significantly more emphasis on the victimizing influence of correctional policies and practices than the characteristics of incarcerated individuals themselves.[5] In many instances, this focus may be due to the types of stories *The New York Times* chooses to tell. However, one should also consider whether such a representation of systematic responsibility could be related to an attempt to avoid reporting stories in ways that blame victims.

LIMITATIONS & IMPLICATIONS FOR FUTURE RESEARCH

While a significant amount of data was gathered in our analysis of *The New York Times* articles on victimization due to incarceration, some of the steps taken to gather details about the different victims and/or incidents mentioned in each article limited our ability to quantify and analyze the attributes of individual incidents. In many cases, articles contained references to more than one type of victimization. As noted in our description of article attributes, many articles also referenced multiple victims, and in some cases, different types of victims (e.g., correctional officers as well as prisoners). The same was often true of perpetrators. This sometimes produced results in which multiple incidents, victims, and victim characteristics were all associated with each other without a clear indication of which victims went with which incidents, which characteristics went with which victims, and which pairs of victims and perpetrators went together.

---

[5] While not discussed in our literature review, it should be noted that criminal justice scholarship certainly does not ignore the concept of systematic victimization within the correctional system. Such research, however, is more likely to be associated with scholarship and debates related to the broader correctional theories and policies rather than the study of victimization within the system itself (Cullen & Jonson, 2017).

In some cases, this resulted in what appeared to be associations between certain types of victims and victimizations which did not occur (such as correctional officers and solitary confinement). Overall, this limited our ability to compare specific types of incidents involving different types of victims or different victim-offender relationships, either to each other or to findings in empirical research.

Because *The New York Times* articles detailing general patterns of victimization do not always differentiate between types of victimization, their victims, and their perpetrators in their own reporting, this association of multiple victims and types of victimization is not completely unavoidable. To allow for comparisons of different victim-offender relationships and/or different victims of specific types of victimization, alternate approaches to coding might be considered in future studies. One approach might be to focus solely on one type of victimization within the correctional system, such as sexual assault. In doing this, victimization could be more specifically coded as prisoner-on-prisoner, prisoner-on-staff, or staff-on-prisoner. Additionally, characteristics for different types of victims and/or offenders could be coded under separate categories—such as prisoner-victim characteristics versus correctional officer-victim characteristics—ensuring traits stay associated with the correct type of victim. Due to the prevalence of portrayals of systematic victimization in *The New York Times* articles, future studies might also consider focusing more specifically on systematic abuses. In doing so, the coding of specific policies or practices considered victimizing could yield more valuable insight into what aspects of the system or types of rights violations are portrayed most often. Due to the establishment of most correctional policies at the state level, such studies might also add value by coding the states represented in each article.

Another set of limitations that should be considered are our original search terms and exclusion criteria. In light of the broader range of types of victimization that appeared in our search results, future studies should consider using search terms representing other forms of victimization that appeared in the articles analyzed, and which might have appeared more frequently if they were included in the search terms. Additionally, while our study did not examine indirect victimization, future studies might consider such portrayals—examining what individuals and/or communities are portrayed as indirect victims, the extent of their portrayal, and the nature of their victimization. As noted earlier, our use of the search phrase "sexual assault" may not have captured articles that used the term "rape." As such, future studies should consider adding "rape" to their search terms. In terms of our exclusion criteria, while victimization at both immigrant detention centers and military prisons overseas was excluded, such delineations may not be made in the formation of public perceptions of victimization within the correctional system. Thus, their portrayals in the media may be important to include in such a study as well.

CONCLUSION

In sum, this analysis demonstrates that media coverage of victimization within the correctional system as presented in The New York Times is, in many ways, reflective of key victimization characteristics and risk factors featured in empirical literature. At the same time, the coverage is also driven by a distinct perspective that focuses on the victimizing nature of a number of widespread policies and practices and emphasizes systematic responsibility. In its portrayal of victims of incarceration, The New York Times offers attention to prisoners and correctional staff in relative proportion to their rate of victimization reflected in empirical literature. In most cases, both types of victims are also portrayed as "worthy" of their victim status, with offenders' past crimes often downplayed or presented as immaterial to their right to be protected from violence and correctional officers rarely blamed for their own injury. In fact, prisoners and correctional officers are also rarely blamed when they are the perpetrators of violence, demonstrating a perspective throughout the articles that blames the correctional system over any individual. The result is a body of articles that conveys the correctional system as victimizing, the prisoners within it as deserving of more rights than they are granted, and the system in need of considerable reform. However, while such a message is one reformers are likely to embrace, we must also consider the limitations of such broad depictions of blame in facilitating the type of informed change that is needed to actually fix any system. Ultimately, *The New York Times'* depiction of victimization within the correctional system reminds us that victimization in prisons and jails is much like victimization outside of correctional facilities. Victimization is a complex event resulting from interconnected individual, cultural, structural, and systematic elements that are unlikely to ever be fully captured in print.

REFERENCES

Austin J., Fabelo T., Gunter A., & McGinnis K. (2006). *Sexual violence in the Texas prison system* (NCJ 215774). Washington, DC: The JFA Institute. Retrieved from https://www.ncjrs.gov/pdffiles1/nij/grants/215774.pdf

Beck, A. J. (2014a). *Prison Rape Elimination Act of 2003: PREA data collection activities, 2014* (NCJ 245694). Washington, DC: U.S. Bureau of Justice Statistics. Retrieved from https://www.bjs.gov/content/pub/pdf/pdca14.pdf

Beck, A. J. (2014b). *Sexual victimization in prisons and jails reported by prisoners, 2011–12: Supplemental tables: Prevalence of sexual victimization among transgender adult prisoners* (NCJ 241399). Washington, DC: Bureau of Justice Statistics. Retrieved from https://www.bjs.gov/content/pub/pdf/svpjri1112_st.pdf

Beck, A. J., Berzofsky, M., Caspar, R., & Krebs, C. (2013). *Sexual victimization in prisons and jails reported by prisoners, 2011–12* (NCJ 241399). Washington, DC: Bureau of Justice Statistics. Retrieved from https://www.bjs.gov/content/pub/pdf/svpjri1112.pdf

Beck, A. J., & Hughes, T. A. (2005). *Prison Rape Elimination Act of 2003: Sexual violence reported by correctional authorities, 2004* (NCJ 210333). Washington, DC: Bureau of Justice Statistics. Retrieved from https://www.bjs.gov/content/pub/pdf/svrca04.pdf

Beck, A. J., & Rantala, R. R. (2016). *Sexual victimization reported by juvenile correctional authorities, 2007–12* (NCJ 249145). Washington, DC: Bureau of Justice Statistics. Retrieved from https://www.bjs.gov/content/pub/pdf/svrjca0712.pdf

Beck, A. J., Rantala, R. R., & Rexroat, J. (2014). *Special report: Sexual victimization reported by adult correctional authorities, 2009–11* (NCJ 243904). Washington, DC: Bureau of Justice Statistics. Retrieved from https://www.bjs.gov/content/pub/pdf/svraca0911.pdf

Blitz, C. L., Wolff, N., & Shi, J. (2008). Physical victimization in prison: The role of mental illness. *International Journal of Law & Psychiatry, 31*, 385–393. doi:10.1016/j.ijlp.2008.08.005

Bottoms, A. E. (1999). Interpersonal violence and social order in prisons. *Crime and Justice, 26*, 205–281. doi:0192-3234/1999/0026-0006$02.00

Boudoukha, A. H., Altintas, E., Rusinek, S., Fantini-Hauwel, C., & Hautekeete, M. (2013). Prisoners-to-staff assaults, PTSD and burnout: Profiles of risk and vulnerability. *Journal of Interpersonal Violence, 28*(11), 2,332–2,350. doi:10.1177/0886260512475314

Boxer, P., Middlemass, K., & Delorenzo, T. (2009). Exposure to violent crime during incarceration: Effects on psychological adjustment following release. *Criminal Justice and Behavior, 36*(8), 793–807. doi:10.1177/0093854809336453

Bureau of Justice Statistics. (2017). *Census of state and federal adult correctional facilities, 2005* [Data file and code book] ICPSR24642-v3. Retrieved from https://doi.org/10.3886/ICPSR24642.v3

Bureau of Prisons. (2017). *Prisoner prison safety.* [Datasets for May 2004–December 2015]. Retrieved from https://www.bop.gov/about/statistics/statistics_prisoner_safety.jsp

Cullen, F. T., & Jonson, C. L. (2017). *Correctional theory: Context and consequences* (2nd ed.). Thousand Oaks, CA: SAGE.

Cunningham, M. D., Sorensen, J. R., Vigen, M. P., & Woods, S. O. (2010). Prisoner homicides: Killers, victims, motives, and circumstances. *Journal of Criminal Justice, 38*(4), 348–358. doi:10.1016/j.jcrimjus.2010.03.008

Daquin, J., Daigle, L., & Listwan, S. (2016). Vicarious victimization in prison. *Criminal Justice and Behavior, 43*(8), 1018–1033. doi:10.1177/0093854816650479

Dye, M. (2010). Deprivation, importation, and prison suicide: Combined effects of institutional conditions and prisoner composition. *Journal of Criminal Justice, 38*(4), 796–806. doi:10.1016/j.jcrimjus.2010.05.007

Ferdik, F. V., & Smith, H. P. (2017). *Correctional officer safety and wellness literature synthesis* (NCJ 250484). Washington, DC: National Institute of Justice. Retrieved from https://www.ncjrs.gov/pdffiles1/nij/250484.pdf

Gibbons, J. J., & Katzenbach, N. de B. (2006). *Confronting confinement: A report of the commission on safety and abuse in America's prisons.* New York: Vera Institute of Justice. Retrieved from https://www.vera.org/publications/confronting-confinement

Hayes, L. (2012). National study of jail suicide: 20 years later. *Journal of Correctional Health Care: The Official Journal of the National Commission on Correctional Health Care, 18*(3), 233–245. doi:10.1177/1078345812445457

Kerbs, J., & Jolley, J. (2007). Prisoner-on-prisoner victimization among older male prisoners. *Crime and Delinquency, 53*(2), 187–218. doi:10.1177/0011128706294119

Konda, S., Tiesman, H., Reichard, A., & Hartley, D. (2013). U.S. correctional officers killed or injured on the job. *Corrections Today, 75*(5), 122–125. Retrieved from https://www.ncbi.nlm.nih.gov/pmc/articles/PMC4699466/

Lahm, K. F. (2009). Prisoner assaults on prison staff: A multilevel examination of an overlooked form of prison violence. *The Prison Journal, 89*(2), 131–150. doi:10.1177/0032885509334743

Lahm, K. F. (2015). Predictors of violent and nonviolent victimization behind bars: An exploration of women prisoners. *Women & Criminal Justice, 25*(3), 273–291. doi:10.1080/08974454.2014.989304

Noonan, M. E. (2016). *Mortality in state prisons, 2001–2014—statistical tables* (NCJ 250150). Washington, DC: Bureau of Justice Statistics. Retrieved from https://www.bjs.gov/index.cfm?ty=pbdetail&&iid=5866

Noonan, M. E., Rohloff, H., & Ginder, S. (2015). *Mortality in local jails and state prisons, 2000–2013—statistical tables* (NCJ 248756). Washington, DC: Bureau of Justice Statistics. Retrieved from https://www.bjs.gov/index.cfm?ty=pbdetail&iid=5341

Obidoa, C., Reeves, D., Warren, N., Reisine, S., & Cherniack, M. (2011). Depression and work family conflict among corrections officers. *Journal of Occupational and Environmental Medicine, 53*(11), 1294–1301. doi:10.1097/JOM.0b013e3182307888

Pérez, D., Gover, A., Tennyson, K., & Santos, S. (2010). Individual and institutional characteristics related to prisoner victimization. *International Journal of Offender Therapy and Comparative Criminology, 54*(3), 378–394. doi:10.1177/0306624X09335244

Pritchard, D., & Hughes, K. (1997). Patterns of deviance in crime news. *Journal of Communication, 47*(3), 49–67.

Sontag, D. (2015). Judge denies transgender inmate's request for transfer. *The New York Times.* Retrieved from https://www.nytimes.com/2015/04/21/us/judge-denies-ashley-diamonds-a-transgender-inmate-request-for-transfer.html

Sorensen, J. R., Cunningham, M. D., Vigen, M. P., & Woods, S. O. (2011). Serious assaults on prison staff: A descriptive analysis. *Journal of Criminal Justice, 39*(2), 143–150. doi:10.1016/j.jcrimjus.2011.01.002

Steiner, B., Ellison, J. M., Butler, H. D., & Cain, C. M. (2017). The impact of prisoner and prison characteristics on prisoner victimization. *Trauma, Violence & Abuse, 18*(1), 17–36. doi:10.1177/1524838015588503

Steiner, B., & Wooldredge, J. (2017). Individual and environmental influences on prison officer safety. *Justice Quarterly, 34*(2) 324–349. doi:1080/07418825.2016.1164883

Stephan, J. J. (2008). *Census of state and federal correctional facilities 2005* (NCJ222182). Washington, DC: Bureau of Justice Statistics.

Stephan, J. J., & Karberg, J. C. (2003). *Census of state and federal correctional facilities 2000* (NCJ 198272). Washington, DC: Bureau of Justice Statistics.

Suto, I., & Arnaut, G. (2010). Suicide in prison: A qualitative study. *The Prison Journal, 90*(3), 288–312. doi:10.1 177/0032885510373499

Williams, T., & Schwirtz, M. (2013). Death in prison of man who held Ohio women captive prompts investigations. *The New York Times.* Retrieved from https://www.nytimes.com/2013/09/05/us/ariel-castro-cleveland-kidnapper-found-dead-in-prison-cell.html

Wilson, J. Q. (2017). Incapacitation: Locking up the wicked. In F. T. Cullen & C. L. Jonson (Eds.), *Correctional theory: Context and consequences* (2nd ed.). Thousand Oaks, CA: SAGE.

Wolff, N., Blitz, C., Shi, J., Siegel, J., & Bachman, R. (2007). Physical violence inside prison: Rates of victimization. *Criminal Justice and Behavior, 34,* 588–599. doi:10.1177/0093854806296830

Wolff, N., & Shi, J. (2009). Contextualization of physical and sexual assault in male prisons: Incidents and their aftermath. *Journal of Correctional Health Care: The Official Journal of the National Commission on Correctional Health Care, 15*(1), 58–77. doi:10.1177/1078345808326622

Wolff, N., Shi, J., & Bachman, R. (2008). Measuring victimization inside prisons: Questioning the questions. *Journal of Interpersonal Violence, 23*(10), 1343–1362. doi:10.1177/0886260508314301

Wolff, N., Shi, J., & Siegel, J. (2009). Understanding physical victimization inside prisons: Factors that predict risk. *Justice Quarterly, 26,* 445–475. doi:10.1080/07418820802427858

Wooldredge, J., & Steiner, B. (2012). Race group differences in prison victimization experiences. *Journal of Criminal Justice, 40*(5), 358–369. doi:10.1016/j.jcrimjus.2012.06.011

Wooldredge, J., & Steiner, B. (2013) Violent victimization among state prison prisoners. *Violence and Victims, 28*(3), 531–551. doi:10.1891/0886-6708.11-00141

Wooldredge, J., & Steiner, B. (2014). A bi-level framework for understanding prisoner victimization. *Journal of Quantitative Criminology, 30*(1), 141–162. doi:10.1007/s10940-013-9197-y

World Prison Brief. (2017). World Prison Brief data—highest to lowest [Dataset]. Retrieved from http://www.prisonstudies.org/world-prison-brief-data

Zweig, J. M., Yahner, J., Visher, C. A., & Lattimore, P. K. (2014). Using general strain theory to explore the effects of prison victimization experiences on later offending and substance use. *The Prison Journal, 95*, 84–113. doi:10.1177/0032885514563283

KEY TERMS

- *Correctional Facility:* Secure government facilities, such as a federal/state prison or local jails, used to hold individuals charged with or convicted of a crime for the purposes of punishment and/or rehabilitation. Does not include less secure community facilities such as halfway houses, work release centers, or drug rehab facilities.

- *Deprivation Theory:* A theoretical framework which attempts to explain victimization according to characteristics of the prison environment, their alleviation or exacerbation of unsatisfied prisoner needs, and the emergence of different individuals as victims or aggressors based on the prioritization of their own needs.

- *Importation Theory:* A theoretical framework which seeks to explain in-prison victimization risk through the individual characteristics and backgrounds prisoners already possess before they are incarcerated.

- *Lifestyle/Opportunity Theory:* A criminological theory which argues that crime, and in turn victimization, is the result of the convergence of a suitable/attractive victim, a motivated offender, and the lack of guardianship in the same place at same time.

- *PREA:* The Prison Rape Elimination Act, passed by Congress in 2003, which resulted in mandated data collection and research on prison rape; nationwide standards for the prevention, detection, and response to prison rape; and federally funded training and assistance to comply with those mandates.

- *Victim Blaming:* Statements or actions which suggest that a victim is either wholly or partially responsible for the crime committed against them, in some cases portraying them as deserving of their victimization.

- *Victim/Offender Overlap:* An empirically supported relationship between victimization and offending which recognizes that characteristics or behaviors which predispose an individual to (or are involved in) offending also increase an individual's risk of victimization.

THE NEW YORK TIMES ARTICLES

Associated Press. (2001). Guards quell riot at California prison. *The New York Times.* Retrieved from https://www.nytimes.com/2001/12/21/us/guards-quell-riot-at-california-prison.html

Marshall, C. (2005). Panel on prison rape hears victims' chilling accounts. *The New York Times.* Retrieved from https://www.nytimes.com/2005/08/20/politics/panel-on-prison-rape-hears-victims-chilling-accounts.html

Sontag, D. (2015). Transgender woman cites attacks and abuse in men's prison. *The New York Times.* Retrieved from https://www.nytimes.com/2015/04/06/us/ashley-diamond-trans-gender-inmate-cites-attacks-and-abuse-in-mens-prison.html

Williams, T. (2015). Prison officials join movement to curb solitary. *The New York Times.* Retrieved from https://www.nytimes.com/2015/09/03/us/prison-directors-group-calls-for-limiting-solitary-confinement.html

Williams, T. (2015). Report details physical abuse of mentally ill prisoners by guards in America's prisons. *The New York Times.* Retrieved from https://www.nytimes.com/2015/05/12/us/mentally-ill-prison-inmates-are-routinely-physically-abused-study-says.html

Wollan, M. (2008). Judges to decide whether crowded California prisons are unconstitutional. *The New York Times.* Retrieved from https://www.nytimes.com/2008/12/08/us/08calif.html

DISCUSSION QUESTIONS

1. When comparing other types of victimization/victims within the correctional system, how are their portrayals in research and the media similar? How are they different?

2. Certain types of victimization were given more coverage and/or more prominent coverage by *The New York Times* than others. Why do you think this is the case?
3. Deprivation, importation, and lifestyle/opportunity theories are all theories considered in empirical research on in-prison violence/victimization. Which one of these theories would you say *The New York Times* coverage tends to support? Why?
4. Much of victimization within correctional facilities occurs "behind the walls." How do you think this impacts *The New York Times* coverage? Would you advocate for increased visibility within correctional facilities, such as the use of correctional officer body cameras? Why or why not?
5. *The New York Times* articles frequently place responsibility for victimization on the system. Do you think this has more to do with the types of victimization they choose to report on or the way they choose to report it? What do those choices reflect?

SECTION II

Violence in Everyday Life

CHAPTER 4

Victims of Youth Homicide Offenders

Carol Burciaga, Department of Criminal Justice, Seattle University;
William Parkin, Department of Criminal Justice, Seattle University

INTRODUCTION

Civilization has historically been intrigued by children who commit murder. These rare types of homicides are reflected in the Greek mythology literature of Oedipus, Orestes, and Alcmaeon (Heide, 1992, 2013). Research regarding children who commit homicide has been investigated for more than 70 years (Bender, 1959; Bender & Curran, 1940; Sellers & Heide, 2012). Not only have juvenile homicide offenders become more prevalent in research, they have also become more frequently featured in the news throughout the world, mainly within the United States (Heide, 2003). This may be related to the fact that the United States has the highest rates for homicide offenses among Western countries (Loeber & Ahonen, 2013; Loeber & Farrington, 2011). Some of the youth may be directly or vicariously exposed to a culture of violence, influencing their behaviors and actions (DiCataldo & Everett, 2008). It has been argued that juveniles who are exposed to violence become desensitized to it and look to violent activities to bring excitement to their daily lives. According to Heide (1995), youth who are chronically bored, lack self-esteem, and lack parental role models will engage in criminal activities as a way to become socially accepted. Often, juvenile homicide offenders have criminal histories including prior arrests (Heide, 2003). These violent tendencies tend to influence the way they cope with particular situations and how they react to being victims of poverty, abuse, neglect, and violence. It is important for society to have a full understanding of the different factors that may play into a juvenile committing murder so there can be less judgment of the juveniles and more of a focus on ways to help them and prevent future violence.

The present study focuses on the incident, suspect, and victim characteristics of homicides committed by juvenile offenders in the United States and featured within *The New York Times*. We examine how the coverage of such violence compares to the patterns found in official data and scholarly research. Research on preadolescent homicide offenders dates back more than 70 years (Bender, 1959; Bender & Curran, 1940; Sellers & Heide, 2012) and these events are frequently featured in the news media (Heide, 2003). The journalists that cover these stories provide information to their viewers and, based on how they cover their stories (using particular terminology, headlines, and facts), their audiences will be provided a framework for how to think about and understand these events. Due to this, it is important to explore how the media represents juvenile homicide offenders, how that coverage compares to the data collected by academics and policymakers, and the possible implications that may arise when the coverage and the statistical data are not aligned.

LITERATURE REVIEW

Homicide can be best understood by the simple statement of 'taking another person's life' (Hickey, 2003). For a deeper understanding of what constitutes a homicidal offense, it is best to look to the Federal Bureau of Investigation's (FBI) classifications regarding this serious criminal act of violence. The act of homicide, per the FBI's Uniform Crime Report[1] (Federal Bureau of Investigation [FBI], 2004), is organized into three different classifications based on the facts of the agency's investigation: **murder and**

---

[1] The FBI collects data for their Uniform Crime Reporting (UCR) Program, which includes data at the local, state, and national level. According to the U.S. Department of Justice, this data is then utilized by law enforcement personnel, policymakers, researchers, and public stakeholders in order to focus on the current concerns within their respective communities (Banks & Regoeczi, 2014). Over time, the FBI decided to collect more information on the reported homicides, which resulted in the Supplementary Homicide Report (SHR) (Banks & Regoeczi, 2014). The first FBI UCR SHR was published in 1962 and at that time only included demographics on the victims (age, sex, and race), weapon utilized, and the circumstance (FBI, 2004). Throughout the years, the SHR has developed by adding additional variables and more detailed information regarding each homicidal incident including the date of the incident, jurisdiction, demographics of the victim(s) and offender(s), the relationship between the victim(s) and offender(s), weapon(s) utilized, and the circumstances of the incident.

non-negligent manslaughter, negligent manslaughter, and **justifiable homicide**.

Some situations regarding homicide offenses can be difficult to categorize due to the circumstances in which the offense took place as well as considering the culpability of the offender. These situations become even more difficult to categorize when the offender is considered a juvenile or youth. The age of a **juvenile** is a fluid variable in this report since it differs per jurisdiction, and this is discussed further in the literature review. These violent offenses are viewed differently because it is not considered normal for young individuals to commit such heinous crimes against other individuals. There are many perspectives presented in the literature on juvenile homicide because the topic is very complex and dynamic; however, this research focuses on the characteristics of the offenders, their victims, and the homicide event.

CHARACTERISTICS OF YOUTH HOMICIDE OFFENDERS

Juveniles who commit homicide vary in age, gender, race, and mental competence. Most literature includes case studies that involve juvenile male and female homicide offenders. However, the male offenders always dominate the sample size. Juvenile males, especially juvenile Black males, are disproportionately accounted for as homicide offenders and victims, regardless of their age (Goetting, 1989; Loeber & Ahonen, 2013). For most homicides that involve juvenile offenders, both offender and victim are of the same gender, with males being the most common (Goetting, 1989; Jerin & Moriarty, 2010). The intelligence of these youths varies, but they typically face problems regarding education such as cognitive deficits, learning disabilities, as well as engaging in disruptive behaviors within their classroom (Heide, 2003). In addition, while homicidal juveniles use an array of weapons to carry out their transgressions, the most frequently utilized weapon is a firearm.

Age of Youth Homicide Offenders

Juvenile homicide offenders are considered to be under the age of 18 at the time of their offense. Once a juvenile reaches the age of 18, they are considered to be an adult. Each classification then has an effect on their case and sentencing. Since there is no definitive age range that corresponds with youth and juvenile terminology, most research and literature reports on homicidal youth up to the age of 18. However, there are age differences across jurisdictions when it comes to charging a youth as an adult.

According to the U.S. Department of Justice's Office of Juvenile Justice and Delinquency Prevention (Griffin, Addie, Adams & Firestine, 2011), each state has the ability to transfer juvenile offenders from juvenile court to adult criminal court depending on their age and what crime they have been charged with. Some states (such as Alaska, Delaware, Rhode Island, and Washington) can transfer a juvenile, regardless of their age, to adult criminal court for any criminal offense (Griffin et al., 2011). There are also states that have minimum transferal ages, except when the offense is murder. For example, in Idaho, while a juvenile can be transferred to adult criminal court for any criminal offense at the age of 14, if they are charged with murder, the state does not maintain an age restriction for transferal (Griffin et al., 2011). Finally, some states have a specific minimum age restriction for transferring a juvenile to adult criminal court if the criminal offense is murder (e.g., Indiana and Vermont (10 years old); Colorado (12 years old); New Hampshire (13 years old); and Arkansas, Louisiana, New Jersey, and Wisconsin (14 years old) (Griffin et al., 2011).

The FBI has been able to provide statistics on juveniles arrested for homicide over the years, which has provided some indication as to what age these young offenders commit homicide. According to the FBI's Supplementary Homicide Report data (SHR) (Puzzanchera, Chamberlin, & Kang, 2017)[2], between 2001 and 2015, there were 230 homicide offenders between the ages of 5 and 12, and 8,105 between the ages of 13 and 17. These numbers, as well as the race and sex distribution of these offenders, can be found in Table 4.1. In addition, as a point of comparison, the same demographics are provided for adults, 18 years of age and older. Importantly, we break the youth homicide offenders into two groups, preteen and teen, in an effort to tease out some of the differences that might be a result of

---

[2] Please note, all SHR data presented in the tables comes from Puzzanchera, Chamberlin, & Kang (2017).

TABLE 4.1 Supplementary Homicide Report Offender Characteristics by Offender Age Groups, 2001–2015

		CHILD (5–12)		TEENAGER (13–17)		ADULT (18+)	
		%	n	%	n	%	n
Offender Race	American Indian or Alaskan Native	3.9	9	2.4	193	2.1	2,647
	Asian or Pacific Islander	0.0	0	0.1	8	0.5	570
	Black	40.4	93	56.1	4,543	44.9	56,328
	White	52.2	120	40.5	3,280	51.4	64,530
	Unknown	3.5	8	1.0	81	1.1	1,374
Offender Sex	Female	13.9	32	7.3	588	10.1	12,647
	Male	83.5	192	92.4	7,491	89.7	112,506
	Unknown	2.6	6	0.3	26	0.2	296
Total		100.0	230	100.0	8,105	100.0	125,449

being pre- or post-pubescent, as well as being in an elementary or primary school and a junior high, middle, or high school.

Sex of Youth Homicide Offenders

Many juvenile homicide offenses are committed by males, and their victims are also usually male (Goetting, 1989). According to the FBI's SHR (Table 4.1), between 2001 and 2015, 83.5 percent of child offenders were male, 92.4 percent of teenage offenders were male, and 89.7 percent of offenders 18 or older were male. Males tend to engage in more risk-taking activities and are also considered to be more aggressive than females, especially during their adolescent years. These negative lifestyle choices can be examined in the arrest rates for male youth offenders. Male juvenile homicide offenders are typically involved in confrontational assaults which then lead to homicide offenses (Brookman, 2005). These altercations can involve money, drugs, gangs and their territory, love interests, alpha personalities, and a desire to prove their worth amongst their peers and community. The most common situation involving juvenile homicide offenders is when a boy or group of boys murders another young boy or male teenager (Adler & Polk, 2001; Heide, Solomon, Sellers, & Chan, 2011; Jerin & Moriarty, 2010; Sellers & Heide, 2012). Additionally, male offenders are more likely than female offenders to be involved in crime-related homicides (Heide, Roe-Sepowitz, Solomon, & Chan, 2012; Heide et al., 2011; Loper & Cornell, 1996; Sellers & Heide, 2012). A crime-related homicide occurs when somebody gets killed during the commission of another crime (Heide et al., 2011; Sellers & Heide, 2012). For example, if a juvenile was robbing someone and ended up killing them, this incident would be considered a crime-related homicide.

Juvenile homicide cases where the offender is a female are quite rare (Brookman, 2005). Female youth tend to be less aggressive and violent than their male counterparts, which can be partially seen in their arrest rates for violent offenses. Female offenders are more likely to commit homicide during conflict-related incidents such as arguments over money, youth gang-related killings, and lovers' triangle arguments (Heide et al., 2012; Heide et al., 2011; Loper & Cornell, 1996; Sellers & Heide, 2012) as well as during the commission of a felony offense such as robbery (Heide, 2003). In situations where the homicide is gang related, the female offender typically plays a secondary role and their codefendant is typically male (Heide, 2003). In addition, a female may have an accomplice when the female plans on killing a family member (Heide et al., 2012; Sellers & Heide, 2012). A study using 30 years of arrest data found that female homicide offenders were more likely to utilize accomplices to kill their family members than their male counterparts (Heide et al., 2012; Sellers & Heide, 2012).

Race of Youth Homicide Offenders

Black juvenile males are overrepresented, as offenders and victims, in homicide offenses compared to White juvenile males (Goetting, 1989; Loeber & Ahonen, 2013). The SHR demonstrates a similar pattern for homicide offenses that occurred between 2001 and 2015. Child offenders were White 52.2 percent of the time, compared to 40.4 percent who were

Black, 3.9 percent American Indian or Alaskan Native, and less than 1 percent for Asian or Pacific Islander. For the teenager category, an even larger percentage was Black (56.1%), compared to 40.5 percent for White.

Violence is more frequent in lower socioeconomic neighborhoods, which are often disproportionately made up of minority populations. Unfortunately, these low-income neighborhoods do not provide enough opportunities for employment and they have a high occurrence of unlawful activities that predict violence and crime such as drug dealing; gang activity; and fencing, buying, and selling guns. These activities typically involve high levels of contestations as well as violence towards others as a means of survival. Since these minority youths are more often exposed to these risk factors, when compared to White male youths, the likelihood of them becoming involved in violence and crime is much higher (Loeber & Ahonen, 2013). In addition, most juvenile homicide offenders and their victims are of the same race, which is consistent with crime research that finds most crime is intraracial (Goetting, 1989).

Weapons Used by Youth Homicide Offenders

The weapons that youths use to commit homicide vary on the circumstance as well as the age and gender of the offender and the victim. Some weapons that are used may indicate more of a personal aggression towards the victim due to the proximity between the offender and victim. The choice of weapon will also depend on the juvenile's access to the weapon. Characteristically, the weapons that are used by homicidal youth include firearms, knives, personal weapons, fire, and objects such as rope or cords.

Firearms are the most used weapon in murder cases within the United States (Goetting, 1989). They are commonly found in homes and are easily accessible to obtain within the streets. They are also frequently mentioned in the media, including sitcoms, news broadcastings, movies, music, and video games. The exposure and access to firearms has increased over time which has assisted in the rise of homicides by juveniles (DiCataldo & Everett, 2008). Many studies have found that firearms are the primary weapon of choice in juvenile homicide offenses (Heide, 1992, 1995; Shumaker & Prinz, 2000). Studies show that both male and female juvenile homicide offenders use firearms; however, males are more likely to use them overall (Heide, Roe-Sepowitz, Solomon, & Chan, 2012; Heide et al., 2011; Loper & Cornell, 1996; Rowley, Ewing, & Singer, 1987; Sellers & Heide, 2012). A study conducted by Sellers and Heide (2012) utilized the FBI SHR data from 1976–2007 and found that more than half (54.4%) of male juvenile homicide offenders used a firearm compared to their female counterparts (16.7%). And a more recent study conducted by Heide (2014) focused on the crime of patricide and step-patricide, utilizing the same dataset, and found that 60.0 percent of male juveniles used a firearm to kill their father or stepfather compared to the 57.4 percent of female juveniles. Firearms can provide a quick and efficient way to end somebody's life and do not require as much physical power to do so.

Using more personal weapons, such as knives or fists, requires the offender to have the physical capability, and many juveniles do not have that ability (Heide, 1995). Also, homicide offenders that use more personal weapons will likely need to be emotionally detached to perform such an intimate deed (Heide, 1995). A study by DiCataldo and Everett (2008) discovered most homicides committed by juvenile offenders use firearms, followed by knives. The use of knives indicates a close-up interaction between the offender and victim which can imply an aggressive and personal attack. Most studies have found that knives are used primarily by female juvenile homicide offenders (Heide et al., in press; Heide et al., 2011; Loper & Cornell, 1996; Rowley, et al., 1987; Sellers & Heide, 2012; Synder & Sigmund, 1999, 2006). A study by Sellers and Heide (2012) concluded that a fifth of juvenile females used a knife in their murders compared to a tenth of juvenile males.

The use of personal weapons is the third most common method of juvenile homicide offenders and is used primarily by females (Heide et al., in press; Heide et al., 2011; Loper & Cornell, 1996; Rowley, et al., 1987; Sellers & Heide, 2012; Synder & Sigmund, 1999, 2006). Sellers and Heide (2012) found that young females (41.7%) used personal weapons more frequently than juvenile males (11.9%) when committing murder. Juvenile females do not normally have the strength to murder somebody older than themselves with their hands or feet; however, they would be able to use their strength to murder infants or young children. Young juvenile females may use this method when they are killing their newborn children since the infants are unable to fight back and defend themselves. They may also use asphyxiation as well. The method of asphyxiation is rarely used; however, when it is used, the offender is typically female (Heide et al., 2011; Sellers & Heide, 2012).

CHARACTERISTICS OF THE VICTIMS OF YOUTH HOMICIDE OFFENDERS

Although juvenile homicide offenders kill both familial and nonfamilial individuals, most literature focuses on **victim-offender relationships** where juveniles kill their own family members (e.g., matricide, parricide). There is no specific terminology used when the relationship between the offender and victim is nonfamilial. This may be due to the limited research regarding the different types of victims relating to the juvenile homicide offenders, including acquaintances, friends, teachers, and strangers. Hickey (2003) utilized juvenile murder reports submitted to the FBI from 1980 through 1999. Over half (55%) of the victims were acquaintances, 31 percent were strangers, 12 percent were other family members, and 2 percent were parents. Similarly, analysis from 1984 data showed that 49 percent of victims killed by juveniles were acquaintances, 33 percent were strangers, 9.4 percent were other family members, and 8.3 percent were parents or stepparents (Ewing, 1990; Holinger, Offer, Barter, & Bell, 1994). Many of the juvenile homicide offenses are one-on-one incidents (Goetting, 1989) where the juvenile offender has had some prior relationship with the victim or has some knowledge of who the victim is (DiCataldo & Everett, 2008).

There is also a relationship between the juvenile's gender and the victim-offender relationship. An analysis conducted by Sellers and Heide (2012) found that for youths six to ten years of age, the gender of the offender varied based on the relationship they had with the victim. When family members were the victims, preadolescent female offenders accounted for 65.4 percent of the slayings, while preadolescent males accounted for 44.3 percent. When a friend, acquaintance, or other individual was killed, male juvenile homicide offenders accounted for 43.9 percent of the killings, with females accounting for 34.9 percent. In all cases where the victim-offender relationship was strangers, the offenders were male.

Also, there are different situational and dispositional factors that are related to the demographics of the juvenile offenders and their victims. Juveniles that kill, typically murder individuals who they have had an extensive history with, specifically when their relationship involves continuous interpersonal conflicts (Cornell, 1989; Cornell, Benedek, & Benedek, 1987; Ewing, 1990; Holinger et al., 1994; Shumaker & Prinz, 2000). Many continuous conflicts will emanate from familial relationships due to the fact that it is difficult for juveniles to leave their families. Also, younger offenders may not understand the significance of death and will turn to murder to solve temporary problems (Heide, 2003; Sellers & Heide, 2012).

Data on Victims of Youth Offenders from the Supplementary Homicide Report

Table 4.2 presents victim information about individuals killed by youth offenders between 2001 and 2015 reported in the SHR. Several noticeable differences can be observed between the victims based on the age of the offenders. First, more than 50 percent of victims killed by a child (5–12) are children themselves (0–12). This is compared to 5.5 percent and 6.3 percent for the teenager (13–17) and adult categories (18+), respectively. In addition, victims of children were more often White, female, and of the same race, when compared to those killed by teenagers and adults. Finally, victims of children were much more likely to be related to the offender. When comparing across the offender types, victims of teenagers were more similar to adult victims than to the victims of child killers.

The SHR also provides situational-level data (Table 4.3). Once again broken down by the age of the offenders, there are clear differences across the categories. For the situation (i.e., the number of victims and offenders), teenage offenders were more likely to attack a single victim in groups, while child and adult offenders had a similar percentage of incidents that involved a single victim and a single offender. For the weapon type,

TABLE 4.2 Supplementary Homicide Report Victim Characteristics by Offender Age Groups, 2001–2015

		CHILD (5–12)		TEENAGER (13–17)		ADULT (18+)	
		%	n	%	n	%	n
Victim Age	Child (0–12)	52.2	120	5.5	449	6.3	7,948
	Teenager (13–17)	10.9	25	22.8	1,845	3.5	4,443
	Adult (18+)	33.9	78	71.0	5,753	89.0	111,650
	Unknown	3.0	7	0.7	58	1.1	1,408
Victim Race	American Indian or Alaskan Native	2.2	5	1.1	88	1.0	1,207
	Asian or Pacific Islander	0.9	2	1.9	157	1.9	2,413
	Black	40.9	94	48.5	3,929	41.8	52,484
	White	54.8	126	47.6	3,861	54.1	67,890
	Unknown	1.3	3	0.9	70	1.2	1,455
Victim Sex	Female	26.1	60	15.2	1,231	26.4	33,138
	Male	73.5	169	84.6	6,860	73.5	92,154
	Unknown	0.4	1	0.2	14	0.1	157
Victim-Offender Same Race	Same Race	90.0	207	81.2	6,584	83.7	105,009
	Different Race	6.1	14	17.0	1,381	14.3	17,981
	Unknown	3.9	9	1.7	140	2.0	2,459
Victim-Offender Relationship	Acquaintance	24.3	56	35.4	2,867	33.0	41,390
	Family	50.4	116	12.6	1,022	11.5	14,390
	Friend	13.9	32	6.1	497	4.3	5,388
	Intimate	0.4	1	1.6	129	15.7	19,750
	Stranger	3.5	8	25.9	2,097	21.2	26,539
	Unknown	7.4	17	18.4	1,493	14.3	17,992
Total		100.0	230	100.0	8,105	100.0	125,449

TABLE 4.3 Supplementary Homicide Report Situational Characteristics by Offender Age Groups, 2001–2015

		CHILD (5–12)		TEENAGER (13–17)		ADULT (18+)	
		%	n	%	n	%	n
Victim-Offender Count	Single victim/single offender	80.9	186	64.6	5,234	78.1	97,963
	Single victim/multiple offenders	13.0	30	31.2	2,531	16.8	21,135
	Multiple victims/single offender	5.2	12	2.3	187	3.7	4,662
	Multiple victims/multiple offenders	0.9	2	1.9	153	1.3	1,689
Circumstance	All other manslaughter by negligence	5.2	12	0.8	67	1.1	1,376
	Arson	2.6	6	0.2	19	0.2	237
	Children playing with gun	17.8	41	1.7	141	0.0	23
	Circumstances undetermined	15.7	36	21.3	1,723	19.8	24,877
	Felon killed by private citizen	2.2	5	1.1	93	2.9	3,583
	Other	29.1	67	14.3	1,155	15.7	19,745
	Other—not specified	3.9	9	3.1	252	3.3	4,190
	Other—Specified	6.1	14	32.1	2,602	23.6	29,663
	Other arguments	13.9	32	23.8	1,930	32.8	41,125
	Other negligent handling of gun	3.5	8	1.5	123	0.5	630
Weapon	Blunt object	3.9	9	3.7	301	4.6	5,810
	Bodily weapon	10.9	25	5.9	475	8.3	10,403
	Fire	6.1	14	0.6	50	0.6	720
	Firearm	62.2	143	69.4	5,627	60.9	76,380
	Knife	9.1	21	14.0	1,135	15.9	19,888
	Other	7.8	18	6.4	517	9.8	12,248
Total		100.0	230	100.0	8,105	100.0	125,449

children were more likely to use bodily weapons to kill. This could be connected back to the victim-level data that showed more than 50 percent of their victims were children. In these cases, children acting out violently against siblings or friends could explain the increased number of observations in these categories.

METHODS & DATA

To have a better understanding of how these violent incidents are presented in the media, a content analysis was completed based on articles in *The New York Times*. The articles analyzed were published between January 1, 2001, and December 31, 2015, and were linked to juvenile homicide offenses within the United States of America. The articles were accessed through the ProQuest database and were chosen based on the following Boolean key terms search: "pubid (11561) AND (homicide* OR murder* OR kill*) AND (child* OR preadolescent* OR adolescent* OR juvenile* OR boy OR girl OR teen* OR preteen*) AND "National Desk" AND pd (20010101–20151231)." More than 1,200 articles were initially included; however, some were excluded based on the article's content. Articles were excluded for the following reasons: only included individuals 18 years of age or older; did not speak of an actual juvenile homicide event; published loose, vague, or general information about homicide; or did not give an indication the offender was a juvenile. Articles that included individuals who were over the age of 17 were included if there was another offender under the age of 18. One event included a juvenile and adult, however, some of those articles were not included due to the original reports of the juvenile being an adult; once the articles published the juvenile was not in fact an adult, they were included in the analysis. This was done because the content analysis is concerned with the framing of crime stories only when the offender is known to be a juvenile. In total, there were 250 articles that were relevant based on this inclusion criterion.

To analyze a full representation of these violent incidents, articles that mentioned a juvenile committing homicide were included; there were certain incidents that *The New York Times* had reported on multiple times and each article was coded individually. Information was not coded if it was not specifically stated nor if such information was known only by reading previous articles on the same incident. For example, if there were two articles published about the same incident and one mentioned the name of the offender and one did not, the variable was only filled in for the article that provided the name while the other article received an "N/A" for this variable; this ensured there were no assumptions being made per article or variable. In one instance there were 16 articles coded about the same incident involving a 12-year-old male killing a 6-year-old female. All 16 articles published the sex of both offender and victim. For each article coded, the data was entered separately but when counting the grand total of how many male offenders or female victims were in this study, this incident only contributed one male and one female to the grand total. To supplement, in order to gather a grand total count of juvenile homicide incidents, offenders, and victims that were reported on within *The New York Times*, the incident and its corresponding variables were only counted once despite being reported on multiple times. This was achieved by giving each incident a unique incident number starting at one. This information was then aggregated to report not only the information presented in the articles, but the information that potentially presented in multiple articles about one incident. These variables included offender age, victim age, victim race, victim sex, victim-offender relationship, the number of offenders/victims in an incident, the circumstances surrounding the homicide, the weapon used, and several geographic and temporal variables.

In addition to information about the victims, offenders, and incidents, data on each homicide event's newsworthiness were also collected. According to Surette (1998), newsworthiness is defined as a set of criterions that are established by a news organization that allows their producers to decide which events are reported on and which events are published to the public (as cited in Gruenewald, Pizarro, & Chermak, 2009, p. 263). Newsworthiness is valuable for understanding why certain incidents are reported and covered in the news compared to others. When news reporting stations cover homicide incidents there are common variables that are included such as age, ethnicity, and gender (Gruenewald et al., 2009). Consequently, these variables can be attributed to stereotypes that feed into certain social ideologies and prejudices against particular ethnicities and genders, which then affects how people view others that fall into those certain categories (Gruenewald et al., 2009). In addition, Gruenewald et al., (2009) states the newsworthiness criterion affects the public and their knowledge of what crime is happening within their communities, which may or may not be an accurate representation of the issue(s); specific criterion can affect the public's perception and anxiety of crime resulting in heightened fears of particular neighborhoods and/or people based on their appearance. Understanding the concept of news-worthiness can bring attention to the way news reporters report on events within their corresponding communities. Newsworthy measures included the number of articles published about each incident, the average word count per incident, and whether articles about the incident were published on the front page.

RESULTS

INCIDENT-LEVEL CHARACTERISTICS
ACROSS OFFENDER AGE GROUPS

To begin, Table 4.4 presents victim characteristics across the offender age groups. Over the 15-year period, the newspaper reported on 95 incidents: 25 where an offender was a child, 65 where the offender was a teenager, and five where the age was not specified but the offender was identified as a juvenile. Setting aside the unknown group, there are several differences across the child offenders and teenage offenders. First, the majority of child offenders killed an individual who was a teenager (48%), where a small minority of victims of teenage offenders were in that category (16.9%). In the case of victim race, although the majority of both the child and teenage offender victims did not have their race reported (9% vs. 81.5%, respectively), in 13.8 percent of the teenage offender cases, it was made clear, either through the language or a photo, that the victim was

TABLE 4.4 Incident-Level Victim Characteristics by Offender Age Groups, 2001–2015

		CHILD (5–12)		TEENAGER (13–17)		UNKNOWN	
		%	n	%	n	%	n
Victim Age	Child (0–12)	40.0	10	40.0	26	20.0	1
	Teenager (13–17)	48.0	12	16.9	11	20.0	1
	Adult (18+)	4.0	1	20.0	13	40.0	2
	Unknown	8.0	2	23.1	15	20.0	1
Victim Race	American Indian or Alaskan Native	0.0	0	0.0	0	0.0	0
	Asian or Pacific Islander	0.0	0	1.5	1	0.0	0
	Black	0.0	0	3.1	2	0.0	0
	White	8.0	2	13.8	9	0.0	0
	Unknown	92.0	23	81.5	53	100.0	5
Victim Sex	Female	40.0	10	32.3	21	0.0	0
	Male	56.0	14	58.5	38	0.0	0
	Unknown	4.0	1	9.2	6	100.0	5
Victim-Offender Relationship	Acquaintance	28.0	7	27.7	18	20.0	1
	Family	48.0	12	13.8	9	0.0	0
	Friend	8.0	2	1.5	1	0.0	0
	Intimate	0.0	0	0.0	0	0.0	0
	Stranger	4.0	1	29.2	19	40.0	2
	Unknown	12.0	3	27.7	18	40.0	2
Total		100.0	25	100.0	65	100.0	5

White, compared to only about 3 percent of the incidents where a Black victim was identified. For both the child and teenage offender categories, the majority of the victims were male (56% vs. 58.5%, respectively). Finally, the victims of child offenders were reported as family members almost half of the time, compared to only 13.8 percent of the time for the victims of teenage offenders. For the same variable, incidents about teenage offenders identified their relationship with the victim as strangers or having an unknown relationship nearly 30 percent of the time for each category—a percentage much higher than the incidents involving the child offenders.

For the incident-level situational characteristics, there are also differences across the two categories of youth offenders (Table 4.5). For example, 96 percent of the child offenders acted alone, compared to only two thirds of teenage offenders. Similarly, only 12 percent of incidents with a child offender had multiple victims, compared to 27.7 percent of teenage offenders. One quarter of incidents with child offenders were caused by the offender playing with a gun, while two of the 25 incidents were the result of arson. For the weapon type, a firearm was used in 60 percent of the incidents where a child was the offender and only 46.4 percent of those with a teenage offender. Interestingly, except for the "Other" category, there are not large differences between the other weapon types across offender age groups.

COMPARISON OF ARTICLE- & INCIDENT-LEVEL RESULTS TO THE SHR

Although the prior section provides the frequencies of victim and homicide incident characteristics that are reported in *The New York Times*, Tables 4.6 and 4.7 provide context for the coverage of these incidents. Specifically, they show how those characteristics change if they are weighted by the number of times they are reported in the newspaper. In other words, these additional tables present information about each article, while the previous tables presented information on each unique incident, regardless of how many articles were published on the homicide. This is important because, all things being equal, events that are reported in multiple articles will become more salient to readers than homicide events that are only reported on once. In addition, we also compare how often those characteristics appeared in the SHR during the 2001 through 2015 time period under study.

TABLE 4.5 Incident-Level Situational Characteristics by Offender Age Groups, 2001–2015

		CHILD (5–12)		TEENAGER (13–17)		UNKNOWN	
		%	n	%	n	%	n
Victim-Offender Count	Single victim/single offender	84.0	21	47.7	31	3.2	3
	Single victim/multiple offenders	4.0	1	24.6	16	2.1	2
	Multiple victims/single offender	12.0	3	18.5	12	0.0	0
	Multiple victims/multiple offenders	0.0	0	9.2	6	0.0	0
Circumstance	Arson	8.0	2	0.0	0	0.0	0
	Children playing with gun	24.0	6	1.5	1	0.0	0
	Circumstances undetermined	32.0	8	44.6	29	2.1	2
	Other—not specified	24.0	6	9.2	6	0.0	0
	Other—specified	0.0	0	32.3	21	1.1	1
	Other arguments	4.0	1	13.8	9	0.0	0
Weapon	Blunt object	8.0	2	12.3	8	0.0	0
	Bodily weapon	4.0	1	4.6	3	0.0	0
	Fire	0.0	0	1.5	1	0.0	0
	Firearm	60.0	15	46.2	30	4.2	4
	Knife	16.0	4	12.3	8	1.1	1
	Other	12.0	3	23.1	15	0.0	0
Total		100.0	25	100.0	65	100.0	95

TABLE 4.6 Victim Characteristics of Youth Homicide Offenders for Articles, Incidents & SHR, 2001–2015

		ARTICLES		INCIDENTS		SHR	
		%	n	%	n	%	n
Victim Age	Child (0–12)	16.8	42	38.9	37	6.8	569
	Teenager (13–17)	11.6	29	25.3	24	22.4	1,870
	Adult (18+)	35.2	88	16.8	16	70.0	5,831
	Unknown	36.4	91	18.9	18	0.8	65
Victim Race	American Indian or Alaskan Native	0.0	0	0.0	0	1.1	93
	Asian or Pacific Islander	0.4	1	1.1	1	1.9	159
	Black	0.8	2	2.1	2	48.3	4,023
	White	10.0	25	11.6	11	47.8	3,987
	Unknown	88.8	222	85.3	81	0.9	73
Victim Sex	Female	26.0	65	32.6	31	15.5	1,291
	Male	56.0	140	54.7	52	84.3	7,029
	Unknown	18.0	45	12.6	12	0.2	15
Victim-Offender Relationship	Acquaintance	20.0	50	27.4	26	35.1	2,923
	Family	20.8	52	22.1	21	13.7	1,138
	Friend	6.8	17	3.2	3	6.3	529
	Intimate	0.0	0	0.0	0	1.6	130
	Stranger	12.8	32	23.2	22	25.3	2,105
	Unknown	39.6	99	24.2	23	18.1	1,510
Total		100.0	250	100.0	95	100.0	8,335

In Table 4.6, the data shows that incidents involving a child as a victim are disproportionately represented in *The New York Times* when compared to the distribution of similar cases in the SHR. Incidents involving youth homicide offenders are also disproportionately less likely to appear in *The*

New York Times if the victim was 18 years or older. The story is slightly different if one takes into account the amount of times these types of victims are presented in articles about the incidents. For example, although incidents with child victims occur more than five times as often in *The New York Times* incident-level data than in the SHR, they appear in the article-level data slightly less than 2.5 times as often as in the SHR. This is to say that, although the incidents with child victims are covered at a higher rate when compared to the population of youth homicide incidents reported in the SHR, there are not as many articles about these incidents as compared to other types of cases.

For race, the victims are White or Black close to 48 percent of the time in the SHR data; however, the race of the victim is known as Black in only 2.1 percent of the incidents reported in *The New York Times* and less than 1 percent of the articles. For White victims, their race is known as such for 11.6 percent of incidents and 10 percent of the articles. For the sex of the victim, female victims are overrepresented in *The New York Times* at both the article and incident levels of analysis. In 26 percent of the articles and 32.6 percent of the incidents the victim was a female, compared to only 15.5 percent of victims of youth homicide offenders being female. Finally, specific to the victim-offender relationship, victims and offenders who were acquaintances were less likely to be covered in *The New York Times,* while those who were family members were more likely to be covered when compared to how often those relationships occurred in the SHR.

At the situational level (Table 4.7), incidents with multiple victims and multiple offenders were covered more often when compared to the SHR, as were incidents with multiple victims and multiple offenders. However, incidents with single victims, regardless of the number of offenders, were covered less often at both the incident and article level when compared to how often they occurred in the SHR. For the type of weapon used, although firearms were used nearly 70 percent of the time by youth homicide offenders in the United States between 2001 and 2015, only 53.2 percent of *The New York Times* articles identified a firearm being used, while only 51.6 percent of the total incidents covered had a firearm as the

TABLE 4.7 Situational Characteristics of Youth Homicide Offenders for Articles, Incidents & SHR, 2001–2015

		ARTICLES		INCIDENTS		SHR	
		%	n	%	n	%	n
Victim-Offender Count	Single victim/ single offender	40.4	101	57.9	55	65.0	5,420
	Single victim/ multiple offenders	17.6	44	20.0	19	30.7	2,561
	Multiple victims/ single offender	23.2	58	15.8	15	2.4	199
	Multiple victims/ multiple offenders	15.2	38	6.3	6	1.9	155
	Unknown	3.6	9	6.3	6	1.9	155
Circumstance	Arson	4.8	12	2.1	2	0.3	25
	Children playing with gun	3.2	8	7.4	7	2.2	182
	Circumstances undetermined	44.4	111	41.1	39	21.1	1,759
	Other—not specified	0.0	0	12.6	12	3.1	261
	Other—specified	42.4	106	23.2	22	49.7	4,146
	Other arguments	5.2	13	10.5	10	23.5	1,962
Weapon	Blunt object	8.0	20	10.5	10	3.7	310
	Bodily weapon	10.4	26	4.2	4	6.0	500
	Fire	1.2	3	1.1	1	0.8	64
	Firearm	53.2	133	51.6	49	69.2	5,770
	Knife	14.0	35	13.7	13	13.9	1,156
	Other	13.2	33	18.9	18	6.4	535
Total		100.0	250	100.0	95	100.0	8,335

murder weapon. Blunt objects and other types of weapons were the only categories that appeared to be disproportionately covered in *The New York Times* compared to their relative frequencies in the SHR.

THE NEWSWORTHINESS OF VICTIMS OF
YOUTH HOMICIDE OFFENDERS

In addition to the above results comparing coverage to the prevalence of youth homicide events, the final set of tables use the number of articles, average word count, and whether an article appeared on the front page of The New York Times at least once as measures for newsworthiness. In the first table (Table 4.8), which presents these variables across victim characteristics, incidents with females were more likely to have only one article published about the female's death. Specifically, 74.2 percent of incidents with women only had one article published, compared to only 59.6 percent of incidents where the victim was male. Similarly, only 6.5 percent of incidents where the victim was female were printed on the front page, compared to 10.5 percent of incidents with male victims. When age was considered, incidents with child victims only had one article published 83.3 percent of the time. For the other age categories, it appears that the older the victims were, the more coverage they received. Incidents with adult victims had the highest number of articles (more than five, 16.2% of the time), largest word counts (greater than 500, 27% of the time), and were on the front page more often than any other of the known victim age groups (10.8% had at least one article on the front page). Finally, for the known victim-offender relationships, stranger relationships appeared to be the least newsworthy.

The situational variables presented in Table 4.9 have two interesting findings. First, for the circumstances variable, all homicide incidents that involved a child playing with a gun (n = 7) only had one article published about them, the majority were less than 100 words (57.1%), and none of these were published on the front page of The New York Times. The second finding of interest is related to the victim-offender count. Incidents with multiple victims and multiple offenders were more likely to have more than five articles printed about the event (33.3%), the articles were longer (50% had more than 500 words), and information about a larger number of incidents was published on the front page (16.7% of the incidents had at least one article published on the front page).

TABLE 4.8 Incident-Level Newsworthiness Measures for Victim Characteristics

| | | ARTICLE COUNT | | | | | | AVERAGE WORD COUNT | | | | | | | | FRONT PAGE | | | | TOTAL | |
| | | 1 | | 2–5 | | >5 | | <100 | | 100–199 | | 200–499 | | ≥500 | | NO | | YES | | | |
		%	n	%	n	%	n	%	n	%	n	%	n	%	n	%	n	%	n	%	n
Victim Sex	Female	74.2	23	19.4	6	6.5	2	25.8	8	25.8	8	19.4	6	29.0	9	93.5	29	6.5	2	100.0	31
	Male	59.6	34	26.3	15	14.0	8	26.3	15	26.3	15	22.8	13	24.6	14	89.5	51	10.5	6	100.0	57
	Unknown	57.1	4	28.6	2	14.3	1	28.6	2	28.6	2	14.3	1	28.6	2	85.7	6	14.3	1	100.0	7
Victim Age	Child (0–12)	83.3	20	12.5	3	4.2	1	29.2	7	37.5	9	12.5	3	20.8	5	91.7	22	8.3	2	100.0	24
	Teenager (13–17)	50.0	8	37.5	6	12.5	2	25.0	4	18.8	3	37.5	6	18.8	3	93.8	15	6.3	1	100.0	16
	Adult (18+)	64.9	24	18.9	7	16.2	6	27.0	10	21.6	8	24.3	9	27.0	10	89.2	33	10.8	4	100.0	37
	Unknown	50.0	9	38.9	7	11.1	2	22.2	4	27.8	5	11.1	2	38.9	7	88.9	16	11.1	2	100.0	18
Victim-Offender	Acquaintance	50.0	13	42.3	11	7.7	2	11.5	3	26.9	7	38.5	10	23.1	6	88.5	23	11.5	3	100.0	26
Relationship	Family	71.4	15	19.0	4	9.5	2	28.6	6	14.3	3	14.3	3	42.9	9	90.5	19	9.5	2	100.0	21
	Friend	66.7	2	0.0	0	33.3	1	33.3	1	0.0	0	0.0	0	66.7	2	66.7	2	33.3	1	100.0	3
	Stranger	72.7	16	22.7	5	4.5	1	36.4	8	31.8	7	9.1	2	22.7	5	90.9	20	9.1	2	100.0	22
	Unknown	65.2	15	13.0	3	21.7	5	30.4	7	34.8	8	21.7	5	13.0	3	95.7	22	4.3	1	100.0	23
Total		64.2	61	24.2	23	11.6	11	26.3	25	26.3	25	21.1	20	26.3	25	90.5	86	9.5	9	100.0	95

TABLE 4.9 Incident-Level Newsworthiness Measures for Situational Variables

| | | ARTICLE COUNT | | | | | | | AVERAGE WORD COUNT | | | | | | | | FRONT PAGE | | | | TOTAL | |
| | | 1 | | 2–5 | | >5 | | <100 | | 100–199 | | 200–499 | | ≥500 | | NO | | YES | | | |
		%	n	%	n	%	n	%	n	%	n	%	n	%	n	%	n	%	n	%	n
Weapon	Blunt object	70.0	7	20.0	2	10.0	1	10.0	1	40.0	4	20.0	2	30.0	3	90.0	9	10.0	1	100.0	10
	Bodily weapon	25.0	1	25.0	1	50.0	2	25.0	1	25.0	1	25.0	1	25.0	1	75.0	3	25.0	1	100.0	4
	Fire	0.0	0	100.0	1	0.0	0	0.0	0	0.0	0	100.0	1	0.0	0	100.0	1	0.0	0	100.0	1
	Firearm	61.2	30	24.5	12	14.3	7	28.6	14	20.4	10	24.5	12	26.5	13	87.8	43	12.2	6	100.0	49
	Knife	69.2	9	23.1	3	7.7	1	15.4	2	38.5	5	23.1	3	23.1	3	100.0	13	0.0	0	100.0	13
	Other	77.8	14	22.2	4	0.0	0	38.9	7	27.8	5	5.6	1	27.8	5	94.4	17	5.6	1	100.0	18
Circumstances	Arson	0.0	0	50.0	1	50.0	1	0.0	0	0.0	0	0.0	0	100.0	2	50.0	1	50.0	1	100.0	2
	Children playing with gun	100.0	7	0.0	0	0.0	0	57.1	4	0.0	0	14.3	1	28.6	2	100.0	7	0.0	0	100.0	7
	Circumstances undetermined	66.7	26	23.1	9	10.3	4	33.3	13	23.1	9	23.1	9	20.5	8	92.3	36	7.7	3	100.0	39

	%	n	%	n	%	n	%	n	%	n	%	n	%	n	%	n	%	n	%	n
Other—not specified	50.0	6	41.7	5	8.3	1	8.3	1	41.7	5	16.7	2	33.3	4	66.7	8	33.3	4	100.0	12
Other—specified	68.0	17	20.0	5	12.0	3	28.0	7	20.0	5	24.0	6	28.0	7	96.0	24	4.0	1	100.0	25
Other arguments	50.0	5	30.0	3	20.0	2	0.0	0	60.0	6	20.0	2	20.0	2	100.0	10	0.0	0	100.0	10
Victim-Offender Count: Multiple Victims / Multiple Offenders	50.0	3	16.7	1	33.3	2	16.7	1	16.7	1	16.7	1	50.0	3	83.3	5	16.7	1	100.0	6
Multiple Victims / Single Offender	46.7	7	40.0	6	13.3	2	20.0	3	26.7	4	13.3	2	40.0	6	86.7	13	13.3	2	100.0	15
Single Victim / Multiple Offenders	63.2	12	26.3	5	10.5	2	31.6	6	31.6	6	26.3	5	10.5	2	89.5	17	10.5	2	100.0	19
Single Victim / Single Offender	70.9	39	20.0	11	9.1	5	27.3	15	25.5	14	21.8	12	25.5	14	92.7	51	7.3	4	100.0	55
Total	64.2	61	24.2	23	11.6	11	26.3	25	26.3	25	21.1	20	26.3	25	90.5	86	9.5	9	100.0	95

ANALYZING VICTIMS OF YOUTH HOMICIDE OFFENDERS

When youth homicide offenders kill, *The New York Times* dispropor-tionately reports more on victims who are children or female compared to how often these victims appear in the SHR. However, incidents with females had few articles published about them and were less often printed on the front page of the paper. Therefore, although female victims were more likely to appear in the paper, when compared to how often they appeared in the SHR, their coverage was not as in-depth or as prominent as male victims. Specific to age, more than 80 percent of child victims only appeared in one article, the largest percentage across the age groups. In these cases, it appears that although the age of the child may have impacted the newsworthiness of a homicide event, the stories themselves were not newsworthy enough to be covered across multiple articles.

Also, when compared to the SHR, homicide events with family victim-offender relationships are also disproportionately covered. For age and sex, the child and female categories are the smallest in the SHR data and it makes sense that the media would cover them more often than other categories as they are relatively unique compared to other types of homicides committed by youth offenders. The overall newsworthiness of victim-offender relation-ships however do not appear to clearly favor one type of relationship over another, outside of the initial comparison to the SHR data.

In the vast majority of the cases, the race of the victim is never reported, however, when it is, the victim is most often identified as White. Editorial policies make it likely in print media that the race and/or ethnicity of a victim or offender will not be mentioned unless this is tied directly to the story. However, in our data, we see that although nearly 90 percent of the cases do not connect a race to the victim, almost all of the remaining incidents identify the victims as White, either within the text or through a photograph. Since the SHR reports that the victims of youth offenders were White approximately 48 percent of the time and Black approxi-mately 48 percent of the time, this presents a skewed perspective to the audience of the victims' race as almost exclusively White. Although not directly comparable, there is evidence from other research that victim race impacts criminal justice policy and procedures (e.g., in the use of the death penalty (Radelet, 1981)).

Specific to situational characteristics, homicide events with multiple victims are also covered more often in *The New York Times* than those with single victims. In fact, incidents with multiple victims and single offenders accounted for almost a quarter of the articles, but only make up 2.4 percent of events in the SHR. These rare, yet deadlier, homicides fit within the ubiquitous statement about traditional media—*if it bleeds, it leads*. For the weapon type, the use of blunt objects to murder a person is reported on disproportionately more in *The New York Times* than it actually occurs in the SHR, which, once again, could be connected to the inherent violence of the act as a measure of newsworthiness. The situational variables compared with the other newsworthiness variables tell a similar story. Incidents with multiple victims were more likely to be on the front page, have multiple published stories, and to have a higher average word count.

CONCLUSION

Juvenile homicide offenses are rare, occurring much less frequently than adult homicides. However, in 95 incidents over a 15-year period, these events were newsworthy enough that *The New York Times* decided to cover the homicides in 250 articles. When compared to homicide data collected by the Federal Bureau of Investigation, homicides committed by juvenile offenders were more likely to be covered if the victim was a child, female, and/or White. These patterns are not unique (see, e.g., Sorenson, Manz, & Berk, 1998). In addition, incidents with multiple victims, family relationships between the victim and the offender, as well as homicides that included the use of blunt objects as a weapon were also more likely to be covered.

This research shows that even for a rare subset of homicides we find similar patterns of coverage that are found in the larger body of literature on crime and media coverage. In addition, although this was not discussed in depth, nor was there an ability to measure it and compare it to official data, the youth offenders in these incidents are most likely also victims in some sense of the word. In addition to the idea of the victim-offender overlap that is found in the criminological literature—the idea that many characteristics that place a person at risk for offending also put them at risk for victimization—most youth who commit acts of violence as severe as homicide have either been psychologically, emotionally, or physically victimized at some point in their lives. However, the media coverage of these events, whether it discusses offender victimization or not, plays an important role in the national narrative of youth violence. If national papers, such as *The New York Times*, misrepresent what a typical victim or a typical offender is, whether purposefully or through the unintentional grind of a business process, it can have real-world implications for criminal justice policy focused on youth violence. Providing a non-distorted picture of youth homicide offenders and their victims, one story at a time, allows the public and policymakers to approach the issue with realistic and much-needed solutions.

REFERENCES

Adler, C., & Polk, K. (2001). *Child victims of homicide*. Cambridge, England: Cambridge University Press.

Banks, D., & Regoeczi, W. (2014, July). *The nation's two measures of homicide*. Washington, DC: Bureau of Justice Statistics. Retrieved from https://www.bjs.gov/content/pub/pdf/ntmh.pdf

Bender, L. (1959). Adolescents who have killed. *American Journal of Psychiatry, 166*(6), 510–513.

Bender, L., & Curran, F. J. (1940). Children and adolescents who kill. *Journal of Criminal Psychopathology, 1*, 297–323.

Brookman, F. (2005). *Understanding homicide*. London, England: SAGE Publications.

Cornell, D. G. (1989). Causes of juvenile homicide: A review of the literature. In E. P. Benedek & D. G. Cornell (Eds.), *Juvenile homicide* (pp. 3–36). Washington, DC: American Psychiatric Press.

Cornell, D., Benedek, E. P., & Benedek, D. (1987). Characteristics of adolescents charged with homicide: Review of 72 cases. *Behavioral Science and the Law, 5*, 11–23.

DiCataldo, F., & Everett, M. (2008). Distinguishing juvenile homicide from violent juvenile offending. *International Journal of Offender Therapy and Comparative Criminology, 52*(2), 158–174.

Ewing, C. P. (1990). *When children kill*. Lexington, MA: Lexington Books.

Federal Bureau of Investigation. (2004). *Uniform crime reporting handbook*. Retrieved from https://ucr.fbi.gov/additional-ucr-publications/ucr_handbook.pdf/at_download/file

Goetting, A. (1989). Patterns of homicide among children. *Criminal Justice and Behavior, 16*(1), 63–80.

Griffin, P., Addie, S., Adams, B., & Firestine, K. (2011). *Trying juveniles as adults: An analysis of state transfer laws and reporting.* Washington, D.C.: United States Department of Justice, Office of Juvenile Justice and Delinquency Prevention. (Juvenile Offenders and Victims: National Report Series Bulletin, September 2011).

Gruenewald, J., Pizarro, J., & Chermak, S. (2009). Race, gender, and the newsworthiness of homicide incidents. *Journal of Criminal Justice, 37,* 262–272.

Heide, K. M. (1992). *Why kids kill parents: Child abuse and adolescent homicide.* Columbus, OH: Ohio State University Press.

Heide, K. M. (1995). Why kids keep killing: The correlates, causes and challenge of juvenile homicide. *Stanford Law & Policy Review, 7*(1), 43–49.

Heide, K. M. (2003). Youth homicide: A review of the literature and a blueprint for action. *International Journal of Offender Therapy and Comparative Criminology, 47*(1), 6–36.

Heide, K. M. (2013). Matricide and stepmatricide victims and offenders: An empirical analysis of U.S. arrest data. *Behavioral Sciences and the Law, 31*(2), 203–214.

Heide, K. M. (2014). Patricide and steppatricide victims and offenders: An empirical analysis of U.S. arrest data. *International Journal of Offender Therapy and Comparative Criminology, 58*(11), 1261–1278.

Heide, K. M., Roe-Sepowitz, D., Solomon, E., & Chan, H. C. P. (2012). Male and female juveniles arrested for murder: A comprehensive analysis of U.S. data by offender gender. *International Journal of Offender Therapy and Comparative Criminology, 56*(3), 356–384.

Heide, K. M., Solomon, E. P., Sellers, B. G., & Chan. H. C. (2011). Male and female juvenile homicide offenders: An empirical analysis of U.S. arrests by offender age. *Feminist Criminology, 6*(1), 3–31.

Hickey, E. (2003). *Encyclopedia of murder & violent crime.* Thousand Oaks, CA: SAGE Publications.

Holinger, P. C., Offer, D., Barter, J. T., & Bell, C. C. (1994). *Suicide and homicide among adolescents.* New York: The Guilford Press.

Jerin, R. A., & Moriarty, L. J. (2010). *The victims of crime.* Upper Saddle River, NJ: Pearson Education, Inc.

Loeber, R., & Ahonen, L. (2013). Invited address: Street killings: Prediction of homicide offenders and their victims. *Journal of Youth & Adolescence, 42*(11), 1640–1650.

Loeber, R., & Farrington, D. (2011). *Young homicide offenders and victims: Development, risk factors, and prediction from childhood.* New York: Springer.

Loper, A., & Cornell, D. (1996). Homicide by juvenile girls. *Journal of Child and Family Studies, 5*(3), 323–336.

Puzzanchera, C., Chamberlin, G., and Kang, W. (2017). Easy access to the FBI's supplementary homicide reports: 1980–2015. Retrieved from http://www.ojjdp.gov/ojstatbb/ezashr/

Radelet, M. L. (1981). Racial characteristics and the imposition of the death penalty. *American Sociological Review, 46,* 918–927.

Rowley, J. C., Ewing, C. P., & Singer, S. I. (1987). Juvenile homicide: The need for an interdisciplinary approach. *Behavioral Sciences & the Law, 5*, 1–10.

Sellers, B. G., & Heide, K. M. (2012). Male and female child murderers: An empirical analysis of U.S. arrest data. *International Journal of Offender Therapy and Comparative Criminology, 56*(5), 691–714.

Shumaker, D. M., & Prinz, R. J. (2000). Children who murder: A review. *Clinical Child and Family Psychology Review, 3*(2), 97–115.

Sorenson, S. B., Manz, J. G., & Berk, R. A. (1998). News media coverage and the epidemiology of homicide. *American Journal of Public Health, 10*, 1510–1514.

Surette, R. (1998). *Media, crime, and criminal justice* (2nd ed.). Belmont, CA: Wadsworth Publishing.

KEY TERMS

- *Justifiable Homicide:* The killing of a felon by a peace officer in the line of duty or the killing of a felon, during the commission of a felony, by a private citizen (FBI, 2004, p. 15–8).

- *Juvenile:* Although the term means a young person, when connected to the criminal justice system, the age at which a person is a juvenile or is under the authority of the juvenile justice system varies between jurisdictions.

- *Murder and Non-Negligent Manslaughter:* The willful (non-negligent) killing of one human being by another. Not including suicides, fetal deaths, traffic fatalities, accidental deaths, assaults to murder, and attempts to murder (FBI, 2004, p. 15–8).

- *Negligent Manslaughter:* The killing of another person through gross negligence. Not including deaths due to an individual's own negligence, accidental deaths not resulting from gross negligence, and traffic fatalities (FBI, 2004, p. 15–8).

- *Victim-Offender Relationships:* In criminological research, an important focus on criminal events is the prior relationship between the victim and the offender. These relationships are typically measured as intimate, familial, acquaintances, and strangers.

THE NEW YORK TIMES ARTICLES

Associated Press. (2002). Youth pleads guilty to murder in California school shootings. *The New York Times.* Retrieved from https://www.nytimes.com/2002/06/21/us/youth-pleads-guilty-to-murder-in-california-school-shootings.html

Associated Press. (2004). National briefing southwest: New Mexico: Charges for boy in family's deaths. *The New York Times.* Retrieved from https://www.nytimes.com/2004/07/10/us/national-briefing-southwest-new-mexico-charges-for-boy-in-family-s-deaths.html

Associated Press. (2009). Maryland: Teenager who killed family is sentenced. *The New York Times.* Retrieved from https://www.nytimes.com/2009/01/24/us/24brfs-TEENAGER-WHOK_BRF.html

Canedy, D. (2001). Sentence of life without parole for boy, 14, in murder of girl 6. *The New York Times.* Retrieved from https://www.nytimes.com/2001/03/10/us/sentence-of-life-without-parole-for-boy-14-in-murder-of-girl-6.html

McKinley, J. (2011). California: Boy accused in killing of his father says he was abused. *The New York Times.* Retrieved from https://www.nytimes.com/2011/05/19/us/19brfs-BOYAC-CUSEDIN_BRF.html

DISCUSSION QUESTIONS

1. What are some of the ways in which we expect to see differences in the way juveniles are portrayed in the media if they are the victim of the crime, the offender, or related/connected to the crime in some other way? How might these portrayals also differ from adult offenders in the situations?

2. What kind of patterns did you expect to see in the data regarding who these youth offenders are and who they victimize? Moreover, how did this expectation compare to data and media portrayals of these victims and offenders?

3. Based on what we know of the victims of juvenile offenders, what are some interventions or policies that could be implemented to reduce these types of homicides?

4. How does an analysis of juvenile homicide offenses illustrate and characterize the symptoms of other, related problems within our society?

5. Are there scenarios where the youth offender might also be considered a victim by society? How might addressing the needs of these victims before they become offenders reduce the frequency of homicides committed by youths?

CHAPTER 5

Victims of Intimate Partner Violence

Chelsea Toby, Department of Criminal Justice, Seattle University;
Leana Bouffard, Department of Sociology, Iowa State University

INTRODUCTION

According to the Bureau of Justice Statistics, incidents of domestic violence accounted for 21 percent of all violent victimizations that occurred
from 2003 to 2012. A small percentage of these incidents occurred between
immediate family members or other relatives, but the large majority of the
violence occurred between **intimate partners** (Truman & Morgan, 2014).
Intimate partner violence (IPV) is limited to violent acts between current
or former spouses, partners, boyfriends, girlfriends, or sexual partners. IPV
affects millions of individuals of all sexes, genders, ethnicities, and sexual
orientations. It is such a pervasive and serious problem that it has been
deemed a public health concern by the Centers for Disease Control and
Prevention (CDC) (Breiding, Basile, Smith, Black, & Mahendra, 2015).

It is important to recognize that the controlling and abusive behaviors
that define IPV include more than just physical violence (Washington State
Department of Health, n.d.). The CDC identifies four main types of IPV:
physical violence, sexual violence, stalking, and psychological aggression.
Physical violence is the use of physical force that has the potential to cause
harm, injury, or death. It includes behaviors such as shoving, hitting, grab-
bing, choking, and the use (or threat of use) of a weapon. Sexual violence,
such as rape and other unwanted sexual contact, are acts that occur without the victim's consent or when the victim is unable to give consent (i.e.,
when they are intoxicated/incapacitated). Stalking is a pattern of unwel-
come attention or contact, such as unsolicited emails or gifts, spying, or
damage to personal property that causes the victim to fear for their safety.
Finally, psychological aggression is verbal or non-verbal communication

that intends to mentally or emotionally harm an individual, such as name-calling, mind games, or threats of violence, as well as exploiting an individual's vulnerabilities, such as their immigration status or disabilities. Whether it is abuse that goes on for years or an act that occurs only once, violence between intimate partners has the potential to cause long-lasting harm (Breiding et al., 2015).

VICTIMS OF IPV

According to the 2010 **National Intimate Partner and Sexual Violence Survey** (NISVS) conducted by the CDC, over 10 million people are victims of physical violence from an intimate partner each year in the United States, or an average of about 20 people per minute (Breiding et al., 2015). A substantial amount of research has been done specifically addressing the diversity of IPV victims. While IPV has no boundaries in who it affects, some populations are at greater risk than others. The sections below synthesize peer-reviewed literature that categorically investigates victim characteristics and the unique challenges victims face when deciding whether or not to report the abuse to law enforcement.

SEX

There is much debate in the literature about whether or not there is gender symmetry in the perpetration of IPV, that is, if it is committed equally by men and women. These studies rely on self-disclosed reports of abusive behavior towards intimate partners and reveal that just as many women confess to battering as men (Carlyle, Scarduzio, & Slater, 2014; Kimmel, 2002). This would mean that both law enforcement data and national self-report data that indicate that the far majority of victims are women are highly skewed. For example, according to the most recent **National Crime Victimization Survey** (NCVS) conducted by the U.S. Census Bureau, 76 percent of nonfatal IPV victims were female and 24 percent were male between 2003 and 2012 (Truman & Morgan, 2014). If more women are perpetrators of IPV, then there should be many more male victims than the official statistics are capturing. Carlyle et al. (2014) present a possible explanation for the lack of recognition of women as abusers and men as victims, stating that "stereotypes characterizing women as the weaker gender are perhaps functioning to excuse women's aggression, and ideas of masculinity constrain men's ability to make sense of, and seek help for, abuse perpetrated by women" (p. 2399). But other researchers suggest interpreting these results with caution. They have criticized these studies for neglecting to take into account violence perpetrated by women in self-defense or retaliation against abusive male partners (Hamilton & Worthen, 2011; Kimmel, 2002).

Perhaps a distinction lies in the type of intimate partner violence that is being measured. Some scholars argue that violence between intimate partners should not be viewed as a single phenomenon and, as such, have outlined a typology that identifies the different types of IPV. This typology, in addition to exploring the varying motivations or circumstances that lead to IPV, also helps to explain why the results of some studies reflect gender symmetry while others do not. The first category, "**coercive controlling violence**" (also referred to as "patriarchal terrorism" and "intimate terrorism"), refers to IPV that is part of a general pattern of power and control used by one partner to terrorize the other. This type of violence, not always physical in nature, has been found to occur more frequently, is more likely to escalate over time, and has more severe outcomes than other types of IPV. While female perpetrators of this type of IPV do exist, it is largely committed by husbands against their wives, argued to be a manifestation of our culture's patriarchal traditions in which men have the right to control their women by any means necessary (thus the term "patriarchal terrorism") (Johnson, 1995; Kelly & Johnson, 2008).

Authors, like Johnson (1995), have found that data showing gender asymmetry in IPV perpetration typically are measuring incidents of coercive controlling violence, while data that show a more gender-balanced perpetration of IPV are most likely measuring a different type of IPV called "**situational couple violence**" (also referred to as "common couple violence"). The main difference between situational couple violence and coercive controlling violence is that situational couple violence is not rooted in a relationship-wide pattern of coercion and control. Instead, this type of IPV occurs occasionally when conflict gets out of hand and one or both partners have poor control of their anger, resulting in less frequent minor violence that is less likely to escalate. Neither sex is more or less likely to initiate this type of violence in their relationship (Johnson, 1995; Kelly & Johnson, 2008). Regardless of the numbers, it is important to recognize that both women and men can suffer abuse at the hands of an intimate partner.

In general, crimes that occur between individuals in close relationships are reported less frequently than those occurring between strangers (Felson & Pare, 2005). Forty-six percent of IPV incidents measured by the NCVS were not reported to the police (Truman & Morgan, 2016). Fleury, Sullivan, Bybee, and Davidson (1998) found that the reasons for underreporting this type of abuse are complex; a majority of the women in their sample gave multiple reasons for why they did not report their victimization. Afraid of retaliation (Felson & Pare, 2005; Fleury et al., 1998; Logan & Valente, 2015), fear that the police would do nothing (Logan & Valente, 2015), use of alcohol or drugs by the victim (Felson & Pare, 2005), and lack of access to a phone (Fleury et al., 1998) are just some examples. Men are even less likely than women to report abuse by an intimate partner (Felson & Pare, 2005), citing privacy concerns and the belief that the incident was trivial as reasons for their underreporting (Felson, Messner, Hoskin, & Deane, 2002).

AGE

Rates of IPV are highest for individuals between the ages of 18 and 24 (CDC, n.d.; Truman & Morgan, 2014). According to the NISVS, one in five women and nearly one in seven men who ever experienced intimate partner violence first experienced some form of IPV between the ages of 11 and 17 (Black et al., 2011). For older women, research has shown that, while their exposure to physical/sexual violence from their intimate partners decreases later in life, the threat of non-physical forms of IPV persists. Older generations of victims face similar challenges in leaving their abusive partners as younger victims do, but age can often be accompanied by increased financial dependence and stronger attachments to home and community that make leaving an even more difficult decision (Harbison, 2008). Additionally, the traditional construction of family matters as private and a wife's duty of subservience to her husband that many older women identify with decreases the likelihood that a victim will reach out for help (Roberto, McPherson, & Brossoie, 2014).

RACE/ETHNICITY

The NCVS reported that Black and multiracial non-Hispanic individuals experienced the most IPV (Truman & Morgan, 2014); the NISVS differentiated the victim's race by sex. So, while Black and multiracial non-Hispanic women had the highest rates of victimization, it was Black (in the 12 months prior to the survey) and American Indian or Alaska Native (lifetime) men who reported more incidents of IPV (Breiding, Chen, & Black, 2014). Both surveys illustrate that racial minorities are at higher risk of being victimized by an intimate partner. It is not that certain races/ethnicities are innately more susceptible to this type of violence, but that their susceptibility is linked to the environment in which many find themselves. Sokoloff and Dupont (2005) reiterate this point when they write, "one major underlying reason for the greater level of domestic violence among African Americans is not attributable to racial and cultural factors but to the high and extreme levels of poverty in Black communities" (p. 48). It is the social and economic marginalization of these communities that fosters the risk factors for IPV (West, 2004).

Yoshioka and Choi (2005) note that cultural factors can affect the options available to women in abusive relationships. They argue that culturally some women are socialized to put the needs of their family and community above their own and, therefore, are more limited in how they can address an abusive situation when compared to a woman from a more individualistic culture. Language barriers can also prevent some victims from reporting IPV to the police as evidenced by studies that found the level of English proficiency predicts the help-seeking behaviors of Latin American victims (Pitts, 2014; West, Kantor, & Jasinski, 1998). Finally, the immigration status of the victim can compromise their ability to seek help. Victims may worry that reporting the abuse to police will also reveal their undocumented status and put them at risk of deportation. Knowledge of unstable immigration status can also be used by the abuser to threaten victims into silence (Reina, Lohman, & Maldonado, 2014).

SEXUAL ORIENTATION/GENDER IDENTITY

Research has found that there are many similarities between cis (opposite)-gender and same-gender IPV (McClennen, 2005), the majority of these studies focusing on LGBTQ youth in dating relationships. While some studies suggest that it is just as prevalent in same-sex couples as it is in heterosexual couples (Burke, Jordan, & Owen, 2002), more recent studies show that both male and female sexual minorities have greater odds of being victimized by their partners than heterosexuals (Dank, Lachman, Zweig, & Yahner, 2013; Goldberg & Meyer, 2013; Koeppel & Bouffard, 2014; Langenderfer-Magruder, Walls, Whitfield, Brown, & Barrett, 2016; Martin-Storey, 2015). In their evaluation of three studies regarding same-sex partner abuse, including their own study of gay male partner abuse, McClennan, Summers, and Vaughan (2002) found that substance abuse was a common correlate of IPV. In about two thirds of the abuse reported by gay and lesbian victims, one or both of the partners was under the influence of drugs and/or alcohol. Multiple explanations were given for the source of conflict in their relationships, but two of the most common responses were related to feelings of jealousy and the victim's or perpetrator's desire for more independence in the relationship.

The NISVS provides additional insight into the victimization of sexual minorities through its inclusion of the experiences of bisexual men and women. According to the survey, in comparison to heterosexual and homosexual individuals, a higher proportion of both bisexual men and women report experiencing rape, physical violence, and/or stalking during their lifetime (Breiding et al., 2014). There is very little information on the victimization of transgender individuals in their personal relationships; the U.S. Transgender Survey is one of the few measures available. The most recent survey conducted in 2015 found that more than half of the transgender respondents had experienced some form of IPV, while about a quarter of those experiences were considered severe physical violence (James et al., 2016).

LGBTQ individuals may face extra barriers in the decision to leave an abusive partner or seek help. For those individuals who are still closeted, the threat of being "outed" can be used by the abusive partner to maintain control. This tactic is also applicable to transgender victims who may be fearful of their assigned sex being revealed to the community or their employers. Real or perceived homophobia/transphobia in a victim's community can make it difficult to reach out for help from police or social services for fear of further harassment (Greenberg, 2012; Langenderfer-Magruder, Whitfield, Walls, Kattari, & Ramos, 2016; Sokoloff & Dupont, 2005).

INDIVIDUALS WITH DISABILITIES

Studies indicate that individuals with mental and physical disabilities are at higher risk of being victimized by an intimate partner than their counterparts without disabilities (Scherer, Snyder, & Fisher, 2016). For example, Smith (2008) found that about twice as many respondents with disabilities, both male and female, reported being victims of IPV behaviors such as unwanted sex and physical abuse. The deaf community has been a population of particular interest to researchers. Specifically in samples of college students, deaf students have been found twice as likely as those with no hearing disabilities to have suffered abuse, both physical and emotional, by an intimate partner (Anderson & Leigh, 2011; Porter & Williams, 2011). Deaf adults surveyed by Pollard, Sutter, and Cerulli (2014) revealed that deaf men were more likely to experience physical abuse and forced sex than deaf women, although both sexes reported victimization rates higher than those in the general population. Emotional abuse was the most prevalent type of IPV reported by the respondents.

LAW ENFORCEMENT FAMILIES

"A concern of both the criminal justice system and the general public has been the issue of how police officers can effectively handle complaints involving domestic violence if they themselves are perpetrators of IPV"

(Erwin, Gershon, Tiburzi, & Lin, 2005, p. 14). Perpetrators and victims of IPV can be found in all professions, but law enforcement officers are in a unique professional paradox. On the one hand, they are responsible for responding to and protecting possible victims of family violence. On the other hand, there is a high risk that the violence that they experience and engage in as part of their job can "spill over" into their personal lives, thus becoming the abusers victims need protection from (Anderson & Lo, 2011; Johnson, Todd, & Subramanian, 2005). Johnson et al. (2005) describes law enforcement as having a "warrior mentality culture," an authoritarian work culture that values and rewards control, aggression, and immediate action (p. 11). Unfortunately, the behaviors and attitudes that are expected and reinforced when an officer is engaged with a suspect can be difficult for some to turn off once they are off duty. Family members can become easy targets when officers are unable or unwilling to address the inevitable stress they face daily in their jobs (Anderson & Lo, 2011).

There are unique barriers to reporting that a victim faces when their abusive partner is in law enforcement. When the abuser works for the very system that the victim is supposed to contact for protection, it is less likely that the victim will feel either comfortable reporting the abuse or confident that their accusations will be given due consideration, particularly when that system is known for its code of silence. Research into the law enforcement subculture reveals that the strong sense of solidarity that develops between an officer and their colleagues inevitably creates a "closed shop" environment, where officers are extremely reluctant to report the actions of their fellow officers (Alpert, Noble, & Rojek, 2002). Reporting the misdeeds of another officer is tantamount to betrayal in the eyes of the group. Therefore, victims whose abusers are police officers know that their reports of IPV are being addressed by their abuser's comrades, and that these officers may do nothing or write a false report in adherence to the code of silence (Johnson et al., 2005). Furthermore, the victim knows that, as a police officer, their abuser has easy access to a firearm which could be used as retribution for reporting. Additionally, the skills that are taught to make a person an effective police officer, such as interrogation techniques and the physical restraint of suspects, can be utilized outside the realm of police work as tools of abuse toward an intimate partner (Avila, 2015). All of these conditions create extra pressure for victims to remain silent.

THE FAR-REACHING EFFECTS OF INTIMATE PARTNER VIOLENCE

When considering the effects of IPV on its victims, perhaps the most obvious is bodily injury that is a direct result of an intimate partner's use of physical force. The prevalence of physical injury will be examined first, but it will be followed by a discussion of other ramifications associated with IPV, ramifications that are long-lasting and can reach beyond the primary victim.

HOMICIDE

The most severe outcome of IPV is death. According to the FBI's Uniform Crime Reports for 2015, 18.1 percent of homicides in which the victim-offender relationship was known were committed by (ex-)wives, (ex-) husbands, boyfriends, or girlfriends (Federal Bureau of Investigation [FBI], 2016). From 1980 to 2008, a larger percentage of female homicide victims (41.5%) than male homicide victims (7.1%) were killed by an intimate partner. This dynamic remains the same regardless of the victim's age group (12–17, 18–24, ... 60 or older). An interesting change that occurred over that 28-year period is related to the offenders involved in the intimate partner homicides. In 1980, more than half of intimate homicides were committed by spouses, while about a quarter were committed by a boyfriend or girlfriend. By 2008, the number of intimate homicides committed by spouses was about equal to those committed by boy/girlfriends (Cooper & Smith, 2011).

It is important to note that the FBI statistics referenced above do not include the number of homicides committed by ex-boyfriends, ex-girlfriends, and those in homosexual relationships. Therefore, the numbers are arguably lower than statistics that would encompass all of the relationships that the CDC includes in its definition of intimate partners.

INJURIES

Non-lethal physical violence between intimate partners occurs more frequently than violence that ends in homicide and results in injuries more often than the violence between immediate family members or other relatives (Truman & Morgan, 2014). NISVS data from 2010 to 2012 found that nearly one in four women, and one in seven men, had experienced severe physical violence by an intimate partner during their lifetime (Smith et al., 2017). The type of physical attacks that both male and female victims most commonly report are being knocked down, slapped, or hit, and the most common injuries are bruises or cuts (Catalano, 2013). More serious injuries, such as broken bones or unconsciousness, are less common (Catalano, 2013; Truman & Morgan, 2014).

HEALTH PROBLEMS

In general, individuals victimized by intimate partners report significantly more health problems than individuals that have not experienced abuse from an intimate partner (Breiding et al., 2014; Breiding et al., 2015; CDC, n.d.; Tolman & Rosen, 2001). For example, those with a history of IPV are more likely to report chronic diseases, such as heart disease, stroke, joint disease, asthma, irritable bowel, and diabetes (Breiding et al., 2014; Breiding et al., 2015) and are more likely to binge drink or smoke (Breiding et al., 2015). Reports of frequent headaches and difficulty sleeping are also more common among IPV victims (Breiding et al., 2014; CDC, n.d.). Certainly not reducing the prevalence of health problems is the finding that IPV victims are less likely to have seen their doctor in the last year (Breiding et al., 2015).

INTERRELATIONSHIP WITH HIV

Among the wide range of health conditions that are reported by IPV victims, the increased risk of human immunodeficiency virus (HIV) infection in particular has received scholarly attention due to the health crisis it has become for women, especially women of color (Machtinger, Wilson, Haberer, & Weiss, 2012). The two most common methods of HIV transmission are high-risk heterosexual contact and injection drug use, behaviors that those with histories of IPV report engaging in more frequently than those without histories of IPV (CDC, 2014). Inconsistent condom use, in particular, is more likely to occur in sexual relationships where IPV is present. "The lack of condom use by women [is] associated with fear and the woman's lack of power to negotiate her safety due to IPV" (Phillips, Walsh, Bullion, Reid, Bacon, & Okoro, 2014, p. S42).

In addition to being a consequence of IPV, HIV has also been found to be a risk factor for IPV. In other words, individuals who are HIV positive may be at greater risk of abuse from their partners. A recent meta-analysis conducted by Machtinger et al. (2012) estimated the rate of IPV among HIV-positive women to be more than twice the rate found in the general population. Other studies found rates of IPV to be similar among HIV-positive and HIV-negative women, but the reported frequency and severity of IPV episodes was higher for those with HIV (Gielen et al., 2007).

CHILDREN

Children whose parents are involved in IPV are at increased risk of being physically victimized themselves (Boeckel, Blasco-Ros, Grassi-Oliveira, & Martínez, 2014), but there are also many ways in which children can be affected by IPV without being the primary target. Such effects can take place as early as when a child is in utero. Research suggests that pregnant women exposed to IPV are at an increased risk of low infant birth weight and preterm birth, two conditions that are associated with infant mortality (Shah & Shah, 2010). Cha and Masho (2014) found that women who reported being a victim of IPV before or during pregnancy were less likely to receive adequate prenatal care compared to those women who reported no IPV. Quality prenatal care is integral to improving pregnancy outcomes (Cha & Masho, 2014).

After evaluating 3,750 cases of IPV that occurred in the state courts of 16 large urban counties, Smith and Farole (2009) found that there was a direct witness in more than 40 percent of the incidents brought to court, and children accounted for half of those witnesses. A child exposed to IPV is at higher risk for emotional and behavioral problems (i.e., aggressive, antisocial), poor academic performance, and low social competence

(Edleson, 2011). It is argued that caregivers who are coping with their own physical or psychological abuse may be less able to meet the developmental needs of their children (Boeckel et al., 2014) or may be a hindrance to the establishment of proper attachment between parent and child (Fusco, 2015), both of which can lead to the problems discussed above.

THE CURRENT STUDY

In American culture, the news plays an influential role in shaping the public's understanding of a wide range of issues. As Bullock and Cubert (2002) note, "news coverage can be framed to convey a particular understanding of reality" (p. 479). Journalists make choices in the topics they cover, the words they use, and the facts they present, all of which play a role in influencing how these issues are viewed by their audiences (Bullock & Cubert, 2002). The purpose of the current study is to explore the representation of intimate partner violence in the news in order to compare the "reality" as presented by journalists with the reality presented by the scholarly research described above.

METHODS

The New York Times newspaper database was searched via ProQuest for articles related to intimate partner violence from 2001 to 2015. Multiple key search terms were used in an effort to capture the mass majority of articles that encompass the relationships and types of actions that the CDC has defined as IPV. A total of 1,905 articles matched the search criteria. In order to be included in the content analysis, at least 50 percent of the article had to (1) be about a specific case/incident that occurred between spouses, ex-spouses, boyfriends/girlfriends, or ex-boyfriends/girlfriends; and (2) involve behavior that could be identified as physical violence, sexual violence, stalking, or psychological aggression. Articles that were follow-ups to a particular IPV incident, such as stories about searching for the suspect or trial proceedings, were included as well. Based on the inclusion criteria, a total of 280 articles remained for the content analysis.

DATA

Each of the 280 articles were coded for multiple variables. First, information about the article itself was gathered, including the location (page) that the article was printed and the number of words in the article. Next, characteristics of the victim were identified, such as name, sex, age, and ethnicity. It was noted if there were additional victims involved in the incident that did not meet the IPV relationship criteria, but these individuals were not counted toward the total victim count. As with the victims, the characteristics of the perpetrator or suspect were also recorded. The relationship between the victim and perpetrator as well as the outcome of each incident for the victim (killed, injured, stalked, threatened) were identified. The final variables were created to capture thematic characteristics of the articles, such as the type of IPV described (more than one category could be coded for), whether or not the article noted a history of violence between the individuals involved, and whether or not the incident was identified or referred to as domestic violence or abuse. None of the included articles contained the phrase or a close variation of "intimate partner violence." Therefore, the more common terminology of domestic violence was tracked instead since many of the relationships under IPV would also fall under the domestic violence umbrella.

RESULTS

Described among the 280 articles was the victimization of 122 individuals (see Table 5.1). The vast majority of victims were female (81%). Unfortunately for the present analysis, the age of 44 (36%) of the victims was not included in the article(s); the highest percentage of victims with known ages was in the 31–50 age range (32%). Eighty-eight (72%) of the victims were killed, 21 (17%) were injured, 11 (9%) were threatened with harm but not injured, and two (2%) were stalked. Regarding the relationship between the victim and perpetrator, 73 (60%) individuals experienced IPV by a spouse, nine (7%) by an ex-spouse, 27 (22%) by a boy/girlfriend, and 12 (10%) by an ex-boy/girlfriend. All but one of the victims was in a heterosexual relationship. In nine (7%) of the cases, the perpetrator worked in law enforcement at the time of the incident or the article mentioned they had previously worked in that field.

TABLE 5.1 Unique Intimate Partner Violence Victims as Reported in *The New York Times* (*N* = 122)

SEX	AGE	RELATION TO SUSPECT	OUTCOME	# ARTICLES	WORD TOTAL
F	42	Wife	Injured	4	1896
F	58	Wife	Killed	1	305
F	22	Wife	Killed	8	4722
F	31	Girlfriend	Killed	1	435
F	34	Wife	Killed	11	2739
M	51	Husband	Injured	2	834
F	44	Wife	Killed	19	7514
M	40	Husband	Killed	1	84
M	NA	Boyfriend	Killed	1	76
M	NA	Husband	Killed	1	96
F	31	Wife	Killed	3	249
F	NA	Ex-Girlfriend	Stalked	1	80
M	44	Husband	Killed	10	8186
F	27	Wife	Killed	46	18115
F	35	Wife	Killed	4	1261
F	39	Wife	Killed	1	440
F	54	Wife	Killed	1	1180
F	NA	Wife	Killed	1	87
F	NA	Ex-Wife	Threatened	1	943
F	NA	Ex-Wife	Threatened	1	674
F	33	Wife	Injured	2	186
M	34	Husband	Killed	2	153
F	NA	Girlfriend	Killed	1	70
M	NA	Husband	Killed	2	195
M	39	Boyfriend	Killed	1	114
F	27	Wife	Killed	5	716

TABLE 5.1 (*Continued*)

SEX	AGE	RELATION TO SUSPECT	OUTCOME	# ARTICLES	WORD TOTAL
F	23	Girlfriend	Killed	1	117
F	21	Girlfriend	Killed	1	148
F	NA	Girlfriend	Injured	1	107
M	NA	Husband	Killed	3	2113
F	NA	Ex-Girlfriend	Killed	1	98
F	NA	Ex-Wife	Killed	1	83
M	25	Boyfriend	Killed	1	98
F	NA	Girlfriend	Injured	1	102
F	36	Ex-Girlfriend	Killed	1	102
F	33	Wife	Killed	3	320
F	27	Wife	Killed	1	130
F	27	Wife	Killed	4	472
M	31	Husband	Killed	10	2745
F	24	Wife	Killed	3	789
F	26	Girlfriend	Killed	1	90
F	39	Wife	Killed	4	943
M	70	Husband	Killed	2	495
F	19	Ex-Girlfriend	Killed	1	239
M	85	Ex-Boyfriend	Killed	1	109
F	28	Girlfriend	Killed	1	117
F	49	Wife	Killed	2	414
M	NA	Boyfriend	Killed	1	90
F	26	Girlfriend	Killed	3	323
F	30	Wife	Killed	1	616
F	NA	Wife	Killed	2	456
F	43	Wife	Killed	2	973
F	20	Ex-Girlfriend	Injured	1	654

(*continued*)

TABLE 5.1 Unique Intimate Partner Violence Victims as Reported in *The New York Times* (*N* = 122) (*Continued*)

SEX	AGE	RELATION TO SUSPECT	OUTCOME	# ARTICLES	WORD TOTAL
F	18	Ex-Girlfriend	Killed	1	746
F	NA	Wife	Killed	2	226
F	43	Ex-Wife	Killed	1	211
F	33	Wife	Killed	2	287
F	16	Spiritual Wife	Injured	3	1814
F	NA	Girlfriend	Injured	1	151
F	NA	Wife	Injured	1	123
F	NA	Wife	Killed	1	137
F	30	Wife	Injured	1	1724
F	NA	Ex-Wife	Killed	1	459
F	43	Wife	Killed	2	1550
F	30	Wife	Killed	1	654
F	NA	Wife	Threatened	1	64
F	30	Wife	Threatened	1	120
F	NA	Wife	Killed	2	152
F	47	Wife	Killed	1	193
F	NA	Wife	Threatened	1	274
F	NA	Ex-Girlfriend	Stalked	2	563
F	NA	Ex-Wife	Killed	1	429
F	29	Ex-Girlfriend	Killed	1	1177
F	54	Wife	Killed	1	327
M	NA	Husband	Killed	1	1195
M	57	Husband	Killed	1	295
F	NA	Wife	Killed	1	134
F	34	Wife	Killed	1	577
F	22	Ex-Girlfriend	Killed	2	1210

TABLE 5.1 *(Continued)*

SEX	AGE	RELATION TO SUSPECT	OUTCOME	# ARTICLES	WORD TOTAL
F	43	Wife	Injured	1	722
F	54	Wife	Killed	1	264
F	33	Girlfriend	Killed	1	568
F	NA	Ex-Wife	Killed	1	577
F	NA	Wife	Injured	8	3562
M	35	Boyfriend	Threatened	1	449
F	NA	Wife	Killed	1	330
F	65	Wife	Killed	1	1157
F	NA	NA	Killed	1	141
F	32	Wife	Killed	3	540
F	73	Wife	Killed	1	134
F	27	Wife	Injured	1	1466
F	NA	Girlfriend	Killed	1	162
M	30	Ex-Boyfriend	Killed	2	492
F	NA	Wife	Injured	1	63
F	NA	Wife	Threatened	1	382
F	NA	Girlfriend	Threatened	3	1217
M	46	Boyfriend	Killed	1	96
F	NA	Wife	Killed	1	76
F	91	Wife	Killed	1	82
F	34	Girlfriend	Injured	1	862
F	52	Religious Wife	Threatened	1	1419
M	NA	Husband	Killed	1	99
F	40	Wife	Killed	1	375
F	39	Wife	Killed	1	690
F	27	Girlfriend	Killed	2	1549
F	NA	Wife	Killed	1	79

(continued)

TABLE 5.1 Unique Intimate Partner Violence Victims as Reported in *The New York Times* (N = 122) (*Continued*)

SEX	AGE	RELATION TO SUSPECT	OUTCOME	# ARTICLES	WORD TOTAL
F	35	Wife	Killed	1	155
F	NA	Wife	Injured	1	806
F	NA	Wife	Injured	4	2255
M	45	Husband	Killed	1	167
F	33	Ex-Wife	Killed	2	1192
F	NA	Girlfriend	Threatened	1	455
M	34	Boyfriend	Killed	1	158
F	NA	Ex-Girlfriend	Threatened	1	267
F	78	Wife	Injured	1	593
M	36	Husband	Injured	1	135
F	40	Ex-Girlfriend	Killed	1	937
F	NA	Girlfriend	Injured	1	1275
F	41	Girlfriend	Killed	1	138
F	24	Girlfriend	Injured	1	297
F	NA	Wife	Killed	1	198
F	49	Wife	Killed	1	771

ANALYSIS OF INTIMATE PARTNER VIOLENCE

The majority of people do not peruse scholarly research in order to educate themselves about the problems in their communities. Instead, the public has come to rely on the news to illuminate and explain societal issues (Carlyle et al., 2014). Thus, the decision of what is considered newsworthy and how these topics are written about has the potential to impact society's interest in and understanding of these issues.

VICTIM CHARACTERISTICS

How do the victims identified in *The New York Times* articles compare to those described in IPV literature? Both sources depict women as being disproportionately affected by IPV. In the articles, 81 percent of the victims were female, and 88 percent of them were either injured or killed in the confrontation with their intimate partner. The majority of the incidents written about in the articles occurred between current or prior spouses, which is contrary to research that identifies current or former boy/girl-friends as most likely to experience IPV.

For a little over a third of the victims, age was not mentioned in the article(s) written about them. The next most frequent age category coded for was 31 to 50 years of age. Empirical research and national surveys indi-cate that the majority of those that are victims of IPV first experience the abuse between 18 and 24 years of age, which means that many of the incidents written about were likely not capturing the initial victimization for that individual. Readers would not have been aware of this, however, because a majority of the stories are presented as isolated incidents, with only 52 (19%) of the 280 articles mentioning a history of violence between the intimate partners involved. Most of the articles presented a mere snap-shot into the lives of the victims, portraying an uncharacteristic outburst of their intimate partner rather than putting the incident within a context of patterned behavior.

Only one of the articles involved a homosexual relationship and none of the victims were identified as having a disability, in contrast to empirical studies that show an equal, if not higher, prevalence of IPV among these two populations. Some may think, is that not a good thing? After all, no group would want to be associated with the commission of violence, but a lack of media attention also keeps these victims hidden behind closed doors. Without understanding the extent of this issue, without acknowl-edging that IPV is a problem within all groups of people, the diverse needs of IPV victims will be ignored. The public will associate IPV with a certain type of victim in a certain type of relationship, and efforts to curtail this abuse will be tailored to those specific individuals. Additionally, victims of IPV may not even know that what they are experiencing is reprehen-sible because they never see or read about "someone like them" being in a similar situation. For example, based on the disproportionate amount of IPV being written about between heterosexual couples, this type of abuse may be perceived as something that only occurs between a man and a woman.

TYPE OF VIOLENCE

About 89 percent of the incidents described in these articles were coded as physical violence (see Table 5.2), and the vast majority of incidents in this category involved the victim being killed. While deadly outcomes, such as a man shooting his wife after she cooked his eggs wrong (Associated Press, 2010) or a woman poisoning her boyfriend with antifreeze (Associated Press, 2007), certainly work to shock readers, homicide is much less prevalent as a form of IPV than its popularity in the media suggests. For example, according to the NISVS, nearly half of both men and women have experienced psychological aggression in their lifetime (Breiding et al., 2014), but a mere 7 percent of articles in this study involved that form of IPV. Threatening to deport a boyfriend (Parker, 2012) or telling an ex-wife not to call the police or her children would be harmed (Hart, 2004) may be less dramatic than a boyfriend chopping up his girlfriend with an ax (Reuters, 2006), but such circumstances better reflect the reality of IPV. Focusing on physical violence can also limit the definition of IPV in the minds of the public. "[The] skewing of coverage toward only physically violent forms of IPV helps perpetuate the misconception that violence has to be physical to be considered IPV" (Carlyle et al., 2014, p. 2411). As long as murder continues to dominate news reporting, it will be difficult for readers to fully grasp the extent of IPV and recognize that all the encompassing behaviors, not just those that cause physical harm, are a form of abuse and violence.

TERMINOLOGY

Although all the articles included in the analysis described an incident that fits the definition of intimate partner violence, none of the incidents were labeled as such among *The New York Times* articles. The absence of specific IPV terminology led to a broader search for terminology related to domestic violence (domestic abuse, domestic dispute, etc.). Out of all the articles (n = 280), only 26 (9%) contained domestic violence verbiage at all

TABLE 5.2 Descriptive Statistics of Intimate Partner Victim Articles (*N* = 122)

	MEASURES	*f* (%)
Age of Victim	NA	44 (36.1)
	<18	1 (0.8)
	18–30	25 (20.5)
	31–50	39 (32.0)
	> 50	13 (10.7)
Sex of Victim	Female	99 (81.1)
	Male	23 (18.9)
Age of Suspect	NA	20 (16.4)
	<18	0 (0.0)
	18–30	18 (14.8)
	31–50	61 (50.0)
	> 50	23 (18.9)
Sex of Suspect	Female	22 (18.0)
	Male	100 (82.0)
Type of IPV*	Physical Violence	108 (88.5)
	Sexual Violence	7 (5.7)
	Stalking	2 (1.6)
	Psychological Aggression	9 (7.4)
Relationship	NA	1 (0.8)
	Spouses	73 (59.8)
	Ex-Spouses	9 (7.4)
	Boy/Girlfriend	27 (22.1)
	Ex-Boy/Girlfriend	12 (9.8)
Sexual Orientation	Heterosexual	121 (99.2)
	Homosexual	1 (0.8)
Law Enforcement	Yes	9 (7.4)
	No	113 (92.6)

* More than one category could be selected per incident

(for example, writing that the suspect had a history of domestic violence), while only 15 (5%) used it specifically to label the incident being described. A great deal of time and effort is being spent by researchers to collect data for studies and surveys about IPV, such as the NCVS and NISVS that have been discussed in this chapter. There appears to be agreement among experts that IPV is a significant public health problem, but by failing to identify certain behaviors as IPV, the concerns about the prevalence of this type of violence and its many consequences are not being effectively communicated to the public.

An additional phraseological theme that emerged in the articles was the use of quoted remarks from individuals that knew the intimate partners involved, or lived in the same community, to express disbelief at what had occurred. Comments such as "I never saw the evil" (Chapman, 2010, A15), "He looked like a normal person" (Southall, 2014, A17), and "It's unusual, and it's not reflective of the values of our community" (Lacey, 2011, A15) are all examples of the kinds of quotes typically selected for the articles. The implication of including these remarks is twofold. On the one hand, some accurately illustrate the elusive nature of IPV behavior because it often occurs in the private sphere, in the home. It is not always loud or destructive, so unless one is privy to the personal relationship involved, they probably would not know such abuse was occurring. On the other hand, these remarks perpetuate the stereotype that perpetrators of IPV somehow look different or are only found in certain types of neighbor-hoods. Although, as discussed earlier in the chapter, there are populations that are at higher risk for experiencing IPV, no community is immune to this type of violence, and it can be perpetrated by all types of people. The decision to use quotes from the public instead of, say, quotes from experts or including study results that reveal the diverse nature of IPV, means that these stories do little to bring awareness to the realities of this issue.

CONCLUSION

Intimate partner violence has the potential to affect the lives of a wide range of individuals of different sexes, ages, ethnicities, and sexual orientations; both victims and perpetrators of IPV are heterogeneous and can be found in any profession and in any community. As a major source of facts for the public, it is important to study whether and how the news media presents the issues that concern the well-being of communities and the individuals living within them. Based on the current analysis of *The New York Times* articles, there is a disconnect between the concerns of governmental agencies, like the CDC which identifies IPV as a public health issue, and what is considered newsworthy. While one of the main functions of the news is to report on current events, it is also a business, and as such is incentivized to feed the public's appetite for crime and courtroom drama. Focusing on the remarkable does not preclude the use of visual/verbal cues that can provide a context for, and better understanding of, all the information that readers/viewers are attempting to process. Both entertainment and insight can be achieved simultaneously without detriment to either. Abusive behavior between intimate partners is a subject that deserves our attention, but how can we hope to address it if people are not able to define it or recognize it?

REFERENCES

Alpert, G. P., Noble, J. J., & Rojek, J. (2002). Solidarity and the code of silence. In R. Dunham & G. Alpert (Eds.), *Critical issues in policing* (pp. 106–121). Long Grove, IL: Waveland Press, Inc.

Anderson, M. L., & Leigh, I. W. (2011). Intimate partner violence against deaf female college students. *Violence Against Women, 17*, 822–834.

Anderson, A. S., & Lo, C. C. (2011). Intimate partner violence within law enforcement families. *Journal of Interpersonal Violence, 26*(6), 1176–1193.

Associated Press. (2007, March 28). Life term in antifreeze death. *The New York Times,* p. A13.

Associated Press. (2010, September 12). Enraged over breakfast, Kentucky man kills 5. *The New York Times,* p. A29.

Avila, A. (2015). When the batterer wears a badge: Regulating officer-involved domestic violence as a line-of-duty crime. *American Journal of Criminal Law, 42*(3), 213–239.

Black, M. C., Basile, K. C., Breiding, M. J., Smith, S. G., Walters, M. L., Merrick, M. T., ...Stevens, M. R. (2011). *The national intimate partner and sexual violence survey: 2010 summary report.* Retrieved from Centers for Disease Control and Prevention, Division of Violence Prevention website: https://www.cdc.gov/violenceprevention/nisvs/

Boeckel, M. G., Blasco-Ros, C., Grassi-Oliveira, R., & Martínez, M. (2014). Child abuse in the context of intimate partner violence against women: The impact of women's depressive and posttraumatic stress symptoms on maternal behavior. *Journal of Interpersonal Violence,* 29(7), 1201–1227.

Breiding, M. J., Basile, K. C., Smith, S. G., Black, M. C., & Mahendra, R. (2015). *Intimate partner violence surveillance: Uniform definitions and recommended data elements.* Retrieved from Centers for Disease Control and Prevention, Division of Violence Prevention website: http://www.cdc.gov/violenceprevention/pdf/intimatepartnerviolence.pdf

Breiding, M. J., Chen, J., & Black, M. C. (2014). *Intimate partner violence in the United States 2010.* Retrieved from Centers for Disease Control and Prevention, Division of Violence Prevention website: http://www.cdc.gov/violenceprevention/nisvs/

Bullock, C. F., & Cubert, J. (2002). Coverage of domestic violence fatalities in Washington State. *Journal of Interpersonal Violence, 17*(5), 475–499.

Bureau of Justice Statistics. (n.d.). *Data collection: National crime victimization survey.* Retrieved from http://www.bjs.gov

Burke, T. W., Jordan, M. L., & Owen, S. S. (2002). A cross-national comparison of gay and lesbian domestic violence. *Journal of Contemporary Criminal Justice, 18*(3), 231–257.

Carlyle, K. E., Scarduzio, J. A., & Slater, M. D. (2014). Media portrayals of female perpetrators of intimate partner violence. *Journal of Interpersonal Violence, 29*(13), 2394–2417.

Catalano, S. (2013). *Intimate partner violence: Attributes of victimization, 1993–2011* (NCJ 243300). Retrieved from Bureau of Justice Statistics website: http://www.bjs.gov/content/pub/pdf/ipvav9311.pdf

Centers for Disease Control and Prevention, National Center for Injury Prevention and Control, Division of Violence Prevention. (2014). *Intersection of intimate partner violence and HIV in women.* Retrieved from http://www.cdc.gov/violenceprevention/pdf/ipv/13_243567_green_aag-a.pdf

Centers for Disease Control and Prevention, National Center for Injury Prevention and Control, Division of Violence Prevention. (n.d.). *An overview of intimate partner violence in the United States—2010 findings.* Retrieved from http://www.cdc.gov/violenceprevention/pdf/ipv-nisvs-factsheet-v5-a.pdf

Cha, S., & Masho, S. W. (2014). Intimate partner violence and utilization of prenatal care in the United States. *Journal of Interpersonal Violence, 29*(5), 911–927.

Chapman, K. J. (2010, April 2). 3 relatives dead, child feared speaking up, police say. *The New York Times,* p. A15.

Cooper, A., & Smith, E. L. (2011). *Homicide trends in the United States, 1980–2008* (NCJ 236018). Retrieved from Bureau of Justice Statistics website: http://www.bjs.gov/content/pub/pdf/htus8008.pdf

Dank, M., Lachman, P., Zweig, J. M., & Yahner, J. (2013). Dating violence experiences of lesbian, gay, bisexual, and transgender youth. *Journal of Youth and Adolescence, 43,* 846–857.

Edleson, J. L. (2011). *Emerging responses to children exposed to domestic violence.* Retrieved from National Online Research Center on Violence Against Women website: http://www.vawnet.org

Erwin, M. J., Gershon, R. R. M., Tiburzi, M., & Lin, S. (2005). Reports of intimate partner violence made against police officers. *Journal of Family Violence, 20*(1), 13–19.

Federal Bureau of Investigation. (2016). *Crime in the United States 2015.* Retrieved from Uniform Crime Reporting website: https://ucr.fbi.gov/

Felson, R. B., Messner, S. F., Hoskin, A. H., & Deane, G. (2002) Reasons for reporting and not reporting domestic violence to the police. *Criminology, 40*, 617–647.

Felson, R., & Pare, P. (2005). *The reporting of domestic violence and sexual assault by nonstrangers to the police* (Document No. 209039). Retrieved from National Criminal Justice Reference Service website: https://www.ncjrs.gov/pdffiles1/nij/grants/209039.pdf

Fleury, R. E., Sullivan, C. M., Bybee, D. I., & Davidson, W. S. (1998). "Why don't they just call the cops?": Reasons for differential police contact among women with abusive partners. *Violence and Victims, 13*(4), 333–346.

Fusco, R. A. (2015). Socioemotional problems in children exposed to intimate partner violence: Mediating effects of attachment and family supports. *Journal of Interpersonal Violence.* doi:10.1177/0886260515593545

Gielen, A. C., Ghandour, R. M., Burke, J. G., Mahoney, P., McDonnell, K. A., & O'Campo, P. (2007). HIV/AIDS and intimate partner violence: Intersecting women's health issues in the United States. *Trauma, Violence, & Abuse, 8*(2), 178–198.

Goldberg, N. G., & Meyer, I. H. (2013). Sexual orientation disparities in history of intimate partner violence: Results from the California Health Interview Survey. *Journal of Interpersonal Violence, 28*, 1109–1118.

Greenberg, K. (2012). Still hidden in the closet: Trans women and domestic violence. *Berkeley Journal of Gender, Law, & Justice, 27*(2), 198–251.

Hamilton, M., & Worthen, M. G. F. (2011). Sex disparities in arrest outcomes for domestic violence. *Journal of Interpersonal Violence, 26*(8), 1559–1578.

Harbison, J. (2008). Stoic heroines or collaborators: Ageism, feminism, and the provision of assistance to abused old women. *Journal of Social Work Practice, 22*, 221–234.

Hart, A. (2004, January 9). Suspect in four family deaths is found shot. *The New York Times*, p. A12.

James, S. E., Herman, J. L., Rankin, S., Keisling, M., Mottet, L., & Anafi, M. (2016). *The report of the 2015 U.S. transgender survey: Executive summary*. Retrieved from National Center for Transgender Equality website: http://www.transequality.org

Johnson, L. B., Todd, M., & Subramanian, G. (2005). Violence in police families: Work-family spillover. *Journal of Family Violence, 20*(1), 3–12.

Johnson, M. P. (1995). Patriarchal terrorism and common couple violence: Two forms of violence against women. *Journal of Marriage and the Family, 57*(2), 283–294.

Kelly, J. B., & Johnson, M. P. (2008). Differentiation among types of intimate partner violence: Research update and implications for interventions. *Family Court Review, 46*(3), 476–499.

Kimmel, M. S. (2002). "Gender symmetry" in domestic violence: A substantive and methodological research review. *Violence Against Women, 8*(11), 1332–1363.

Koeppel, M., & Bouffard, L. A. (2014). *The consequences of intimate partner violence victimization by sexual orientation* (Report No. 2014-02). Retrieved from Sam Houston State University, Crime Victim's Institute website: www.crimevictimsinstitute.org

Lacey, M. (2011, June 3). Gunman in southern Arizona kills six, including ex-wife and her lawyer, police say. *The New York Times*, p. A15.

Langenderfer-Magruder, L., Walls, N. E., Whitfield, D. L., Brown, S. M., & Barrett, C. M. (2016). Partner violence victimization among lesbian, gay, bisexual, transgender, and queer youth: Associations among risk factors. *Child & Adolescent Social Work Journal, 33*, 55–68.

Langenderfer-Magruder, L., Whitfield, D. L., Walls, N. E., Kattari, S. K., & Ramos, D. (2016). Experiences of intimate partner violence and subsequent police reporting among lesbian, gay, bisexual, transgender, and queer adults in Colorado: Comparing rates of cisgender and transgender victimization. *Journal of Interpersonal Violence, 31*(5), 855–871.

Logan, T., & Valente, R. (2015). *Who will help me? Domestic violence survivors speak out about law enforcement responses.* Retrieved from National Domestic Violence Hotline website: http://www.thehotline.org/resources/law-enforcement-responses/

Machtinger, E. L., Wilson, T. C., Haberer, J. E., & Weiss, D. S. (2012). Psychological trauma and PTSD in HIV-positive women: A meta-analysis. *AIDS and Behavior, 16*(8), 2091–2100.

Martin-Storey, A. (2015). Prevalence of dating violence among sexual minority youth: Variation across gender, sexual minority identity and gender of sexual partners. *Journal of Youth and Adolescence, 44*, 211–214.

McClennen, J. C. (2005). Domestic violence between same-gender partners: Recent findings and future research. *Journal of Interpersonal Violence, 20*(2), 149–154.

McClennen, J. C., Summers, A. B., & Vaughan, C. (2002). Gay men's domestic violence: Dynamics, help-seeking behaviors, and correlates. *Journal of Gay & Lesbian Social Services, 14*(1), 23–49.

Parker, A. (2012, February 19). Arizona sheriff is accused of threatening ex-boyfriend. *The New York Times*, p. A19.

Phillips, D. Y., Walsh, B., Bullion, J. W., Reid, P. V., Bacon, K., & Okoro, N. (2014). The intersection of intimate partner violence and HIV in U.S. women: A review. *Journal of the Association of Nurses in AIDS Care, 25*(1), S36–S49.

Pitts, K. M. (2014). Latina immigrants, interpersonal violence, and the decision to report to police. *Journal of Interpersonal Violence, 29*(9), 1661–1678.

Pollard Jr., R. Q., Sutter, E., & Cerulli, C. (2014). Intimate partner violence reported by two samples of deaf adults via a computerized American Sign Language survey. *Journal of Interpersonal Violence, 29*(5), 948–965.

Porter, J., & Williams, L. M. (2011). Intimate violence among underrepresented groups on a college campus. *Journal of Interpersonal Violence, 26*, 3210–3224.

Reina, A. S., Lohman, B. J., Maldonado, M. M. (2014). "He said they'd deport me": Factors influencing domestic violence help-seeking practices among Latina immigrants. *Journal of Interpersonal Violence, 29*(4), 593–615.

Reuters. (2006, June 7). Ax murderer executed. *The New York Times*, p. A19.

Roberto, K. A., McPherson, M. C., & Brossoie, N. (2014). Intimate partner violence in late life: A review of the empirical literature. *Violence Against Women, 19*(12), 1538–1558.

Scherer, H. L., Snyder, J. A., & Fisher, B. S. (2016). Intimate partner victimization among college students with and without disabilities: Prevalence of and relationship to emotional well-being. *Journal of Interpersonal Violence, 31*(1), 49–80.

Shah, P. S., & Shah, J. (2010). Maternal exposure to domestic violence and pregnancy and birth outcomes: A systematic review and meta-analysis. *Journal of Women's Health, 19*(11), 2017–2031.

Smith, D. L. (2008). Disability, gender and intimate partner violence: Relationships from the behavioral risk factor surveillance system. *Sexuality and Disability, 26*, 15–28.

Smith, E. L., & Farole, D. J. (2009). *Profile of intimate partner violence cases in large urban counties* (NCJ 228193). Retrieved from Bureau of Justice Statistics website: https://www.bjs.gov/content/pub/pdf/pipvcluc.pdf

Smith, S. G., Chen, J., Basile, K. C., Gilbert, L. K., Merrick, M. T., Patel, N., ... Jain, A. (2017). *The national intimate partner and sexual violence survey: 2010-2012 state report.* Retrieved from Centers for Disease Control and Prevention, Division of Violence Prevention website: https://www.cdc.gov/violenceprevention/pdf/NISVS StateReportBook.pdf

Sokoloff, N. J., & Dupont, I. (2005). Domestic violence at the intersections of race, class, and gender: Challenges and contributions to understanding violence against marginalized women in diverse communities. *Violence Against Women, 11*(1), 38–64.

Southall, A. (2014, April 20). Ex-officer killed wife, police say; Children ran for help. *The New York Times,* p. A17.

Tolman, R. M., & Rosen, D. (2001). Domestic violence in the lives of women receiving welfare: Mental health, substance dependence, and economic well-being. *Violence Against Women, 7*(2), 141–158.

Truman, J. L., & Morgan, R. E. (2014). *Non-fatal domestic violence, 2003-2012* (NCJ 244697).

Retrieved from Bureau of Justice Statistics website: http://www.bjs.gov/content/pub/pdf/ndv0312.pdf

Truman, J. L., & Morgan, R. E. (2016). *Criminal victimization, 2015* (NCJ 250180). Retrieved from Bureau of Justice Statistics website: https://www.bjs.gov/content/pub/pdf/cv15.pdf

Washington State Department of Health. (n.d.). *Domestic violence.* Retrieved from http://www.doh.wa.gov/YouandYourFamily/InjuryandViolencePrevention/SexualandDomesticViolence/DomesticViolence

West, C. M. (2004). Black women and intimate partner violence: New directions for research. *Journal of Interpersonal Violence, 19*(12), 1487–1493.

West, C. M., Kantor, G. K., & Jasinski, J. L. (1998). Sociodemographic predictors and cultural barriers to help-seeking behavior by Latina and Anglo American battered women. *Violence and Victims, 13*(4), 361–375.

Yoshioka, M. R., & Choi, D. Y. (2005). Culture and interpersonal violence research: Paradigm shift to create a full continuum of domestic violence services. *Journal of Interpersonal Violence, 20*(4), 513–519.

KEY TERMS

- *Coercive Controlling Violence*: Systematic and intentional terrorization of one's partner based on a relationship dynamic of power and control. It includes more than just physical violence, such as isolation, economic subordination, and other control tactics. Originally called "patriarchal terrorism," the term was later changed to acknowledge that not all coercive control is a product of patriarchal traditions (a man's right to control/own "their" woman) and is not exclusively perpetrated by men (although it more often results in injuries to women) (Johnson, 1995; Kelly & Johnson, 2008).

- *Intimate Partner*: A person with whom one has a close personal relationship, such as a current or former spouse, dating partner, or sexual partner. The relationship commonly involves at least one of the following characteristics: emotional connectedness, identity as a couple, regular contact, familiarity/knowledge of each other's lives, and ongoing physical/sexual contact. It is important to note that intimate partners do not have to be cohabitating or be sexually intimate (Breiding et al., 2015).

- *National Crime Victimization Survey (NCVS)*: A yearly survey conducted by the U.S. Census Bureau for the Bureau of Justice Statistics and administered to individuals aged 12 and over from a nationally representative sample of about 134,690 households. First launched in 1973, this survey asks respondents if they have ever been a victim of nonfatal personal crime or property crime and, if so, gathers information about the characteristics of the offender and the crime itself (Bureau of Justice Statistics, n.d.).

- *National Intimate Partner and Sexual Violence Survey (NISVS)*: A national random digit dial telephone survey of English and Spanish-speaking individuals aged 18 and over launched by the CDC in 2010 measuring lifetime victimization, as well as victimization in the 12 months prior to the survey. This survey collects information not previously measured in a national population-based survey (for example, incidents of psychological aggression and types of sexual violence other than rape), and is also the first survey to simultaneously measure national- and state-level estimates of violence for all states (Breiding et al., 2014).

- *Physical Violence:* Personally, or coercing another person into, using physical force with the intent of causing death, disability, injury, or harm. Examples include, but are not limited to, scratching, slapping, punching, shoving, choking, burning, biting, use of restraints, and use of a weapon (Breiding et al., 2015).

- *Psychological Aggression*: Verbal and non-verbal communication that is intended to exert control over another person and/or harm another person mentally or emotionally. Often covert and manipulative in nature, these non-physical acts may not be readily perceived as aggression. Examples include name-calling, limiting access to money and friends, excessive monitoring of emails/social media, threatening to disclose immigration status or sexual orientation, and refusing to use birth control (Breiding et al., 2015).

- *Sexual Violence:* Penetration or touching of a sexual manner, either committed or attempted, in which a victim either does not freely give consent, or is unable to consent (due to age, disability, intoxication, etc.) or refuse (due to threats of violence, intimidation, misuse of authority, etc.) the sexual act. Non-contact unwanted sexual experiences are also included, such as unwanted exposure to pornography, sexual comments, the sending of sexually explicit photographs, or unwanted filming of a sexual act (Breiding et al., 2015).

- *Situational Couple Violence*: Occasional outbursts of violence mostly arising from arguments/conflicts between partners that "get out of hand." Unlike coercive controlling violence, this type of violence is not derived from a dynamic of power and control, and it is considered less severe in nature and in its repercussions (Johnson, 1995; Kelly & Johnson, 2008).

- *Stalking*: Acts of repeated and unwanted attention/contact including, but not limited to, receiving phone calls, text messages, emails, and gifts, as well as being watched or followed. Sneaking into another's home, the damaging of personal property, and harming or threatening to harm pets, are also considered stalking tactics. This pattern of behavior causes the victim to be fearful or concerned about their own safety or the safety of someone else (Breiding et al., 2015).

THE NEW YORK TIMES ARTICLES

Associated Press. (2007). Ohio: Bond set for officer accused in killings. *The New York Times*. Retrieved from https://www.nytimes.com/2007/06/26/us/26brfs-pregnant.html

Associated Press. (2007). Professor pleads guilty. *The New York Times*. Retrieved from https://www.nytimes.com/2007/11/27/us/27brfs-PROFESSORPLE_BRF.html

Associated Press. (2007). Wife guilty of manslaughter in minister's killing. *The New York Times*. Retrieved from https://www.nytimes.com/2007/04/20/us/20minister.html

Schmidt, M. S. (2015). Secret service officer faces charges in a break-in. *The New York Times*. Retrieved from https://www.nytimes.com/2015/04/11/us/service-officer-faces-charges-in-a-break-in.html

Urbina, I. (2009). Ex-mayor denies stalking woman. *The New York Times*. Retrieved from https://www.nytimes.com/2009/07/07/us/07barry.html

DISCUSSION QUESTIONS

1. Name the four types of IPV identified by the CDC, and give an example of each.
2. With the knowledge that IPV typically begins occurring at a young age, what sorts of preventative measures should be implemented to address it? Who should be responsible for implementing them? Parents? Schools?
3. Do you think that a more accurate representation of IPV in the media would have an effect on victim reporting? Why or why not?
4. How might an increase in victim reporting change the behavior of the various actors in the criminal justice system (police, prosecutors, etc.)?

CHAPTER 6

Victims of Sexual Violence

Andrea Giuffre, Department of Criminal Justice, Seattle University;
David Patrick Connor, Independent Criminologist

INTRODUCTION

The most widely accepted estimates of **sexual violence** (also termed sexual assault) approximate that 18 percent of women and three percent of men in the United States are victims of sexual violence in their lifetime (Devore & Sachs, 2011; Harrell et al., 2009; Tjaden & Thoennes, 2000). Studies have shown that sexual assault victimization rates have remained constant since the 1990s (Basile, Chen, Black, & Saltzman, 2007). Even so, these estimates are thought to capture only part of the prevalence of violent sex crimes. This is because sex crimes are widely underreported, sexual assault is not clearly defined, and survey methodology is not consistent with respect to measuring the prevalence of sexual violence (Devore & Sachs, 2011).

Most authorities estimate that only around 15 percent to 40 percent of victims report their sexual assault (Rosen & Golden, 1992). This phenomenon is thought to be due to the fact that after sexual assault occurs, such victimization may cause many mental health and general health problems. Some of the most common mental health and general health issues include, but are not limited to, functional gastrointestinal disorders, chronic pain, depression, substance abuse disorders, and post-traumatic stress disorders (Devore & Sachs, 2011). Moreover, sexual assault crimes are arguably very personal, almost always trauma related, and responsible for the highest incidences of post-traumatic stress disorder development (Norris & Beutler, 1992). Child sexual assault victims often grow up to become highly involved with substance abuse and fall into depression (Murphy et al., 1988; Ullman, 2016). The National Sexual Violence Resource Center (2016) describes that sexual violence violates a person's trust and their feelings of safety. From an emotional standpoint, victimization may cause feelings of guilt, shame, fear, numbness, shock, and isolation (National Sexual Violence Resource Center, 2016).

Many victims of sexual violence seek help and resources from community organizations, although few victims report their assaults to the police (Patterson & Campbell, 2010). Tjaden and Thoennes (2000) estimate that around 36 percent of female rape victims seek medical treatment of some kind after the assault. For those that *do* report their assaults, withdrawal of participation during investigation is common due to lasting detrimental mental health effects of participating in the criminal justice system. These effects are commonly referred to as **secondary victimizations** because of the similar impact that they may have on the victim compared to the initial victimization (Patterson & Campbell, 2010).

Along those lines, Hanson and colleagues (2003) suggest that the disclosure of abuse may increase the likelihood of psychological problems that make it difficult for victims to cope. Poor mental health after sexual violence has been associated with younger age, lower income, lower educational attainment, lack of emotional support, and lack of health insurance (Vandemark & Mueller, 2008). There is consistent evidence that victim satisfaction with criminal justice organizations and representatives corresponds to positive mental health outcomes (Kunst, Popelier, & Varekamp, 2015). Further, the impact of sexual assault extends beyond those immediately impacted by sex crimes, such as the victim's family members, friends, and significant others. Those working to help victims, such as advocates, therapists, and researchers, may also experience vicarious trauma (Campbell & Wasco, 2005).

With respect to the absence of a clear definition for sexual assault, **sexual assault** *may* be defined as any type of physical sexual contact without appropriate legal consent. Within this definition, various models of legal consent dominate American discourse and many different laws govern sexual assault crimes in American society (Decker & Baroni, 2011). Other definitions are more complicated, stating that sexual violence includes any sexual act, attempt to obtain a sexual act, unwanted sexual comments or advances, or acts to traffic, or otherwise directed, against a person's sexuality using coercion, by any person regardless of their relationship to the victim, in any setting, including but not limited to home and work (World Health Organization, 2002). Consent is often defined as words or actions by a legally or functionally competent individual that give informed approval of sexual activity. A victim's age, illness, mental or physical disability, being asleep or unconscious, or intoxication by way of alcohol or drugs (whether voluntary or involuntary) may prevent an individual from being able to consent to sexual activity. Moreover, victims may be unable to refuse sexual activity and thereby unable to give consent because of the use of weapons, physical violence, threats of physical violence, intimidation, pressure, or misuse of authority (Basile, Smith, Breiding, Black, & Mahendra, 2014).

The #MeToo movement, Time's Up organization, and very public allegations of sexual assault against high-powered celebrities have brought new fire to a national discussion on sexual violence. Despite public disagreement over what may constitute sexual violence, various forms of media have provided a platform for a greatly needed dialogue about how best to address many forms of sexual violence. But, by the same token, media create dominant "realities" that can reinforce dominant power relations and shape personal beliefs and perceptions of events. Therefore, media play a large role in shaping public opinion and the policy responses that follow (Easteal, Holland, & Judd, 2015). In order to parse out some of the influence that media may have on the discourse around sexual violence, this chapter relies on an interpretive content analysis of newspaper articles that discuss sexual violence.

This chapter is structured as an interpretive content analysis, identifying common themes among articles in *The New York Times* depicting specific instances of sexual assault in the years 2001 to 2015. Then, the analyses compare *The New York Times'* depictions of sexual assault to current sexual assault trends. This chapter will strive to situate media depictions of sexual assault within discussions of sexual assault in a criminal justice research context. Thus, the chapter "interprets" media through identification and analysis of common thematic elements (Drisko & Maschi, 2016). Last, this chapter will make recommendations for the effective consumption of newspaper articles in criminal justice research and policy contexts.

LITERATURE REVIEW

VICTIM CHARACTERISTICS

A review of the scholarly literature suggests that there are some attributes common among many victims of sexual violence. Victims of sexual violence are generally female youth (Acierno, Resnick, & Kilpatrick, 1997). For females, low-income status and being African American are significant risk factors for sexual victimization (Acierno et al., 1997; Gross, Winslett, Roberts, & Gohm, 2006; Kalof, 2000). Some studies have found that Native American or Hispanic females are at an increased risk for sexual victimization (Kalof, 2000; Sochting, Fairbrother, & Koch, 2004). In many studies that utilize self-reports from college students, the number of prior sexual partners was a significant predictor of assault for women (Harrell et al., 2009).

Interestingly, the literature provides a clear picture that prior sexual assault is a significant predictor for future sexual violence (Harrell et al., 2009). What is more, childhood sexual abuse is usually related to an increased risk of becoming sexually victimized as an adult (Humphrey & White, 2000; Siegel & Williams, 2003; Sochting, et al., 2004). The severity of past sexual abuse can impact the severity of future sexual abuse, and women who have multiple experiences of sexual abuse have an even higher risk for victimization (Gidycz, Hanson, & Layman, 1995; Merrill et al., 1999; Smith, White, & Holland, 2003). A **compounding effect** is commonly referenced in the literature, wherein childhood sexual victimization increases the odds of adolescent victimization, which subsequently increases the odds of adult assault (Humphrey & White, 2000).

Among male victims of sexual violence, physical, psychiatric, and cognitive disabilities represent significant risk factors for sexual victimization (Stermac, Del Bove, & Addison, 2004; Stermac, Sheridan, Davidson, & Dunn, 1996). At the same time, men who participate in athletics during college have been found to be more likely to experience serious sexual assault (Tewksbury & Mustaine, 2001). Further, alcohol and drug use is reported as another risk factor for both male and female victims of sexual violence in college settings and some community settings (Harrell et al., 2009; Tewksbury & Mustaine, 2001).

OFFENDER CHARACTERISTICS

Beyond what is known about victims of sexual violence, prior research offers some insight about the characteristics of many perpetrators of sexual violence. People who engage in sexual violence are likely to be male; may possess a hostile, masculine attitude; and potentially hold calloused and/or aggressive sexual beliefs (Abbey, McAuslan, Zawacki, Clinton, & Buck, 2001; Bernat, Wilson, & Calhoun, 1999; Hall et al., 2006; McConaghy & Zamir, 1995; Wheeler, George, & Dahl, 2002). A history of coerciveness and committing assault are also predictors of participating in sexual violence against others (Abbey, Parkhill, BeShears, Clinton-Sherrod, & Zawacki, 2006; Loh, Gidycz, Lobo, & Luthra, 2005). Some studies have found that the experience of childhood sexual abuse can predict perpetration of sexual assault (Abbey et al., 2006; Casey, Beadnell, & Lindhorst, 2009; Senn, Desmarais, Verberg, & Wood, 2000). More commonly, studies have found that a composition of multiple types of childhood abuse increases the likelihood of sexual assault perpetration in adulthood (Abbey, Jacques-Tiura, & Lebreton, 2011; Malamuth, Linz, Heavey, Barnes, & Acker, 1995; Thompson, Koss, Kingree, Goree, & Rice, 2011). Alcohol use is one of the most common situational risk factors for offenders (Abbey, Clinton-Sherrod, McAuslan, Zawacki, & Buck, 2003; Abbey & McAuslan, 2004; Zawacki et al., 2003). When people have a higher number of sexual partners, this may increase their likelihood of engaging in sexual violence (Abbey & McAuslan, 2004; Abbey et al., 2001).

The results are mixed with respect to how group membership may influence one's proclivity toward sexual violence. Belonging to a group, such as a fraternity, athletic organization, or military service branch, has shown to either increase the likelihood of sexual assault perpetration or reduce the likelihood of sexual assault perpetration (Harrell et al., 2009).

In general, when considering the influence of group membership on likelihood of perpetration of sexual assault, men's likelihood of perpetrating sexual assault depends on the level of rape-supportive attitudes among peers within their social groups (Fabiano, Perkins, Berkowitz, Linkenbach, & Stark, 2003; Humphrey & Kahn, 2000).

OFFENSE CHARACTERISTICS

In terms of offense characteristics that are common in instances of sexual violence, studies largely focus on the victim-offender relationship and the physical context of the victimization. The relationship between victims and offenders of sexual violence may vary based on whether or not victims are women or men. For female victims, an intimate partner is most often the perpetrator of sexual violence (Acierno et al., 1997; Gross et al., 2006; Jones, Wynn, Kroeze, Dunnuck, & Rossman, 2004). Some studies suggest that greater intimacy may actually increase the level of violence of a sexual assault (Tjaden & Thoennes, 2000). Within these relationships, male perpetration of assault against female victims is the most common (Harrell et al., 2009). Women are likely to be physically attacked by known individuals, such as husbands or ex-husbands, boyfriends, relatives, and acquaintances (Acierno et al., 1997; Gross et al., 2006). In contrast, men are slightly more likely to be victimized by strangers (Acierno et al., 1997).

With respect to the physical context of sexual violence, there is some evidence that sexual victimization is more likely to occur in specific environments and locations. Perhaps not surprisingly, private spaces appear to be less safe than public spaces. Past studies have found that most reported sexual assaults occur at private residences (i.e., homes, apartments, fraternity houses, and residence halls) or in parked cars (Balemba & Beauregard, 2012; Hewitt & Beauregard, 2014; Sochting et al., 2004). Research has shown that sexual assault is more prevalent in secluded areas (Sochting et al., 2004).

However, the context of sexual assault depends on many factors (Balemba & Beauregard, 2012; Hewitt & Beauregard, 2014). Balemba and Beauregard (2012) discuss that when a victim is kidnapped and is dressed provocatively, the offense may be more likely to occur outside. Balemba and Beauregard (2012) also mention that offenses are more likely to occur at night when the victim is an adult, and the crime is more likely to happen on a weekday when the victim is a stranger. Additionally, if an offender did not use physical force on their victim, the offense is more likely to occur in a private location (Balemba & Beauregard, 2012). In essence, the types of sexual crimes committed and strategies used to secure a victim depend on which spatial or temporal aspect of a crime is examined (Hewitt & Beauregard, 2014). Ultimately, sexual assault can take place in almost any location and depends on many complex situational factors.

MEDIA DEPICTIONS OF SEXUAL VIOLENCE

Media depictions of sexual violence often portray a particularly dark picture of the frequency and severity of sex crimes. Acts of sexual violence involving children and other especially heinous acts of sexual violence are more likely to be covered by the media (Galeste, Fradella, & Vogel, 2012; Jenkins, 1998; Zgoba, 2004). For example, in an analysis of newspaper coverage of child sexual abuse, Mejia, Cheyne, & Dorfman (2012) found that media reports typically do not cover stories about child sexual abuse that are not violent or brutal in nature. Further, analyses of crime stories from newscasts conducted by Dowler (2006) show that many media depictions of sexual violence portray a heightened sense of fear of sex crimes. When the media portray heinous acts of sexual violence (often against children) and combine those depictions with a sense of extreme fear, the acts may be personalized by the general public. When personalization of the aforementioned acts occurs, the public may come to view that such crimes frequently *reoccur* and a **moral panic** may ensue (Connor & Tewksbury, 2017).

Other myths about sex offenders are exceedingly prevalent in media coverage of sexual violence. The public tends to accept the media's myths as conventional wisdom and perpetuate certain false stereotypes of sex offenders (Connor & Tewksbury, 2017; Harrell et al., 2009). Sex offenders are often portrayed as not having a relationship with their victims, anticipated to repeat offend, specialize in particularly heinous sexual offenses, belong to a stereotypically homogenous group, and be unable to be rehabilitated (Connor & Tewksbury, 2017). Mejia, Somji, Nixon, Dorf-man, & Quintero (2015) demonstrate this "othering" of sex offenders in a study of newspaper articles where approximately one fifth of the articles analyzed portrayed sex offenders as subhuman. This characterization of sex offenders as subhuman, or the "other," may be termed "**folk deviling.**"

In sum, media depictions of sexual violence have been found to depart from what criminal justice researchers have discovered are the most preva-lent sexual violence characteristics. Media tend to cover especially heinous acts of sexual violence (Galeste et al., 2012; Jenkins, 1998; Mejia et al., 2012; Zgoba, 2004), generally with a heightened sense of fear (Dowler, 2006). Essentially, media can be seen as perpetuating myths about the incidents themselves and about victims. Media tend to perpetuate myths about offenders in the same way, distancing relevant criminal justice research from the public's understanding of sexual violence. Sex offenders are often publicly conceived of as the "other" and ostracized by society (Connor & Tewksbury, 2017).

METHODOLOGY & RESULTS

In the following analysis, we intend to shed light on the various ways that the media portrays acts of sexual violence. Specifically, the analysis below utilizes newspaper content from *The New York Times* during the first decade and a half of the 21st century to examine how acts, victims, and offenders of sexual violence are depicted in a major media outlet. Our analysis was conducted to explore and expose any gaps between media portrayal of sexual violence and the empirical reality of sexual violence.

The articles examined in the present study were obtained from the Pro-Quest Research Library database. The database was searched for all articles pertaining to "sexual violence," "sexual assault," "sexual abuse," "rape," "raping," and "rapist" within the National Desk section of *The New York Times* from January 1, 2001, to December 31, 2015. Among the 2,535 articles that matched the aforementioned criteria, 1,882 articles did not focus on particular instances of sexual violence. Because the present study attempted to understand how *The New York Times* frames specific episodes of sexual violence in recent years, these 1,882 articles were subsequently excluded. The remaining 653 articles described one or more particular instances of sexual assault and were thus included in the present study. The articles that were included in the analyses may have included anecdotes about other instances of sexual assault, but nonetheless focused on one specific occurrence. The "main" instance or portrayal of sexual assault was the only instance coded in the analysis.

To begin, each article was categorized based on its publication year. Between 2001 and 2005, particular episodes of sexual assault were reported at a high level. In the following few years, there was a drastic decrease in the number of articles containing information about distinct instances of sexual violence. Then, particular instances of sexual violence continued to increase in coverage in *The New York Times*. The greatest number of articles containing specific instances of sexual violence were published in *The New York Times* in 2002 (n = 151). Most of the articles that featured specific acts of sexual assault were published in *The New York Times* in the first quarter of the study period of interest (between 2002 and 2005) and the last quarter of the study period of interest (between 2012

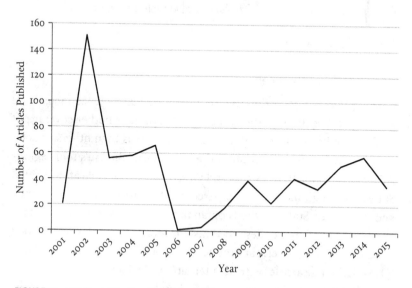

FIGURE 6.1   Number of *The New York Times* Articles Depicting Sexual Violence from the Years 2001–2015.

and 2015). This suggests that these crimes severely fluctuated in media attention over the study period of interest, perhaps with large scandals gaining mass media attention.

Analysis of articles shows that there were three primary content areas that were emphasized in *The New York Times* when it came to reporting on specific crimes of sexual violence. Throughout this 15-year period, offense characteristics, victim characteristics, and offender characteristics emerged as themes. When describing offense characteristics, articles described where the crimes occurred and the relationship between victims and offenders. At the same time, articles focused on victim characteristics centered on their age, race, sex, occupation, and religion, as well as how many people experienced victimization. Further, articles that discussed offender characteristics similarly noted their age, race, sex, occupation, and religion, as well as how many people engaged in sexual violence. Thus, this analysis includes the following variables: age of victim/offender, race of victim/offender, sex of victim/offender, occupation of victim/offender, religion of victim/offender, and number of victims/offenders. An indication of newsworthiness (i.e., whether or not an article appeared on the front page of *The New York Times*) was also included in the analysis.

OFFENSE CHARACTERISTICS

Location of Sexual Violence

One approach to reporting the location of sexual violence focused on geographical position of the crimes. To determine whether coverage of sexual assaults was more common in certain areas than others, articles were coded for representation of the U.S. Census Bureau's four regions (i.e., Midwest, Northeast, South, and West) and areas outside of the United States. Although more than 80 percent of the articles ($n = 571$) identified the United States as the geographical location of sexual assaults, a small number of articles described instances of sexual violence that took place inside "Asia," "Central America," "Europe," the "Middle East," and "Oceania." These articles with an international incident location depicted a combination of American/international victim(s) and American/

international offender(s). Nevertheless, victim or offender or both victim and offender were American.

An example of this kind of international article is titled, "Ex-Soldier Gets Life Sentence for Iraq Murders." This article, published in 2009, discusses the rape and murder of a 14-year-old Iraqi girl by a former American soldier. Nearly one third of the articles centered on sexual assaults that occurred inside the western region of the United States. Nonetheless, when articles described the geographic position of sexual victimization, each of the four U.S. regions were more commonly represented than the rest of the world.

A second approach to reporting the location of sexual violence focused on the physical setting where such crimes transpired. A total of 454 articles explicitly described the physical setting of specific instances of sexual assaults. As displayed by Table 6.1, articles most commonly identified churches, homes, and college and university campuses as places where sexual assaults occurred. At the same time, hotels, schools, property owned by the military, and hospitals were not unusual locations for sexual violence. The "other" category represented additional physical settings where sexual assaults occurred, but were mentioned in no more than five articles, including summer and youth camps, parking lots, prisons/correctional facilities, residential care centers, public transit, courthouses, outdoor recreational areas, and homeless encampments. Based on media reporting of sexual violence, it appeared that these offenses happen in a variety of physical settings, especially in closed environments. An example of the most common location of sexual violence depicted is shown in the 2002 article, "Bail Is Reduced for Boston Priest." This article describes that Reverend Paul Shanley sexually abused a boy at a Catholic church in Newton, Massachusetts, from the years 1983 to 1990.

Victim/Offender Relationship

The association between victims and perpetrators of sexual violence was a focal point in more than one half of the articles. Specifically, 404 articles described whether victims and offenders were strangers or known to

TABLE 6.1 Descriptive Statistics at the Incident Level (n = 653)

VARIABLE	RESPONSE	n (%)
Geographic position	West	204 (32.2%)
	Northeast	185 (28.3%)
	South	100 (15.3%)
	Midwest	82 (12.6%)
	Europe	7 (1.1%)
	Central America	5 (0.8%)
	Middle East	4 (0.6%)
	Asia	1 (0.2%)
	Oceania	1 (0.2%)
	Not reported	65 (10.0%)
Location	Church	194 (29.7%)
	Home	93 (14.2%)
	Campus	50 (7.7%)
	Hotel	34 (5.2%)
	School	32 (4.9%)
	Military	29 (4.4%)
	Hospital	9 (1.4%)
	Other	13 (2.0%)
	Not reported	199 (30.5%)
Relationship type	Known	366 (56.0%)
	Strangers	38 (5.8%)
	Not reported	249 (38.1%)

each other. An overwhelming majority of these articles (n = 366) reported that victims were familiar with their perpetrators. For instance, an article published in 2003 titled, "At Age 11, Girl Says, She Voluntarily Left With Male Neighbor," discusses the kidnapping and rape of a young girl by a neighbor with whom she was familiar.

VICTIM CHARACTERISTICS (TABLE 6.2)

Age

Most of the articles ($n = 599$) established whether or not victims of sexual violence were minors, adults, or a combination of minors and adults. Over two thirds of the articles described sexual assault victims who were under the age of 18, and approximately one quarter of the articles stated that such victims were adults. Only 13 articles discussed victims who were not solely minors or adults. One article that typifies those depicting sexual violence against children is titled, "New Arrest Adds Unexpected Turn in Child-Killing Case," and it was published in 2005. This article discusses that an Indiana girl was abducted, raped, and murdered by a 38-year-old factory worker.

Race

Only 53 articles provided details on the racial identities of victims of sexual violence. These articles utilized seven distinct categories to racially describe victims. Fifteen articles portrayed White victims. Black victims were the second most commonly portrayed ($n = 11$), and Hispanic victims were the third most commonly portrayed ($n = 8$). Six articles described multiple victims who were identified with differing racial identities (e.g., White and Black). Very few articles portrayed victims as Native American, Latin, Middle Eastern, and Asian people. For example, the Jaycee Dugard case is covered in the 2009 article titled, "'91 Kidnapping and Rape Victim Reunited With Family; 2 Are Charged in Abduction." A picture of the victim is included with this analysis, showing that she is White.

Sex

Most of the articles ($n = 573$) described the biological sex of people who were victimized during specific instances of sexual violence. These articles most commonly focused on female victims ($n = 324$), but a minority of them looked at male victims ($n = 191$). An even smaller number of articles portrayed female and male victims that were victimized by the same per-petrator(s). An example of this small section of articles portraying both

TABLE 6.2 Descriptive Statistics at the Victim Level (*n* = 653)

VARIABLE	RESPONSE	*n* (%)
Age	Minor	431 (66.0%)
	Adult	155 (23.7%)
	Minor & adult	13 (2.0%)
	Not reported	54 (8.3%)
Race	White	15 (0.6%)
	Black	11 (0.4%)
	Hispanic	8 (0.3%)
	Native American	6 (0.2%)
	Multiple	6 (0.2%)
	Latino	3 (0.1%)
	Middle Eastern	2 (0.1%)
	Asian	2 (0.1%)
	Not reported	600 (91.9%)
Sex	Female	324 (49.6%)
	Male	191 (29.3%)
	Female & male	58 (8.9%)
	Not reported	80 (12.3%)
Religion	Catholic	204 (31.2%)
	Fundamentalist Mormon	19 (2.9%)
	Christian	7 (1.1%)
	Jehovah's Witness	2 (0.3%)
	Amish	1 (0.2%)
	Fundamentalist Christian	1 (0.2%)
	Lutheran	1 (0.2%)
	Mormon	1 (0.2%)
	Not reported	417 (63.9%)
Number of victims	Single	341 (52.2%)
	Multiple	312 (47.8%)

female and male victims is the article, "Child Abuse at Reservation Is Topic for 3 Lawmakers." Published in 2013, this article describes the rape and murder of a 9-year-old girl and her 6-year-old brother at the Spirit Lake Indian Reservation.

Religion

The majority of articles did not describe victims' religions. However, of the articles that mentioned victim religion, many portrayed victims as Catholic and a small number portrayed victims as Fundamentalist Mormon. The articles that portrayed victims as Fundamentalist Mormon generally referred to cases of arranged marriage and statutory rape. For example, an article published in 2005 is titled, "After Fleeing Polygamist Community, an Opportunity for Influence" which mentions that a 16-year-old girl was forced to marry a 28-year-old man in the Fundamentalist Church of Jesus Christ of Latter-day Saints.

Number

Articles utilized in this study were practically split among those that portrayed multiple or single victims. These data portray sexual assault as a widespread problem, common to many individuals. One article published in 2003 and titled, "Rapist of Victims 11 to 79 Is Sought by Police in Miami" describes that one serial rapist assaulted six women and girls from the ages of 11 to 79.

Occupation

Wide variation existed with respect to articles that described victims' occupations (see Table 6.3). Indeed, victims were portrayed as having a variety of occupations, suggesting that anyone may be a victim of sexual violence. Most minors cannot legally hold an occupation. Therefore, the victim occupation for articles mentioning solely minor victims unable to hold an occupation due to their age were not included in this level of the analysis.

However, when victim occupation was described in articles, victims of sexual violence were most commonly portrayed as students, military

TABLE 6.3 Victim Occupation

VARIABLE	RESPONSE	n (%)
Occupation	Student	56 (21.2%)
	Military personnel	44 (16.7%)
	Hotel worker	20 (7.6%)
	Sex worker	8 (3.0%)
	Nun	2 (0.8%)
	Peace Corps volunteer	2 (0.8%)
	Teacher	2 (0.8%)
	Waitress	2 (0.8%)
	Court employee	1 (0.4%)
	Dorm counselor	1 (0.4%)
	Factory worker	1 (0.4%)
	Forest service worker	1 (0.4%)
	Housekeeper/nanny	1 (0.4%)
	Laundry service worker	1 (0.4%)
	Legal assistant	1 (0.4%)
	Janitor	1 (0.4%)
	Professor	1 (0.4%)
	Senator	1 (0.4%)
	University basketball program staff; former model	1 (0.4%)
	Yoga instructor	1 (0.4%)
	Not reported	116 (43.9%)
	Total	264 (100.0%)
Occupation aggregated	Student	56 (37.8%)
	Military personnel	44 (29.7%)
	Hotel worker	20 (13.5%)
	Other	20 (13.5%)
	Sex worker	8 (5.4%)
	Total	148 (100.0%)

personnel, hotel workers, and sex workers. One article titled, "In Florida Student Assaults, an Added Burden on Accusers" was published in 2014 and considers the rape of a female student by a university football player.

OFFENDER CHARACTERISTICS

Age

Most of the articles (n = 605) established whether or not perpetrators of sexual violence were minors, adults, or a combination of minors and adults (see Table 6.4). The clear majority of articles mentioned that offenders were adults at the time of the offense(s) (~89% of articles utilized). Only six articles discussed offenders who were not solely minors or adults. An example of an article depicting offenders that were both minors and adults is titled, "A Brutal Attack Outside a School Continues to Horrify One Year Later." This article was published in 2010 and discusses the gang rape of a girl outside her school by both minor and adult offenders.

Race

Similar to victim race, many of the articles did not focus on offenders' race. However, the articles that did mention offender race focused on White, Black, Hispanic, and Native American. A few cases with multiple offenders specifically mentioned multiple races. About one tenth of the offenders described were portrayed as White (around 11%). A number of offenders were portrayed as Black (4%). As the same case with victims, offenders were portrayed as belonging to a particular race either through a picture included in the article or physical description of the offender. The 2014 article, "Despite Earlier Confession, Suspect in Indiana Killings Refuses to Speak in Court" includes a picture of the offender, who is Black.

Sex

Most of the articles (n = 603) described the biological sex of people who victimized others during specific instances of sexual violence. Offenders were most commonly portrayed as male. Only a small number of articles described perpetrators of sexual violence as a combination of male and

TABLE 6.4 Descriptive Statistics at the Offender Level (*n*=653)

VARIABLE	RESPONSE	*n* (%)
Age	Adult	578 (88.5%)
	Minor	21 (3.2%)
	Minor & adult	6 (0.9%)
	Not reported	48 (7.4%)
Race	White	69 (10.6%)
	Black	26 (4.0%)
	Hispanic	8 (1.2%)
	Multiple	2 (0.3%)
	Asian	1 (0.2%)
	Latino	1 (0.2%)
	Native American	1 (0.2%)
	Not reported	545 (83.5%)
Sex	Male	579 (88.7%)
	Female & male	21 (3.2%)
	Female	3 (0.5%)
	Not reported	50 (7.7%)
Religion	Catholic	209 (32.0%)
	Fundamentalist Mormon	21 (3.2%)
	Christian	5 (0.7%)
	Jehovah's Witness	2 (0.3%)
	Jewish	2 (0.3%)
	Amish	1 (0.2%)
	Fundamentalist Christian	1 (0.2%)
	Lutheran	1 (0.2%)
	Mormon	1 (0.2%)
	Not reported	410 (62.8%)
Number of offenders	Single	483 (74.0%)
	Multiple	123 (18.8%)
	Gang	39 (6.0%)
	Not reported	8 (1.2%)

female offenders. Three female offenders were mentioned in the articles. The article, "Caught in the Gray Area of a Child-Abuser Database" was published in 2011 and discusses instances of sexual assault on the part of a mother and father.

Religion

The majority of articles did not describe offenders' religions. However, of the articles that mentioned offender religion, perpetrators of sexual violence were most commonly described as Catholic or Fundamentalist Mormon. An article, "Los Angeles Archdiocese to Dismiss Priest Over Admission of Molesting Girl" was published in 2011 and highlights the rape of a teenage girl by a Catholic priest.

Number

Some offenders were portrayed as acting in a gang-type offense (i.e., multiple offenders acting together). Other articles included mention of multiple offenders acting independently or single offenders acting independently. Most of the offenders portrayed were single actors (~74%). The remaining fourth of articles mentioned multiple offenders acting independently, those acting in a gang-type offense, or situations where the number of offenders was unknown. The 2015 article titled, "Vanderbilt Rape Trial Didn't Stir Vanderbilt" depicts the sexual assault of an unconscious woman by two former Vanderbilt football players, which is considered gang rape.

Occupation

Wide variation existed with respect to articles that described offenders' occupations. Seventy-one distinct offender occupations were mentioned throughout the articles (see Table 6.5). Perpetrators of sexual violence who were described in the articles were most likely to be priests ($n = 202$), military personnel ($n = 47$), basketball players ($n = 36$), pop stars ($n = 36$), students ($n = 20$), and students who were also football players ($n = 17$). Celebrities in general, such as Bill Cosby (mentioned in the 2014 article "For Some Fans, Accusations of Rape Crumble Bill Cosby's Wholesome Image"), have also been the focus of much media attention. Additionally, because of

TABLE 6.5 Offender Occupation (*n*=288)

	n (%)
Priest	202 (70.1%)
Military personnel	47 (16.3%)
Basketball player	36 (12.5%)
Pop star	36 (12.5%)
Student	20 (6.9%)
Student and football player	17 (5.9%)
FLDS leader	8 (2.8%)
Student and Phi Kappa Psi member	8 (2.8%)
Unemployed	8 (2.8%)
Film director	7 (2.4%)
Pediatrician	7 (2.4%)
Teacher	7 (2.4%)
Actor	6 (2.1%)
Football coach	5 (1.7%)
Bus driver	3 (1.0%)
Car collector; "eccentric millionaire;" oil heir	3 (1.0%)
Church leader	3 (1.0%)
Police officer	3 (1.0%)
Politician	3 (1.0%)
Production line supervisor	3 (1.0%)
Factory worker	2 (0.7%)
Football player	2 (0.7%)
Former teacher; wrestling coach; Speaker of the House	2 (0.7%)
Judge	2 (0.7%)
Nun	2 (0.7%)
Nursing assistant	2 (0.7%)
Pimp	2 (0.7%)
Priest; teacher	2 (0.7%)

TABLE 6.5 (Continued)

	n (%)
Republican state legislator; corn and soybean farmer	2 (0.7%)
Truck driver	2 (0.7%)
Camp counselor	1 (0.3%)
Catholic clergy member	1 (0.3%)
Concrete layer	1 (0.3%)
Congressman	1 (0.3%)
Construction worker	1 (0.3%)
Food warehouse worker	1 (0.3%)
Forest service worker	1 (0.3%)
Former priest	1 (0.3%)
Geneticist	1 (0.3%)
Handyman	1 (0.3%)
Headmaster	1 (0.3%)
Hospital worker	1 (0.3%)
Inmate	1 (0.3%)
Insurance adjuster	1 (0.3%)
Lawyer; Virginia House delegate	1 (0.3%)
Leader of homeless encampment	1 (0.3%)
Monk	1 (0.3%)
Janitor	1 (0.3%)
Pastor	1 (0.3%)
Pilot	1 (0.3%)
Pipe fitter	1 (0.3%)
Pizza deliveryman	1 (0.3%)
Plumber/carpenter	1 (0.3%)
Prince; Professor	1 (0.3%)
Owner of printing business	1 (0.3%)

(continued)

TABLE 6.5 Offender Occupation (*n*=288) (*Continued*)

	n (%)
Owner of printing business; aide for adults with developmental disabilities	1 (0.3%)
Prison guard	1 (0.3%)
Professor	1 (0.3%)
Ranch helper	1 (0.3%)
Reverend	1 (0.3%)
School employee	1 (0.3%)
Scout leader	1 (0.3%)
Security guard; steel mill worker; casino worker; tech worker	1 (0.3%)
Senator	1 (0.3%)
Sheriff	1 (0.3%)
Spiritual leader	1 (0.3%)
State employee; employee of the Department of Corrections	1 (0.3%)
Teacher's aide	1 (0.3%)
Truck painter	1 (0.3%)
Yoga instructor	1 (0.3%)
Not reported	148 (51.4%)

a combined minor status and legal inability to hold a job, minor offenders were left out of this level of the analysis. The articles suggest that offenders come from all walks of life and make up a very heterogeneous group.

NEWSWORTHINESS

Approximately 12 percent (*n* = 77) of the articles included in this analysis (*n* = 653) appeared on the front page of *The New York Times*. Of those 77 articles appearing on the front page, approximately 43 percent (*n* = 33) concerned church scandals of sexual abuse, approximately 10 percent (*n* = 8) concerned celebrity scandals of sexual abuse, approximately nine percent (*n* = 7) concerned military scandals of sexual abuse, and only about five percent

(n = 4) concerned college and school scandals of sexual abuse. With the articles concerning church scandals of sexual abuse representing almost one half of the front page stories related to sexual violence, a case can be made that *The New York Times* deemed church-related sexual abuse scandals as the most "newsworthy" type of scandal.

Front Page & Victim Age

In another way, the majority (~62%) of *The New York Times* articles covering sexual violence that appeared as front page news depicted minor victims (see Table 6.6). Front page sexual violence stories in *The New York Times* typically covered heinous acts against children. For instance, an article published in 2002 titled, "Man Arrested in California Case of Child's Abduction and Killing," described the sexual assault and murder of 5-year-old Samantha Runnion. The author writes that the kidnapped child's "abused body was left in a gruesome pose in the hills southeast of this suburban city" and that, "investigators said it had been posed in a provocative fashion, leading them to believe that the killer was a sexual predator who was likely to strike again." The author also discusses that the

TABLE 6.6 Contingency Table Examining Newsworthiness and Victim Age

			VICTIM AGE			
			ADULT	MINOR	MINOR & ADULT	NOT REPORTED	TOTAL
Front page	No	Count	137	383	11	45	576
		% Within front page	23.8	66.5	1.9	7.8	100.0
		% Of total	21.0	58.7	1.7	6.9	88.2
	Yes	Count	18	48	2	9	77
		% Within front page	23.4	62.3	2.6	11.7	100.0
		% Of total	2.8	7.4	0.3	1.4	11.8
Total		Count	155	431	13	54	653
		% Within front page	23.7	66.0	2.0	8.3	100.0
		% Of total	23.7	66.0	2.0	8.3	100.0

suspect was accused of assaulting children in the past, but was acquitted. This article depicts a particularly horrific act against a child on the front page of the newspaper perhaps to garner readership.

Front Page & Number of Victims

Front page articles of *The New York Times* depicting sexual violence were almost split between those depicting single and multiple victims of the same perpetrator(s) (see Table 6.7). Articles portraying multiple victims did so in a manner that would suggest serial offenders. For instance, an article published in 2008 titled, "Accusations Of Sex Abuse Trail Doctor," depicts 43 separate sexual abuse claims against a well-known pediatrician, Dr. Melvin D. Levine. The claims of abuse presented in this article discuss events that range from 1967 onward. This article depicts many acts against children on the front page of the newspaper perhaps to garner readership.

Front Page & Number of Offenders

Almost one fourth of front page *The New York Times* articles depicting sexual violence portrayed multiple offender or gang offender type

TABLE 6.7 Contingency Table Examining Newsworthiness and Number of Victims

			VICTIM AGE		
			MULTIPLE	SINGLE	TOTAL
Front page	No	Count	276	300	576
		% Within front page	47.9	52.1	100.0
		% Of total	42.3	45.9	88.2
	Yes	Count	36	41	77
		% Within front page	46.8	53.2	100.0
		% Of total	5.5	6.3	11.8
Total		Count	312	341	653
		% Within front page	47.8	52.2	100.0
		% Of total	47.8	52.2	100.0

perpetration of sexual violence (see Table 6.8). This spread of stories involving multiple perpetrators is at the higher end of estimates of the prevalence of sexual assaults involving multiple offenders. Franklin (2004) discusses that the precise percentage of sexual violence committed by multiple perpetrators in the United States is unknown, but estimates range from 10 percent to 30 percent. Government crime victimization data, which relies on officially reported sexual violence, reveals that around 10 percent of sexual violence is committed by multiple perpetrators at one time (Franklin, 2004). An example of this kind of article is titled, "Navy Hearing in Rape Case Raises Alarm." Published in 2013, this article discusses the rape of a female midshipman by three United States Naval Academy football players. Similar to other front page news articles depicting highly extraordinary cases, this article appears to portray an exceptional case of gang rape.

TABLE 6.8 Contingency Table Examining Newsworthiness and Number of Offenders

			NUMBER OF OFFENDERS				
			GANG	MULTIPLE	SINGLE	NOT REPORTED	TOTAL
Front page	No	Count	35	109	425	7	576
		% Within front page	6.1	18.9	73.8	1.2	100.0
		% Of total	5.4	16.7	65.1	1.1	88.2
	Yes	Count	4	14	58	1	77
		% Within front page	5.2	18.2	75.3	1.3	100.0
		% Of total	0.6	2.1	8.9	0.2	11.8
Total		Count	39	123	483	8	653
		% Within front page	6.0	18.8	74.0	1.2	100.0
		% Of total	6.0	18.8	74.0	1.2	100.0

ANALYSIS OF SEXUAL VIOLENCE

The acts of sexual violence portrayed by *The New York Times* followed prior research that sexual violence tends to occur in private spaces (Sochting et al., 2004). For example, offenses in *The New York Times* articles were reported as taking place in many closed environments, including college campuses, churches, homes, military facilities, schools, medical centers/hospitals, prisons/correctional facilities, residential care centers, public transit, and summer camps. The sex offenses described in *The New York Times* articles were also spread relatively evenly across the midwestern, northeastern, southern, and western regions of the United States. A slightly higher number of *The New York Times* articles portrayed the Northeast and West as locations for sexual violence in line with current research suggesting that reported instances of rape cluster in urban areas such as large, coastal cities. However, it should be noted that clusters of rape reports appear either because there are many rapes in an area or because a high proportion of rapes are reported to the police (Amin, Nabors, Nelson, Saqlain, & Kulldorff, 2015).

The victim-offender relationships portrayed by *The New York Times* are also in line with prior research on sexual violence. Similar to prior research that describes intimate partner violence as the most common type of sexual violence (Acierno et al., 1997; Gross et al., 2006; Jones et al., 2004), most of the relationships described in *The New York Times* articles were among people who were familiar with each other prior to the offense. Only about six percent of articles portrayed a stranger relationship. Despite common myths about "stranger danger," victims and offenders seem to know each other in most cases.

Over one half of *The New York Times* articles described sexual assault victims under the age of 18. Most sexual assault victims are youth, so *The New York Times'* portrayal of sexual violence accurately reflects current empirical research. Generally speaking, the articles in *The New York Times* focused on female victims, which is in line with prior research describing a majority of sexual assault victims as female (Acierno et al., 1997, Devore & Sachs, 2011; Harrell et al., 2009; Tjaden & Thoennes, 2000). However, many of *The New York Times* articles ($n = 260$) did not discuss victims' race, which has been found to impact the likelihood of sexual assault. Low-income status and African American ethnicity are significant risk factors for female sexual victimization (Acierno et al., 1997; Gross et al., 2006; Kalof, 2000). Some studies have found that Native American or Hispanic females are at an increased risk for sexual victimization as well (Kalof, 2000; Sochting et al., 2004).

Of the articles that did mention race, the category with the most mentions was White, which does not match prior research discussing that race has an impact on sexual assault (Acierno et al., 1997; Gross et al., 2006; Kalof, 2000; Sochting et al., 2004). *The New York Times* articles portrayed sexual assault as common among female youth, but severely neglected to include race as an important factor for sexual victimization. Considering the fact that women put at a structural disadvantage from an economic and racial standpoint are further impacted negatively by criminal justice apparatus outcomes (Kaukinen & DeMaris, 2005), it is beneficial to discuss sexual assault victims' race. By including race in the discussion of sexual violence, criminal justice actors can target resources for the prevention, reduction, and management of sexual violence in communities where assistance is most needed.

Relevant factors to the likelihood of victimization such as income level, prior number of sexual partners, prior sexual assaults, childhood sexual abuse, and alcohol and drug use were largely left out of *The New York Times'* discussion regarding victim characteristics as well. Although *The New York Times* portrayed many victims as female youth, many relevant demographic and behavioral characteristics were not mentioned. Instead, information on victims' religions was included in many of the articles (*n* = 236). Because of this disparity, individuals consuming repeated newspaper media mentioning particular victim characteristics may fall prey to believing myths and stereotypes about what constitutes the "typical" victim. The perpetuation of stereotypes is particularly harmful because such stereotypes may produce a "moral panic." Ultimately, moral panics can skew the attention of victims' resources in a manner such that those most vulnerable do not receive proper attention by criminal justice professionals, medical professionals, mental health professionals, and so forth (Jenkins, 1998).

Future research should focus more on religious group participation as a factor in the likelihood of sexual assault victimization so that media depictions of religious group influence on sexual assault can be verified. Future reporting such as that of *The New York Times* should include more relevant demographic and behavioral characteristics of victims so as not to perpetuate myths about what a stereotypical sexual assault victim may look like. Victim demographic and behavioral characteristics are exceedingly important to understand in the context of sexual assault when considering the implementation of targeted preventative programs. For example, if a myth is perpetuated that mostly White, college females are targets of sexual violence, many resources will be allocated to this population instead of more affected populations such as minority, low-income females.

Most offenders portrayed in *The New York Times* were male ($n = 579$), in line with current research suggesting that males perpetrate most sexual assaults (Abbey et al., 2001; Bernat et al., 1999; Hall et al., 2006; McConaghy & Zamir, 1995; Wheeler, et al., 2002). However, offender characteristics cited in *The New York Times* articles are not representative of factors relevant to the propensity to commit sexual assault. While *The New York Times* focused on the offender age, race, occupation, religion, and number of offenders, prior research suggests that behavioral factors and alcohol use are relevant to the likelihood that an individual will offend sexually (Abbey et al., 2003; Abbey et al., 2001; Abbey & McAuslan, 2004; Bernat et al., 1999; Hall et al., 2006; Loh, et al., 2005; McConaghy & Zamir, 1995; Piquero, Piquero, Terry, Youstin, & Nobles, 2008; Wheeler et al., 2002). Piquero and colleagues (2008) note that a combination of sexual offending and antisocial behavior has been found to occur across different phases of the life course. Thus, antisocial behavior is a relatively stable factor in sexual offending (Piquero et al., 2008). Media outlets should be careful not to stereotype offenders' demographic characteristics, as offenders come from many walks of life (this is evidenced by the multitude of offender occupations portrayed by *The New York Times*).

The most striking part of this data is that *The New York Times* portrayed offenders as a part of an organized religion, the military, athletic team, or student group. Because prior data are mixed on whether belonging to a group increases the likelihood of sexual assault perpetration (Harrell et al., 2009), more research should be conducted to determine the level of rape-supportive attitudes among individuals within such groups. As Piquero and colleagues (2008) have noted, scandals such as that of the sex abuse in the Catholic Church in the early 2000s "reinforced many stereotypes about offenders, making it difficult for professionals to reestablish awareness of the full spectrum of offenders" (p. 585).

While members of the Catholic clergy may make up a unique type of offenders, criminal justice researchers should keep in mind that sexual maltreatment makes up only 10 percent of reported child abuse cases (Piquero et al., 2008). Along the same lines, the Catholic Church sex abuse scandals led to "zero-tolerance" policies for priests, reinforcing publicly held beliefs that sex offenders are untreatable and offend throughout their lives (Finkelhor, 2003). In fact, research has suggested quite the opposite. For example, empirical research demonstrates that cognitive-behavioral treatments can reduce sexual offense recidivism up to 40 percent (Hanson, Kievit, Saunders, & Smith, 2003). And sex offenders are not generally recidivistic or specialized (Sample & Bray, 2003; Zimring, Piquero, & Jennings, 2007). But, due to the widespread media coverage of heinous acts of sexual violence against children within the Catholic Church, the public internalized myths about sexual offending to produce such "zero-tolerance" policies. The American public increasingly came to view that such crimes frequently *reoccur* (Piquero et al., 2008) and a moral panic ensued. In the early 2000s, Catholic priests were "folk deviled" and ostracized from society. An example of this is clearly seen in the article, "An Ousted Priest, His Offense Long Past, Wistfully Departs," published in 2002 by *The New York Times*.

CONCLUSION

In conclusion, *The New York Times* did portray many acts of sexual violence involving children and focused on many irrelevant demographic characteristics of both victims and offenders. For example, *The New York Times* focused heavily on very heinous acts of sexual violence against female children, without regard for victim race, income level, prior number of sexual partners, prior sexual assaults, childhood sexual abuse, and alcohol and drug use. In a similar manner, *The New York Times* focused heavily on offenders belonging to organized groups, without regard for the behavioral or cultural characteristics for such groups and alcohol or drug use of offenders.

This content analysis reveals some major gaps between what is discussed in the media about characteristics of sexual assault and what is empirically relevant to the likelihood that sexual assault will occur. As mentioned previously, future empirical research should focus on breaking down the stereotypes of victims and offenders to include more information on the widespread nature of both victim and offender demographics. With more accurate information on sexual assault victim characteristics, researchers could help identify the most vulnerable populations and concentrate supportive and therapeutic services in places with the highest need for such services. With more accurate information on sexual offender characteristics, researchers could help identify the populations most at risk for offending to open up the ability to create targeted preventative programs and concentrated therapeutic services. These programs and services would ideally reduce the number of instances of sexual assaults.

Ultimately, this content analysis demonstrates that certain instances of sexual violence in recent years as portrayed in *The New York Times* may be overly sensationalized and may only provide a glimpse of the entire picture of the problem, especially concerning relevant risk factors for sexual assault. Readers should be wary of the danger of irrelevant risk factors mentioned within media reporting on sexual assault and consume media reports of sexual assault with an awareness of its limitations that may be similar to those found in official statistics. It is important to remember that sex crimes are widely underreported, conceptions of sexual assault are not always well-defined, and inconsistent measurement of such phenomena often make understanding its prevalence highly difficult (Devore & Sachs, 2011). Nonetheless, analyzing media reporting may be one approach to understanding and subsequently addressing sexual violence. Such an approach may help shed light on the gaps between what is discussed in the media about characteristics of sexual assault and what is empirically relevant to its likelihood of occurrence. These distinctions may guide directions for future research, sexual assault prevention, and treatment for victims and offenders so that sexual violence may be reduced.

REFERENCES

Abbey, A., Clinton-Sherrod, A., McAuslan, P., Zawacki, T., & Buck, P. (2003). The relationship between the quantity of alcohol consumed and the severity of sexual assaults committed by college men. *Journal of Interpersonal Violence, 18*(7), 813–833. doi:10.1177/0886260503253301

Abbey, A., Jacques-Tiura, A., & Lebreton, J. (2011). Risk factors for sexual aggression in young men: An expansion of the confluence model. *Aggressive Behavior, 37*(5), 450–64. doi:10.1002/ab.20399

Abbey, A., & McAuslan, P. (2004). A longitudinal examination of male college students' perpetration of sexual assault. *Journal of Consulting and Clinical Psychology, 72*(5), 747–756. doi:10.1037/0022-006X.72.5.747

Abbey, A., McAuslan, P., Zawacki, T., Clinton, A., & Buck, P. (2001). Attitudinal, experiential, and situational predictors of sexual assault perpetration. *Journal of Interpersonal Violence, 16*(8), 784–807. doi:10.1177/088626001016008004

Abbey, A., Parkhill, M., BeShears, R., Clinton-Sherrod, A., & Zawacki, T. (2006). Cross-sectional predictors of sexual assault perpetration in a community sample of single African American and Caucasian men. *Aggressive Behavior, 32*(1), 54–67. doi:10.1002/ab.20107

Acierno, R., Resnick, H., & Kilpatrick, D. (1997). Health impact of interpersonal violence 1: Prevalence rates, case identification, and risk factors for sexual assault, physical assault, and domestic violence in men and women. *Behavioral Medicine, 23*(2), 53–64. doi:10.1080/08964289709596729

Amin, R., Nabors, N., Nelson, A., Saqlain, M., & Kulldorff, M. (2015). Geographical clusters of rape in the United States: 2000–2012. *Statistics and Public Policy, 2*(1), 87–92. doi:10.1080/2330443X.2015.1092899

Balemba, S., & Beauregard, E. (2012). Where and when? Examining spatiotemporal aspects of sexual assault events. *Journal of Sexual Aggression, 19*(2), 1–20. doi:10.1080/13552600.2012.703702

Basile, K., Chen, J., Black, M., & Saltzman, L. (2007). Prevalence and characteristics of sexual violence victimization among U.S. adults, 2001–2003. *Violence and Victims, 22*(4), 437–448. doi:10.1891/088667007781553955

Basile, K., Smith, S., Breiding, M., Black, M., & Mahendra, R. (2014). *Sexual violence surveillance: Uniform definitions and recommended data elements.* Atlanta, GA: National Center for Injury Prevention and Control. Retrieved from https://www.cdc.gov/violenceprevention/pdf/sv_surveillance_definitionsl-2009-a.pdf

Bernat, J., Wilson, A., & Calhoun, K. (1999). Sexual coercion history, calloused sexual beliefs and judgments of sexual coercion in a date rape analogue. *Violence and Victims, 14*(2), 147–160.

Campbell, R., & Raja, S. (1999). Secondary victimization of rape victims: Insights from mental health professionals who treat survivors of violence. *Violence and Victims, 14*(3), 261–275.

Campbell, R., & Wasco, S. M. (2005). Understanding rape and sexual assault: 20 years of progress and future directions. *Journal of Interpersonal Violence, 20*(1), 127–131. doi:10.1177/0886260504268604

Casey, E., Beadnell, B., & Lindhorst, T. (2009). Predictors of sexually coercive behavior in a nationally representative sample of adolescent males. *Journal of Interpersonal Violence. 24*(7), 1129–1147. doi:10.1177/0886260508322198

Cohen, S. (2014). *Folk devils and moral panics: The creation of the Mods and Rockers*. London: Routledge.

Connor, D. P., & Tewksbury, R. (2017). Public and professional views of sex offender registration and notification. *Criminology, Criminal Justice, Law & Society, 18*(1), 1–27.

Decker, J. F., & Baroni, P. G. (2011). "No" still means "yes": The failure of the "non-consent" reform movement in American rape and sexual assault law. *Journal of Criminal Law and Criminology, 101*(4), 1081.

Devore, H. K., & Sachs, C. J. (2011). Sexual assault. *Emergency Medicine Clinics of North America, 29*(3), 605–620. doi:10.1016/j.emc.2011.04.012

Dowler, K. (2006). Sex, lies, and videotape: The presentation of sex crimes in local television news. *Journal of Criminal Justice, 34*(4), 383–392. doi:10.1016/j.jcrimjus.2006.05.004

Drisko, J., & Maschi, T. (2016). *Content analysis*. New York: Oxford University Press.

Easteal, P., Holland, K., & Judd, K. (2015). Enduring themes and silences in media portrayals of violence against women. *Women's Studies International Forum, 48*(1), 103–113. doi:10.1016/j.wsif.2014.10.015

Fabiano, P. M., Perkins, H. W., Berkowitz, A., Linkenbach, J., & Stark, C. (2003). Engaging men as social justice allies in ending violence against women: Evidence for a social norms approach. *Journal of American College Health, 52*(3), 105–112. doi:10.1080/07448480309595732

Finkelhor, D. (2003). The legacy of the clergy abuse scandal. *Child Abuse & Neglect, 27*(11), 1225–1229. doi:10.1016/j.chiabu.2003.09.011

Franklin, K. (2004). Enacting masculinity: Antigay violence and group rape as participatory theater. *Sexuality Research & Social Policy, 1*(2), 25–40. doi:10.1525/srsp.2004.1.2.25

Galeste, M. A., Fradella, H. F., & Vogel, B. (2012). Sex offender myths in print media: Separating fact from fiction in U.S. newspapers. *Western Criminology Review, 13*(2), 4–24.

Gidycz, C., Hanson, K., & Layman, M. (1995). A prospective analysis of the relationships among sexual assault experiences: An extension of previous findings. *Psychology of Women Quarterly, 19*(1), 5–29. doi:10.1111/j.1471-6402.1995.tb00276.x

Gross, A., Winslett, A., Roberts, M., & Gohm, C. (2006). An examination of sexual violence against college women. *Violence against Women, 12*(3), 288–300. doi:10.1177/1077801205277358

Hall, G. C., Nagayama, D., David S., Eap, S., Teten, A. L., & Sue, S. (2006). Initiation, desistance, and persistence of men's sexual coercion. *Journal of Consulting and Clinical Psychology, 74*(4), 732–742. doi:10.1037/0022-006X.74.4.732

Hanson, R., Kievit, L., Saunders, B., & Smith, D. (2003). Correlates of adolescent reports of sexual assault: Findings from the National Survey of Adolescents. *Child Maltreatment, 8*(4), 261–272. doi:10.1177/1077559503257087

Harrell, M. C., Werber, L., Adelson, M., Gaillot, S. J., Lynch, C., & Pomeroy, A. (2009). *A compendium of sexual assault research*. Santa Monica, CA: RAND.

Hewitt, A., & Beauregard, E. (2014). Sexual crime and place: The impact of the environmental context on sexual assault outcomes. *Journal of Criminal Justice, 42*(5), 375–383. doi:10.1016/j.jcrimjus.2014.05.003

Humphrey, J. A., & White, J. W. (2000). Women's vulnerability to sexual assault from adolescence to young adulthood. *Journal of Adolescent Health, 27*(6), 419–424. doi:10.1016/s1054-139x(00)00168-3

Humphrey, S., & Kahn, A. (2000). Fraternities, athletic teams, and rape: Importance of identification with a risky group. *Journal of Interpersonal Violence, 15*(12), 1313–1322. doi:10.1177/088626000015012005

Jenkins, P. (1998). *Moral panic: Changing concepts of the child molester in modern America*. New Haven, CT: Yale University Press.

Jones, J. S., Wynn B. N., Kroeze, B., Dunnuck, C., Rossman, L. (2004). Comparison of sexual assaults by strangers versus known assailants in a community-based population. *American Journal of Emergency Medicine, 22*(6), 454–459. doi:10.1197/aemj.9.5.382

Kalof, L. (2000). Ethnic differences in female sexual victimization. *Sexuality and Culture, 4*(4), 75–98. doi:10.1007/s12119-000-1005-9

Kaukinen, C., & DeMaris, A. (2005). Age at first sexual assault and current substance use and depression. *Journal of Interpersonal Violence, 20*(10), 1244–1270.

Kunst, M., Popelier, L., & Varekamp, E. (2015). Victim satisfaction with the criminal justice system and emotional recovery. *Trauma, Violence, & Abuse, 16*(3), 336–358. doi:10.1177/1524838014555034

Loh, C., Gidycz, C., Lobo, T., & Luthra, R. (2005). A prospective analysis of sexual assault perpetration. *Journal of Interpersonal Violence, 20*(10), 1325–1348. doi:10.1177/0886260505278528

Malamuth, N., Linz, D., Heavey, C., Barnes, G., & Acker, M. (1995). Using the confluence model of sexual aggression to predict men's conflict with women: A 10-year follow-up study. *Journal of Personality and Social Psychology, 69*(2), 353–369. doi:10.1037/0022-3514.69.2.353

McConaghy, N., & Zamir, R. (1995). Heterosexual and homosexual coercion, sexual orientation and sexual roles in medical students. *Archives of Sexual Behavior, 24*(5), 489–502. doi:10.1007/BF01541830

Mejia, P., Cheyne, A., & Dorfman, L. (2012). News coverage of child sexual abuse and prevention, 2007–2009. *Journal of Child Sexual Abuse, 21*(4), 470–487. doi:10.1080/10538712.2012.692465

Mejia, P., Somji, A., Nixon, L., Dorfman, L., & Quintero, F. (2015). *What's missing from the news on sexual violence? An analysis of coverage, 2011–2013*. Berkeley, CA: Berkeley Media Studies Group.

Merrill, L., Newell, C., Thomsen, C., Gold, S., Milner, J., Koss, M., & Rosswork, S. (1999). Childhood abuse and sexual revictimization in a female Navy recruit sample. *Journal of Traumatic Stress, 12*(2), 211–225. doi:10.1023/A:1024789723779

Murphy, S., Kilpatrick, D., Amick-Mcmullan, A., Veronen, L., Paduhovich, J., Best, C., ... Saunders, B. (1988). Current psychological functioning of child sexual assault victims: A community study. *Journal of Interpersonal Violence, 3*(1), 55–79. doi:10.117/088626088003001005

National Sexual Violence Resource Center (2016). *The impact of sexual violence.* Fact sheet retrieved from https://www.nsvrc.org/publications/nsvrc-publications-sexual-assault-awareness-month-fact-sheets/impact-sexual-violence

Norris, F., & Beutler, L. E. (1992). Epidemiology of trauma: Frequency and impact of different potentially traumatic events on different demographic groups. *Journal of Consulting and Clinical Psychology, 60*(3), 409–418. doi:10.1037//0011-006x.60.3.409

Patterson, D., & Campbell, R. (2010). Why rape victims participate in the criminal justice system. *Journal of Community Psychology, 38*(2), 191–205. doi:10.1002/jcop.20359

Piquero, A., Piquero, N., Terry, K., Youstin, T., & Nobles, M. (2008). Uncollaring the criminal: Understanding criminal careers of criminal clerics. *Criminal Justice and Behavior, 35*(5), 583–599. doi:10.1177/0093854808314361

Rosen, R. A., & Golden, P. (1992). Meeting the needs of the sexual assault victim. *Annals of Emergency Medicine, 21*(6), 741–742.

Sample, L. L., & Bray, T. M. (2003). Are sex offenders dangerous? *Criminology and Public Policy, 3*(1), 59–82. doi:10.1111/j.1745-9133.2003.tb00024.x

Senn, C., Desmarais, S., Verberg, N., & Wood, E. (2000). Predicting coercive sexual behavior across the lifespan in a random sample of Canadian men. *Journal of Social and Personal Relationships, 17*(1), 95–113. doi:10.1177/0265407500171005

Siegel, J., & Williams, L. (2003). Risk factors for sexual victimization of women. *Violence Against Women, 9*(8), 902–930. doi:10.1177/1077801203255130

Smith, P. H., White, J. W., & Holland, L. J. (2003). A longitudinal perspective on dating violence among adolescent and college-age women. *The American Journal of Public Health, 93*(7), 1104–1109. doi:10.2105/ajph.93.7.1104

Sochting, I., Fairbrother, N., & Koch, W. (2004). Sexual assault of women. *Violence Against Women, 10*(1), 73–93. doi:10.1177/1077801203255680

Stermac, L., Del Bove, G., & Addison, M. (2004). Stranger and acquaintance sexual assault of adult males. *Journal of Interpersonal Violence, 19*(8), 901–915. doi:10.1177/0886260504266887

Stermac, L., Sheridan, P. M., Davidson, A., & Dunn, S. (1996). Sexual assault of adult males. *Journal of Interpersonal Violence, 11*(1), 52–64. doi:10.1177/088626096011001004

Tewksbury, R., & Mustaine, E. (2001). Lifestyle factors associated with the sexual assault of men: A routine activity theory analysis. *The Journal of Men's Studies, 9*(2), 153–182. doi:10.3149/jms.0902.153

Thompson, M., Koss, M., Kingree, J., Goree, J., & Rice, J. (2011). A prospective mediational model of sexual aggression among college men. *Journal of Interpersonal Violence, 26*(13), 2716–2734. doi:10.1177/0886260510388285

Tjaden, P., & Thoennes, N. (2000). *Full report of the prevalence, incidence, and consequences of violence against women: Findings from the National Violence Against Women Survey.* Washington DC: U.S. Department of Justice.

Ullman, S. (2016). Sexual revictimization, PTSD, and problem drinking in sexual assault survivors. *Addictive Behaviors, 53*(1), 7–10. doi:10.1016/j.addbeh.2015.09.010

Vandemark, L., & Mueller, M. (2008). Mental health after sexual violence: The role of behavioral and demographic risk factors. *Nursing Research, 57*(3), 175–181. doi:10.1097/01.nnr.0000319498.44499.53

Wheeler, J. G., George, W. H., & Dahl, B. J. (2002). Sexually aggressive college males: Empathy as a moderator in the "Confluence Model" of sexual aggression. *Personality and Individual Differences, 33*(5), 759–775. doi:10.1016/S0191-8869(01)00190-8

World Health Organization. (2002). *World report on violence and health.* Retrieved from http://apps.who.int/iris/bitstream/10665/42495/1/9241545615_eng.pdf

Zawacki, T., Abbey, A., Buck, P., McAuslan, P., Clinton Sherrod, A., & Giancola, Peter R. (2003). Perpetrators of alcohol-involved sexual assaults: How do they differ from other sexual assault perpetrators and nonperpetrators? *Aggressive Behavior, 29*(4), 366–380. doi:10.1002/ab.10076

Zgoba, K. M. (2004). Spin doctors and moral crusaders: The moral panic behind child safety legislation. *Criminal Justice Studies, 17*(4), 385–404. doi:10.1080/1478601042000314892

Zimring, F. E., Piquero, A. R., & Jennings, W. G. (2007). Sexual delinquency in Racine: Does early sex offending predict later sex offending in youth and young adulthood? *Criminology & Public Policy, 6*(3), 507–534. doi:10.1111/j.1745-9133.2007.00451.x

KEY TERMS

- *Compounding Effect of Victimization:* Childhood victimization increases the odds of adolescent victimization, which subsequently increases the odds of adult victimization (Humphrey & White, 2000).

- *Folk Devil:* An individual or group labeled as outside the central core values of consensual society and posing a threat to both the values of society and society itself (Cohen, 2014).

- *Moral Panic:* A condition, episode, person, or group of persons is defined as a threat to societal values and interests in symbolic form by the media, resulting in responses from authorities and policymakers as well as social changes within the community (Cohen, 2014).

- *Secondary Victimization:* Negative experiences with the criminal justice apparatus and/or community agencies, which produce further traumatization of victims (Campbell & Raja, 1999).

- *Sexual Violence/Assault:* "Any sexual act, attempt to obtain a sexual act, unwanted sexual comments or advances, or acts to traffic, or otherwise directed, against a person's sexuality using coercion, by any person regardless of their relationship to the victim, in any setting, including but not limited to, home and work" (World Health Organization, 2002, p. 149).

THE NEW YORK TIMES ARTICLES

Baker, A., & Stelloh, T. (2012) With teachers' aide accused of abuse, parents are seeking answers. *The New York Times.* Retrieved from http://www.nytimes.com/2012/02/12/nyregion/parents-seek-answers-after-teachers-aide-is-charged-with-abuse.html

Hurdle, J. (2012). Accuser describes attack by priest in Pennsylvania. *The New York Times.* Retrieved from http://www.nytimes.com/2012/04/05/us/accuser-describes-rape-attempt-by-philadelphia-priest.html

Lovett, I. (2014). Felony charges are filed in case of 2004 disappearance. *The New York Times.* Retrieved from https://www.nytimes.com/2014/05/23/us/rape-and-kidnap-charges-in-case-of-2004-disappearance.html

Oppel, Jr., R. A. (2014). Army general apologizes to victims of misconduct before being sentenced. *The New York Times.* Retrieved from https://www.nytimes.com/2014/03/20/us/general-apologizes-to-sexual-misconduct-victims.html

Robbins, J. (2013). Trial of former college quarterback accused of rape starts Friday in Montana. *The New York Times.* Retrieved from http://www.nytimes.com/2013/02/07/us/rape-trial-of-jordan-johnson-starts-friday.html

DISCUSSION QUESTIONS

1. What role do media, such as *The New York Times*, play in the moral panic surrounding sexual violence?
2. How may information about offense, victim, and offender characteristics be beneficial to reducing and preventing sexual assault?
3. What may happen when media reports of sexual violence are different than descriptions of sexual violence found in research?

CHAPTER 7

Victims of Workplace Violence

Kelly Szabo, Department of Criminal Justice, Seattle University;
Mary K. Stohr, Department of Criminal Justice & Criminology,
Washington State University

INTRODUCTION

On December 2, 2015, Syed Rizwan Farook and his wife opened fire at a San Bernardino County holiday party, killing 14 people. Many of the victims were Syed Farook's co-workers. It seems there are always news stories about an employee who goes on a shooting spree and kills a group of co-workers at a factory or post office or conference room before killing themselves. With so much focused media coverage, we tend to believe that this type of crime happens every day, but how often does it actually occur, and in which occupations does it happen the most? Furthermore, how is the media reporting on these incidents?

This chapter explores the topic of **workplace violence** by addressing these and other questions in two ways. First, a review of current literature and government statistics on workplace violence will be examined for the years 2001 through 2015. Second, these findings will provide context for a content analysis of a sample of workplace violence articles extracted from *The New York Times* for the same years. The intent is to define workplace violence, analyze its impact, and examine how the reporting of workplace violence by a major media source compares to the available literature and governmental data. In addition, findings will be viewed through various theoretical lenses as a way to understand workplace violence and its subsequent media coverage.

LITERATURE REVIEW

DEFINITIONS & TYPES OF WORKPLACE VIOLENCE

The definition of workplace violence can vary. Some definitions are broad, while others are very specific. The Occupational Safety and Health Administration (OSHA, 2002) provides the following definition:

> Workplace violence is violence or the threat of violence against workers. It can occur at or outside the workplace and can range from threats and verbal abuse to physical assaults and homicide, one of the leading causes of job-related deaths. (p. 1)

The Federal Bureau of Investigation's (2002) definition consists of "murder or other violent acts by a disturbed, aggrieved employee or ex-employee against coworkers or supervisors" (p. 11). The U.S. Department of Labor's website provides a more specific definition as "an action (verbal, written, or physical aggression) which is intended to control or cause, or is capable of causing, death or serious bodily injury to oneself or others, or damage to property" including "abusive behavior toward authority, intimidating or harassing behavior, and threats" (U.S. Department of Labor, n.d.). Such actions include, but are not limited to, homicide, suicide, stalking, robbery, assault, harassment, and sexual assault (FBI, 2002; Thornton, Voigt, & Harper, 2013). Still, other definitions of workplace violence include organizations as offenders, if employees of those organizations are killed or injured due to negligence by the organization itself (Knefel & Bryant, 2004).

Workplace violence is a broad subject within the literature. As a way to organize and make sense of its reach, workplace violence has been categorized by researchers into different types, depending upon who perpetrates the violence (Booth, Vecchi, Finney, Van Hasselt, & Romano, 2009; FBI, 2002; Injury Prevention Research Center [IPRC], 2001; Lipscomb, Silverstein, Slavin, Cody, & Jenkins, 2002; Tiesman, Gurka, Konda, Coben, & Amandus, 2012). **Type 1**, also known as stranger-on-employee workplace violence, encompasses criminal intent. In instances of stranger-on-employee violence, the assailant has no official connection with the employee or business experiencing the violence. Examples under this type often include robbery, shoplifting, or trespassing (Booth et al., 2009; IPRC, 2001; Lipscomb et al., 2002; Tiesman et al., 2012). **Type 2** workplace violence consists of violence, or the threat of violence, by a customer or client toward an employee, business, or organization. In this instance, there is a legitimate relationship between the assailant and the employee, business, or organization. Assailants can include customers, clients, patients, passengers, students, and inmates, to name a few (IPRC, 2001; Libscomb et al., 2002; Tiesman et al., 2012). **Type 3** workplace violence includes those incidents where an employee or ex-employee uses violence or the threat of violence toward current or former co-workers or supervisors (IPRC, 2001; Tiesman et al., 2012). These instances might be spurred by stress, personal or religious differences, or a sense of injustice about such things as losing out on a promotion or being fired (IPRC, 2001; Tiesman et al., 2012). Lastly, **Type 4** workplace violence refers to those assailants from outside of the workplace who have a personal or domestic relationship with an employee or other member of a business or organization, and then commit or threaten to commit a violent act at the victim's place of work (IPRC, 2001; Tiesman et al., 2012). Domestic workplace violence is typically domestic violence that migrates to the workplace (FBI, 2002; Versola-Russo & Russo, 2009). Examples include, but are not limited to, violence perpetrated by spouses, significant others, exes, or by others connected to victims in the workplace through a personal relationship.

PREVALENCE OF WORKPLACE VIOLENCE

According to OSHA's (2002) Fact Sheet, it is estimated that two million American workers experience workplace violence each year. Others claim the occurrence of workplace violence is rare (Piquero, Piquero, Craig, & Clipper, 2013). Those events that do occur often do not normally grab national headlines. In 2016, there were 500 intentional workplace homicides in the United States and about 447 per year, on average, from 2011 through 2017 (Bureau of Labor Statistics [BLS], 2017a, 2017b, 2018). In addition, there were 34,750 intentional, nonfatal, workplace violence injuries that required time off from work in 2015 (BLS, 2016). This equates to roughly eight workplace violence homicides per week, and approximately 668 intentionally violent workplace injuries per week. One must keep in mind, however, that these statistics do not include workplace violence that goes unreported or incidents that do not require time off work for the victim.

OCCUPATIONS IN WHICH WORKPLACE VIOLENCE IS MOST PREVALENT

Workplace violence can occur in any occupation, and in any job location, whether one works in an office cubicle or in an outdoor environment (Lipscomb et al., 2002; Occupational Safety and Health Administration, 2002). There are, however, certain occupations that are correlated with higher instances of workplace violence. Back in 1996, the Occupational Safety and Health Administration (OSHA) released a list of occupations with the highest levels of risk. Included are occupations with public contact, in particular those that involve the exchange of money; the delivery of passengers, goods, and services; or those involving a mobile workplace (taxi drivers and police officers). In addition, occupations where one is working with volatile or unstable persons, working in isolation, working late at night or in the early morning, working in high-crime areas, guarding valuables, and working in community-based settings are also considered to be at a higher level of risk for workplace violence (National Institute for Occupational Safety and Health, 1996).

More recent statistics reflect a general decline in workplace violence between 1993 and 2009; however, the violent trend of certain occupations remains unchanged (Harrell, 2011). The rate of workplace violence by occupation is highest in law enforcement (18.9%), followed by retail sales (13.2%), medical (10.2%), and teaching (9%) (Harrell, 2011).

The Healthcare Industry

One occupation that is particularly fraught with incidents of workplace violence is the healthcare industry. In particular, nurses appear to be particularly susceptible to physical assaults, threats, and harassment. In one study, 8,444 nurses completed an online survey regarding both Type 2 (customer/client-on-employee) and Type 3 (employee-on-employee or co-worker) workplace violence (Ulrich, Lavandero, Woods, & Early, 2014). Results showed that roughly 73 percent of nurses reported Type 2 violence in the form of verbal abuse by either patients, families of patients, or significant others of patients. In addition, almost 23 percent of nurses reported physical abuse by patients. In the same study, Type 3 non-physical violence (verbal abuse) by fellow co-workers such as doctors and fellow RNs was reported by 27 percent of respondents. These results are similar to yet another nationwide survey of nurses, which found that female certified registered nurse anesthetists were frequently victims of workplace aggression, particularly younger RNs (Sakellaropoulos, Pires, Estes, & Jasinski, 2011).

Workplace violence within the healthcare industry goes beyond the realm of nurses. Other workers who may experience such abuse include nurse's aides, doctors, and security staff (Dougherty, 2015; Gates et al., 2011; Kowalenko et al., 2012). One cross-sectional study in the Midwest surveyed a sample of 2,131 workers within the healthcare industry (Findorff, McGovern, Wall, Gerberich, & Alexander, 2004). Positions surveyed included both clinical (e.g., hospital nurses, patient care assistants, physicians) as well as clerical (e.g., accountants, computer programmers, and technicians). Findings showed that those jobs with greater patient contact, such as intensive care workers, emergency room workers, and those in the mental health field, resulted in a higher risk of Type 2 (customer/client-on-employee) violence, both physical and non-physical (Findorff et al., 2004).

Lastly, studies show that workplace violence between clients and employees within the healthcare industry also includes those who work outside the hospital setting (Payne & Appel, 2007; Respass & Payne, 2008; Ringstad, 2009). In one study, Payne and Appel (2007) analyzed data from the Bureau of Labor Statistics (BLS). Results showed that nursing home caretakers had the highest rates of assault victimization when compared to home healthcare workers, hospital workers, workers in doctor's offices, and "all workers in private industry in the United States" (Payne & Appel, 2007, p. 49).

Social Service Workers

Social service workers make up a large portion of the **high-risk occupations** outlined by OSHA and, according to some researchers, experience the highest frequency of workplace violence (Harrell, 2011; Respass & Payne, 2008; Warchol, 1998). Police officers, court employees, domestic violence advocates, drug and alcohol service providers, children and youth service providers, mental health providers, developmental disability service providers, school social workers, and family service providers are just a portion of jobs that make up social services. One study explored threats to rehabilitation counselors in Montana (Davis, 2008). Results revealed that one in five counselors had been threatened with damage to their property, one in three had been threatened with physical violence, and some had received threats against their own family members (Davis, 2008).

Taxi Drivers

The occupation of taxi driver contains certain attributes that place it within the higher risk categories of OSHA's dangerous occupation list (National Institute for Occupational Safety and Health, 1996). Taxi drivers, chauffeurs, and other for-hire drivers deal with the transaction of cash, many times in high-crime or isolated areas, often at night, and often with clients who are under the influence of alcohol (Occupational Safety and Health Administration, 2002). The opportunity for victimization is abundant (Schwer, Mejza, & Grun-Rehomme, 2010). To put this into perspective, within the state of Nevada there were 2,037,478 taxi trips in March of 2017 (Nevada Taxi Cab Authority, 2017). Even greater still are the 474,000 taxi trips per day within New York City in 2015 (New York City Taxi and Limousine Commission, 2016).

Drivers can fall victim to many different crimes, including verbal abuse, robbery, assault, and even homicide (Occupational Safety and Health Administration, 2010; Schwer et al., 2010). Although the annual homicide rate for taxi drivers and chauffeurs has declined from approximately 18 per 100,000 in 1997 to approximately 11 per 100,000 in 2007, driving a taxi continues to carry a workplace violence risk 21 times greater than any other occupation (U.S. Department of Labor, 2010).

TYPES OF VIOLENCE EMPLOYED & WHO'S KILLING WHO

According to the Bureau of Labor Statistics, workplace homicide was the fifth leading cause of death in 2016, with 500 intentional homicides (BLS, 2017b). These workplace homicide incidents included 394 shootings; 38 stabbing, cutting, slashing, or piercing incidents; 35 hitting, kicking, beating, or shoving crimes; 10 strangulations, and six multiple acts by other persons (BLS, 2017a).

Of the perpetrators in these crimes, 39 were co-workers, 15 were former co-workers, six were work associates, and two were former work associates (BLS, 2017a). In addition, there were 152 robbers, 23 acquaintances, 40 clients or customers, seven patients, two students, and seven inmates or detainees in custody (BLS, 2017a). Lastly, there were 43 relatives or domestic partners, in which 35 of those were spouses and four were an immediate family member other than the spouse. Another 50 assailants were not apprehended (BLS, 2017a).

States differ in their numbers of intentional workplace homicide, with some states reporting more instances and other states reporting less. In 2013, California and Texas reported the highest number of intentional workplace homicides, with 43 incidents each (BLS, 2017a). California had a slightly higher number of reported intentional workplace homicides in 2014 and 2016, with 45 and 46, respectively, while Texas reported 39 incidents in 2014 and 45 incidents in 2016 (BLS, 2017a). In 2015, Texas reported the most incidents, with 46 intentional workplace homicides, one more than California (BLS, 2017a). New Hampshire, Idaho, and Vermont reported the lowest incidents of workplace homicide, with each state recording one incident during the four-year span from 2013 through 2016 (BLS, 2017a). Over a seven-year period, from 2011 through 2017, there were about 447 workplace homicides on average per year, nationally (BLS, 2018).

According to the Bureau of Labor Statistics (2017b), assailants of female victims of workplace homicide between 2011 and 2016 were mostly relatives or domestic partners (40%). Regarding male workplace homicide victims, the most common assailants were robbers (33%) (BLS, 2017b). Men typically have made up the bulk of victims, with 84 percent in 2013, 83 percent in 2014, 85 percent in 2015, and 82 percent in 2016 (BLS, 2017a). Women were less likely to be victims, with 16 percent in 2013, 17 percent in 2014, 15 percent in 2015, and 18 percent in 2016 (BLS, 2017a).

Between 2013 and 2016, the age range of workplace homicide victims has included those under the age of 16 to 65 and over (BLS, 2017a). The majority of victims fell within the range of 25 to 54, with 343 in 2016 alone, making up 69 percent of all workplace homicides (BLS, 2017a). The age range of 45 to 54 had the most homicides for a single age category, with 120 total in 2016 (BLS, 2017a).

With regard to race or ethnic origin, Whites (non-Hispanic) made up the majority of workplace homicide victims, with 188 in 2013, and increasing to 241 in 2016 (BLS, 2017a). Blacks or African Americans were the next highest, with 100 in 2013, and increasing to 128 in 2016 (BLS, 2017a). Hispanic or Latino were at 67 in 2013, and increased to 69 in 2016, while Asians were at 42 in 2013, and increased to 52 in 2016 (BLS, 2017a).

VICTIMS OF TYPE 3 (EMPLOYEE-ON-EMPLOYEE) WORKPLACE VIOLENCE

So what does the literature say about co-worker violence? How prevalent is it compared to stranger, client, or domestic violence-related violence in the workplace? According to some studies, co-worker violence is the least frequent (Scalora, Washington, Casady, & Newell, 2003; Tiesman et al., 2012). Type 3 workplace violence can result from bullying, sexual harassment, general aggression, name-calling, insults, denial of promotion, denied privileges, and denied training opportunities, among others (Hinduja, 2007; Sakellaropoulos et al., 2011). One particular study looked at workplace homicides of women in the United States over a six-year period (n = 544). The authors found that homicide by a co-worker happened in 14 percent of the sampled cases, whereas the majority of the workplace homicides (39%) were a result of stranger violence (Tiesman et al., 2012). In 33 percent of the cases, women were killed by personal/domestic relations, and 14 percent of the workplace homicides were committed by customers, clients, patients, or others (Tiesman et al., 2012).

Another study analyzed nonfatal workplace risks that come from internal threats (employees, co-workers, and supervisors) and external threats (customers and strangers) (Scalora et al., 2003). Findings revealed that 67 percent of cases involved external threats, such as customers and strangers, whereas over 32 percent of cases involved internal threats such as disgruntled employees taking vengeance on fellow employees or supervisors, or domestic violence. Of the internal threats, 21 percent were domestic violence related (Scalora et al., 2003).

GENDER DIFFERENCES

Empirical studies have resulted in mixed findings on the prevalence of gender and workplace violence. As mentioned earlier, more males than females are killed or injured due to workplace violence (BLS, 2017a; Scalora et al., 2003). Although men are killed in the workplace more often by strangers, women are killed more often at the hands of a domestic partner (BLS, 2017a, 2017b; Tiesman et al., 2012). As for nonfatal workplace violence, some studies have found that, in clinical environments, male and female workers shared an equal probability of being physically or sexually assaulted by a patient (Hatch-Maillette, Scalora, Bader, & Bornstein, 2007). In addition, female staff are more likely than males to be victims of verbal, physical, or sexual threats (Hatch-Maillette et al., 2007).

Studies on women and socioeconomic status have also revealed that workplace violence does not discriminate among levels of occupation or education (Potter & Banyard, 2011). An exploratory study of employed women in New Hampshire (n = 1,079) found that 69 percent experienced either one or a combination of sexual assault, physical violence by an intimate partner, emotional abuse, sexual harassment, or stalking (Potter & Banyard, 2011). The participants in the study were educated women, including post-graduate degrees (21%), college degrees (31%), technical school (26%), and high school diplomas (22%). Furthermore, 46 percent of respondents lived in households with an annual income above $51,000 a year, and 29 percent had household income levels over $100,000. In essence, workplace violence perpetrated against women is not limited to lower levels of education or lower levels of employment (Potter & Banyard, 2011).

MASS SHOOTINGS IN THE WORKPLACE

The most newsworthy type of workplace violence, the mass workplace shooting, seldom takes place. When it does, however, the assailant many times will commit suicide before they can be apprehended (Lankford, 2013; Lester, 2014).

Two separate studies were found in the literature that examined the incidents of mass workplace shootings. One study examined the average amount of victims and found that, out of 28 incidents, there was a mean average of 4.54 killed (SD of 5.74) and 3.04 injured (SD of 4.08) (Lester, 2014). The other study reviewed workplace shootings and found that the assailants averaged 37.11 to 41.66 years of age (Lankford, 2013). In addition, the majority of workplace shooting assailants were male, and casualties averaged 5.94 (Lankford, 2013). Of those who committed suicide, 11 percent left suicide notes prior to their attacks, while 91 percent of the incidents ended in suicide (Lankford, 2013). Interestingly, these two studies differed in their findings in terms of casualty rates and successful suicide of the perpetrator: Lankford (2013) found no significant relationship between casualty rates and successful suicide by the perpetrator, whereas Lester (2014) found the opposite to be true.

CAPTIVE-TAKING INCIDENTS

One study examined the subject of workplace violence involving captive-taking (Booth et al., 2009). The cases for this study (n = 15) were retrieved from the FBI's Hostage/Barricade Database System (HOBAS). Five of the cases were deemed Type 1 violence (stranger), six were deemed Type 2 (customer/client), one was Type 3 (co-worker–on–co-workers), and in three cases the perpetrator of the violence was unknown (Booth et al., 2009, pp. 80–81).

Of the total victims, few were physically hurt, and none were killed (Booth et al., 2009). Eleven cases had between one and nine captives, and four cases had more than 10 captives. There were 198 victims in total, and they mostly (12 cases) involved White female victims. Ages of victims ranged from 7 to 68 years (it should be noted that it is unlikely those victims under the legal working age were employees at the workplace). In addition, the majority of captives "were not abused" (Booth et al., 2009, pp. 87–88).

In almost 80 percent of these cases, the assailant and the victims had no relationship to one another, and in only one case was there a workplace relationship. Over half of victims were released or escaped, while 97.5 percent were released without injury (Booth et al., 2009).

THEORETICAL EXPLANATIONS

When workplace violence occurs, we often try to make sense of why it happens. One way is to apply our theoretical knowledge of crime. Routine activities theory (Cohen & Felson, 1979) and general strain theory (Agnew, 1992) are sometimes mentioned as explaining why workplace violence may occur and the factors that place some at higher risk than others.

ROUTINE ACTIVITIES THEORY

Routine activities theory views crime as needing three things: a suitable target, an absent guardian, and a motivated offender; take any of these three factors away from the equation, and crime is less likely to happen (Cohen & Felson, 1979). The application of target hardening, or the removal of a suitable target, for stranger workplace violence, has been successful in some instances because it reduces the opportunities for robberies and robbery-related homicides (Casteel, Peek-Asa, Greenland, Chu, & Kraus, 2008; Casteel, Peek-Asa, Howard, & Kraus, 2004). In addition, target hardening with metal detectors, fences, security cameras, and self-defense training are just some of the proposed steps by some researchers for reducing Type 2 (customer/client-on-employee) workplace violence within the healthcare field (Philip, 2016). Therefore, workplace violence, according to this theory, would be less likely if the victim were absent or less accessible, if there were people (or other security measures) around to protect the victim(s), and if likely offenders were less inclined to engage in this violence.

GENERAL STRAIN THEORY

General strain theory posits that people resort to crime as a result of strain experienced in their lives (Agnew, 1992). A removal of positively valued goals, or the continuous presence of negatively valued goals, may drive a person to become strained, which may lead to anger, which in turn can lead to crime. Actions such as rejection, denial of promotion, denied privileges, or denied training are examples of not just the removal of positive stimuli, but the presence of negative stimuli. Discrimination, loss of financial support, or bullying might also drive one to commit crime. Financial strain or a dependence upon drugs might drive one to rob a convenience store or bank. Feelings of unhappiness over a service, or being cheated out of money, might cause one to become angry and threaten a business owner or employee.

One study focused on conflict, prejudice, and ethno-violence in the workplace to see what influences they had on stress levels, health, and interpersonal relationships (Hinduja, 2007). Workplace violence in this research was bifurcated into two categories: covert harassment and overt harassment. Covert harassment included such things as denying an individual a raise, denying training opportunities, and treating one as though they did not exist. Thirty-eight percent of respondents stated they were kept from getting a raise, over 21 percent stated they were denied training, and over 35 percent felt they were treated as though they did not exist (Hinduja, 2007).

Overt harassment in this study included destroying or damaging personal items, physical attacks or threats of attack, and name-calling or insults (Hinduja, 2007). Almost 9 percent stated they had personal belongings that had been damaged or destroyed, over 12 percent stated they had been attacked or threatened, and almost 40 percent had been called names or insulted (Hinduja, 2007). Moreover, some respondents admitted that both the covert and overt harassment caused some level of aggressive or negative emotions (Hinduja, 2007). This study supports the idea that there can be both overt and covert stresses on the job, which, if not dealt with on a professional level, could lead to anger. This anger could then lead to incidents of workplace violence (Bowen, Privitera, & Bowie, 2011; Hinduja, 2007).

FRAMING THEORY

Besides looking through the lenses of strain theory and routine activities theory to explain why crimes take place, we are also interested in understanding why *The New York Times* reported more on certain workplace violence incidents than others. For this, we can use framing theory, which posits that we not only frame our realities with our own views and opinions, but that we are able to influence, and be influenced by, the frames of others (Goffman, 1974). It is hoped that analyzing these *The New York Times* articles for evidence of "framing" will make it easier to determine if there is undue bias in their selection or reporting. When it comes to the media, studies suggest that framing can have a persuasive effect on consumers who consider themselves "knowledgeable" regarding world events (Lecheler & de Vrees, 2012) and can also influence the trust in media when it comes to certain aspects of political framing (Hopmann, Shehata, & Strömbäck, 2015). Framing theory can also be used as a tool, as a way to identify and understand differing news coverage (de Vreese, 2005). Moreover, in *Mediating the Message*, Shoemaker and Reese (1996) break down different possible framing influences such as individual beliefs, organizational/ownership policies and routines, economics, news sources, advertisers, target audience, and others. By analyzing such things as the wording of a headline, the number of articles written per workplace violence type, or the overarching article content pattern, it may be possible to identify framing in action.

THE IMPACT OF WORKPLACE VIOLENCE

Workplace violence has the capacity to affect everyone. At the organizational level, in particular, workplace violence effects can include financial loss, property damage, medical costs, lost productivity, lawsuits, and damage to company trust (Henson, 2010; Hinduja, 2007; Lipscomb et al., 2002; Versola-Russo & Russo, 2009). In addition, employee absenteeism, employee attrition (Davis, 2008), employee turnover (Hatch-Maillette et al., 2007), employee burnout (Bass et al., 2016), and public and internal police investigations all might occur as a result of the violence (Booth et al., 2009).

RESEARCH SUMMARY

Workplace violence is rare, but it can occur in almost any work environment, though certain types of occupations tend to be more prone to it. There are four main types, which include stranger-on-employee, customer/client-on-employee, co-worker–on–co-worker, and personal/domestic relation-on-employee. Contrary to popular belief, co-worker–on–co-worker workplace violence (including mass workplace shootings) is the rarest form, along with customer/client-on-employee. The most common form is stranger-on-employee, followed by domestic relationships-on-employee.

Tens of thousands of workers were intentionally injured in 2016 while at work, and 500 were murdered. These victims were mostly White males, between the ages of 25 and 54. Men were more likely to die at the hands of strangers, while women were more likely to be killed by domestic partners.

Policy implications for workplace violence lie in creating safety procedures that:

1. target harden retail businesses and others to discourage robberies;
2. create and ensure a safe workplace where employees are treated with dignity and respect to avoid stresses and strains that might create a disgruntled employee;
3. implement workplace policies and safety plans/procedures that reduce discrimination and violence, and familiarize employees with the telltale signs of unstable customers or clients; and
4. implement workplace policies and procedures to handle and support those employees who might be in a domestic violence situation outside of work.

These four recommendations are likely to result in the reduction of workplace violence.

Finally, there is still much within the realm of workplace violence that is not included in the literature (Piquero et al., 2013). For instance, there is not much research on the most prevalent type of workplace violence, which is violence committed by strangers. In addition, studies that focus on other high-risk industries, such as bartending, adult entertainment, fast food, and airlines, are needed (Piquero et al., 2013).

CONTENT ANALYSIS

So far this chapter has explored the topic of workplace violence by reviewing the current literature, as well as empirical studies and government statistics. In this next section, a content analysis of a sample of workplace violence articles from *The New York Times* will reveal which incidents are reported, and which are not, as compared to the literature and government statistics. In addition, this analysis will reveal *how* these workplace violence stories are reported. *The New York Times* articles will also allow for a glimpse into the impact that workplace violence has on businesses and surrounding communities. Furthermore, it is hypothesized that rarer workplace violence types will receive more articles than those which are known, through the data, to happen more often.

RESEARCH METHODOLOGY

METHODS

A total of 1,700 *The New York Times* articles were selected using search terms related to workplace violence. The search terms entered into LexisNexis included the following SQL command: *"National Desk" AND (employee OR worker OR ex-employee) AND (murders OR opens fire OR kills OR killed OR wounded OR injured)*; the term *victim* was purposely omitted to avoid flagging articles that covered victimization in other contexts. In order to narrow the focus to current events, the years searched were limited to 2001 through 2015. Articles were then selected if they reported on any type of violence or crime that was committed specifically against an employee in the context of his or her job duties, or as a direct result of job duties performed by the employee.

It is important to note that as there are other chapters within this book devoted to specific forms of violence, some articles were excluded from this particular sample. For example, workplace violence in law enforcement, including deaths and injuries of police officers, corrections officers, or other local, state, or federal law enforcement officers while on the job were excluded; however, prosecutors were included. Also, random incidents of workplace violence, such as the DC sniper deaths, were excluded, as they did not fit the definition of true workplace violence as used in this analysis. In addition, articles about incidents of crime or violence that took place in a workplace setting but were specifically targeted towards non-employees were also excluded. An example of this is the Denver movie theater shootings that were directed at audience members. Finally, articles on incidents officially labeled terrorism were excluded, such as the 9/11 fatalities in the Twin Towers. The final sample of articles that fit the criteria for workplace violence was 227 (n = 227).

The articles were coded in order to extract information on how victims of workplace violence are reported in the mainstream media. Data were collected on several variables, including type of workplace violence, occupation of the victim, the reported victim's age and gender, and manner of victimization (shot, stabbed, etc.). Data were also gathered on the number of words per article and the total number of victims reported. Lastly, data were collected on the outcome for the perpetrator (apprehended, killed, suicide), any claims regarding workplace violence for the particular incident, and any reported effects. Other auto-coded variables were included, such as the page number of the article, date of publication, number of pages, author, and other automatically coded information available from downloading the articles.

It is important to point out that not all variables were available for every article. For example, gender and age were both difficult to code. Many times this information was not disclosed in the article, and in these instances the variable was coded as NR (not reported).

HIGH-PROFILE CASES

There were four high-profile cases included in these articles that are important to note. One of these was the Fort Hood shooting in Texas, which totaled 13 articles, as well as the shooting of Congresswoman Gabrielle Giffords and her constituents in Arizona, which totaled 12 articles. Other high-profile cases included the BP oil rig explosion in the Gulf of Mexico, with nine articles, and the Virginia Tech shooting, with eight articles.

THE RESULTS

AFFECTED OCCUPATIONS

Occupations in which *The New York Times* sample articles reported incidents of workplace violence included the following: accounting (accountants and those working in an accounting office), attorney, banking (tellers, managers, or other bank personnel), court stenographer, education, employment agent, fitness instructor, food service, forestry, hairdresser, high tech (aerospace, computers, engineering), industrial (factories, plants, large production facilities), insurance, journalism (reporter, editor), judge, legal (law office staff other than attorney), liquor sales (bartender, liquor store employee), maintenance worker, manufacturing (semiconductor, printing facilities), mental health, military, mining, oil worker, politician, postal service (delivery, sorting), property management, prosecutor, religious affiliation (nonprofit organizations, religious leaders), retail, security guard, and social work (child protective services). There were 12 articles that either did not report or were unclear about job type or occupation, and they were coded as NR (not reported).

UNIT OF ANALYSIS

There was much discussion as to whether article or incident would be the best unit of analysis for the content analysis portion of this chapter. Both were found to have strengths and limitations, but because the intent of this analysis was to view numbers of articles written on workplace violence as a whole, the final decision came down to article as the main unit of analysis. While the total sample size of articles was 227, the total number of incidents relating to those articles was 112. For informational and contextual purposes, Table 7.1 includes each reported occupation, the number of related incidents, and number of articles devoted to each.

TABLE 7.1 Incidents per Occupation vs Articles per Occupation

OCCUPATION	NUMBER OF INCIDENTS	NUMBER OF ARTICLES
Employment Agent	1	1
Insurance	1	1
Court (Judge, Stenographer)	1	3
Accounting	1	1
Banking	1	3
Attorney/Legal	1	1
Property Management	1	1
Hairdresser	1	2
Oil Worker	1	10
Fitness Instructor	1	1
Forestry	1	1
Public Health Inspector	1	4
Maintenance Worker	2	3
Mental Health	2	2
Mining	2	8
Journalism	3	8
Politician	3	15
Manufacturing	3	3
Liquor Sales	3	3
Military	3	14
Social Work	4	4
Religious Affiliation	4	6
Postal Service	4	5

TABLE 7.1 *(Continued)*

OCCUPATION	NUMBER OF INCIDENTS	NUMBER OF ARTICLES
High Tech	4	20
Security Guard, Education	5	5
Healthcare	6	6
Prosecutor	6	13
Education	7	23
Food Service	7	8
Retail	12	23
Industrial	17	26
Unspecified (Office)	3	3
Total	112	227

As for article as unit of analysis, there were coding challenges. Some articles reported on two separate incidents within the same article, which affected some results of data collected; however, clarifications within the content analysis are made frequently to address these. In addition, other articles reported two separate occupations that were victimized during the same incident and could not be separated. As a result, the following occupation combinations were coded as their own occupational category: judge and court stenographer, security guard and education, property management and high tech, and prosecutor and postal service worker. Each one of these combinations was coded as one article.

Table 7.2 lists all affected occupations and the total article counts for each. Workplace violence victimization within industrial plants was reported the most, with 26 articles (11.5%), followed by retail, with 23 articles (10.1%), and education, with 22 articles (9.7%). Also on the high end of incidents were high tech (7.5%), politician (6.6%), and military (U.S. soil) (6.2%), with 17, 15, and 14 articles, respectively. On the lower end of incidents, some occupations, such as insurance, accounting, and employment agent, were reported in only one article (0.4%).

TABLE 7.2 Occupation by Articles, Words, and Gender

OCCUPATION	ARTICLES	PERCENT	WORDS	PERCENT	MALE	FEMALE
Industrial	26	11.5	11,849	6.9	2	1
Retail	23	10.1	12,919	7.5	3	1
Education	22	9.7	25,205	14.6	3	9
High tech	17	7.5	12,018	7.0	14	10
Politician	15	6.6	20,302	11.8	0	1
Military	14	6.2	12,966	7.5	0	0
Prosecutor	12	5.3	10,418	6.0	4	9
Oil worker	10	4.4	6,677	3.9	0	0
Mining	8	3.5	6,516	3.8	7	2
Journalism	8	3.5	7,869	4.6	4	3
Food Service	8	3.5	2,283	1.3	17	5
Healthcare	6	2.6	2,895	1.7	31	17
Religious Affiliation	6	2.6	3,875	2.2	0	1
Postal Service	4	1.8	2,252	1.3	6	5
Social Work	4	1.8	511	.3	2	2
Security Guard	4	1.8	2,599	1.5	1	2
Judge & Court Stenographer	3	1.3	3,200	1.9	3	0
Banking	3	1.3	1,312	.8	10	0
Liquor sales	3	1.3	1,649	1.0	1	2
Manufacturing	3	1.3	1,152	.7	10	1
Maintenance	3	1.3	1,698	1.0	30	0
Hairdresser	2	.9	839	.5	16	9
Mental health	2	.9	5445	3.2	0	0
Employment agent	1	.4	364	.2	10	14
Security Guard & Education	1	.4	1476	.9	2	4
Attorney & Legal	1	.4	40	.2	2	0
Accounting	1	.4	410	.2	20	3

TABLE 7.2 *(Continued)*

OCCUPATION	ARTICLES	PERCENT	WORDS	PERCENT	MALE	FEMALE
Insurance	1	.4	59	.03	1	1
Property Management & High Tech	1	.4	381	.2	4	1
Forestry	1	.4	104	.1	16	29
Fitness Instructor	1	.4	658	.4	2	0
Prosecutor & Postal Service	1	.4	348	.2	1	0
Not reported	12	5.3	12,091	7.00	3	3
Total	227	100	172,788	100	225	135

Occupations were also broken down by total word count. The majority of printed words was greatest for education (14.6%), followed by politician (11.8%), retail (7.5%), and military (7.5%). Some lower word count articles based on occupation included attorney and legal, with 40 words (0.2%), insurance, with 59 words (0.03%), and forestry, with 104 words (0.1%). There were also a total of 12,091 words for those articles whose occupations were not reported (7%).

Lastly, Occupation was broken down by reported victim gender. For those articles that reported gender, there were a total of 225 male victims and 135 female victims noted. It is important to remember that the above gender victim counts and occupation word counts do not represent totals from the incidents themselves, as many of these articles reported on the same incident multiple times, and therefore mention the same occupation(s) and victim(s) multiple times.

WORKPLACE VIOLENCE BY TYPE

As indicated in Table 7.3, the type of workplace violence was broken down among five typologies. There were a total of 56 (24.7%) articles reporting on Type 1 workplace violence, or those incidents perpetrated by strangers. Type 2 workplace violence, where incidents were perpetrated by clients or

TABLE 7.3 Type by Articles, Words, and Front Page

TYPE	ARTICLES	PERCENTAGE	WORDS	PERCENTAGE	FRONT PAGE
Co-worker	90	39.7	62,973	36.5	12
Stranger	56	24.7	43,275	25.1	6
Client	45	19.8	42,417	24.6	8
Negligence	20	8.8	13,405	7.8	3
Domestic Violence	7	3.1	4,103	2.4	1
Multiple types	1	.4	381	.2	0
Not specified	8	3.5	6,234	3.6	1
Total	227	100	172,788	100	31

customers, was reported in 45 (19.8%) articles. Type 3 workplace violence, which consists of co-workers as perpetrators, was reported in 90 (39.7%) articles total. And Type 4 workplace violence, where domestic violence spills over into the workplace, was reported in seven (3.1%) articles. Lastly, because there were articles that reported on victimization resulting from organizational negligence, a fifth type of workplace violence was created for this category. Type 5 was reported in a total of 20 (8.8%) articles.

In addition, workplace violence type was cross-referenced with Occupation. As the results reported on Table 7.4 would indicate, education was the only occupation that spanned Types 1 through 4. Food service, healthcare, security guard, postal service, religious affiliation, and liquor sales, spanned Types 1 through 3. Retail spanned Types 1, 3, and 4, while industrial spanned Types 1, 3, and 5. Forestry and oil worker, however, were exclusive to Type 5 (negligence). From the data in Table 7.4, it appears that workplace violence was reported more often when Type 3 co-worker violence was involved.

ARTICLE THEME

Articles were also classified into one of seven themes. Articles were assigned to Incident Account when the main focus of the article was

TABLE 7.4 Type by Occupation

STRANGER	CLIENT	CO-WORKER	DOMESTIC VIOLENCE	NEGLIGENCE
Education	Education	Education	Education	Industrial
Food service	Food service	Food service	Retail	Mining
Healthcare	Healthcare	Healthcare	Manufacturing	Forestry
Security guard	Security guard	Security guard	Hairdresser	Oil worker
Postal service	Postal service	Postal service		
Religion-based	Religion-based	Religion-based		
Retail	Liquor sales	Retail		
Industrial	Legal	Industrial		
Journalism	Employment agent	Journalism		
Liquor sales	Court reporter	Liquor sales		
Accounting	Insurance	Legal		
Nursing home nurse	Mental health	Manufacturing		
Fitness	Prosecutor	Mining		
Banking	Social worker	High Tech		
Politician	Judge	Maintenance		
		Health Inspector		
		Military		
		Printer		

on the facts of the incident or a retelling of the account. Investigation Update was assigned when the article provided new information in the investigation of the incident. Legal Case Update was assigned to those articles where a legal case was pending and new information on that case was presented. Examples include any reports on scheduled court appearances, hearing updates, attorney statements, sentencing, and executions.

The category of Perpetrator Highlights was assigned to those articles that primarily reported on the perpetrator of the crime. This included any background, life history, or articles that dealt with the "how" or the "why" behind the perpetrator's actions. Similarly, Victim Highlights included those articles that focused on the victims of the crimes, or contained a substantial amount of victim information, such as the names of the victims, their ages, backgrounds, and future plans unrealized, for example. Articles were also flagged as Victim Highlights when they focused on subject matter such as memorial services, heroic actions by the victims, and their individual personalities. It should be noted that article themes were coded inductively rather than using post hoc quantitative structure or specific qualitative measurements.

Policy Impact and Community Impact were assigned to those articles that, as a result of the incident, either drove policy changes within the place of work, school, or legislature, or those articles that reported on impact to the community as a whole. Articles that tended to lean more towards one of these themes were classified as such, even though many articles had more than one theme.

Listed in Table 7.5, the majority of articles fell into the Incident Account theme, with a total article count of 89 (39.2%). Legal Case Update had the next highest article count, with 38 (16.7%), and Investigation Update had a total of 35 articles (15.4%). Perpetrator Highlights made up 26 reported articles (11.5%), while Community Impact and Policy Impact had article counts of 16 (7.1%) and 13 (5.7%), respectively. Victim Highlights was the least common theme, with 10 articles total (4.4%).

MODE OF VIOLENCE

Articles were also coded for the mode of violence perpetrated. Modes of workplace violence included victimization by firearm (shooting, mass shooting), explosion (mine, oil rig, refinery), knife, car crash, bomb (improvised explosive device), and a combination of knife and sexual assault. Articles on victimization by firearm were found to be the most prevalent, with 194 (85.5%). Second were articles where the reporter focused on explosions, with 20 (8.8%), and third were articles that included a discussion of victimization by knife, with seven (3.1%).

TABLE 7.5 Theme by Articles, Words, and Front Page

THEME	ARTICLES	PERCENTAGE	WORDS	PERCENTAGE	FRONT PAGE
Incident Account	89	39.2	50,619	29.3	10
Perpetrator Highlights	26	11.5	38,290	22.2	8
Legal Case Update	38	16.7	25,079	14.5	5
Investigation Update	35	15.4	23,988	13.9	5
Community Impact	16	7.1	14,209	8.2	1
Policy Impact	13	5.7	10,422	6.0	1
Victim highlights	10	4.4	10,181	5.9	1
Total	227	100	172,788	100	31

In Table 7.6, the breakdown of Mode of Violence by Gender is listed. Articles reporting on firearm violence had a total of 191 males reported as victims and a total of 127 females reported as victims. In addition, there were a total of 31 males reported as victims of explosions and a total of seven females reported as victimized by knife. Again, these numbers are tallied per article and not incident, and therefore they do not represent true victim counts. Also included is data on the frequency of the different modes of violence being featured on the front page of *The New York Times*. Articles of victimization by firearm were on the front page 27 times, whereas articles on explosions were front page news three times, and victimization by knife made it on the front page once.

ANALYSIS OF VICTIMS OF WORKPLACE VIOLENCE

When it comes to workplace violence, what do the findings of this content analysis say about how and what is reported by *The New York Times*?

TABLE 7.6 Mode of Violence by Gender, Words, and Front Page

MODE	MALE	FEMALE	ARTICLES	WORDS	PERCENT	PAGE A1
Firearm	191	127	194	147,913	85.6	27
Explosion	31	0	20	13,414	7.8	3
Knife	2	7	7	7874	4.6	1
Knife & Sexual Assault	1	0	1	102	.1	0
Car Crash	1	0	1	104	.1	0
Bomb	1	0	1	759	.4	0
Not Reported	0	1	3	2622	1.5	0
Total	225	135	227	172,788	100	31

To begin, although 227 articles focused on some type of workplace violence, there were zero articles that included the term "workplace violence" within its headline. Even within the body of the articles, less than a handful had any reference to workplace violence as a definition of the incident. Instead the articles featured other characterizations of the violence. "Shooting" was the most prevalent reference to the violence, with 155 articles. "Shooting rampage" was another characterization, as was "deadly rampage," "massacre," "attack," "slaying," "shooting spree," "murder," "blowout," "shooting massacre," and "negligence," to name a few. Again, these characterizations, though descriptive, are not necessarily indicative of the presence of workplace violence.

HIGH-RISK OCCUPATIONS

As mentioned in the literature review, OSHA reported that occupations with public contact are at most risk for workplace violence victimization. Those jobs that deal in the exchange of money; delivery of passengers, goods, and services; and working with unstable persons are included. When analyzing the occupation makeup of workplace violence articles in

The New York Times, many fell within these OSHA categories, but a significant number did not. Perhaps this is due to differences in newsworthiness in general, as well as the limitation of the sample of articles.

Out of a total sample of 227 articles, many of the reported occupations fell within the high-risk category. Occupational categories included banking, retail, education, food service, liquor sales, social work, postal service, health inspection, and hairdresser, in addition to physical fitness, employment agent, security, and healthcare. Of these, workplace violence in retail and education had the most articles, with 23 and 22 articles, respectively. The next highest number of articles was from workplace violence in the legal field (attorneys), with 13 articles. Food service was reported in seven articles, security in five articles, while banking tied with social work and postal service with four articles each.

By contrast, the occupation with the most articles of all did not fall within the typical high-risk for violence categories listed by OSHA. Industrial, including plant and factory workers, was covered the most, with 25 articles. In addition, workplace violence victimization in the military (on U.S. soil) made up 15 articles, while the political designation had 14 articles and high tech (computer programmers, engineers, aerospace) made up 17 articles.

The 2009 Fort Hood shooting, which fell into the military category, resulted in 43 victims. It is likely that the sheer volume of victims, as well as the value placed on the military personnel and the label of terrorism that eventually defined the violence, brought the total number of articles to 13. Similarly, the shooting of Congresswoman Gabrielle Giffords, along with bystanders and constituents, may have grabbed the attention of those in high places of power, bringing the total article count in the sample to 12. In contrast, the mining explosion at the Upper Big Branch Mine took the lives of 29 men, and yet its total article count from the sample was six. This may be an example of the media framing certain workplace violence incidents as more newsworthy than others. Either way, without such high-profile incidents, these normally low-risk occupational categories might have substantially less articles each, which would more accurately reflect workplace violence statistics on those occupations.

WORKPLACE VIOLENCE TYPE

It is apparent after examining the prevalence of each type of workplace violence that, from the sample, there were more *The New York Times* articles produced for those types of workplace violence that are statistically less likely to occur and less articles on those types that were more likely to occur.

The most frequent type of workplace violence, as reported through the literature and statistics, is Type 1 stranger violence for men, followed by Type 4 domestic violence for women. An analysis was conducted on the frequency of articles pertaining to each workplace violence type, as illustrated in Table 7.3. The type most frequently reported in articles was Type 3 co-worker violence, which, according to the literature, is the least prevalent of the four types. In addition, the second most common type of workplace violence, Type 4 (domestic violence), was reported in a total of seven articles. The reason for this discrepancy may also be due to its newsworthiness. Most articles on co-worker workplace violence reported on cases that involved many victims, which is apt to attract more media attention; those cases in which there are only one or two victims may not catch the attention of national media outlets, or even the local community, depending upon location.

Type 2 client workplace violence is as rare as co-worker violence, yet there were as many as 40 articles dedicated to it alone. In addition, although Type 1 stranger workplace violence is the most frequent type, it was second to co-worker workplace violence, which had 58 articles written. Again, those stories that are out of the ordinary may have the saleable appeal that newspapers are looking for.

Type 5, which was created for the purposes of this analysis, includes injuries or death caused by negligence on the part of an employer. Under Type 5, there were two high-profile cases: the Upper Big Branch mine explosion on April 5, 2010, and the BP oil rig explosion five days later on April 10, 2010. In the sample, there were six articles that reported on the Upper Big Branch explosion, and there were nine articles that reported on the BP oil rig explosion. Twenty-nine men were killed in the Upper Big Branch explosion, while 13 were killed in the BP oil rig explosion. Although the casualties of both incidents were great, the BP oil rig explosion had more articles written, even though the casualties were less than half of the other. This may have been due to the nature of not only the explosion itself, but the environmental impact of its uncapped oil well, resulting in more media attention.

ARTICLE THEMES

Thematic analysis allowed the researchers to determine which article themes were more popular within the sample. It is apparent that Initial Reporting and Follow-up articles on the account of the incident were most popular. This is not surprising, as many times an incident warrants further coverage, depending upon its circumstances. Similarly, articles that focused on the perpetrator of the violence were also popular; there will always be interest in the quest to find out the "who" and the "why" of certain high-profile incidents. The victim-themed articles, however, were not afforded the same words, article counts, or front page status that the former themes were afforded (see Table 7.5). Articles solely devoted to the victims of workplace violence were rare. Follow-up articles that focused on recounting the details of the incident, or those that gave in-depth reporting on all aspects of the perpetrator, were not only more often published in *The New York Times*, but they were the only article types to make the front page. Articles on victims were not.

MODE OF VIOLENCE

In the 2014 report on workplace violence deaths, the Bureau of Labor Statistics included all ways in which victims of workplace violence are intentionally harmed or killed. Shootings were the most prevalent, with stabbings second, assaults third, and multiple acts of violence fourth. True to these numbers, more articles revolved around shootings, with 197 articles total.

Twenty-one articles were written about injuries and deaths caused by corporate or organizational negligence, including explosions and a car crash. According to the Bureau of Labor statistics, however, explosions and car crashes are not listed as intentional workplace violence. In addition, these incidents had relatively high victim totals and high levels of policy and community impact.

Injuries and deaths by knife were covered in seven articles, while Multiple Acts of Violence (knife and sexual assault) was covered in one article. One knife incident involved a victim that was beheaded with a machete, but it resulted in a total of two articles within the sample. In light of its graphic nature, one might expect more than two articles on such an incident. Even still, neither of the two articles focused on the victim.

IMPACT

Despite the disparity in coverage between those incidents of workplace violence that occur more regularly than others, or the infrequency of victim-focused pieces, there were some insights that many of the articles provided, especially in terms of impact. For example, the articles that focused on the Gabrielle Giffords shooting contained examples of how this particular incident of workplace violence can affect the job of politicians. Public speaking, which was once considered a relatively safe action, suddenly became something that other politicians might be thinking twice about. In one article, a Florida representative named Steve Southerland reacts to the presence of police officers mingled within the crowd:

> "I've got to have contact with people," he said. "I look in their faces and see their hope, and I touch their hands and I hug them around the shoulders, and that's important. If I had to sit behind a computer answering e-mails or responding to letters from constituents, I wouldn't be doing this job." (Williams, 2011, p. A12)

In addition, fear from the shooting had impacted the community as well. The articles states, "public appearances by members of Congress have been canceled in recent weeks because businesses have expressed concerns about the safety of their employees" (Williams, 2011, p. A12).

In an article that focused on the one-year anniversary of the shooting at Sandyhook Elementary in Newtown, Connecticut, the author focused on community impact and how Newtown was still in the midst of healing. A portion of the articles states:

> Beyond the desire for keeping their grief private, the town's business owners are concerned about their economic well-being. Last December, media vehicles clogged streets, making it difficult to get to shops during the important Christmas season. "Even the places you could get to, you didn't want to because you'd have a microphone or TV camera in your face," said Jim Morely, a board member of Newtown Savings Bank. (Berger, 2013, p. 29)

Similarly, there was a lower profile incident where a hairdresser was killed at work by her ex-husband. Two articles on this incident were found in the sample, and one took note of the impact on the community and workplace. The article states, "The Police Department had to call in reinforcements from a half-dozen neighboring forces to help seal the area, control crowds, help traumatized family members and deal with a crush of news media" (Lovett & Nagourney, 2011, p. A18).

Incidents of workplace violence can also impact policy. In an article on the naval shipyard shooting in Washington, DC, the author reports:

> The independent review called the overall security process at the Pentagon installations outdated, with too much focus on keeping a secure perimeter against outside threats and not enough on examining the potential threats from people granted secret-level clearance to enter the installations. (Cooper, 2014, p. A13)

It was recommended that the Pentagon review security clearances and revoke 10 percent of them, while making it clear that mental health service is an option for those employees who might need it (Cooper, 2014).

Another article, which focused on the killing of seven in a Lockheed Martin plant, made note of previous racially motivated workplace violence inflicted by the perpetrator onto his co-workers for years prior to the incident (Hart, 2004). It also states that the federal Equal Employment Opportunity Commission (EEOC) found that the company should have dealt with the perpetrator earlier (Hart, 2004). Moreover, even after the incident, the EEOC found that "the company's response since the shootings has been inadequate and that the Black employees at the plant still endure a hostile environment" (Hart, 2004, p. A14).

MISCELLANEOUS

Other findings from the sample of *The New York Times* articles should be mentioned. First, victim counts of workplace violence only included those who were injured or killed, while it is likely that a very few were counted when verbally or physically threatened. In addition, only two articles included any quotes from qualified professionals regarding workplace violence as a way of putting the particular incident into perspective. Instead, quotes from witnesses, police officers, and community members were most prevalent.

THEORETICAL ANALYSIS OF WORKPLACE VIOLENCE

ROUTINE ACTIVITIES THEORY VS. GENERAL STRAIN THEORY

Overall, it appears that more articles covered workplace violence that is best explained by general strain theory. Employee-on-employee crimes, domestic violence crimes, and customer/client-on-employee crimes primarily involved some type of human strain that drove the commission of the crime reported. Conversely, the least amount of *The New York Times* articles from the sample were for crimes explained by routine activities theory. These were mostly workplace violence incidents involving strangers born out of an opportunity, such as robberies. In comparing these two theories with the number of articles in the sample, one could argue that crime by opportunity does not pique one's curiosity or interest as much as the "dark" realm of human strain. *The New York Times* article counts could act as a mirror of sorts, reflecting people's captivation with crime, though that is highly dependent upon the context of the crime.

FRAMING THEORY

Does framing theory offer an explanation for the higher number of sampled *The New York Times* articles reported on some workplace violence types versus others? In framing theory, an individual's reality is not only influenced by one's own perspective, but by others' perspectives as well (Goffman, 1974). When this theory is applied to the sample of *The New York Times* articles in this study, it follows that the journalists themselves could have been influenced by other forces (Goffman, 1974; Shoemaker & Reese, 1996). This might include a journalist subculture of sorts, or political affiliations that they or their organization might have (Shoemaker & Reese, 1996). They might be influenced by basic economics, such as stories that will generate the most revenue (Shoemaker & Reese, 1996). Also, *The New York Times'* organizational policies could have an influence on the journalists (Shoemaker & Reese, 1996). Therefore, it could be possible that some journalists have framed these workplace violence incidents as a means of influencing readers. After a thorough review of the sampled articles, however, we have concluded that framing theory does not lend itself well to explaining the differences in the number of *The New York Times* workplace violence articles.

If framing were present in some of the sampled articles, we could possibly see indications of bias within some of the headlines. For example, in a framed headline of an article involving gun violence in the workplace setting, one might see a headline that reads, *Gun-toting Husband Shoots Wife at Work*. In this case we might automatically visualize a man with a large gun collection. Compare that to a different headline which reads, *Distraught Husband Shoots Wife at Work*. In this headline, we immediately wonder why the husband was distraught. In each of these examples, readers can be pulled in a different direction. Upon examining each sampled *The New York Times* headline, there is no indication that any are worded in such a way as to deliberately frame the series of workplace violence events in a different light other than what happened. The bulk of headlines state the general known facts of the incidents, without embellishments or bringing in personal opinions or political agendas. Examples include *Shelter Manager Fatally Shot* or *Prayer Leader Killed During Service*. Even the headlines that go beyond stating facts of the incident do not appear to include anything that is overtly biased. For example, one headline states, *Eye-Opening to Jaw-Dropping: Twists Multiply in Shooting Case*. While one could argue that "eye-opening to jaw-dropping" material is relative to who is reading the story, the article itself does lay out abnormal facts that most might consider unusual. In another headline, *Oregon Killer Described as Man of Few Words, Except on Topic of Guns*, one could argue that the journalist is framing gun violence as being associated with those who are quiet and keep to themselves. But in context with the story, this headline is describing the perpetrator as he was described by others. In addition, headline terms such as "shooting rampage," "massacre," and "slaying," though clearly violent characterizations, could arguably be defended as accurate descriptions of the events that took place, though they do tend to grab the reader's attention.

Another indication of framing might be the number of articles written on a certain workplace violence incident. As mentioned earlier, there do tend to be more articles written when there are many victims. Such incidents in the sample include Sandyhook (26 fatalities), Virginia Tech (32 fatalities), Fort Hood (45 total victims), the BP oil rig explosion (11 fatalities), and the Upper Big Branch coal mine explosion (29 fatalities). These examples involved incidents of employees shooting multiple co-workers, clients (students) shooting staff, domestic violence, and organizational negligence. These article numbers are explainable, however, as one could reasonably conclude that incidents with high numbers of victims will garner more follow-up articles than those stories with, say, one or two victims. Along the same lines, the Gabrielle Giffords shooting had a total of four victims, but it involved a politician and constituents, one of them being a child. It could be argued that this type of story grabs the attention of the media because it combines politics and the death of an innocent child. It also involves survival against heavy odds, since Gabrielle Giffords did not die from her serious injuries. As such, it could be seen as reasonable that many follow-up stories were written in addition to the initial article.

Despite the fact that there were many articles written on rarer workplace violence incidents, *The New York Times* did report on the more common types of workplace violence as well. Within the sample, there were a number of articles on workplace violence in retail (23) as well as healthcare occupations (6). On the other hand, it would appear that *The New York Times* did not always take the opportunity to report multiple articles on incidents that were extremely rare. For instance, both the pizza delivery man who was killed by a bomb strapped around his neck and the co-worker who decapitated his co-worker with a machete only received one and two articles each, respectively. So, for this content analysis, it is unknown why there is such a discrepancy in the number of workplace violence articles when broken down by type. Perhaps it is simply the case that human interest is more often piqued by rare incidents than by those that happen all the time.

STUDY LIMITATIONS

There were a number of study limitations in this content analysis. As mentioned earlier in the discussion section, victim gender, age, and numbers were extremely difficult to pin down, since many articles varied in their reporting of these data. As a result, these data did not provide any significant information that could be useful for this content analysis. Also, the selection of articles for this analysis was limited in that it was a cross-sectional sample; it is unknown if other articles existed that would have changed the end counts of articles on each workplace violence type or article themes. In addition, only articles from *The New York Times* were sampled. As such, it would be incorrect to assume that all media outlets follow the same pattern. Future content analyses would benefit from pulling from a larger random sample that included not only print, but also televised and Internet coverage of other newspapers and news organizations. With that being said, *The New York Times* was chosen for this analysis on the merits of being a nationally distributed paper, covering all

50 states. According to *The New York Times* website, print and digital readership total circulation in May of 2015 was 2,178,674 for Monday through Friday and 2,624,277 for Sunday. As such, its articles could be regarded as more or less representative of the type of media coverage found when it comes to important and emerging topics within the United States.

CONCLUSION

The utilization of *The New York Times* articles for this content analysis allows for a unique glimpse into how the media reports on workplace violence. Gathering this data may help to put the reporting of workplace violence victimization into perspective. The findings of this content analysis suggest that the media tends to inflate the true scope of workplace violence in certain occupations and types and conflates the role of the victim, perhaps in an attempt (whether intentional or not) to influence the reader and shape their attitudes about those incidents deemed more important or newsworthy. Articles on workplace violence are more likely to feature high-profile incidents of mass shootings with high mortality rates, while those incidents not involving firearms will have less coverage. Furthermore, articles that focus on the perpetrator are more frequent than articles that focus on the victims. The reporting of workplace violence effects is often covered, but mostly for high-profile cases.

REFERENCES

Agnew, R. (1992). Foundation for a general strain theory of crime and delinquency. *Criminology, 30*(1), 47–88.

Bass, B. I., Chen, P. Y., Cigularov, K. P., Henry, K. L., Li, Y., & Tomazic, R. G. (2016). The effects of student violence against school employees on employee burnout and work engagement: The roles of perceived school unsafety and transformation leadership. *International Journal of Stress Management, 23*(3), 318–336.

Berger, J. (2013). As a school shooting's first anniversary nears, Newtown asks for privacy. *The New York Times*. Retrieved from https://www.nytimes.com/2013/12/08/nyregion/as-a-school-shootings-first-anniversary-nears-newtown-asks-for-privacy.html

Cooper, H. (2014). Pentagon finds Washington Navy Yard killings could have been prevented. *The New York Times*. Retrieved from https://www.nytimes.com/2014/03/19/us/navy-yard-rampage-could-have-been-prevented-pentagon-review-says.html

Booth, B., Vecchi, G. M., Finney, E. J., Van Hasselt, V. B., & Romano, S. J. (2009). Captive-taking incidents in the context of workplace violence: Descriptive analysis and case examples. *Victims and Offenders, 4,* 76–92. doi:10.1080/15564880802675935

Bowen, B., Privitera, M. R., & Bowie, V. (2011). Reducing workplace violence by creating healthy workplace environments. *Journal of Aggression, Conflict and Peace Research, 3*(4), 185–198. doi:10.1108/17596591111187710

Bureau of Labor Statistics. (2016). *Nonfatal occupational injuries and illnesses requiring days away from work, 2015.* Retrieved from https://www.bls.gov/news.release/pdf/osh2.pdf

Bureau of Labor Statistics. (2017a). *Workplace homicides with assailant and circumstance, 2011–2016.* Retrieved February 10, 2018, from https://www.bls.gov/iif/oshcfoi1.htm#other

Bureau of Labor Statistics. (2017b). *Number of fatal work injuries by employee status, 2003–2016,* pp. 1–20. Retrieved February 10, 2018, from https://www.bls.gov/iif/oshwc/cfoi/cfch0015.pdf

Bureau of Labor Statistics. (2018). *National census of fatal occupational injuries in 2017.* Retrieved January 3, 2019, from https://www.bls.gov/news.release/pdf/cfoi.pdf

Casteel, C., Peek-Asa, C., Greenland, S., Chu, L. D., & Kraus, J. F. (2008). A study of the effectiveness of a workplace violence intervention for small retail and service establishments. *Journal of Occupational and Environmental Medicine, 50*(12), 1365–1370. doi:10.1097/JOM.0b013e3181845fcf

Casteel, C., Peek-Asa, C., Howard, J., & Kraus, J. F. (2004). Effectiveness of crime prevention through environmental design in reducing criminal activity in liquor stores: A pilot study. *Journal of Occupational and Environmental Medicine, 46*(5), 450–458. doi:10.1097/01.jom.0000126025.14847.b1

Cohen, L. E., & Felson, M. (1979). Social change and crime rate trends: A routine activity approach. *American Sociological Review, 44,* 588–608.

Davis, A. (2008) A survey of threats received by rehabilitation counselors in Montana. *Journal of Rehabilitation, 74*(4), 3–8.

de Vreese, C. H. (2005). News framing: Theory and typology. *Information Design Journal + Document Design 13*(1), 51–62. doi:10.1075/idjdd.13.1.06vre

Dougherty, D. (2015). *Inspection guidance for inpatient healthcare settings.* OSHA. Retrieved from https://www.osha.gov/dep/enforcement/inpatient_insp_06252015.html

Federal Bureau of Investigation. (2002). *Workplace violence: Issues in response.* Washington, DC: U.S. Department of Justice. Retrieved from https://www.fbi.gov/stats-services/publications/workplace-violence

Findorff, M. J., McGovern, P. M., Wall, M., Gerberich, S. G., & Alexander, B. (2004). Risk factors for work related violence in a health care organization. *Injury Prevention, 10,* 296–301. doi:10.1136/ip.2003.004747

Gates, D., Gillespie, G., Kowalenko, T., Succop, P., Sanker, M., & Farra, S. (2011). Occupational and demographic factors associated with violence in the emergency department. *Advanced Emergency Nursing Journal, 33*(4), 303–313. doi:10.1097/TME.0b013e3182330530

Goffman, E. (1974). *Frame analysis: An essay on the organization of experience.* Boston, MA: Northeastern University Press.

Harrell, E. (2011). *Workplace violence, 1993–2009.* Washington, DC: U.S. Department of Justice. Retrieved from http://www.bjs.gov/content/pub/pdf/wv09.pdf

Hart, A. (2004, July 13). National briefing south: Mississippi: Company cited in worker killings. *The New York Times*, p. A14.

Hatch-Maillette, M. A., Scalora, M. J., Bader, S. M., & Bornstein, B. H. (2007). A gender-based incident study of workplace violence in psychiatric and forensic settings. *Violence and Victims, 22*(4), 449–462.

Henson, B. (2010). Preventing interpersonal violence in emergency departments: Practical applications of criminology theory. *Violence and Victims, 25*(4), 553–565. doi:10.1891/0886-6708.25.4.553

Hinduja, S. (2007). Workplace violence and negative affective responses: A test of Agnew's general strain theory. *Journal of Criminal Justice, 35*, 657–666. doi:10.1016/j.jcrimjus.2007.09.002

Hopmann, D. N., Shehata, A., & Strömbäck, J. (2015). Contagious media effects: How media use and exposure to game-framed news influence media trust. *Mass Communication and Society, 18*, 776–798. doi:10.1080/15205436.2015.1022190

Injury Prevention Research Center. (2001, February). *Workplace violence: A report to the nation.* Retrieved from https://www.public-health.uiowa.edu/iprc/resources/workplace-violence-report.pdf

Knefel, A. M., & Bryant, C. D. (2004). Workplace as combat zone: Reconceptualizing occupational and organizational violence. *Deviant Behavior, 25*, 579–601. doi:10.10800=016396200497884

Kowalenko, T., Cunningham, R., Sachs, C. J., Gore, R., Barata, I. A., Gates, D., ... McClain, A. (2012). *The Journal of Emergency Medicine, 43*(3), 523–531. doi:10.1016/j.jemermed.2012.02.056

Lankford, A. (2013). A comparative analysis of suicide terrorists and rampage, workplace, and school shooters in the United States from 1990 to 2010. *Homicide Studies, 17*(3), 255–274.

Lecheler, S., & de Vreese, C. H. (2012). News framing and public opinion: A mediation analysis of framing effects on political attitudes. *Journalism & Mass Communication Quarterly, 89*(2), 185–204. doi:10.1177/1077699011430064

Lester, D. (2014). Murder-suicide in workplace violence. *Psychological Reports: Disability & Trauma, 115*(1), 28–31. doi:10.2466/16.17.PR0.115c14z4

Lipscomb, J., Silverstein, B., Slavin, T. J., Cody, E., & Jenkins, L. (2002). Perspectives on legal strategies to prevent workplace violence. *Journal of Law, Medicine & Ethics, 30*(3), 166–172.

Lovett, I., & Nagourney, A. (2011, October 13). 8 killed in salon shooting in southern California. *The New York Times*, p. A18.

National Institute for Occupational Safety and Health. (1996, July). Current bulletin #57: Violence in the workplace: Risk factors and prevention strategies. Department of Health and Human Services. (NIOSH) Publication No. 96-10. Retrieved from https://www.cdc.gov/niosh/docs/96-100/homicide.html

Nevada Taxi Cab Authority. (2017). *Nevada taxi cab industry statistics, November 2017.* Retrieved from http://taxi.nv.gov/uploadedFiles/taxinvgov/content/About_Us/ALL/Statistics/2017_November_Statistics.pdf

New York City Taxi and Limousine Commission (NYTLC). (2016). *Taxicab fact book.* Retrieved from http://www.nyc.gov/html/tlc/downloads/pdf/2016_tlc_factbook.pdf

Occupational Safety and Health Administration. (2002). *Workplace violence: OSHA fact sheet.* Washington, DC: U.S. Department of Labor. Retrieved from https://www.osha.gov/OshDoc/data_General_Facts/factsheet-workplace-violence.pdf

Occupational Safety and Health Administration. (2015). *Guidelines for preventing workplace violence for healthcare and social service workers.* Washington. DC: U.S. Department of Labor. Retrieved from https://www.osha.gov/Publications/osha3148.pdf

Payne, B. K., & Appel, J. K. (2007). Workplace violence and worker injury in elderly care settings: Reflective of a setting vulnerable to elder abuse? *Journal of Aggression, Maltreatment & Trauma, 14*(4), 43–56. doi:10.1300/J146v14n04_03

Philip, J. P. (2016). Workplace violence against health care workers in the United States. *The New England Journal of Medicine, 374*(17), 1661–1669. doi:10.1056/NEjMra1501998

Piquero, N. L., Piquero, A. R., Craig, J. M., & Clipper, S. J. (2013). Assessing research on workplace violence, 2000–2012. *Aggression and Violent Behavior, 18*, 383–394.

Potter, S. J., & Banyard, V. L. (2011). The victimization experiences of women in the workforce: Moving beyond single categories of work or violence. *Violence and Victims, 26*(4), 513–532. doi:10.1891/0886-6708.26.4.513

Respass, G., & Payne, B. K. (2008). Social services workers and workplace violence. *Journal of Aggression, Maltreatment & Trauma, 16*(2), 131–143. doi:10.1080/10926770801921287

Ringstad, R. (2009). CPS: Client violence and client victims. *Child Welfare, 88*(3), 127–144.

Sakellaropoulos, A., Pires, J., Estes, D., & Jasinski, D. (2011). Workplace aggression: Assessment of prevalence in the field of nurse anesthesia. *American Association of Nurse Anesthetists Journal, 79*(4), 51–57.

Scalora, M. J., Washington, D. O., Casady, T., & Newell, S. P. (2003). Nonfatal workplace violence risk factors: Data from a police contact sample. *Journal of Interpersonal Violence, 18*(3), 310–327. doi:10.1177/0886260502250092

Schwer, R. K., Mejza, M. C., & Grun-Rehomme, M. (2010). Workplace violence and stress: The case for taxi drivers. *Transportation Journal, Spring*, 5–23.

Shoemaker, P. J., & Reese, S. D. (1996). *Mediating the Message.* White Plains, NY: Longman.

Thornton, W. E., Voigt, L., & Harper, D. W. (2013). *Why Violence?: Leading Questions Regarding the Conceptualization and Reality of Violence in Society.* Carolina Academic Press.

Tiesman, H. M., Gurka, K. K., Konda, S., Coben, J. H., & Amandus, H. E. (2012). Workplace homicides among U.S. women: The role of intimate partner violence. *National Institute for Occupational Safety and Health, Analysis and Field Evaluations, 22*(4), 277–284. doi:10.1016/j.annepidem.2012.02.009

Ulrich, B. T., Lavandero, R., Woods, D., & Early, S. (2014). Critical care nurse work environments 2013: A status report. *Critical Care Nurse, 34*(4), 64–79. doi:http://dx.doi.org/10.4037/ccn2014731

U.S. Department of Labor. (n.d.) *DOL workplace violence program—appendices.* Retrieved from http://www.dol.gov/oasam/hrc/policies/dol-workplace-violence-program-appendices.htm

U.S. Department of Labor. (2010). *OSHA fact sheet: Preventing violence against taxi and for-hire drivers.* Retrieved from https://www.osha.gov/Publications/taxi-driver-violence-factsheet.pdf

Versola-Russo, J. M., & Russo, F. (2009). When domestic violence turns into workplace violence: Organizational impact and response. *Journal of Police Crisis Negotiations, 9,* 141–148. doi:10.1080/15332580902865193

Warchol, G. (1998). *Workplace violence, 1992–1996.* Bureau of Justice Statistics Special Report. Washington, DC: U.S. Department of Justice. Retrieved from http://www.bjs.gov/content/pub/pdf/wv96.pdf

Williams, T. (2011, February 7). After Tucson rampage, a struggle to stay in reach. *The New York Times,* p. A12.

KEY TERMS

- *High-Risk Occupations:* Occupations with public contact, in particular those that involve the exchange of money; delivery of passengers, goods, and services; or working with unstable persons (OSHA, 1996). In addition, occupations where one is working in isolation, working late at night or in the early morning, working in high-crime areas, guarding valuables, or working in community-based settings (OSHA, 1996).

- *Type 1 Workplace Violence:* Also known as stranger-on-employee workplace violence, encompasses criminal intent. In instances of stranger-on-employee violence, the assailant has no official connection with the employee or business experiencing the violence. Examples under this type often include robbery, shoplifting, or trespassing (Booth et al., 2009; IPRC, 2001; Lipscomb et al., 2002; Tiesman et al., 2012).

- *Type 2 Workplace Violence:* Also known as customer or client violence, includes the threat of violence by a customer or client toward an employee, business, or organization. In this instance, there is a legitimate relationship between the assailant and the employee, business, or organization. Assailants can include customers, clients, patients, passengers, students, and inmates, to name a few (IPRC, 2001; Libscomb et al., 2002; Tiesman et al., 2012).

- *Type 3 Workplace Violence:* Also known as co-worker violence, includes those incidents where an employee or ex-employee uses violence or the threat of violence toward current or former co-workers or supervisors (IPRC, 2001; Tiesman et al., 2012). These instances might be spurred by stress, personal or religious differences, or a sense of injustice about such things as losing out on a promotion or being fired (IPRC, 2001; Tiesman et al., 2012).

- *Type 4 Workplace Violence:* Also known as domestic/personal violence, refers to those assailants from outside of the workplace who have a personal or domestic relationship with an employee or other member of a business or organization, and then commit or threaten to commit a violent act at the victim's place of work (IPRC, 2001; Tiesman et al., 2012). It is typically domestic violence that migrates to the workplace (FBI, 2002; Versola-Russo & Russo, 2009). Examples include, but are not limited to, violence perpetrated by spouses, significant others, exes, or by others connected to victims in the workplace through a personal relationship.

- *Workplace Violence:* "An action (verbal, written, or physical aggression) which is intended to control or cause, or is capable of causing, death or serious bodily injury to oneself or others, or damage to property" including "abusive behavior toward authority, intimidating or harassing behavior, and threats" (U.S. Department of Labor, n.d.).

THE NEW YORK TIMES ARTICLES

Fountain, J. W. (2001). Ex-worker opens fire at Illinois plant; 5 are killed. *The New York Times.* Retrieved from https://www.nytimes.com/2001/02/06/us/ex-worker-opens-fire-at-illinois-plant-5-are-killed.html

Fountain, J. W. (2002). Five people shot to death in Nebraska bank holdup. *The New York Times.* Retrieved from https://www.nytimes.com/2002/09/27/us/five-people-shot-to-death-in-nebraska-bank-holdup.html

Hart, A. (2004). National briefing south: Mississippi: Company cited in worker killings. *The New York Times.* Retrieved from https://www.nytimes.com/2004/07/13/us/national-briefing-south-mississippi-company-cited-in-worker-killings.html

Kleinfield, N. R. (2002). Before deadly rage, a lifetime consumed by a troubling silence. *The New York Times.* Retrieved from https://www.nytimes.com/2007/04/22/us/22vatech.html

Lovett, I. (2011). Custody battle may have fueled killings at salon, victims' kin say. *The New York Times*. Retrieved from https://www.nytimes.com/2011/10/14/us/suspect-in-california-salon-killings-was-in-bitter-custody-battle-victims-kin-say.html

DISCUSSION QUESTIONS

1. Prior to reading this chapter, how did you define workplace violence? How much of a role do you believe the media played in your view and definition? Has your definition of workplace violence now changed? Why or why not?

2. Were you surprised by the level of workplace violence in certain occupations as reported in the literature? Which occupations do you believe would seem to have more or less workplace violence? Why?

3. From your experience with workplace violence as reported by the media, how does the coverage of victims and perpetrators of workplace violence differ, if at all?

4. Do you believe corporate negligence to be a legitimate form of workplace violence? Why or why not?

5. What are some constructive ways in which workplace violence can be avoided or combatted in each of the four main workplace violence types discussed (employee-on-employee, customer/client-on-employee, stranger-on-employee, and domestic violence)?

CHAPTER 8

Victims of School Violence

Maurya Hiden, Department of Criminal Justice, Seattle University;
John Brent, School of Justice Studies, Eastern Kentucky University

INTRODUCTION

Over the past two decades school violence has become a pressing topic
driving research initiatives, policy changes, and political debates. Despite
its many forms, recent news reports regarding school violence has focused
primarily on the occurrence of school shootings. Without a doubt, these are
tragic events that target some of the most vulnerable and innocent while
deepening people's fears and insecurities. That stated, media reports privi-
leging high-profile shootings over other—perhaps more prevalent—forms
of violence may not only create false constructions of school violence but
may also misguide policy recommendations. Given recent shifts in policy
and practices, it appears that crime has become an organizing principle
shaping school operations. Just as Simon (2007, p. 213) reminds us, "When
a problem for 10 percent becomes a paradigm for all, it is the mark of the
hold of crime over our contemporary political imagination."

This issue becomes more pressing when considering that media representations of school violence can provoke "moral panics" that bring
about heightened security measures, punitive disciplinary policies, and
sweeping policy changes. As part of their response to publicized shootings, schools across the nation have adopted security measures that range
from hall passes and mandatory sign-ins/outs for guests, to the addition
of school resource officers (SROs) and metal detectors (Casella, 2006;
Perumean-Chaney & Sutton, 2013). Schools have also escalated disciplinary
responses in the form of exclusionary practices and zero-tolerance policies
(see Hirschfield & Celinska, 2011; Kupchik, 2010). These policy outcomes
are interesting given that they often decrease feelings of safety among

students while also negatively impacting immediate and future outcomes at the student and school level.

Still further, Schildkraut and Hernandez (2014) reveal that—after the Columbine school shooting in 1999—over 800 bills related to firearms were introduced, yet only 10 percent were passed. In 2008 following the Virginia Tech shooting, President George W. Bush signed the National Instant Criminal Background Check (NICS) Improvement Amendment. In 2014, the Office of Justice Programs alongside the National Institute of Justice established the Comprehensive School Safety Initiative (CSSI). Among other focus areas, this initiative targeted school violence via evidence-based models and ongoing program evaluation. Even after the wake of the Newtown, Connecticut, school shooting, the political discourse emphasized great security over alternative "responsive responses" that demonstrate effectiveness (Kupchik, Brent, & Mowen, 2015).

There can be little doubt that school violence has social, cultural, and political complexities that are often overlooked, underreported, or unacknowledged in news reports. Given the influential role of the media and significant impact of school violence, the purpose of this chapter is to examine whether news reports of school violence align with findings in the empirical literature. In the following pages, this chapter gathers research regarding school violence—specifically noting its forms, who it impacts, how often it occurs, and how the media, government, and school officials respond to such events. This review is then juxtaposed against media reports of school violence. In order to accomplish this, data for this chapter come from a content analysis of a sample of *The New York Times* articles published between 2001 and 2015. Lastly, comparisons are made between these two sources and concluding remarks and recommendations are offered.

LITERATURE REVIEW

A PICTURE OF SCHOOL VIOLENCE, BROADLY

If we define "school violence" as meaning more than school shootings, what does it entail? Broadly, **school violence** has been defined as any type of aggressive activity that harms or impacts the learning environment (Johnson & Barton-Bellessa, 2014) and as "a subset of youth violence, a broader public health problem ... the intentional use of physical force or power, against another person, group, or community, with the behavior likely to cause physical or psychological harm" (Centers for Disease Control and Prevention, 2012, pg. 1). Therefore, aside from shootings, school violence includes a wide range of misconduct, including assault, fighting, rape, sexual assault, robbery, bullying, carrying a weapon to school, threatening, property offenses, and crimes against the school—among many others (Bureau of Justice Statistics, 2014; CDC, 2012; Finkelhor, Vanderminden, Turner, Shattuck, & Hamby, 2014).

In order to capture the nature of occurrence of school violence, the Bureau of Justice Statistics (BJS) and the National Center for Education Statistics (NCES) joined forces to conduct the **Indicators of School Crime and Safety Survey (ISCS)**. According to the 2016 ISCS, in the 2013–2014 academic year 65 percent of public schools reported one or more violent incidents. For students between the ages of 12 and 18, 21 percent reported being bullied at school, seven percent were the target of hate-related words, seven percent experienced cyberbullying, two percent experienced theft, and roughly 1 percent reported serious violent victimization. For youth in Grades nine through 12, eight percent reported being in a physical fight at school, six percent were threatened or injured with a weapon on school grounds, and four percent reported carrying weapons on school property. The report also found 48 school-associated violent deaths, including 26 homicides, 20 suicides, one legal intervention death, and one undetermined cause. Of these 48 school-related deaths, 12 homicides and eight suicides were school-aged youth between five and 18 years of age.

The Centers for Disease Control (CDC) also reports on school violence for youth Grades nine through 12. According to the School Associated Violent Death Study (1994–1999), roughly two percent of all school-aged homicides happened on school grounds, commuting to/from school, or during a school-related event. The CDC also finds that 22 percent of females and 18 percent of males reported being a victim of bullying, 22 percent of females and 11 percent of males experienced cyberbullying, 12 percent of students reported being in a fight, roughly seven percent indicated that they had been threatened or injured with a weapon, and just over five percent of students reported they carried a weapon to school. In the 2009–2010 school year, 17 homicides of youth between five and 18 years old occurred at school—a rate of youth homicides at school that has remained under two percent since the 1992–1993 school year (CDC, 2012).

Aside from the BJS and the NCES data, researchers utilizing the National Survey of Children's Exposure to Violence (NatSCEV) Series concluded differently, finding that 13.9 percent of students were assaulted, although they did find that 0.4 percent of students were sexually assaulted, a number aligning closely to the BJS and NCES (Finkelhor et al., 2014). A possible reasoning behind the discrepancy could be due to the fact that the BJS statistic is based on students from 12 to 18 years old, while NatSCEV includes children from five to 17 years old.

CORRELATES OF SCHOOL VIOLENCE

Most researchers studying school violence argue that school violence is a reflection of violence in the broader social context, including the students' backgrounds, communities they live in, their family structure, and larger macro factors. Other issues related to victimization in schools pertain to race/ethnicity, generational status, and gender/sexual orientation. Koo, Peguero, and Shekarkhar (2012) chose to utilize data from the Education Longitudinal Study of 2002, and sampled 9,870 first, second, and third generation Latino, Asian American, African American, and White students. They concluded that immigrant youth are less likely to report violence. Compared to American Caucasian males, Caucasian immigrant males were victimized more, and at the highest rate of all immigrants. Overall, African American females were victimized at a higher rate than Asian American, White, and Latina females. When examining geographical and educational settings, researchers identified a higher rate of nonfatal victimizations in schools within urban and suburban communities than those in rural communities (Johnson & Barton-Bellessa, 2014). In addition, middle and high school students experience a higher rate of all types of violent victimization (Finkelhor et al., 2014).

Students are not the only victims of school violence; school administration, including schoolteachers also experience victimization. Seven percent of teachers in the United States are victims of some type of violent act, and four percent of teachers have been physically attacked by a student while at school (Johnson & Barton-Bellessa, 2014; Kajs, Schumacher, & Vital, 2014). A higher rate of male teachers (9%) reported receiving threats of injury than female teachers (7%) (Kajs et al., 2014). In addition, more teachers in the city reported being threatened with injury (10%) than teachers in the suburban (7%) or rural areas (6%) (Thornton, Voigt, & Harper, 2013). Furthermore, a small survey study of a rural midwestern school district identified that 18.2 percent of male teachers avoided current or former students outside of school because of fear or intimidation (Johnson & Barton-Bellessa, 2014).

SCHOOL SHOOTINGS & THEIR IMPACT

As uncommon as they are, **school shootings** receive an abundance of media attention, policy recommendations, and academic research. The reasoning behind this is likely due to the high volume of deaths in one incident, the perceived randomness, and because the victims and the attackers are mostly children—arguably the most vulnerable victims of violence. The school shooting of Columbine High School should be mentioned as it was the beginning of a renewed focus on school shootings in the United States. On April 20, 1999, two students, Dylan Klebold and Eric Harris, claimed the lives of 12 students and one teacher and wounded 24 others.

After four other shootings in 1999, medical professionals, law enforcement agencies, and the general public wanted to know why students engage in school shootings, what the warning signs associated with these horrific acts are, and what could be done to prevent future shootings. The American Psychological Association (APA) (Ferguson, Coulson, & Barnett, 2011) created an online pamphlet describing the warning signs of youth violence, to include hurting animals, fighting, and poor school performance among others. The Federal Bureau of Investigation (FBI) (Ferguson et al., 2011) also created a threat assessment. Broad warning signs included a failed love relationship, attitude of superiority, and a fascination with violent entertainment. Other warning signs included the externalization of blame and having a closed social group—alongside other risk factors.

The general theme in the years after Columbine was a focus on external factors including violent media, Goth culture, issues with society, government, and legislation, rather than internal issues the attacker may have experienced, including depression or psychotic tendencies (Ferguson et al., 2011).

The problem with most research on school shootings is that the attacker usually commits suicide or is killed by law enforcement, so information on the attacker is gathered from other sources. In 2002, the U.S. Secret Service and The Department of Education conducted a report that analyzed 37 school shootings, involving 41 attackers, including 10 interviews with attackers, occurring between 1974 and 2000. The report makes it clear that there is no one reliable "profile" of a school shooter. Contrary to prior research and popular belief, only 15 percent of the attackers expressed "some interest" in violent video games and 59 percent displayed "some interest" in violent media of any kind. In regard to social isolation, most of the attackers had friends, and 41 percent were involved in a mainstream social group. Of all the attackers, 34 percent were described as loners (Ferguson et al., 2011).

Other than being a White male, the most common features of the attackers were internal. Seventy-one of the attackers perceived themselves as wronged, bullied, or persecuted by others. Victims who reciprocate violence, and those who eventually become criminal offenders, are an important part of understanding victimization. Violence is often circular in nature, and the victim-offender population is an important topic to analyze separately in future research. Although few attackers had received mental health services, 98 percent had experienced some major loss prior to the incident, 78 percent had a history of suicide attempts or ideations, and 61 percent had a documented history of significant depression. The researchers of this study identified depression coupled with antisocial behavior as the best predictor of youth violence. In addition, 81 percent of the attackers had informed at least one person of their intent before the act, and in 93 percent of the cases, attackers engaged in behaviors that caused alarm in peers, parents, teachers, or mental health professionals (Ferguson et al., 2011).

Another research study that focused on reasoning behind school shootings discovered three commonalities: marginalization, access to guns, and masculinity. Many school shooters were bullied or ignored in school. In addition, shooters had access to guns and ammunition, whether legally or illegally (Mongon, Hatcher, & Maschi, 2009). One study found that 68 percent of attackers utilized a relative's firearm(s) in the school shooting (Augustyniak, 2005). The last commonality is that attackers experienced attacks on their manhood, including being dumped, bullied, or called "gay." In addition, school shooters do not act on impulse and will often plan for months, which includes a process of pre-contemplation, contemplation, planning, taking action, and following through with the act (Mongon et al., 2009).

Researchers in another study measured the variables associated with shootings and the differences between school levels. The study consisted of 38 random and 96 targeted school shootings in the United States between 1996 and 2009 compared to a control of 138 randomly sampled schools in the United States. The results indicate that fatal shootings are 2.5 times more likely to occur on high school and middle school campuses than college campuses. Shootings are six times more likely to occur at predominately non-White than at predominantly White schools. School shootings are also more likely to occur in schools with higher enrollment rates. Finally, compared to middle and high schools, college campuses are 20 times more likely to have a random shooting than a targeted shooting (Flores-De Apodaca, Brighton, Perkins, Jackson, & Steege, 2012).

SCHOOL SHOOTINGS 2000–2013

The FBI under the Department of Justice recently produced information regarding active shooter cases, including school shootings. The report consisted of all school shootings, kindergarten through college level, which occurred between 2000 and 2013. During this time frame, 37 school shootings occurred: 12 at colleges, 14 at high schools, six at middle schools, four at elementary schools, and one at a K-12 school. All but two of the incidents involved an individual acting alone, and 12 of the 14 high school shootings involved a student shooter. Five of the six middle schools involved a student, and all four of the elementary schools were attacked by an adult shooter. The majority (59%) of shootings occurred in classrooms and hallways. The two shootings with the highest causalities were Virginia Tech (32 killed, 17 wounded) and Sandy Hook Elementary School (27 killed, 2 wounded) (Blair & Schweit, 2014).

Researchers comparing attempted and completed school shootings from 1764 to 2013 discovered that school shootings were most prevalent in the southern region of the United States. When considering individual states, California had the highest number of school attacks, followed by New York and Pennsylvania. In addition, February had the highest number of mass shootings, while April and September had the highest number of attempted shootings. School shooters committed suicide in 31 percent of the incidents, although this number has increased in more recent years (Agnich, 2015). Overall, most of the school shooters were bullied, which often fueled their intent to kill their peers, resulting in a complete circle of violence. The next section will explain the nature of bullying in more depth.

BULLYING

Bullying victimization has become a serious public issue, receiving more attention in the last two decades, especially with the advances in technology which led to the advent of cyberbullying. Often referred to as peer victimization, bullying involves an imbalance of power and aggressive actions or words perpetrated by one or many youth against another youth. Bully victims can experience trauma symptoms including anger, depression, anxiety, dissociation, and post-traumatic stress disorder (Finkelhor, Shattuck, Turner, Ormrod, and Hamby, 2011). The negative consequences of bully victimization can even lead into adulthood (Seals & Young, 2003).

Researchers conducting a study of seven Mississippi public schools, with a high population of African American students, studied the prevalence and type of bullying experienced by 12- to 17-year-olds. The researchers discovered that 24 percent of students had a direct involvement in bullying, either as a bully or a victim. There were twice as many male bullies as female bullies, although they did not differ in the type of bullying they engaged in (physical, threats, name-calling, teasing, and exclusion). The majority (62.5%) of students only bullied when they were in a group, and the most common location of bullying was at lunch and/or recess, followed by the commute to and from school. When bullies did bully a victim one on one, they were usually the same gender (Seals & Young, 2003).

The results of this same study identified verbal bullying as the most prevalent, and seventh graders were more involved in bullying than eighth graders; however, physical bullying remained steady across age groups. Contrary to other studies, African Americans and Caucasians did not differ in bullying experiences. This result could be attributed to the fact that 79 percent of the population was African American. The researchers also found that victims had higher levels of depression and bullies had the highest levels of self-esteem, although this finding was not significant (Seals & Young, 2003).

Another study focused on bullying and violent victimization of school-aged children involved a subset population of the National Survey of Children's Exposure to Violence II (NatSCEV). The NatSCEV is a joint project of the Office of Juvenile Justice and Delinquency Prevention and the Center of Disease Control that surveys children of all ages, involving questions on a range of victimizations. The current study utilized a subset of 3,391 children, ages five to 17. Almost half (48%) of the students had been exposed to at least one form of victimization at school in the past year, the most frequent form was bullying (29.8%). Among those victimized (bullied and/or assaulted), 68 percent reported that school personnel knew about the victimization. In addition, 30 percent of the students experienced intimidation, and 12 percent of those bullied/assaulted were injured (Finkelhor et al., 2014).

Researchers from another study also utilized the NatSCEV, taking a subset of 2,999 students, ages six to 17, focusing on victimization in and outside of school in the last year. This study expanded bullying through six measures of peer victimization including physical assault, which included being hit, punched, kicked, or experiencing any violence within an intimate relationship, identified as dating violence. The next measure was physical intimidation, which included being chased, grabbed, or forced to do something that they did not want to do. Emotional victimization measured violence through experiencing name-calling, teasing, or being excluded. Sexual victimization included the victimization of sexual assault, flashing, and sexual harassment. Property victimization included robbery, theft, and vandalism; Internet harassment was measured separately (Turner, Finkelhor, Hamby, Shattuck, & Ormrod, 2011).

The researchers in this study discovered that all types of victimization were significantly related to increased trauma symptoms, emotional victimization having the greatest effect. In addition, trauma symptoms significantly increased with more than one type of victimization. Physical assault, property crimes, and sexual victimization increased with age, while physical intimidation was more common among elementary students. Emotional victimization was common among elementary, middle school, and high school students, although Black students experienced a significantly higher rate of assault victimization. The specific type of victimization that happened disproportionately (78%) at school, compared to outside of school, was bias attacks (being hit or attacked because of skin color, religion, nationality, physical disability, or sexual orientation) (Turner et al., 2011).

Gender, as it relates to victimization, was also considered by the researchers in this study. Their findings indicate that boys experience more physical victimization, while girls experience emotional and sexual victimization more often. Forty-one percent of all assaults occurred at places other than school-related locations, and boys experienced a higher rate of their most recent victimization outside of school. Those whose last victimization was outside of school were more likely to be injured from the incident and be more afraid. Finally, 82 percent of all emotional victimization happened at school (Turner et al., 2011).

Another researcher seeking to understand bullying experiences and the prevalence of bullying identified bullying as a continuum rather than a dichotomy between those who bully and those who are the victims of bullying. This study surveyed 192 students in Grades three through eight attending rural schools in the Appalachian region during the fall of 2002. Of the students studied, 98 percent were Caucasian, and 43–61 percent of the students attending the schools studied received free or reduced lunch. The survey measured students' experience with direct and indirect bullying acts, as well as the amount of bully and/or victim experiences they were subjected to each month. Direct bullying involved physical aggression, name-calling, teasing, threats, and items taken away. Indirect bullying involved spreading false rumors, using third parties to harm someone, and using relationships to harm someone. A student was identified as a bully if they bullied two to three times each month, and as a bully-victim if they experienced victimization two to three times a month and acted as a bully two to three times a month (Dulmus, Sowers, & Theriot, 2006).

The results from the survey helped to identify 43 percent of the students as victims of bullying. Of these victims, 73 percent were only victims, while 27 percent were identified as bully-victims, which indicate that 11.5 percent of all the students were bully-victims. In addition, 40 to 50 percent of each group believed that school personnel do nothing, little, or fairly little to counteract bullying, a result also found in a separate study (Wilson-Simmons, Dash, Tehranifar, O'Donnell, & Stueve, 2006). For both victims and bully-victims, the most common type of bullying was teasing or name-calling, although bully-victims experienced significantly more teasing and name-calling. Bully-victims were also more likely to be bullied with names or comments based on race or color. They were also more likely to be physically assaulted and have money or items taken or damaged. Bully-victims also experienced more occurrences of bullying on a weekly basis, as well as more forms of bullying. Bully-victims appear to experience a cycle of violence (Dulmus et al., 2006).

METHODS

METHODOLOGICAL APPROACH & DATA

In line with prior working definitions, this chapter defines school violence to include acts of violence committed by students individually or collectively, committed against other students, school personnel, or the school itself, with most occurrences happening on school grounds. Other locations may include commutes to and from school as well as after-school programs or school-related events. The definition of school will include private and public schools, kindergarten through college level, as well as any schools located on Native American reservations.

A content analysis was conducted using articles pertaining to school violence published in *The New York Times* over a 15-year period, from 2001 to 2015. In order to identify relevant articles pertaining to the study's focus, the following key terms were used to frame the search: school, shooting, violence, assault, bullying, and fighting. From this search, more than 1,500 articles were found. From these articles, a total of 270 were applicable based on preset exclusion criteria. Specifically, articles were excluded if the violent act occurred in places other than school, near school, or in route to school. Other articles were excluded because the information was a general overview of the prevalence of school violence or was a conclusion of a study about school violence. Finally, articles that focused on gun control, mental health, or other political debates related to school violence were excluded unless they were in direct response to a violent event or a cluster of violent events.

VARIABLES & ANALYSIS

To examine the content of these 270 articles, they were coded for a series of preset variables. From the outset, the date, start page, and word count were auto-coded and included in the analysis. Afterward, the general focus of the article was collected. This item was coded as a school response, community response, story of the event, offender background, victim background, police response, political response, investigation, or court process.

Given the focus of the study, the type of violence was also coded. In line with inclusive definitions of school violence, the analysis includes sexting, assaults, fights, shootings, mass shootings, mass killings, mass stabbings, attempted attacks, planned attacks, bullying, and others. In order to capture where the violent act occurred, the state, school name, and education level (K-college) were also coded.

The next set of variables measured captured whether the article was victim or offender focused. If 50 percent or more of the article referenced the victim(s), it was coded as victim focused; if 50 percent or more of the article referenced the offender(s), it was coded as offender focused. If the article was neither victim nor offender focused, it was coded as neither or left blank if the article did not reference the victims or offenders.

In a similar vein, the number of victims referenced was measured, as well as their names, age, race, and sex. Many of these variables were coded as not applicable (N/A) or unknown because some violent incidents did not involve or identify a victim(s). By way of example, many articles did not mention victim demographics unless the violence was racially motivated. Finally, general themes were also drawn from the articles to include mass shootings and other school shootings, bullying, other forms of school violence, newsworthiness, and response to school violence. The two thematic responses to school violence were mental health and gun control.

The themes were easily extracted from the articles based on the type of school violence each article covered. As you will read in the proceeding pages, mass shootings and other school shootings account for the bulk of the news articles, resulting in one major theme. Sub-themes are also noted within the mass-shooting theme. Much in the same way, bullying as a theme was evident within the articles. Whether as a way to describe the perpetrator of violence (e.g., bullied school shooter) or to draw attention to bullied victims (e.g., bullied children who commit suicide), bullying was a topic that emerged through the articles. Violent victimization as a theme provides the reader with an overview of all school violence, as represented within the articles. Another important theme included in the proceeding pages is newsworthiness. Newsworthiness within this study is based on front-page publications and average word count. As you will read, the incidents of school violence that are considered more newsworthy are not necessarily those that are more likely to occur.

Response to school violence is a theme that can be broken down into two thematic responses: mental health and gun control. As mentioned in preceding pages, following a violent school attack, the public wants to pinpoint the reason perpetrators commit these heinous crimes. This is also why many of the articles in this study are offender focused. Furthermore, the public also frequently demands change through gun policy reform following a major violent attack at a school. As mentioned before, many gun reform policies are introduced following a mass shooting, as seen after the Columbine or Parkland shootings.

FINDINGS

MASS SHOOTINGS

The preponderance of the articles focused on mass shootings—141 out of the 270 articles, or 52.5 percent of the total (see Table 8.1). Although the Columbine school shooting occurred in 1999, the aftermath extends into the 2000s. Twenty-nine articles were dedicated to the Columbine shooting alone, representing 20.5 percent of the mass shooting articles and 10.7 percent of the total articles. Three articles were not about the Columbine shooting; two were threats made against the school at a later date, and one referenced an aggravated assault. Fourteen of the articles on Columbine focused on lawsuits. Lawsuits were filed against the parents of the shooters and the drug company that produced Luvox, a drug Eric Harris had been taking. Lawsuits were filed against the county, makers of violent video games, and the school for their delayed response to the shooting. Another lawsuit involved parents blaming the police department for the death of their son due to a mistaken identity as the shooter. This was eventually dropped because ballistics evidence showed that it was the attackers and not the police who shot the victim.

The mass shooting at Virginia Tech was the subject of the second most number of articles on mass shootings. Twenty-four articles were dedicated to this violent event (17% of the articles on mass shootings and 8.8% of the total articles analyzed). Do note that one article on Virginia Tech was not in response to the mass shooting but was a threat on the school. These articles had a different ring than Columbine, specifically less lawsuits. Although there were a few articles that referenced blame placed on the school administration for their actions or inactions, more articles were

TABLE 8.1 Frequency and Average Word Count of School Violence Articles

REPORTED VIOLENCE	NUMBER OF ARTICLES	PERCENT OF ARTICLES	WORD COUNT PER ARTICLE
Accidental gunshot	1	< 1	333
Assault	1	< 1	100
Attempted attack	7	3	355
Beaten to death	2	< 1	838
Bullying	13	5	987
Drive by shooting	4	2	278
Fighting	2	< 1	369
Harassment	1	< 1	603
Hazing	4	2	544
Homicide and/or suicide	1	< 1	444
Hostage	5	2	424
Mass killing	6	2	1502
Mass shooting	141	52	815
Mass stabbing	2	< 1	523
Planned attack	13	5	515
Sexting	4	2	1528
Sexual assault	1	< 1	754
Shooting	48	18	418
Stabbed to death	2	< 1	258
Suicide	1	< 1	1112
Threats	10	4	607
Weapon	1	< 1	1152

* N = 270 *The New York Times* Articles
* Percent and Word Counts represent rounded figures

dedicated to describing the killer's mental health issues, his "dark" writings, and classmates' and teachers' fears of him.

The next most commonly reported mass shooting was the event at Red Lake High School in 2005, where a student killed nine children and adults, and then killed himself. Twenty articles were dedicated to this event, equating to a total of 14 percent of the mass shooting articles and 7.4 percent of the total articles. More than half of the articles on this event followed the attacker's background and the possible accomplice. The 16-year-old son of the chairman of the Red Lake Band of Chippewas was arrested and charged with conspiracy. He had exchanged emails with the attacker about the event, including conversations about firearms and the school layout, yet did not engage in the actual attack. The articles followed this case of foul play and how it appeared to tear the community apart.

The next three most commonly reported mass shootings were Santana High School, Umpqua Community College, and an Amish schoolhouse in Pennsylvania. Santana High School represented 9.2 percent of mass shooting articles and 4.8 percent of all articles, an event in 2001 where a student killed two and wounded 13 others before being apprehended by the police. The shooting at Umpqua Community College in 2015 represented 8.5 percent of the mass shooting articles and 4.4 percent of the total articles, an event where a student shot and killed 10 and wounded seven others. Finally, in 2006, a middle-aged man took over an Amish schoolhouse, shot 10 young girls, killing five, and then took his own life. The Santana shooting sparked debate on the offender's background; some articles described him as a "loner" and "weird kid" that was bullied, while others described him as a "calculated killer." The Umpqua shooting sparked more political response regarding gun control than other shootings. Over half of the articles on the Amish schoolhouse shooting were about the community's response, and only one article focused on the offender.

More than half of the articles on mass shootings (75) occurred on or near high school campuses, while 32.6 percent (46) happened on or near college campuses. Only two articles referenced mass shootings on or near middle schools, while 10.6 percent (15) of the articles referenced elementary mass shootings. The remainder of the articles referenced more than one school in the article.

The focus of articles on mass school shootings ranged from a story of the event to community and school responses, investigations, the court process, and backgrounds of offenders and victims. The most common focus of mass shooting articles was the community response (24%), court process (21.9%), and offender background (16.3%). Throughout the articles, it appeared that not only was the school affected by the shooting but the entire community was also affected. The court process was also a popular focus; articles followed each step of the court proceedings for the shooters that did not commit suicide. Not only did the articles focus on the court process for the offender, but many articles focused on parents of the attacker and lawsuits against the school and the police. After the major school shootings at Columbine and Virginia Tech, multiple lawsuits were brought against the schools, citing negligence in allowing mentally ill students to attend school and their delayed response to the incident. Some parents were charged for crimes, including the father of the student who shot four students in the lunchroom of Marysville-Pilchuck High School in Washington.

The third most common focus of articles on mass shootings was the offender's background, consisting of 23 articles (16.3%) of the 141 articles on mass shootings. Many focused on the offender's background and referenced mental health issues to explain why they would do such a horrible thing. The offender's background also included stories of their "troubled past" or a life of being a loner. A family friend of the Lake Academy High School mass shooting explained, "He tried so hard to be normal. He had to see his brother in and out of rehab and jail. He just sat there and watched. It's really hard to be normal around that" (Bidgood & Tavernise, 2012, A12). Shooters were also described by their obsession with violent media and Goth culture. As one student described the shooter of the Success Tech Academy, "'He said he was going to take them down,' said Marie Johnson, a 16-year-old junior, describing how Mr. Coon was often mocked for the way he dressed and how he bragged about plans to make targets of his tormenters. 'But we didn't think he was serious.'" (Maag & Urbina, 2007).

On the other hand, some offenders were portrayed as popular kids or successful young men with healthy home environments. The 15-year-old who shot four friends and then took his own life was not the "typical" school shooter, "He was not a loner or a known misanthrope—far from it. He was a football player with a million-dollar smile, popular enough to be elected homecoming prince of his freshman class at Marysville-Pilchuck High School" (Johnson & Dewan, 2014). After the mass shooting at Northern Illinois University many were shocked by who committed the heinous crime, "'He was an exemplary student and a nice guy,' said Kristen Myers, one of his professors when Mr. Kazmierczak was in college here. 'Something dreadful must have happened to him.'" (Davey, 2008).

In sharp contrast, the victim backgrounds made up 2.8 percent (4) of the total articles on mass shootings. These articles were not as in depth as those that discussed the offenders' backgrounds. They usually provided basic information about the victim such as age, name, accomplishments, and what the victim was planning to do in the future.

SCHOOL SHOOTINGS

School shootings, other than mass shootings, were the second most reported violent event in the news articles. This category made up 17.7 percent (48) of all the articles. Shootings ranged in school level, victims, and circumstances. Victims included teachers, principals, vice principals, and students. The majority of the events were not random; the attacker either targeted the victim in advance or the violence resulted from a dispute. The most referenced shooting was the shooting at Lake Worth Middle School in 2001, where a 13-year-old student shot his 35-year-old male teacher between the eyes for not allowing him to come back into the classroom to say goodbye to two girls on the last day of school. All seven of the articles were dedicated to the court process because the shooter was the second 14-year-old in South Florida to be tried as an adult that year for first-degree murder. Some described the shooter as a "calculated killer," as one described, "This defendant's demeanor sends chills up my spine" (Canedy, 2001). Others described him as a "troubled kid," as one individual explained, "He's a child, and that's who committed this crime" (Canedy, 2001).

BULLYING

Bullying was the third most referenced violent event in the articles analyzed, making up 13 articles or 4.8 percent of the total. All 13 articles referenced middle schools and high schools, and eight of the articles focused directly on two female students who committed suicide due to repeated bully victimization. Three articles focused on gay bullying and the need for schools to adopt same-sex curriculum in school, and one article focused on a school district's adoption of a new anti-bullying procedure. Other than the two girls who committed suicide due to bullying, only one article focused on the victim's experience of bullying. This article included a description of a boy who had been bullied repeatedly in middle and high school, which led to his parents filing a lawsuit against the school for showing deliberate indifference to the boy.

Five out of the 13 articles on bullying covered the story of a 15-year-old girl from Ireland who was bullied repeatedly at school and online at a high school in Massachusetts. "They vilified her on web sites and sent her text messages calling her a slut and a whore and telling her she deserved to die, according to Ms. Prince's friends" (Eckholm & Zezima, 2010, A1). Nine male and female students were charged with crimes including harassment, violating civil rights, and statutory rape. Three other articles focused on a 12-year-old middle school girl, living in Florida, who committed suicide by jumping off a building after repeated bully victimization. This case focused mostly on cyberbullying, although the victim was bullied on school grounds as well. Through various phone applications, she received comments from peers such as, "Why are you still alive?" "You're ugly," and "Can u die please?" (Lizette, 2013). This case resulted in a 12-year-old girl and a 14-year-old girl both being charged for aggravated stalking.

VIOLENT VICTIMIZATION

More than half (51.8%) of all the articles referenced some form of violence within high schools (140 out the 270 articles examined). Violence within

TABLE 8.2. Frequency of School Violence in Articles, by School Level

SCHOOL LEVEL	TOTAL	ROUNDED %
College	73	27
College/Elementary	1	< 1
Elementary	20	7
Elementary/MS	1	< 1
Elementary/MS/HS	2	< 1
HS	140	52
HS/College	1	< 1
HS/College/Elem	1	< 1
MS	21	8
MS/HS	8	3
Unknown	1	< 1
MS/HS/College	1	< 1

* N = 270 *New York Times* Articles

college campuses amounted to 27 percent of all the articles, while middle and elementary schools only represented 7.7 percent and 7.4 percent, respectively (see Table 8.2). The remaining articles referenced more than one school level within the article. For college, high school, and elementary school, the most cited violent event was a mass shooting.

Based on the information in the articles, 53 percent of the mass shootings occurred at high schools, 32.6 percent on college campuses, 10.6 percent at elementary schools, and 1.4 percent at middle schools. Articles on shootings occurred most often at high schools, representing 43.7 percent of all shootings. Middle schools represented 29.1 percent, colleges represented 25 percent, and elementary schools represented two percent of all shootings. Articles focusing on bullying only included middle schools and high schools; six were on high schools, three on middle schools, and four focused on both middle schools and high schools. Out of 270 articles, not one article referenced bullying in elementary or college campuses.

When violent events were broken down by state, not surprisingly, Colorado had the highest number of articles, accounting for 12.9 percent (35) of all the articles. A large portion (83%) of these articles were in response to Columbine. The next highest state was California, representing 11.4 percent of all the articles, again partly due to the 13 articles dedicated to the Santana High School shooting. Minnesota (9.6%), Virginia (8.8%), and Pennsylvania (7.4%) followed suit. Each of these states experienced school shootings that resulted in major news media coverage.

The sex of the victim was not always revealed, and unless specifically referenced, sex of the victims was not recorded. The sex of 141 of the victims reported was referenced, and of those referenced, males made up 42.5 percent of the total victims. Females accounted for 24.1 percent of the victims, while females and males referenced in an article made up 33.3 percent of the victim population. Of the articles that included victims (excluding threats, sexting, and planned or attempted attacks), more than half (58.5%) referenced the name or names of the victims. Again, these are only victims that were reported in the articles, not the total victims in each incident.

The race of the victim was almost never cited; only four different incidents identified the race of the victim(s). One article focused on the background of one of the victims of the UC Santa Barbara mass killing, identifying him as a student from Taiwan who was murdered by a roommate known for having issues with other Asian students. Another incident that resulted in five articles referenced a bullied female student who was given the name "Irish Slut" by students who bullied her. Two other incidents cited Black and Hispanic students. One article focused on threats made against Black and Hispanic students by an unknown suspect, while another included a fight between many Black and Hispanic students. In all, the race of victims was only cited when the crime committed was racially motivated or had some racial underpinnings.

NEWSWORTHINESS

A total of 39 articles on school violence were placed on the front page, 27 of which were mass shootings. Although only 13 articles covered bullying, it was the next highest number of front page articles, with a total of four covered on A-1. All four articles covering bullying were from 2008 on, possibly a sign that bullying has started to become more newsworthy in the last eight years. The remaining front-page articles included mass killings (2), sexting (2), a weapon brought to school (1), planned attack (1), shooting (1), and threats (1).

The offender's background was the most common focus for front-page articles, a total of 12 out of the 39. Furthermore, only one front-page article focused on the victim's background, an article on the Umpqua Community College shooting. The article identified and described the nine lives lost, one identified as 20-year-old Treven Taylor. One individual described Taylor in the news report, "All he wanted to do in life was to marry his high school sweetheart, be a firefighter like his dad, and to serve others" (Miller, Philipps, & Turkewitz, 2015). Lucero Alcaraz, 19, also listed as one of the victims, was described by her cousin: "Ms. Alcaraz, whose first name means 'bright star' in Spanish, was an honor student on a scholarship at Umpqua, set on becoming a pediatric nurse" (Miller et al., 2015, A1). Although this article focused solely on the victims, with not even a mention of the shooter, this appears to be the exception and not the rule for newsworthiness.

Another method utilized to measure newsworthiness included the average number of words for each type of school violence. The results from the cross-tabulation of average words per violent type looked much different than the prior results. The violence type that had the highest average number of words was "sexting," with an average of 1,527.8 words per article. Although there were only four total articles on the topic of sexting, there was a lot to discuss. In addition, the four articles on sexting were printed in the last four years, while three were in the last year. This could be evidence that sexting is becoming a school violence topic that is discussed more and will receive more attention in the future. Sexting can be a form of violence when pictures that are sexual in nature are dispersed without the knowledge or permission of the individual in the picture. Articles on mass killings had the second highest number of words on average with 1,502 words, although only six articles focused on mass killings. This could be due to the fact that mass killings occur less often than mass shootings, so when they do happen, it is a topic that is given a lot of attention. These events usually involve stabbings or a combination of stabbing, beating, and shooting.

Even more interesting are the cross-tabulation results of the average number of words per article for mass shootings and other shootings. Although mass shootings and shootings account for the majority of the news articles, the average number of words for the events resulted in 814.5 and 416.6, respectively. A possible explanation for this result could be that these events are rare, yet highly publicized—many articles follow each step of the court process and political response or community response to the event. These articles are often short and repetitive, including a quick update about the case. Although the events are rare, the events seem to live for years through news publication. The Columbine High School mass shooting occurred in 1999, yet it accounted for the most mass shooting articles from 2001 through 2015. Almost anything related to the school shooting was produced by *The New York Times*, even something as short as a 400-word summary of a lawsuit against the shooters' parents.

THEMATIC RESPONSES

Throughout the 270 articles, two clear thematic responses to school violence emerged: mental health and gun control—each being especially prominent for mass shootings. Mental health appears to be an explanation for random violence, especially for mass shootings. Many articles were specifically focused on mental health, while other articles referenced mental health to some degree. Columbine victims' parents sued a drug company, families looked to blame Virginia Tech for not being aware of the shooter's mental health issues, and throughout the court proceedings mental health was cited as a possible reason behind offenders' actions. The killer of the University of California Santa Barbara mass killing was described by an acquaintance as someone who didn't appear to be mentally stable: "We said right from the get-go that that kid was going to lose it someday and just freak out, he said. Everyone made fun of him and stuff" (Lovett & Nagourney, 2014).

Mental health was a popular topic for court processes as well. One shooter was evaluated for an insanity defense, "A 16-year-old who prosecutors say smirked as he pulled the trigger in a school shooting in 2003 in Cold Spring that left two teenagers dead was convicted of murder" (*The New York Times*, 2005). The judge later ruled he was in fact sane at the time of the murder. The Virginia Tech shooter was also known for his mental illness and obsession with "dark writings." "A counselor recommended involuntary commitment, and a judge signed an order saying that he 'presents an imminent danger to self or others' and sent him to Carilion St. Albans Psychiatric Hospital in Radford for an evaluation" (Dewan & Santora, 2007). Mental health was also cited for events that didn't result in a violent incident, "An 11-year-old boy who took a gun and ammunition to school heard voices telling him to shoot a boy who he thought was bullying a friend, the police said in a court document released Thursday" (Associated Press, 2013).

Many articles cited gun control debates following a shooting, especially after a mass shooting. Moreover, out of the articles that focused on the political response to the violent incident, 50 percent of those responses were focused on gun control. After the Virginia Tech shooting, one referenced gun control issues, "'I think after today, what we're doing and what we want the American people to do is start asking our elected officials, 'What are we going to do about this?' Mr. Helmke said" (Toner, 2007).

After the Umpqua Community College shooting President Obama stated, "'[t]hese tragedies must end, and to end them, we must change'" (Gardiner, 2015). Interestingly, 10 out of the 11 articles that focused on gun control were written in the last three years, and five were produced in 2015 alone. This has resulted in the gun control debate becoming a more popular topic and political tool for those running for various public offices.

CONCLUSION

Without any prior knowledge or experience with research on school violence, after reading *The New York Times*, one would logically conclude that shootings, and particularly mass shootings, occur frequently and are a cause for concern in schools across the United States. While shootings and mass shootings are horrific and should be researched to identify methods to prevent future occurrences, one might argue that articles in *The New York Times* disproportionately represent shootings and mass shootings. Shootings and mass shootings together roughly accounted for 70 percent of all the articles about school violence produced from 2001 to 2015, yet only 1 percent of all youth homicides between the ages of five and 18 occur at school (CDC, 2012). In addition, less than 0.5 percent of youth aged 12 to 18 reported serious violent victimization such as rape, sexual assault, robbery, or aggravated assault (BJS, 2014).

Bullying, on the other hand, is underrepresented in *The New York Times* articles compared to the research. Approximately 18.2 to 22 percent of students reported being bullied at school, and seven to 22 percent experienced cyberbullying within the school year (BJS, 2014; CDC, 2012). A total of 13 articles focused on bullying and/or cyberbullying, accounting for less than five percent of the articles. In addition, had the victims of these two cases not committed suicide, the count of articles could have been lower since those articles accounted for 61.5 percent of all the articles on bullying. Although the research identifies bullying as the most common form of school violence, it is not newsworthy unless it results in a death.

According to the research, fighting (12%), carrying a weapon (5.4%), and engaging in assaultive behavior with a weapon (7.4%) are also much more common than shootings (CDC, 2012), yet all together these account for less than five percent of the total articles. Overall the news articles present violence as more prevalent in high schools (51.8%) than middle schools (7.7%), in agreement with the research, although the news articles underrepresented middle school violence.

Shootings are overrepresented, the disproportionate reporting on mass shootings masks other types of violence, and the victims are also somehow lost in the story. Stories on the offender's background greatly outweigh stories on the victim's background, especially when a mass shooting is the focus. In addition, the majority of the front-page articles focus on mass shootings, and many outline the offender's motives, background, and mental stability.

If the community is to begin to understand the type and prevalence of violence experienced by those in educational settings, the news should strive to accurately portray it. Misinformation and misunderstanding can result in sensational views of shootings, fear, and moral panic. Furthermore, if victims continue to be masked by the offenders, court proceedings, and politics, we will continue to lose sight of how violence impacts victims.

REFERENCES

Agnich, L. (2015). A comparative analysis of attempted and completed school-based mass murder attacks. *American Journal of Criminal Justice, 40*(1), 1–22.

Augustyniak, K. (2005). Integration of Federal Bureau of Investigation and United States Secret Service/Department of Education threat assessment models into a conceptual framework for prevention of school violence. *Journal of School Violence, 4*(2), 29–46.

Blair, J. P., & Schweit, K. W. (2014). A study of active shooter incidents, 2000–2013. Washington, DC: Texas State University and Federal Bureau of Investigation, U.S. Department of Justice. Retrieved from https://www.fbi.gov/about-us/office-of-partner-engagement/active-shooter-incidents/a-study-of-active-shooter-incidents-in-the-u.s.-2000-2013

Bureau of Justice Statistics. (2014). Indicators of school crime and safety, 2013. Retrieved from http://www.bjs.gov/index.cfm?ty=pbdetail&iid=5008

Canedy, D. (2001). Florida teenager declares sorry for killing teacher. *The New York Times.* Retrieved from https://www.nytimes.com/2001/07/27/us/florida-teenager-declares-sorrow-for-killing-teacher.html.

Casella, R. (2006). *Selling us the fortress: The promotion of techno-security equipment for schools.* New York: Routledge.

Centers for Disease Control and Prevention. (2012). *Youth violence: Facts at a glance.* Retrieved from http://www.cdc.gov/violenceprevention/youthviolence/schoolviolence/data_stats.html

Davey, M. (2008). Gunman showed few hints of trouble. *The New York Times.* Retrieved from https://www.nytimes.com/2008/02/16/us/16gunman.html

Dewan, S. & Santora, M. (2007). Officials knew troubled state of killer in '05. *The New York Times.* Retrieved from https://www.nytimes.com/2007/04/19/us/19gunman.html

Dulmus, C., Sowers, K., & Theriot, M. (2006). Prevalence and bullying experiences of victims and victims who become bullies (bully-victims) at rural schools. *Victims and Offenders, 1*(1), 15–31.

Ferguson, C., Coulson, M., & Barnett, J. (2011). Psychological profiles of school shooters: Positive directions and one big wrong turn. *Journal of Police Crisis Negotiations, 11*(1), 141–158.

Finkelhor, D., Shattuck, A., Turner, H. A., Ormrod, R., & Hamby, S. L. (2011). Polyvictimization in developmental context. *Journal of Child & Adolescent Trauma, 4*(4), 291–300.

Finkelhor, D., Vanderminden, J., Turner, H., Shattuck, A., & Hamby, S. (2014). At-school victimization and violence exposure assessed in a national household survey of children and youth. *Journal of School Violence, 15*(1), 67–90.

Flores-De Apodaca, R., Brighton, L., Perkins, A., Jackson, K., & Steege, J. (2012). Characteristics of schools in which fatal shootings occur. *Psychological Reports, 110*(2), 363–377.

Gardiner, H. (2015). Obama consoles families in Oregon amid 2 more campus shootings. *The New York Times.* https://www.nytimes.com/2015/10/10/us/politics/obama-consoles-families-in-oregon-amid-2-more-campus-shootings.html

Harper, D., Voigt, L., & Thornton, W. (2012). *Violence: Do we know it when we see it?* Durham, NC: Carolina Academic Press.

Hirschfield, P. J., & Celinska, K. (2011). Beyond fear: Sociological perspectives on the criminalization of school discipline. *Sociology Compass, 5*(1), 1–12.

Johnson, B., & Barton-Bellessa, S. (2014). Consequences of school violence: Personal coping and protection measures by school personnel in their personal lives. *Deviant Behavior, 35*(1), 513–533.

Johnson, K. & Dewan, S. (2014). Tangled portrait of a student emerges in Washington shooting. *The New York Times.* Retrieved from https://www.nytimes.com/2014/10/26/us/contrasting-portraits-emerge-of-jaylen-ray-fryberg-shooter-at-washington-school.html

Kajs, L., Schumacher, G., & Vital, C. (2014). Physical assault of school personnel. *The Clearinghouse, 87*(1), 91–96.

Koo, D., Peguero, A., & Shekarkhar, Z. (2012). Gender, immigration and school victimization. *Victims and Offenders, 7*(1), 77–96.

Kupchik, A. (2010). *Homeroom security: School discipline in an age of fear.* New York: NYU Press.

Kupchik, A., Brent, J. J., & Mowen, T. J. (2015). The aftermath of Newtown: More of the same. *British Journal of Criminology, 55*(6), 1115–1130.

Lizette, A. (2013). Girl's suicide points to rise in apps used by cyberbullies. *The New York Times.* Retrieved from https://www.nytimes.com/2013/09/14/us/suicide-of-girl-after-bullying-raises-worries-on-web-sites.html

Lovett, I., & Nagourney, A. (2014). Video rant, then deadly rampage in California town. *The New York Times.* Retrieved from https://www.nytimes.com/2014/05/25/us/california-drive-by-shooting.html

Maag, C. & Urbina, I. (2007). Student, 14, shoots 4 and kills himself in Cleveland school. *The New York Times.* Retrieved from https://www.nytimes.com/2007/10/11/us/11cleveland.html

Miller, C.C., Philipps, D., & Turkewitz, J. (2015). A snapshot of students lost: Young and old, but all striving. *The New York Times.* Retrieved from https://www.nytimes.com/2015/10/03/us/oregon-shooting-victims-umpqua-community-college-students.html

Mongon, P., Hatcher, S., & Maschi, T. (2009). Etiology of school shootings: Utilizing a purposive, non-impulsive model for social work practice. *Journal of Human Behavior in the Social Environment, 19*(1), 635–645.

Perumean-Chaney, S., & Sutton, L. (2013). Students and perceived school safety: The impact of school security measures. *American Journal of Criminal Justice, 38*(1), 570–588.

Schildkraut, J., & Hernandez, T. (2014). Laws that bit the bullet: A review of legislative responses to school shootings. *American Journal of Criminal Justice, 39*(1), 358–374.

Seals, D., & Young, J. (2003). Bullying and victimization: Prevalence and relationship to gender, grade level, ethnicity, self-esteem and depression. *Adolescence, 38*(152), 735–747.

Simon, J. (2007). *Governing through Crime: How the War on Crime Transformed American Democracy and Created a Culture of Fear.* New York: Oxford University Press.

The New York Times. (2005). National Briefing, Midwest: Minnesota: Teenager is convicted of murder. *The New York Times.* Retrieved from https://www.nytimes.com/2005/07/19/us/national-briefing-midwest-minnesota-teenager-is-convicted-of-murder.html

Thornton, W. E., Voigt, L., & Harper, D. W. (2013). Why Violence?: Leading Questions Regarding the Conceptualization and Reality of Violence in Society. Carolina Academic Press.

Toner, R. (2007). Heading toward 2008: The caucus; Renewed scrutiny for gun controls. *The New York Times.* Retrieved from https://archive.nytimes.com/query.nytimes.com/gst/fullpage-990CE6D9113FF934A25757C0A9619C8B63.html

Turner, H. A., Finkelhor, D., Hamby, S. L., Shattuck, A., & Ormrod, R. K. (2011). Specifying type and location of peer victimization in a national sample of children and youth. *Journal of Youth and Adolescence, 40*(8), 1052–1067.

Wilson-Simmons, R., Dash, K., Tehranifar, P., O'Donnell, L., & Stueve, A. (2006). What can student bystanders do to prevent school violence? Perceptions of students and school staff. *Journal of School Violence, 5*(1), 43–62.

KEY TERMS

- *Bullying Victimization:* Often referred to as peer victimization, bullying involves an imbalance of power and aggressive actions or words perpetrated by one or many youth against another youth. Bully victims can experience trauma symptoms including anger, depression, anxiety, dissociation, and post-traumatic stress disorder (Shattuck & Ormrod, 2011).

- *Indicators of School Crime and Safety Survey (ISCS):* A survey developed and administered by the Bureau of Justice Statistics and the National Center for Education Statistics to measure safety and crime at educational facilities.

- *School Shootings:* Rare events that receive an abundance of media attention, policy recommendations, and academic research.

- *School Violence:* Includes a wide range of misconduct, including assault, fighting, rape, sexual assault, robbery, bullying, carrying a weapon to school, threatening, property offenses, and crimes against the school—among many others (Bureau of Justice Statistics, 2014; CDC, 2012; Finkelhor et al., 2014).

THE NEW YORK TIMES ARTICLES

Barron, J. (2012). Children in Connecticut school were all shot multiple times, officials say. *The New York Times.* Retrieved from https://www.nytimes.com/2012/12/16/nyregion/gunman-kills-20-children-at-school-in-connecticut-28-dead-in-all.html

Barry, D. (2008). A boy the bullies love to beat up, repeatedly. *The New York Times.* Retrieved from https://www.nytimes.com/2008/03/24/us/24land.html

Bidgood, J., & Tavernise, S. (2012). Shooting at Chardon High School kills one and wounds 4. *The New York Times.* Retrieved from https://www.nytimes.com/2012/02/28/us/fatal-school-shooting-in-chardon-ohio-suspect-is-arrested.html

Eckholm, E., & Zezima, K. (2010). Questions for school on bullying and a suicide. *The New York Times.* Retrieved from https://www.nytimes.com/2010/04/02/us/02bully.html

Fitzsimmons, E. G., & Williams, T. (2014). Student stabs 21 people at a high school outside Pittsburgh. *The New York Times.* Retrieved from https://www.nytimes.com/2014/04/10/us/stabbings-franklin-regional-high-school-murrysville.html

DISCUSSION QUESTIONS

1. There is a distinct focus on offenders, not victims, in a vast majority of the articles that cover school shootings. Why is this? What are some of the factors that might lead to this?

2. More recent mass shootings (such as Parkland, which was not included in the analysis as it occurred in 2018) have sparked more advocacy and policy discussions, spearheaded by youth victims, surrounding gun control and mental health. What do you think about these policy areas? What do you think can be done to address school shootings?

3. In your opinion, how does the media's focus on school shootings over other more prevalent types of school violence, such as bullying, impact general discussions of school violence and safety? Why?

4. Are you familiar with recent "active shooter" training being used in all levels of education? Either way, take an opportunity to look up some of the training examples, such as the training found at https://www.alicetraining.com, and discuss how these trainings impact education.

CHAPTER 9

Victims of Virtual Violence

Caitlin M. Healing, Department of Criminal Justice, Seattle University;
Jacqueline B. Helfgott, Department of Criminal Justice, Seattle University

INTRODUCTION

The online world is a vast space that is difficult to control. Every day we are exposed to potential threats online as we place trust in machines to keep our information safe. New technological inventions meant to help users, such as GPS or smartphones, have made it even easier for offenders to track victims without them knowing it and potentially escalate that behavior into harassment or worse. Virtual violence has only recently become a crime of interest to the public, as it did not exist before the creation of the Internet. Crimes that have always existed, like bullying, stalking, and malicious harassment, have effortlessly expanded into cyberspace. In fact, committing these crimes is made even simpler by the anonymity the Internet provides and the ability to victimize from any geographic distance. Roberts (2008) points out that, unlike property crimes that have been facilitated by the creation of the Internet, cyber-stalking is a crime against the person, which has new implications for criminology and criminal justice, as it is a form of violence that is not physical. Simply put, victims are more accessible and vulnerable, and offenders are more able to remain undetected. Despite the ever-growing threat, not much research has been done on virtual violence or the effects it has on victims. In this chapter, we discuss the literature on victims of virtual violence and then provide an analysis of *The New York Times'* depiction of these victims in the media. Comparisons will be drawn to see how accurately victims of virtual violence are represented to the public.

VIRTUAL VIOLENCE

Crime evolves with every societal development and new creation of technology. Electronic media has had a greater influence than suspected in terms of formation of attitudes, values, and behaviors, and it can encourage impulsiveness, have a desensitizing effect, and legitimize violence as a means to an end (Shelton, 1996). Online technologies, which were originally meant as a method of bringing people together through quicker, easier communication, are now being used to bully, harass, stalk, and tease (Bamford, 2004). In-person interpersonal violence is now being taken to the Internet, with the online versions of these attacks sharing many characteristics with the physical versions (Cassidy, Faucher, & Jackson, 2013; Hemphill, Tollit, Kotevski, & Heerde, 2015), but now with added anonymity and ease that the online platform provides. The concept of **"virtual violence"** and the harm it brings to victims is only beginning to be understood. Virtual violence does not have to involve a physical act and can have consequences for victims. Virtual violence has been defined as "all forms of violence that are not experienced physically and, in particular, to encompass the extent to which children increasingly experience violence in more realistic ways than they have before" (American Academy of Pediatrics, Council on Communications and Media, 2016). Technology can be used as a tool to intimidate, threaten, and taunt victims over the Internet—for example through email threats, social media, and other websites. There have been cases where prisoners have used websites and Facebook to intimidate their victims from behind bars (Helfgott, 2008; Associated Press, 2011). During the last decade there has been an increase in online-related crimes, as citizens overestimate the safety of the online world and become susceptible to all kinds of threats and actions. Although there is a wide range of cybercrimes, the focus of this chapter will be on online interpersonal threats, specifically cyberbullying, malicious harassment, and cyberstalking.

CYBERBULLYING

Cyberbullying is only one type of behavior in an ever-growing list of virtual harm and violence (Bamford, 2004; Nuccitelli, 2012). It is broadly defined as "a form of bullying that uses electronic means such as email, mobile phone calls, text messages, instant messenger contact, photos, social networking sites, and personal web pages, with the intent of causing harm to another person through repeated hostile conduct" (Ortega et al., 2012, p. 342). It often encompasses several behaviors, such as "flaming," which is posting offensive and harassing language in a public discussion environment; "outing," which is displaying or forwarding sensitive and personal communication or images; or "exclusion," which is designating someone as a kind of outcast (Bamford, 2004). Nuccitelli (2012) outlines 28 tactics used to cyberbully, including Bamford's definitions and newer tactics. For example, he discusses strategies like "screen name mirroring," where a bully will create a screen name that is nearly identical to the victim's and act as them, or "sending malicious code," where the bully sends viruses or spyware to the victim's computer to harm it (p. 26). Gillespie (2006) points out that these virtual threats are often sexual in nature, frequently utilizing photo-editing programs to make innocent images look pornographic.

Although there are some similarities between cyberbullying and traditional bullying, Hemphill et al. (2015) distinguish the two in that cyberbullies can more easily remain anonymous and have the ability to bully many people at once, regardless of the location or time of day. These factors make cyberbullying particularly threatening and effective.

Characteristics of Victims

Research on cyberbullying is fairly limited due to the short period of time the crime has existed. The lack of research makes it difficult for school officials and service providers to know how to properly handle the increasing number of cases, especially with youth populations (Cassidy et al., 2013). Most research focuses on specific populations, in particular high school students, as juveniles tend to be the most common victims of cyberbullying (Addington, 2013). More recently, cyberbullying and harassment targeting specific groups has been discussed in both the public discourse and academic literature. For example, in 2014, female video game designers were subjected to an international online harassment campaign involving stalking, death and rape threats, hacking personal accounts, and harassment of family and friends. In the case of game designer Zoë Quinn, a massive harassment campaign rooted in domestic violence was launched against her by her abusive boyfriend. He incited a mob attack on Quinn by antifeminist gamers and alt-right supporters, which became a cultural phenomenon known as #GamerGate (Freed, 2017; Todd, 2015; Quinn, 2017).

Prevalence

Statistics on the prevalence of cyberbullying vary greatly depending on the population in the study. Ybarra, Mitchell, Wolak, and Finkelhor (2006) found that 9 percent of the youths they surveyed had been targeted for harassment online, and 32 percent reported chronic harassment (defined as three or more times in the last year). The National Crime Prevention Council (NCPC) (2007) commissioned a study focused on cyberbullying among middle school and high school students in the United States. The study revealed that 43 percent of males and 57 percent of females in their study had experienced cyberbullying. Sontag, Clemans, Graber, and Lyndon (2011) found that 41 percent of the middle school students in their survey experienced cyber victimization. The United States Department of Education (2013) reported results from the 2011 School Crime Supplement (SCS) and National Crime Victimization Survey (NCVS) showing that 9 percent of the students age 12 to 18 surveyed reported being cyberbullied. The Urban Institute (2013) reported that 17 percent of youths in their study reported being victims of cyberbullying, with females experiencing significantly higher rates. Lesbian, gay, bisexual, transgender, and questioning (LGBTQ) youths reported significantly higher rates of cyberbullying than heterosexual youth. Litwiller and Brausch (2013) found rates comparable to previous studies, with 23 percent of adolescent participants reporting being victims of cyberbullying.

Relationship to Offender

In victimization studies, the relationship between the victim and the offender is a key point of interest to researchers. The victim and the offender can be family members, friends, acquaintances, or strangers, and this relationship can give some insight into the nature of the victimization. Addington (2013) found that cases are cleared more often when the victim knows the offender and can identify them. Ybarra et al. (2006) utilized the national Second Youth Internet Safety Survey, which included 1,500 youths and their caregivers about their Internet usage, and found nearly half of the victims knew their offenders before the incident. The NCPC (2010) study found that about three out of four victims were able to figure out who the cyberbully was, and in most cases, it was a friend, someone they knew from school, or someone they knew from somewhere else.

Gender

The genders of both the victim and the offender are important to note when considering those more likely to be victimized and those more likely to victimize others. Barboza's (2015) study of 5,589 students in Grades 5 through 12 found that the odds of being bullied by rumors or by having unwanted, hurtful information posted online are 2.11 and 3.58 times higher, respectively, for females than males. Marcum, Higgins, Freiburger, and Ricketts (2014) found in their study of students at a southeastern university that both sexes were more likely to cyberbully through Facebook if they had been cyberbullied as well. They also found that males and females with low self-control were more likely to cyberbully over Facebook. The NCPC (2010) study found that females were more likely to report negative emotions associated with cyberbullying victimization, especially those between the ages of 13 and 15. Turner, Exum, Brame, and Holt (2013) found that female cyberbullying victims had higher levels of depression than male cyberbullying victims.

Post-Harassment Emotions

Victims feel a wide range of emotions after they are victimized, and people react in a variety of ways. Ybarra et al. (2006) found that 38 percent of the youths in their study who reported being harassed online reported feeling emotionally distressed, upset, and afraid as a result. The likelihood of these emotions increased significantly if the victims were targeted by adults, were asked to send a picture of themselves, received offline threats, or were preadolescents. Students who feel afraid after abuse tend to skip school and have lower self-esteem and poor school performance (Barboza, 2015). A study commissioned by the NCPC (2010) discovered that victims in their sample reported emotions like anger, embarrassment, and fear.

Coping Mechanisms

It is important to look at the variety of ways victims cope with their victimization. Victims cope positively and negatively, and understanding this may assist authorities with therapeutic interventions. Parris, Varjas, Meyers, and Cutts (2012) interviewed students in a southeastern high school about their feelings about coping with cyberbullying. The researchers found three main responses to cyberbullying: reactive coping, which included avoidance, acceptance, justification, and seeking social support; preventive coping, which included talking to potential offenders in person and increasing security and awareness; and feeling that there was no way to prevent cyberbullying.

Randa and Reyns (2014) found that victims of cyberbullying are almost twice as likely to practice avoidance behavior at school. This statistic was negatively correlated with age, in that the older victims were, the less likely they were to practice avoidance behavior at school. Avoidance behavior was positively associated with the "non-White" variable, meaning that reports of avoidance behavior were more likely if the respondent reported their race as something other than White.

Reporting

Reporting refers to victims notifying authorities, whether it is the police or a teacher, of their victimization. This is important to note, as a lack of reporting leads to inaccurate statistics and skews estimates of the prevalence of victimization. It is a common finding in cyberbullying literature that victims rarely notify authorities of their victimization, likely due to the fact that most victims are juveniles and the bullying takes place between schoolmates (Addington, 2013). However, Addington (2013) also found that females are 1.98 times more likely to report to a teacher or other adult than males. Ybarra et al. (2006) found that two in three victims reported incidents of Internet harassment. Moore, Guntupalli, and Lee (2010) found in their study of adolescents' Internet habits that parental regulation of Internet use had no effect on a victim reporting their cyberbullying.

Additional Characteristics

There are several additional characteristics of victims and perpetrators of cyberbullying that are important to examine. Research shows that youth cyberbullying offenders are more likely to become cyberbullying victims (Bauman, Toomey, & Walker, 2013; Ybarra et al., 2006). Wright and Li (2013) discovered the relationship works in the opposite direction as well; victims of cyberbullying deal with their feelings of anger and frustration by cyberbullying others. The researchers also found a two-way relationship between peer rejection and cyber victimization. Furthermore, Ybarra et al. (2006) found that youths who used the Internet for instant messaging, blogging, and chat room usage were more likely to be targeted than those who did not. Barboza (2015) found that Whites were less likely to be highly victimized than non-Whites. Sontag et al. (2011) found that the southeastern middle school students in their study who experienced cyber victimization were less likely to exhibit effortful control and more likely to exhibit symptoms of depression and/or anxiety.

The Urban Institute (2013) reported that cyberbullying victims and perpetrators were nearly three and four times as likely, respectively, as non-victims and non-perpetrators to experience or perpetrate cyber dating abuse against romantic partners. Cyber dating abuse victims and perpetrators were more than two and three times as likely, respectively, to report experiencing or perpetrating cyberbullying against non-intimates. In their study of 5,647 youths, Yahner, Dank, Zweig, and Lachman (2015) found that two thirds of victims of cyberbullying also experienced dating violence. These associations were stronger with cyberbullying than traditional, physical bullying.

Litwiller and Brausch (2013) studied the connections between bullying (both physical and virtual) and suicide, while considering substance use and unsafe sexual behavior as mediators. Their sample consisted of 4,693 public high school students, of which only 3,838 completed all the items. The researchers found that cyberbullying victimization had significant and positive direct effects on substance use, violent behavior, sexual behavior, and suicidal behavior. Additionally, substance use and violent behavior mediated the effects cyberbullying had on suicidal behavior.

CYBERSTALKING

In 1999, the United States Attorney General put out a report about the prevalence of cyberstalking. Law enforcement agencies were seeing a significant rise in cyberstalking, with an estimated 20 percent of all cases involving cyberstalking. At that point nearly 20 years ago, 80 million adults and 10 million children had access to the Internet (United States Attorney General, 1999). Cyberstalkers gain online access to information about a target for the purpose of intimidation and harm (Helfgott, 2008). One out of every 12 women in the United States and one out of every 45 men in the United States were victims of stalking. The report estimated that the proportion could be about the same for cyberstalking, though there were no official statistics at that time. Technology has vastly changed since then, and the prevalence of cyberstalking has increased.

Parsons-Pollard and Moriarty (2009) argue that there is confusion about what constitutes cyberstalking, which then affects how laws against it are written. Cyberstalking is a more recently discussed method of virtual violence and is often considered the "most dangerous type of cybercrime" (Cox, 2014, p. 278). Just as traditional bullying and cyberbullying share some similarities, traditional stalking and cyberstalking do as well. Broadly defined, **cyberstalking** is "the use of the Internet, email, and other electronic communication devices to stalk another person" (Ashcroft, 2001, p. 1). According to this definition, the only difference between traditional stalking and cyberstalking is that cyberstalking is perpetrated online. D'Ovidio and Doyle (2003) add to this definition by including the actions of annoying, alarming, or threatening an individual or group of individuals. Tapp (2011) adds that the behavior is "persistent," "repeated," and "unsolicited" (p. 74). Cyberstalking behaviors are generally characterized by a desire to control the victim (Gerstein & Gerstein, 2011; United States Attorney General, 1999). Philips and Morrissey (2004) caution that cyberstalking can often lead to traditional, in-person stalking and other dangerous behaviors.

Nobles, Reyns, Fox, and Fisher (2014) discuss the difficulties in operationalizing cyberstalking due to the many social media platforms and personal devices like cell phones. From a legal standpoint, it is difficult to prosecute a cyberstalker without considering all of these aspects in the definition. The virtual nature of the crime and its distinction from traditional stalking affects the victim, the laws, the distribution of resources, and how the crime itself is defined (Parsons-Pollard & Moriarty, 2009).

Characteristics of Victims

Because cyberstalking happens in a virtual world, victims can potentially be anyone with Internet access. Due to the relative recency of the Internet, research on virtual violence victimization is limited, but it is rapidly becoming a topic of interest. Existing literature mostly focuses on specific populations, such as college students or adolescents, which makes it difficult to generalize results to all victims (Reyns, 2010). Below is a summary of the existing literature on the topic.

Prevalence

As an offense that has only been in existence for a decade or so, the prevalence of cyberstalking is important to discuss. Nobles et al. (2014) found that 19 percent of the participants in their national study had been victims of cyberstalking, which they argue is consistent with the limited research, despite their obviously small population. Reyns, Henson, and Fisher (2012) found that 40.8 percent of the college students they surveyed had been victims of cyberstalking, and 46.3 percent of the victims were females. The organization Working to Halt Online Abuse (WHOA) has, until recently, received case information on victims of online harassment and cyberstalking. According to their cumulative statistics from completed questionnaires of victims, there were 3,393 reported incidents of cyberstalking/online harassment between the years 2000 and 2011.

Additionally, over the course of that same time period, California consistently had the highest number of victims and, with the exception of one year, the highest number of harassers.

Relationship to Offender

Just as with cyberbullying, the relationship between the cyberstalking victim and offender is important to analyze; however, the relationships between people involved in cyberstalking are different than those involved with cyberbullying. Moriarty and Freiberger (2008) utilized newspaper reports published between 1999 and 2006 to study cyberstalking victimization patterns. Their research found that 60 percent of the victims had no previous relationship with the offender who was cyberstalking them. Reyns et al., (2012) surveyed 974 Midwest undergraduate college students and also found victims most often did not know their offenders. The WHOA organization found nearly equal proportions of victims that knew the offender as those who did not.

Gender

The gender of both victims and offenders of cyberstalking is an important factor. Multiple studies have found that victims were more likely to be female, whereas offenders were more likely to be male (Moriarty & Freiberger, 2008; Reyns et al., 2012). WHOA found consistent results. In contrast, Strawhun, Adams, and Huss (2013) found no significant difference between genders for cyberstalking victimization, but females reported higher rates for cyberstalking perpetration, results not often found in literature. According to Finn (2004), college students who identify as gay, lesbian, bisexual, or transgender are twice as likely to experience cyberstalking or email harassment as their heterosexual counterparts.

Post-Stalking Behavior

Victims of cyberstalking react to their victimization in a variety of ways. The Nobles et al. (2014) study showed that cyberstalking victims participate in more self-protective behaviors, such as taking time away from work or school, changing normal activities, or changing their email address. The likelihood of these behaviors increased if there was fear reported, the victim was female, or there had been an attack.

Additional Characteristics

There are several other interesting points to note about cyberstalking victimization. Nobles et al. (2014) created a national sample and did not focus solely on college students, as many prior studies had done. They also compared traditional stalking incidents with cyberstalking victimization. In 2006, they utilized NCVS data and methods to sample and interview household members, 18 years and older, who had passed initial screening questions. Participants were given a supplemental stalking survey after the initial NCVS interview. The researchers found several interesting results. Cyberstalking victims were younger on average, and there were more White male victims when compared to traditional stalking victims. Cyberstalking victims also had significantly higher household incomes and education levels. Interestingly, victims in the Reyns et al. (2012) study were more likely to be non-White, non-single, and non-heterosexual.

CRIMINOLOGICAL THEORIES & VIRTUAL VIOLENCE

Researchers have not agreed upon one single criminological theory to explain virtual violence, largely due to the short amount of time the crime has even been in existence. This makes it difficult to identify risk factors for victimization (Reyns, 2010). However, there are several theories that can be applied in an attempt to understand the nature of the crime and factors that contribute to it.

GENERAL THEORY OF CRIME

Gottfredson and Hirschi's (1990) **general theory of crime** is viewed as an all-encompassing theory that applies to all types of crime. The basic tenet of this theory is that low self-control, which is caused by poor parenting, leads to criminal behavior when coupled with opportunity. Marcum, Higgins, and Ricketts (2014) discuss the application of this theory to cybercrimes. They discovered that individuals who tested low on self-control measures were more likely to cyberstalk others, were more likely to have difficulty controlling their impulses to cyberstalk, and were less likely to see the negative consequences of those actions. Low self-control is a particularly logical explanation for cyberstalking and cyberbullying, as the behaviors are often found among adolescent populations.

SOCIAL LEARNING THEORY

Akers' (1998) **social learning theory** built upon Sutherland's (1947) theory that criminal behavior is learned. The basic tenet of social learning theory is that criminal behavior is learned through social interactions with peer groups who define criminal behavior as favorable. Individuals weigh rewards and punishments of the behaviors and imitate them. Marcum et al. (2014) discussed the application of social learning theory to cybercrimes. In their study, the researchers found that those who associated with deviant peers were more likely to cyberstalk. This was due to the deviant peers providing favorable definitions of the crime. Again, as cyber harassment is often found among adolescent populations who are particularly susceptible to socially learned behavior, this theory seems particularly applicable.

ROUTINE ACTIVITIES THEORY

Cohen and Felson's (1979) **routine activities theory** focuses on opportunities and situations that lead to crime. This theory argues that there are three elements that must come together for crime: motivated offenders, suitable targets, and a lack of guardianship. Agustina (2015) discusses the application of this theory to cyber violence. The idea here is that victims' behaviors online are fairly predictable, and the personalities of the victims determine their level of risk in the cyber environment. Finally, because cyberspace is so difficult to control, offenders can attack victims easily. The victims' routine activities make them susceptible to virtual abuse, as offenders are able to predict behaviors and find weak spots.

CULTURAL CRIMINOLOGY AND MEDIA, TECHNOLOGY, AND CRIMINAL BEHAVIOR

Few of the traditional criminological theories are equipped to shed light on the nature and unique elements of virtual violence. Helfgott (2008, 2015) suggests that multiple theoretical perspectives and lines of research are necessary to explain and examine media-mediated crimes. Drawing from the literature on cultural criminology (Ferrell, 1995, 1999; Ferrell & Sanders, 1995), the aesthetics of violence (Black, 1991), copycat and performance crime (Coleman, 2004; Surette, 1990, 2002, 2012), and celebrity culture (Harvey, 2002), Helfgott suggests that mass media and computer technology operate as risk factors for certain types of crime. These crimes can range on a continuum: at one end, perpetrators use media sources to get ideas for crime and, at the other end, media and technology elements represent the essence of the behavior to such an extent that the media-mediation itself can be considered a signature element that reflects the very essence of the crime.

This recent theoretical work on media-mediated crime, performance crime (Surette, 2013, 2015), and the notion of media and technology as risk factors for certain types of criminal behavior (Helfgott, 2008, 2015), offer a starting point for further examination of the ways in which media and technology operate as both as a method to commit crime and a signature element that defines the very nature of the crime. The traditional criminological theories such as general learning theory, social learning theory, and routine activity theory offer important frameworks with which to understand the elements of virtual violence that are shared with other types of offenses; however, the centrality of the role of media in this type of criminal behavior requires a more developed understanding of the media-mediated nature of virtual violence.

SUMMARY OF LITERATURE

Virtual violence is a relatively recent topic of interest in the criminal justice world. The creation of the Internet, and all the technological advances that continue to come with it, has opened a door to crimes in the virtual environment. Virtual offenders can more easily remain anonymous while harassing a larger number of people and their reach can extend globally. Future research is needed to examine virtual violence committed by different types of individuals. Much of the research to date utilizes college student samples, and more information is needed to examine different demographic populations and members of specific subcultures (e.g., video gamers, domestic extremist groups). In addition, research is needed to further investigate offender motivation, prevalence, risk factors for victims, and the effects virtual violence has on its victims. Finally, continued development of policy that attends to the empirical research available to date is needed to mitigate the effects of virtual violence. With the constantly changing technological environment, keeping up with changes over time in the use of technology as a tool for victimization will be a challenge. Theory, research, policy, and practice on virtual violence will need to be dynamic and cognizant of the constantly and quickly changing technology field.

METHODOLOGY & RESULTS

For this section, articles from *The New York Times* were analyzed for representation of victims of virtual violence. The purpose of this was to evaluate how accurately the media represents victims of virtual violence when compared to the literature on this topic. Variables were chosen based on items discussed in the literature, as well as variables pertaining to newsworthiness. Newsworthy stories are those that capture human interest, are current, affect larger numbers of people, and occur in closer emotional or geographical proximity. Finally, we draw comparisons between the literature and *The New York Times* articles to discuss the similarities and differences between the representation of victims of violence in the media and what we know empirically about the phenomena.

Based on our search parameters,[1] an initial sample of 1,629 articles was found. After eliminating articles that were irrelevant to the topic, a final

---

[1] To identify the articles for analysis, search parameters were set based upon all aspects of virtual violence that came up in the literature and could possibly come up in *The New York Times* articles. The following keyword search string was used in ProQuest to identify as many

sample of 90 articles was established. Articles were most often removed if they crossed over into other topics (e.g., terrorism), if the crimes occurred outside of the United States, or if they did not actually have to do with virtual violence. Unfortunately, most of the articles were found to not be relevant to this study. Articles that were kept for the sample pertained to violence that occurred online (i.e., cyberbullying, cyberstalking, threats of violence online), violence with an online connection, and videos of violence that were posted online. Cases of online pornography were also kept in the sample, as this is viewed as a form of violence, especially in the cases with juvenile victims.

To analyze these articles, data on 17 variables were collected. The variables include victim characteristics, such as whether or not the victim(s) was mentioned, how many victims there were, and the age, sex, and race of the victim(s). Similarly, offender characteristics were coded, such as how many offenders there were and the age, sex, and race of the offender(s). The relationship between the victim(s) and the offender(s) was also noted, as well as the threat type. To ensure that all forms of virtual violence were included, the parameters for the threat type were expanded to include cyberbullying, cyberstalking, threats of violence, videos or pictures of violence posted online, instances of picture or video distribution that was classified as pornography, and real-life violence that had some connection to the online world. Additional variables included the page number of the article, the overall theme of the article, the state in which the event took place, and whether the authorities were notified. Frequencies were examined to identify common occurrences in the analysis, and cross-tabulations were produced to describe the relationship between variables.

---

articles as possible about virtual victimization: (cyberstalk* OR cyberbull* OR "cyber stalk*" OR "cyber bull*") OR (swatting AND police) OR (online AND (bully OR bullied OR bullies OR bullying)) OR (online AND stalk*) OR ("social media" AND stalk*) OR (online AND threat*) OR ("social media" AND threat*) OR (blackmail* AND online) OR (blackmail* AND "social media") OR (facebook AND (blackmail* OR stalk* OR threat* OR bully OR bullied OR bullies OR bullying)) OR (twitter AND (blackmail* OR stalk* OR threat* OR bully OR bullied OR bullies OR bullying)) OR (myspace AND (blackmail* OR stalk* OR threat* OR bully OR bullied OR bullies OR bullying)) OR (snapchat AND (blackmail* OR stalk* OR threat* OR bully OR bullied OR bullies OR bullying)). Only articles published by the National Desk between January 1, 2001, and December 31, 2015, were used.

Table 9.1 contains the complete list of variables analyzed, as well as their possible responses. Those with responses not listed were open-ended, such as the title of the article or additional comments.

The first variable we looked at, which was related to newsworthiness, was the page number of the articles. All of the articles were in the "A"

TABLE 9.1 Variable and Responses

VARIABLES	POSSIBLE RESPONSES
Article title	—
Was the victim(s) mentioned at least once?	Yes; No
Number of victims	0–999
Number of offenders	0–999
Primary theme of the article	Discussion of victim; Discussion of offender; Court process; Policy/political debate; Discussion of issue overall; Discussion of specific case
Age of victim	0–999
Age of offender	0–999
Sex of victim	Male; Female; Transgender; Not mentioned
Sex of offender	Male; Female; Transgender; Not mentioned
Race of victim	White; Black; Asian; Hispanic; Other
Race of offender	White; Black; Asian; Hispanic; Other
Relationship of victim to offender	Not mentioned; Friend; Family; Current or former romantic partner; Acquaintance; Stranger; Other
Type of threat	Cyberbullying; Cyberstalking; Threats of violence; Video posted of violence; Pornography; Real life violence with some online aspect
State where crime/ event took place	All states in the United States
Were authorities notified?	Yes; No
Article page number	—
Comments	—

section of *The New York Times* and 25 articles, or approximately 28 percent, were on the front page. The second variable examined was the primary theme of the articles (see Table 9.2). The most common theme of the articles was a "discussion of a specific case" (n = 22), such as the case of the San Francisco Police Department officers accused of sending racist and homophobic text messages and forcing fighting matches between inmates (Williams, 2015). Closely behind were the themes of a "discussion of the offender" (n = 20), such as Jarvis Britton of Birmingham, Alabama, who posted threats to the president on Twitter (Brown, 2013); and a "discussion of the issue overall" (n = 20), such as the problem of "swatting," where practical jokers falsely report heinous crimes happening at celebrity homes in order to incite the dispatch of SWAT teams (Nagourney & Lovett, 2013). The inclusion of a "court process," such as the criminal trial of Lori Drew, who is the mother accused of creating a fake MySpace profile and cyberbullying 12-year-old Megan Meier until she committed suicide (Steinhauer, 2008), made up 17.8 percent (n = 16) of the articles. The inclusion of "policy or political debate," such as whether or not "sexting" among teens should be a felony (Eckholm, 2015), was the least common theme, showing up in only three articles (3.3%). Only 10 percent of the articles focused on the victim (n = 9), such as Abraham Biggs, the 19-year-old student from Pembroke Pines, Florida, who live-streamed his own suicide (Stelter, 2008).

TABLE 9.2 Frequencies of Article Themes

	FREQUENCY	PERCENT
Discussion of specific case	22	24.4
Discussion of offender	20	22.2
Discussion of issue overall	20	22.2
Court process	16	17.8
Discussion of victim	9	10.0
Policy/Political debate	3	3.3
Total	90	100.0

TABLE 9.3 Primary Theme of the Article By Placement on Front Page

PRIMARY THEME OF THE ARTICLE	PLACEMENT		TOTAL
	FRONT PAGE	NOT ON FRONT PAGE	
Discussion of specific case	3 (13.6%)	19 (86.4%)	22
Discussion of offender	9 (45%)	11 (55%)	20
Discussion of issue overall	10 (50%)	10 (50%)	20
Court process	0 (0%)	16 (100%)	16
Discussion of victim	3 (33.3%)	6 (66.7%)	9
Policy/political debate	0 (0%)	3 (100%)	3
Total	25	65	90

Table 9.3 shows the relationship between the first two variables discussed: themes of the articles and the number of times they appeared on the front page. The theme that was most commonly seen on the front page (n = 10) is the discussion of the issue overall.

Table 9.4 shows the frequency of the *type of threat discussed* in the article variable. Cyberbullying was the most common type of threat discussed, with 35.6 percent of the articles focusing on it. Threats of violence were the second most common type of threat discussed, at 30 percent of the articles. Cyberstalking was only mentioned in one article (1.1%). Table 9.4 also shows the relationship of the victim to the offender. It is important to note that the relationship "Family" was coded for, but there were no articles analyzed where the victim and the offender were family members. The most common relationship found was the Stranger relationship, with 47.8 percent (n = 43) of the articles focusing on victims and offenders that did not know each other.

Next, the connection between the relationship of the victim and the offender, and the type of threat discussed in the article was examined. Table 9.5 shows the most significant results of this variable. In 19 articles, or 21.1 percent of the total articles, the threats of violence were made online where the victim and the offender were strangers. Additionally,

TABLE 9.4 Frequencies of the Type of Threat Discussed and Victim/Offender Relationship

	FREQUENCY	PERCENT
Cyberbullying	32	35.6
Threats of violence	27	30.0
Real life violence with some online aspect	18	20.0
Pornography	10	11.1
Video posted of violence	2	2.2
Cyberstalking	1	1.1
Total	90	100.0
Stranger	43	47.8
Friend	14	15.6
Acquaintance	13	14.4
Not mentioned	8	8.9
Current or former romantic partner	6	6.7
Other	6	6.7
Total	90	100.0

20 of the 32 cyberbullying articles (62.5%) had offenders that were either friends or acquaintances of the victims.

Table 9.6 shows the final part of the analysis, inspecting the relationship between the primary theme of the article and the number of victims mentioned in the article. First, in 13 of the 20 articles where the focus was on the offender, there were four or more victims. Additionally, in 15 of the 22 articles where the focus of the article was on the discussion of the specific case, there were one to three victims mentioned.

ANALYSIS OF VICTIMS OF VIRTUAL VIOLENCE

This analysis of the media's representation of victims of virtual violence had several interesting results. First, the general topic of virtual violence

TABLE 9.5 Relationship of Victim to Offender By Type of Threat

			TYPE OF THREAT				
RELATIONSHIP OF VICTIM TO OFFENDER	CYBERBULLYING	CYBERSTALKING	THREATS OF VIOLENCE	VIDEO POSTED OF VIOLENCE	PORNOGRAPHY	REAL LIFE VIOLENCE WITH SOME ONLINE ASPECT	TOTAL
Stranger	5 (11.6%)	0 (0%)	19 (44.2%)	1 (2.3%)	5 (11.6%)	13 (30.2%)	43
Friend	10 (71.4%)	0 (0%)	0 (0%)	0 (0%)	3 (21.4%)	1 (7.1%)	14
Acquaintance	10 (76.9%)	0 (0%)	0 (0%)	0 (0%)	0 (0%)	3 (23.1%)	13
Not mentioned	3 (37.5%)	0 (0%)	3 (37.5%)	1 (12.5%)	1 (12.5%)	0 (0%)	8
Romantic partner	0 (0%)	1 (16.7%)	4 (66.7%)	0 (0%)	1 (16.7%)	0 (0%)	6
Other	4 (66.7%)	0 (0%)	1 (16.7%)	0 (0%)	0 (0%)	1 (16.7%)	6
Total	32	1	27	2	10	18	90

TABLE 9.6 Primary Theme of the Article By Number of Victims

PRIMARY THEME OF THE ARTICLE	NUMBER OF VICTIMS			TOTAL
	0	1–3	4 OR MORE	
Discussion of specific case	0 (0%)	15 (68.2%)	7 (31.8%)	22
Discussion of offender	2 (10%)	5 (25%)	13 (65%)	20
Discussion of issue overall	0 (0%)	7 (35%)	13 (65%)	20
Court process	1 (6.25%)	14 (87.5%)	1 (6.25%)	16
Discussion of victim	0 (0%)	9 (100%)	0 (0%)	9
Policy/political debate	0 (0%)	1 (33.3%)	2 (66.7%)	3
Total	3	51	36	90

was prevalent in the news stories, as seen by the number of articles posted on the front page and all others within the A section. This would imply that virtual violence is a topic of interest and has a significant place in reporting. Second, as the analysis showed, the main focus of the articles was the discussion of a specific case. Next were the discussions of the issue overall and of the offender, which both had an equal number of articles. The articles that focused on the issue overall often began with a mention of a specific case or victim and then quickly transitioned into a discussion of the larger issue. In many articles, the focus was on the offender, often in an effort to provide an explanation for the offense or going deep into their personal histories. In very few cases was the focus of articles on the victim, thus the analysis shows that the media does not find victims as newsworthy as offenders or other issues that were covered more frequently.

The next two variables were the frequencies of the type of threat discussed and the frequencies of the relationship of the victim to the offender. Cyberbullying is overwhelmingly the most common form of virtual violence discussed in the literature, and it appeared to be the same in the articles analyzed. Interesting to note, the second most common form of virtual violence discussed in the literature, cyberstalking, was hardly mentioned in the articles. This is particularly concerning, as cyberstalking is viewed as the most dangerous and concerning form of virtual violence. The representation of relationships between victims and offenders was also noteworthy. The literature shows that victims usually know their offenders as friends or acquaintances. However, the articles focused on a lack of relationship, where victims and offenders were strangers. This is likely due to the shocking nature and inability to predict an offense between strangers. The evil offender attacking an innocent stranger is deemed more newsworthy.

Next, the connection between the relationship of the victim and the offender, and the type of threat discussed in the article was examined. The articles reported that most of the cyberbullying cases discussed were between friends or acquaintances. This was consistent with the literature, which shows cyberbullying generally happens between individuals that know each other on some level. However, cyberstalking is drastically underrepresented in the articles, despite the fact that the literature shows it is the second most common and the most dangerous form of virtual violence.

Finally, the relationship between the overall theme of the article and the number of victims mentioned was examined. The goal was to see whether more victims made the focus of the article more victim-related. It was found that more victims actually made the article more offender-focused. When there were fewer victims, the articles were more focused on the case as a whole, not focusing on any particular aspect. Additionally, the articles that focused on the court process more often comprised multiple articles on a specific case, with many articles providing updates of the court proceedings and sentencing. For example, the Megan Meier case was represented in multiple articles. This case was about a 13-year-old girl who committed suicide after her former friend's mother posed as a teenage boy on MySpace, seduced Megan, and then turned on her. The case became high-profile, as it was an adult parent who was the offender and the event led to the child victim's suicide.

After coding the articles, several variables were removed from the analysis. The high-profile cases discussed actually affected several variables. For example, the results of the variable that recorded the state in the United States where the event took place were skewed. As more articles were written on specific cases, the count for those specific states increased, thus giving the appearance that a state had more events. Additionally, the variables for the ages of both the victim(s) and the offender(s) was determined to be useless for analysis. Ages were rarely mentioned at all, unless the case was particularly shocking (e.g., the suicide of Megan Meier). For example, in one article about a mass shooter, the ages of multiple people interviewed were listed, but the age of the offender was not. This is especially noteworthy because the literature focuses so much on age, specifically middle school and high school students. To not mention age is directly in contrast to the literature. The variables for the races of both the victim(s) and the offender(s) were also discarded. Race was rarely explicitly stated in articles.

Overall, the analysis had a few major findings. The focus of *The New York Times* articles is rarely on victims. Many articles look at the case as a whole or focus on the offender. If the victim is mentioned, it is in passing. Additionally, high-profile cases get more attention. This is likely because these cases are particularly shocking and are therefore deemed newsworthy. However, this leads to a misrepresentation of the actual victimization. Multiple articles were written on the same case, especially as the case went through court proceedings. This was even more likely if the case had any connection to terrorism, if the event led to the suicide of the victim, or if there were adult offenders with child victims. Another interesting finding was that race, either of the victim or the offender, was hardly mentioned. It was only mentioned if the motivation was particularly grounded in race. This is particularly surprising, as race is such an important and salient topic of interest. Finally, in comparison to the literature, *The New York Times* had fewer articles where victims were children. The literature shows that victims of virtual violence, especially cyberbullying, are mostly middle school and high school students.

There were a few limitations to this analysis. First, the articles came from only one publication, *The New York Times*. Results from this study may not be indicative of the representation of victims across the media overall. More newspapers, magazines, or other media outlets should be examined for a more thorough conclusion about the representation of victims. Additionally, it is a newspaper, a written publication, and therefore it may not be representative of the multiple platforms of media. When things like space and deadlines come into play, some stories must be prioritized. Finally, a single researcher completed the analysis of the sample articles, leaving open the possibility for bias; other researchers may have coded the analyzed variables differently.

CONCLUSION

Having only been in existence for the last couple of decades, virtual violence is increasingly becoming a topic of interest in the United States. As beneficial as growth in technology is, it also creates a whole new avenue for criminal behavior. Victims are more accessible, and offenders are more hidden than ever. Both victim and offender feel protected behind a computer screen. We are only just beginning to realize the prevalence of virtual violence in our world. Due to its recent emergence, research on this type of violence is limited; however, due to the public's growing interest, the research is increasing. Current virtual violence research concentrates on victimization, looking into characteristics of victims, their coping mechanisms, and their relationships with their offenders. Interestingly, the media often does not focus on this aspect of virtual violence, but instead it frequently spotlights the offenders. The media commonly centers on the characteristics of offenders and their crimes that portray them as evil or even crazy.

This study has several implications for future research. First, more research is needed on other types of virtual violence. The research presented here focuses on cyberbullying and cyberstalking, the two most common forms of virtual violence. However, there are more virtual crimes taking place, as demonstrated by *The New York Times* articles. Other types of violence, such as threats online, pornography-related crimes, and real-life violence with ties to the online world should be reviewed further. Additionally, more research needs to be done on other age, subcultural, or population groups besides middle school and high school students.

Moreover, research should examine why the media deems some cases more newsworthy than others. What characteristics do some victims or offenders have that the media chooses to focus on over others? The media is a for-profit business, but research should examine why some cases are seen as more profitable than others. Finally, it will be important in the advancement of empirical research on virtual violence to establish a theoretical and empirical framework that is dynamic and able to make sense of the ever-changing technological environment and the ways in which this environment impacts both offending behavior in terms of method and motive as well as the nature of victimization of virtual violence.

REFERENCES

Addington, L. A. (2013). Reporting and clearance of cyberbullying incidents: Applying "offline" theories to online victims. *Journal of Contemporary Criminal Justice, 29*(4), 454–474.

Agustina, J. R. (2015). Understanding cyber victimization: Digital architectures and the disinhibition effect. *International Journal of Cyber Criminology, 9*(1), 35–54.

Akers, R. (1998). *Social learning and social structure: A general theory of crime and deviance.* Routledge.

American Academy of Pediatrics, Council on Communications and Media. (2016). Virtual violence. *Pediatrics, 138*(2), 1–4.

Ashcroft, J. (2001). *Stalking and domestic violence: A report to Congress* (NCJ 186157). Washington, DC: U.S. Department of Justice. Retrieved January 26, 2016, from http://www.ncjrs.gov/pdffiles1/ojp/186157.pdf

Associated Press. (2011, November 21). Inmates use Facebook to harass their victims, intimidate victims from behind bars. *New York Daily News.* Retrieved from http://www.nydailynews.com/news/national/inmates-facebook-harass-victims-intimidate-witnesses-behind-bars-article-1.980641

Bamford, A. (2004). Cyber-bullying, AHISA Pastoral Care National Conference. Retrieved from www.ahisa.com.au/documents/conferences/PCC2004/bamford.pdf

Barboza, G. E. (2015). The association between school exclusion, delinquency and subtypes of cyber- and F2F-victimizations: Identifying and predicting risk profiles and subtypes using latent class analysis. *Child Abuse & Neglect, 39,* 109–122.

Bauman, S., Toomey, R., & Walker, J. (2013). Associations among bullying, cyberbullying, and suicide in high school students. *Journal of Adolescence, 36,* 341–350.

Black, J. (1991). *The aesthetics of murder: A study in romantic literature and contemporary culture.* Baltimore: Johns Hopkins University Press.

Brown, R. (2013, July 3). 140 characters spell charges and jail. *The New York Times,* A15.

Cassidy, W., Faucher, C., & Jackson, M. (2013). Cyberbullying among youth: A comprehensive review of current international research and its implications and application to policy and practice. *School Psychology International, 34*(6), 575–612.

Cohen, L. E., & Felson, M. (1979). Social change and crime rate trends: A routine activity approach. *American Sociological Review, 44*, 588–608.

Coleman, L. (2004). *The copycat effect: How the media and popular culture trigger mayhem in tomorrow's headlines.* New York: Paraview Pocket Books.

Cox, C. (2014). Protecting victims of cyberstalking, cyberharassment, and online impersonation through prosecutions and effective laws. *Jurimetrics: The Journal of Law, Science & Technology, 54*(3), 277–302.

D'Ovidio, R., & Doyle, J. (2003). A study on cyberstalking: Understanding investigative hurdles. *FBI Law Enforcement Bulletin, 72*(3), 10–17.

Eckholm, E. (2015, November 15). Prosecutors weigh teenage sexting: Folly or felony? *The New York Times*, A13.

Ferrell, J. (1995). Culture, crime, and cultural criminology. *Journal of Criminal Justice and Popular Culture, 3*(2), 25–42.

Ferrell, J. (1999). Cultural criminology. *Annual Review of Sociology, 25*, 395–418.

Ferrell, J., & Sanders, C. R. (1995). *Cultural criminology.* Boston: Northeastern University Press.

Finn, J. (2004). A survey of online harassment at a university campus. *Journal of Interpersonal Violence, 19*(4), 468–483.

Freed, J. (2017). Gamergate, violence and video games: Re-thinking a culture of misogyny. *Media Report to Women, 45*(3), 6–23.

Gerstein, R., & Gerstein, L. (2011). Cyberstalking: An increasing problem for colleges and universities. *Criminal Justice Research Review, 12*(6), 94–104.

Gillespie, A. A. (2006). Cyber-bullying and harassment of teenagers: The legal response. *Journal of Social Welfare & Family Law, 28*(2), 123–136.

Gottfredson, M. R., & Hirschi, T. (1990). *A general theory of crime.* Stanford University Press.

Harvey, D. (2002). *Obsession: Celebrities and their stalkers.* Dublin, Ireland: Merlin Publishing.

Helfgott, J. B. (2008). *Criminal behavior: Theories, typologies, and criminal justice.* Thousand Oaks, CA: SAGE.

Helfgott, J. B. (2015). Criminal behavior and the copycat effect: Literature review and theoretical framework for empirical investigation. *Aggression and Violent Behavior, 22*, 46–64.

Hemphill, S. A., Tollit, M., Kotevski, A., & Heerde, J. A. (2015). Predictors of traditional and cyber-bullying victimization. *Journal of Interpersonal Violence, 30*(15), 2567–2590.

Litwiller, B., & Brausch, A. (2013). Cyber bullying and physical bullying in adolescent suicide: The role of violent behavior and substance use. *Journal of Youth & Adolescence, 42*(5), 675–684.

Marcum, C. D., Higgins, G. E., Freiburger, T., & Ricketts, M. L. (2014). Exploration of the cyberbullying victim/offender overlap by sex. *American Journal of Criminal Justice, 39*(3), 538–548.

Marcum, C. D., Higgins, G. E., & Ricketts, M. L. (2014). Juveniles and cyber stalking in the United States: An analysis of theoretical predictors of patterns of online perpetration. *International Journal of Cyber Criminology, 8*(1), 47–56.

Moore, R., Guntupalli, N. T., & Lee, T. (2010). Parental regulation and online activities: Examining factors that influence a youth's potential to become a victim of online harassment. *International Journal of Cyber Criminology, 4*(1/2), 685–698.

Moriarty, L. J., & Freiberger, K. (2008). Cyberstalking: Utilizing newspaper accounts to establish victimization patterns. *Victims & Offenders, 3*(2/3), 131–141.

Nagourney, A., & Lovett, I. (2013, April 11). 'Swatting' hoax tests the police and stars alike. *The New York Times*, A1.

National Crime Prevention Council. (2007, February). Teens and cyberbullying: Executive summary of a report on research conducted for NCPC. Retrieved from http://archive. ncpc.org/resources/files/pdf/bullying/Teens%20and%20Cyberbullying%20Research%20 Study.pdf

Nobles, M. R., Reyns, B. W., Fox, K. A., & Fisher, B. S. (2014). Protection against pursuit: A conceptual and empirical comparison of cyberstalking and stalking victimization among a national sample. *Justice Quarterly, 31*(6), 986–1014.

Nuccitelli, M. (2012). Cyber bullying tactics. *Forensic Examiner, 21*(3), 24–28.

Ortega, R., Elipe, P., Mora-Merchán, J. A., Genta, M. L., Brighi, A., Guarini, A., & Tippett, N. (2012). The emotional impact of bullying and cyberbullying on victims: A European cross-national study. *Aggressive Behavior, 38*(5), 342–356.

Parris, L., Varjas, K., Meyers, J., & Cutts, H. (2012). High school students' perceptions of coping with cyberbullying. *Youth & Society, 44*(2), 284–306.

Parsons-Pollard, N., & Moriarty, L. J. (2009). Cyberstalking: Utilizing what we do know. *Victims & Offenders, 4*(4), 435–441.

Philips, F., & Morrissey, G. (2004). Cyberstalking and cyberpredators: A threat to safe sexuality on the Internet. *Convergence: The International Journal of Research into New Media Technologies, 10,* 66–79.

Quinn, Z. (2017). *Crash override: How Gamergate (nearly) destroyed my life, and how we can win the fight against online hate.* New York: PublicAffairs.

Randa, R., & Reyns, B. W. (2014). Cyberbullying victimization and adaptive avoidance behaviors at school. *Victims & Offenders, 9*(3), 255–275.

Reyns, B. W. (2010). A situational crime prevention approach to cyberstalking victimization: Preventive tactics for Internet users and online place managers. *Crime Prevention & Community Safety, 12*(2), 99–118.

Reyns, B. W., Henson, B., & Fisher, B. S. (2012). Stalking in the twilight zone: Extent of cyberstalking victimization and offending among college students. *Deviant Behavior, 33*(1), 1–25.

Roberts, L. (2008). Jurisdictional and definitional concerns with computer-mediated interpersonal crimes: An analysis on cyber stalking. *International Journal of Cyber Criminology, 2*(1), 271–285.

Shelton, D. L. (1996). Virtual violence. *American Medical News, 39*(41), 14–17.

Sontag, L. M., Clemans, K. H., Graber, J. A., & Lyndon, S. T. (2011). Traditional and cyber aggressors and victims: A comparison of psychosocial characteristics. *Journal of Youth & Adolescence, 40*(4), 392–404.

Steinhauer, J. (2008, November 27). Woman found guilty in web fraud tied to suicide. *The New York Times*, A25.

Stelter, B. (2008, November 25). Web suicide viewed live and reaction spur a debate. *The New York Times*, A16.

Strawhun, J., Adams, N., & Huss, M. T. (2013). The assessment of cyberstalking: An expanded examination including social networking, attachment, jealousy, and anger in relation to violence and abuse. *Violence & Victims, 28*(4), 715–730.

Surette, R. (1990). Estimating the magnitude and mechanisms of copycat crime. In R. Surette (Ed.), *The media and criminal justice policy: Recent research and social effects.* Springfield, IL: CC Thomas Publishers.

Surette, R. (2002). Self-reported copycat crime among a population of serious and violent adult offenders. *Crime & Delinquency, 48*(1), 46–69.

Surette, R. (2012). Cause or catalyst: The interaction of real world and media crime models. *American Journal of Criminal Justice, 38*(3), 392–409.

Surette, R. (2013). Pathways to copycat crime. In J. B. Helfgott (Ed.), *Criminal psychology, Vol. 1. Theory and research, Vol. 2. Typologies, mental disorders, and profiles, Vol. 3. Implications for forensic assessment, policing, and the courts, Vol. 4. Implications for juvenile justice, corrections, and reentry* (pp. 251–273). Santa Barbara, CA: Praeger/ABC-CLIO.

Surette, R. (2015). Performance crime and justice. *Current Issues in Criminal Justice, 27*(2).

Sutherland, E. H. (1947). *Principles of Criminology, 4th Ed.* Philadelphia, PA: J. B. Lippincott.

Tapp, H. D. (2011). Because knowledge is power: Stalking and harassment in the digital age. *Kentucky Law Enforcement Magazine, 10*(4), 73–77.

Todd, C. (2015). GamerGate and resistance to the diversification of gaming culture. *Women's Studies Journal, 29*(1), 64–67.

Turner, M. G., Exum, M. L., Brame, R., & Holt, T. J. (2013). Bullying victimization and adolescent mental health: General and typological effects across sex. *Journal of Criminal Justice, 41*(1), 53–59.

United States Attorney General. (1999, August). Cyberstalking: A new challenge for law enforcement and industry. Retrieved from http://www.cyber-rights.org/documents/cyberstalkingreport.htm

United States Department of Education. (2013, August). Student reports of bullying and cyber-bullying: Results from the 2011 school crime supplement to the national crime victimization survey. (Publication No. NCES 2013-329). Retrieved from http://nces.ed.gov/pubs2013/2013329.pdf

Urban Institute. (2013, July). Technology, teen dating violence and abuse, and bullying. Retrieved from https://www.ncjrs.gov/pdffiles1/nij/grants/243296.pdf

Williams, T. (2015, May 8). Inquiry to examine the extent of racial bias in the San Francisco police. *The New York Times*, A13.

Working to Halt Online Abuse. (n.d.) Online harassment/cyberstalking statistics. Retrieved from http://www.haltabuse.org/resources/stats/index.shtml

Wright, M., & Li, Y. (2013). The association between cyber victimization and subsequent cyber aggression: The moderating effect of peer rejection. *Journal of Youth & Adolescence, 42*(5), 662–674.

Yahner, J., Dank, M., Zweig, J. M., & Lachman, P. (2015). The co-occurrence of physical and cyber dating violence and bullying among teens. *Journal of Interpersonal Violence, 30*(7), 1079–1089.

Ybarra, M. L., Mitchell, K. J., Wolak, J., & Finkelhor, D. (2006). Examining characteristics and associated distress related to Internet harassment: Findings from the Second Youth Internet Safety Survey. *Pediatrics, 118*(4), e1169–e1177.

KEY TERMS

- *Cyberbullying:* It is broadly defined as "a form of bullying that uses electronic means such as email, mobile phone calls, text messages, instant messenger contact, photos, social networking sites, and personal web pages, with the intent of causing harm to another person through repeated hostile conduct" (Ortega et al., 2012, p. 342).

- *Cyberstalking:* Broadly defined, cyberstalking is "the use of the Internet, email, and other electronic communication devices to stalk another person" (Ashcroft, 2001, p. 1).

- *General Theory of Crime:* Viewed as an all-encompassing theory that applies to all types of crime. The basic tenet of this theory is that low self-control, which is caused by poor parenting, leads to criminal behavior when coupled with opportunity (Gottfredson & Hirschi, 1990).

- *Routine Activities Theory:* Focuses on opportunities and situations that lead to crime. This theory argues that there are three elements that must come together for crime: motivated offenders, suitable targets, and a lack of guardianship (Cohen & Felson, 1979).

- *Social Learning Theory:* The basic tenet of social learning theory is that criminal behavior is learned through social interactions with peer groups who define criminal behavior as favorable. Individuals weigh rewards and punishments of the behaviors and imitate them (Akers, 1998).

- *Virtual Violence:* The concept of "virtual violence" and the harm it brings to victims is only beginning to be understood. Virtual violence does not have to involve a physical act and can have consequences for victims. Virtual violence has been defined as "all forms of violence that are not experienced physically and, in particular, to encompass the extent to which children increasingly experience violence in more realistic ways than they have before" (American Academy of Pediatrics, Council on Communications and Media, 2016).

THE NEW YORK TIMES ARTICLES

Brown, R. (2013, July 3). 140 characters spell charges and jail. *The New York Times*. Retrieved from https://www.nytimes.com/2013/07/03/us/felony-counts-and-jail-in-140-characters.html

Eckholm, E. (2015, November 15). Prosecutors weigh teenage sexting: Folly or felony? *The New York Times*. Retrieved from https://www.nytimes.com/2015/11/14/us/prosecutors-in-teenage-sexting-cases-ask-foolishness-or-a-felony.html

Nagourney, A., & Lovett, I. (2013, April 11). 'Swatting' hoax tests the police and stars alike. *The New York Times*. Retrieved from https://www.nytimes.com/2013/04/11/us/hollywood-swatting-hoax-strains-both-police-and-stars.html

Steinhauer, J. (2008, November 27). Verdict in MySpace suicide case. *The New York Times*. Retrieved from https://www.nytimes.com/2008/11/27/us/27myspace.html

Stelter, B. (2008, November 25). Web suicide viewed live and reaction spur a debate. *The New York Times*. Retrieved from https://www.nytimes.com/2008/11/25/us/25suicides.html

DISCUSSION QUESTIONS

1. What types of policies or measures could be put into place to help to prevent cyberbullying amongst middle and high school students? What are some of the limitations to any policy aimed at controlling online behavior?
2. Do you think identity theft is a form of virtual violence? Explain your answer.
3. In regard to cases that cross over international boundaries and include victims and/or offenders in different countries, how are offenders brought to justice? How might victims find resolution?

Try searching the web for an example or two and discuss your findings.

4. In your opinion, which of the criminological theories listed by the authors makes the most sense in explaining why people commit virtual violence? Is one type of behavior/crime, such as cyberstalking or cyberbullying, better explained by your selected theory than another? Why?

SECTION III

Violence Against the Other

CHAPTER 10

Victims of Hate Crime

Devan M. Duenas, Department of Criminal Justice, Seattle University;
Jeff Gruenewald, School of Public and Environmental Affairs, Indiana
University-Purdue University, Indianapolis

INTRODUCTION

Scholarly research on **hate crime** (or bias crime) has increased precipi-
tously over the last quarter century. For evidence, one must only look to the
several books and edited volumes covering what has been learned about
hate crime victims, offenders, motives, and criminal justice responses to
these crimes (e.g., Gerstenfeld, Grant, & Chiang, 2003; Hall, 2014; Perry,
2003). The increase in empirical research is due in part to a rise in official reporting by American law enforcement agencies and the publishing
of these reports in the Federal Bureau of Investigation's (FBI) **Uniform
Crime Reports Hate Crime Statistics.**[1] Though not a new form of crime
in the United States, hate crime has been integrated into the public's ver-
nacular over the last 25 years. Even with some increases in the public's
understanding and progress in reporting practices, hate crime remains
underreported by police agencies and is sometimes misunderstood by the
general public.

We suggest in this chapter that continuing ambiguities about hate
crime stem largely from two forces that make defining and describing
the reality of hate crime challenging. First, there is a reluctance by some
law enforcement agencies to report hate crime when it occurs. Decision-
making is shaped not only by the views of officers toward hate crime
laws, but also by agency rules and the sociopolitical contexts in which
their agency operates. A second force shaping perceptions of hate
crime is media coverage. As is the case for other forms of serious crime,

---

[1] The FBI's Hate Crime Statistics reports are available since 1995 at https://ucr.fbi.gov/
hate-crime.

most people never experience the harmful effects of hate crime personally, but instead learn about this form of victimization from various media sources. For this reason, it is important to empirically investigate how hate crime is (mis)represented to audiences by media.

In what follows, we examine how hate crime is constructed by police reporting and news stories, while also recognizing some of the organizational and external forces shaping official and mediated accounts of these crimes. These data sources are comparatively analyzed to identify similarities and differences across sources of information about hate crime. The FBI's current definition of a hate crime as "a criminal offense against a person or property motivated in whole or in part by an offender's bias against a race, religion, disability, sexual orientation, ethnicity, gender, or gender identity"[2] is adopted. We begin by reviewing trends and patterns of official hate crime reports, accounting for potential heterogeneity in the nature of these hate crimes across victim groups. We then content analyze news print stories about hate crime from *The New York Times* published between 2001 and 2015. To guide our analysis, we ask, *how do official reports and news media represent hate crime in the United States, and in what ways do news media reflect patterns and trends in official reporting?*

The chapter unfolds by first addressing the challenges to police reporting of hate crime and how they affect national crime statistics. Second, we review the findings published by the FBI and relevant literature about hate crime. Third, we discuss how news media representations of crime and crime participants are often distorted and why. Fourth, we provide findings from an original content analysis of stories published in *The New York Times* to comparatively examine official and media reporting of hate crime in the United States. Finally, we end this chapter by discussing several ways that researchers, law enforcement, newsmakers, and other experts can improve the quality of hate crime data and advance the study of this important topic.

---

[2] The FBI's definition of hate crime can be found at https://www.fbi.gov/investigate/civil-rights/hate-crimes.

OFFICIAL HATE CRIME REPORTING

Despite several advances in police reporting of hate crime over the past few decades, official data do not provide an accurate assessment of discriminatory crimes in the United States. One issue is the underreporting of hate crime to police (McDevitt, Balboni, Bennett, 2000). While the FBI's UCR Hate Crime Statistics reported an annual average of 8,834 hate crime incidents between 2000 and 2003, one study relying on data from National Crime Victimization Survey (NCVS) found an annual average of 191,000 hate crimes during this time (Harlow, 2005). Comparing police and victimization data,[3] this research has shown that only 44 percent of the hate crime occurring in the United States is reported to the police, while an estimated 60 percent of violent hate crime is reported to police (see also Meuchel-Wilson, 2014; Perry, 2001; Thornton, Voigt, & Harper, 2013; Turpin-Petrosino, 2015; Zaykowski, 2010).

Victim **underreporting** may occur for several reasons, such as victims anticipating that police will minimize their victimization experiences or will be unwilling or unable to help them. Other victims may be hesitant to report because they want to avoid police attention (Perry, 2003). For instance, some groups, such as undocumented immigrants, often choose not to report hate crime victimization out of fear of deportation (Cohen, 2015). Others, including racial minorities or sexual orientation and gender identity minorities, have historically had issues with law enforcement being unsympathetic, unresponsive, or even hostile toward them. It is also possible that some victims may not perceive actions against them as crimes or fear that reporting their victimization will only invite further suffering.

In addition to victim reluctance to report, a lack of uniformity in law enforcement treatment of hate crime also contributes to the unavailability of reliable official crime data (Bell, 2002; Boyd, Berk, & Hamner, 1996; Franklin, 2002; Haider-Markel, 2002; Martin, 1995; Nolan & Akiyama, 1999). In particular, we know that while some large police departments have specialized units or specific officers devoted to investigating possible hate crimes, the vast majority of departments do not (McDevitt et al.,

---

[3] The UCR and the NCVS report similar percentages of hate crime by victim group.

2000). There are also variations in the adoption of hate crime definitions across law enforcement agencies (Jenness & Grattet, 2001). In effect, there remains ambiguity in hate crime policies and enforcement practices (Berk, Boyd, & Hamner, 1994), as police agencies tend to reflect the sociopolitical contexts of their broader communities (Hamm, 1998).

Other research suggests that challenges in sorting complex crime motives and the idiosyncratic views of individual police officers shapes official hate crime reporting practices (Berk et al., 1994; Boyd et al., 1996; Haider-Markel, 2002; Martin, 1996). That is, there are several different ways officers may go about deciding if and how to classify a crime as hate-motivated. Some officers, for instance, may follow the "but for" rule, such that crimes are considered hate crimes only when they would not have occurred but for animus toward victims. Other questions involve whether hate crime can simultaneously involve motives other than prejudice or discrimination. The reality is that police must investigate messy crimes where motives are elusive and clouded by conflicting witness reports, multiple and intersecting statuses of victims, and sometimes provocation from victims.

PATTERNS OF HATE CRIME IN THE UNITED STATES

Despite the challenges of measuring hate crime based on official reports, these data are currently the most comprehensive source of available information on these crimes. In this section, we draw from a national assessment of hate crime conducted annually by the Federal Bureau of Investigation (2015a; 2015b; 2015c) and review what is known about those crimes that target some of the most common victim groups. We begin by noting that an average of 7,009 hate crime incidents were reported per year by law enforcement agencies in the United States over the course of our 15-year study period. During these years, an average of 13,543 agencies participated in the Hate Crime Statistics Program, with only about 1,946 agencies on average reporting one or more hate crimes per year. States reporting the largest average number of incidents during this period included two of the most populous, California and New York, while states with the lowest average of reported incidents included Mississippi, Alabama, Wyoming, and Alaska.

As for whom is responsible for committing hate crime in the United States, official data indicate that the average offender from 2001 to 2015 was White (Non-Hispanic or Latino). This finding also seems to align with previous official statistics and victim surveys (see Harlow, 2005; Meuchel-Wilson, 2014). Hate crime offenders choose to commit crime in a variety of locations, including residences, throughways (e.g., highways, roads, alleys, streets, sidewalks), educational centers, religious institutions, and other public and private locations. Over the course of the 15-year study period, there were an average of 4,198 hate crime incidents against persons and 2,990 incidents against property.

Of the 105,129 hate crime incidents recorded during the study period, approximately 50 percent were committed based on racial bias, about 19 percent being religious based, 17 percent based on bias against the victim's sexual orientation, and the remaining based on ethnicity bias, gender identity bias, and biases against people with disabilities. Of the 52,473 racially motivated hate crimes, a majority of those incidents involved Black victims (35,056), significantly less of these incidents involved Whites (10,592), Asians and Pacific Islanders (2,581), and American Indians and Alaska Natives (1,216). The relative extent to which racial groups are targeted appears to be generally consistent across various studies and reports utilizing official and victim survey data (Harlow, 2005; Messner, McHugh, & Felson, 2004; Meuchel-Wilson, 2014; Perry, 2001; Thornton et al., 2013; Zaykowski, 2010).

Crimes targeting those of varying sexual orientations are another common type of hate crime in the United States. From 2001 through 2015, there were 18,078 hate crimes committed based on victims' sexual orientation. A majority of these incidents were against homosexual males (61%), with another 20 percent of incidents targeting homosexual females. Perpetrated by both strangers and persons known to victims, researchers have noted that anti-sexual orientation and gender identity victimization often involves excessive violence (Gruenewald, 2012; Thornton et al., 2013; Turpin-Petrosino, 2015) and results in severe psychological distress to both immediate and secondary victims (Thornton et al., 2013; Turpin-Petrosino, 2015).

As another common form of hate crime in the United States, anti-religious hate crimes have totaled 19,825 over the course of our study period. The two most prevalent victim groups were persons of Jewish descent (65%) and Muslims (13%), while fewer crimes targeted Catholics (5%) and Protestants (3%). Despite hate crimes targeting Jews representing the largest proportion of religious-based hate crime, there is relatively little empirical research on these crimes. In contrast, there has recently been a flurry of studies examining anti-Muslim hate crime in the United States. (Byers & Jones, 2007; Deloughery, King, & Asal, 2012; Disha, Cavendish, & King, 2011; King & Sutton, 2013; Swahn, et al., 2003). Scholars have explored the significant increase in this form of hate crime following the terrorist attacks of September 11, 2001, finding that anti-Muslim hate crime has steadily decreased since the attacks, though not returning to pre-9/11 levels. In addition, research has indicated that members of other religions (i.e., Sikhs) have been victimized in part due to misperception of victims' cultural and religious backgrounds (Levin & McDevitt, 2002).

MEDIA REPRESENTATIONS OF CRIME

Not all novel forms of crime, like hate crime, receive elevated media coverage, especially when they fail to follow well-established "normal crime" story scripts (Gilliam & Iyengar, 2000; Sudnow, 1965). Crime story scripts are shaped by cultural expectations about the characteristics of typical offenders, victims, and circumstances of crime. For instance, research has found that racial minorities are more likely to be portrayed as criminals than as victims, while Whites are more commonly depicted as law enforcers, heroes, or tragic victims of crime (Entman, 1990, 1992). Studies have also shown that racial minority crime victims are less likely to receive media attention in comparison to White crime victims, especially those of high socioeconomic status. Victims of crime who are thought to be above suspicion or especially vulnerable (e.g., elderly victims or children) are also considered worthy victims and are more likely to receive media attention, while those considered socially deviant, criminal, or failing to meet social expectations receive more negative and relatively less attention (Lundman, 2003; Pritchard & Hughes, 1997).

THE CURRENT STUDY

To date, there has been little research on how news media represent hate crime in the United States. While hate crime is a rare form of crime, we know little about if and to what extent statistical infrequency affects the newsworthiness of this topic. Based on prior research, it seems plausible that some forms of hate crime, such as those considered novel or serious, will receive more news media attention. To investigate these and other related questions, we examine how depictions of hate crime in articles published from the National Desk section of *The New York Times* between 2001 and 2015 correspond with official crime statistics and other academic findings. Articles were downloaded from an online news index and included in this study if they contained the keywords "hate crime," "bias crime," or "bias-motivated crime." From this pool of articles, we systematically gathered information pertinent to hate crime victims and event circumstances. The selected articles cover specific hate crimes and community and criminal justice system responses to hate crime. We exclude editorials and other opinion pieces that did not focus on these issues as well as duplicated newswire stories. Out of a total of 472 articles initially identified, 203 articles met our inclusion criteria and are included in our analysis.

ATTRIBUTES OF *THE NEW YORK TIMES* HATE CRIME ARTICLES

To begin, we note the yearly frequency of published hate crime stories in *The New York Times* (see Figure 10.1). Our findings show that yearly prevalence of hate crime coverage has varied significantly since 2001, largely due to increased attention to media sensationalism of certain high-profile cases. For instance, a relatively large number of articles (n = 33) were

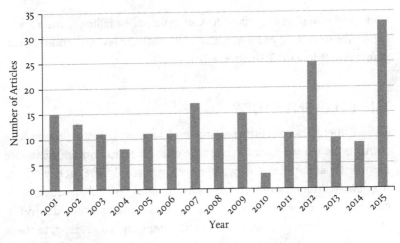

FIGURE 10.1 Number of *The New York Times* Hate Crime Articles by Year

published in 2015 in response to the mass shooting at a predominantly Black church in Charleston, South Carolina.

In 2012, the elevated coverage (n = 25 articles) was largely due to an attack on an Ohio Amish community. Periods of increased hate crime coverage also occurred in 2001 and 2002 primarily covering anti-Muslim retaliation hate crimes committed in response to the 9/11 terrorist attacks.

We also examined the types of victim groups mentioned in *The New York Times* articles. Hate crime targeting five different victim groups were identified, including victims selected based on their race or ethnicity, religion, sexual orientation or gender identity, other identity markers, or based on multiple identity markers. There were also a number of articles in which the source of hate was not specified. Of the 203 articles, 171 (84%) reported on a single hate crime, while another 32 articles (16%) reported on multiple hate crimes. Articles mentioning more than one hate crime often sought to establish a pattern of behavior, addressing how a particular incident compared to similar crimes. Among the articles, 70 (35%) indicated race/ethnicity as the victim group targeted. Another 45 articles (22%) discussed hate crimes targeting victims based on their religion. Hate crime targeted at victims due to their sexual orientation or gender identity was mentioned in 25 (12%) of *The New York Times* articles.

In one article, "other" was noted as the source of bias. This particular article described a man who shot a security guard of a conservative policy think tank in Washington, DC. In this incident, the security guard who was shot and wounded was not necessarily the target of the offender's bias; rather, the article notes that the offender worked at a center whose values and politics ran counter to that of the institution for which the guard worked (Emery, 2012). In seven articles (3%), multiple victim groups were mentioned, while in the remaining 55 articles (27%) a specific victim group was not mentioned.

VICTIM CHARACTERISTICS

Our analysis of *The New York Times* hate crime articles also yielded information on victims. Across all articles, victims of hate crime were identified a total of 446 times. Some victims are counted multiple times as several articles may report on the same hate crime. We also note that a specific number of hate crime victims was not provided in about 10 percent of *The New York Times* articles. Taking into account these issues, we provide information on the number of victims for three of the most represented victim groups: race or ethnicity, religion, and sexual orientation or gender identity (see Table 10.1). Of the 70 articles depicting hate crimes targeting racial or ethnic minorities, the most common category included Black victims (n = 39 articles). Several of these articles focused on a shooting that occurred at the Emanuel African Methodist Episcopal Church in Charleston, South Carolina, on June 17, 2015. The shooting resulted in the deaths of nine Black parishioners (Horowitz, Corasaniti, & Southall, 2015; Stewart & Perez-Pena 2015). In addition, eight articles reported stories on Hispanic or Latino victims, while less common were Alaskan Native victims (n = 2 articles), Native American victims (n = 2 articles), victims of other races or ethnicities[4] (n = 2 articles), and White victims (n = 2 articles). Only one article reported on the victimization of an individual of Asian descent, and only one article discussed the victimization of a mixed race individual. The six articles listed as "N/A" included articles discussing the

---

[4] This category encompassed people of Middle Eastern descent (e.g., Afghan, Egyptian, Iraqi, Jordanian, Palestinian, Syrian, Yemeni, etc.), though victims may have been targeted because they were reportedly perceived as "Arab" or "Muslim" by offenders.

TABLE 10.1 Number of Articles by Specific Victim Types for Most Represented Groups

RACE OR ETHNICITY (n=70)	FREQUENCY (%)	RELIGION (N=45)	FREQUENCY (%)	SEXUAL ORIENTATION OR GENDER IDENTITY (N=25)	FREQUENCY (%)
Black	39 (56%)	Amish	15 (33%)	Male	18 (72%)
Hispanic/Latino	8 (11%)	Muslim	11 (24%)	Transgender	4 (16%)
N/A	6 (9%)	Not Specified	9 (20%)	Female	3 (12%)
Various	4 (6%)	Jewish	3 (7%)		
Not Specified	3 (4%)	Christian	2 (5%)		
Alaskan Native	2 (3%)	Various	2 (5%)		
Native American	2 (3%)	Hindu	1 (2%)		
Other	2 (3%)	N/A	1 (2%)		
Asian	1 (1%)	Sikh	1 (2%)		
Mixed	1 (1%)				
White	2 (3%)				

property destruction targeting a particular group based on race or ethnicity, such as historically Black churches. The four articles listed as victims of "various" denote stories discussing victims of various racial or ethnic backgrounds. Finally, three articles did not list the race or ethnicity of victims, yet still indicated that race or ethnicity was the source of bias for the crime.

An additional 45 news articles focused on religious bias crime. As previously mentioned, several articles covered an attack against the Amish such that over 30 percent of all religious hate crime articles center on this group. Several of these articles depicted a series of attacks in which the beards and hair of Amish men and women were cut, an act the articles described as a form of religious humiliation. The long beards and hair worn by the men and women, respectively, of the Amish faith are considered central to their Amish identity (Eckholm, 2012). Eleven articles depicted Muslim victims (24%), while the remaining religious bias articles focused on Jewish victims (7%), Christian victims (4%), Hindu victims (2%), and Sikh victims (2%). The two articles listed as "various" again focused on multiple victims of varying religions. The one article listed as "N/A" discussed the targeting of a "Muslim store." Lastly, 20 percent of the articles did not specify the religion of the victim yet indicated that it was the motivating factor of the crime.

The third most common type of victim group mentioned in *The New York Times* articles published about hate crime were victims targeted because of their sexual orientation or gender identity. These victims were most often male (72%) and depicted as homosexuals. Only four of the articles discussed the victimization of transgender individuals, all of which were described as biological males who identified as females. In addition, only three (12%) articles published on sexual orientation and gender identity hate crime involved female victims. One such article depicts the physical abuse a woman endured at the hands of her brothers who felt that her lesbian relationship brought shame to their family (Janofsky, 2001). Her family then tried to kidnap her and take her back to their home country of Jordan. This article demonstrates the point made previously that those victimized based on their sexual orientation or gender identity are sometimes victimized by those close to them and that these crimes involve excessive violence (Gruenewald, 2012; Thornton et al., 2013; Turpin-Petrosino, 2015). The article also provides an example of the psychological distress that these victims endure as the victim's former romantic partner noted that both of them had been traumatized by the experience (Janofsky, 2001).

We also examined the types of crimes mentioned in *The New York Times* articles across different victim groups. Crime types included those committed against persons, property, and a combination of persons and property (or "mixed") (see Table 10.2). We found that for crimes against persons, the largest percentage of crimes targeted racial and ethnic minorities (36%), followed by religious minorities (21%), and sexual orientation or gender identity victims (15%).

Among articles reporting on hate property crimes, 35 percent discussed targeting religious institutions, including churches, mosques, and temples. Other property crimes targeted structures based on animus toward racial and ethnic minorities (23%). Such cases usually involved homes or businesses that were targeted for arson and vandalism due to the racial or ethnic identity of the inhabitant. In 11 (42%) of the articles on property crimes, it was not possible to discern a source of bias. The remaining four *The New York Times* articles focused on the victimization of both people and property. The majority (75%) of these articles encompassed multiple sources of bias, usually discussing multiple hate crimes varying in victim type and underlying motive.

TABLE 10.2   Article Counts for Victim Type by Victim Group

CRIME TYPE		RACE/ ETHNICITY	RELIGION	SEXUAL ORIENTATION/ GENDER IDENTITY	OTHER	NOT SPECIFIED	MULTIPLE	TOTAL
Person	(n)	63	36	25	1	44	4	173
	(%)	36.4	20.8	14.5	0.6	25.4	2.3	100
Property	(n)	6	9	0	0	11	0	26
	(%)	23.1	34.6	0.0	0.0	42.3	0.0	100
Mixed	(n)	1	0	0	0	0	3	4
	(%)	25.0	0.0	0.0	0.0	0.0	75.0	100

TABLE 10.3 Victim Mention by Victim Group

VICTIM MENTION		RACE/ ETHNICITY	RELIGION	SEXUAL ORIENTATION/ GENDER IDENTITY	OTHER	NOT SPECIFIED	MULTIPLE	TOTAL
Named	(n)	44	20	19	0	44	1	128
	(%)	34.4	15.6	14.8	0.0	34.4	0.8	100
Not	(n)	24	19	6	1	10	0	60
Named	(%)	40.0	31.7	10.0	1.6	16.7	0.0	100
Mixed	(n)	2	6	0	1	6	0	15
	(%)	13.3	40.0	0.0	6.7	40.0	0.0	100

We also examined whether victims of hate crime were mentioned by name. Our findings revealed that 63 percent of articles did mention victim names, while an additional 12 percent of articles mentioned the names of some victims while omitting the names of others. In Table 10.3, we provide information on the extent to which articles mentioned victims by name across varying target groups.

Across the 128 articles that mentioned victim names, 34 percent were articles on racial or ethnic hate crimes, while others targeted religious groups (16%), and sexual orientation or gender identity minorities (15%). Another 34 percent of *The New York Times* articles mentioning victim names did not specify a particular target group. Articles that did not mention victim names followed a similar pattern with 40 percent of articles focusing on racial or ethnic minorities, 32 percent on religious groups, and 10 percent on victims of sexual orientation or gender identity crimes.

The final variable that we examined measured whether articles focused primarily on the victims of hate crimes. Our results indicated that out of the 203 articles, only 51 (25%) were focused on victims. Table 10.4 provides the percentages of articles focusing on victims across victim groups. Of victim-focused articles, 29 percent focused on race or ethnicity bias crimes, 12 percent on sexual orientation or gender identity minorities, and six percent on religious groups. Nearly half of articles in which the victim was the focus did not specify the type of bias involved.

TABLE 10.4 Victim Focus by Victim Group

VICTIM FOCUS		RACE/ ETHNICITY	RELIGION	SEXUAL ORIENTATION/ GENDER IDENTITY	OTHER	NOT SPECIFIED	MULTIPLE	TOTAL
Yes	(n)	15	3	6	0	25	2	51
	(%)	29.4	5.9	11.8	0.0	49.0	3.9	100
No	(n)	55	42	19	1	30	5	152
	(%)	36.2	27.6	12.5	0.7	19.7	3.3	100

Instead, these articles often generally provided details about victims based on information from family members, acquaintances, and other witnesses.

Among the 152 articles that were not victim-focused, 36 percent involved racial or ethnic hate crime, followed in frequency by religious hate crime (28%), and sexual orientation or gender identity hate crime (13%). The remaining 20 percent of articles that were not victim-focused failed to specify a particular victim group.

ANALYSIS OF VICTIMS OF HATE CRIMES

One of the key purposes of this chapter was to investigate the extent to which coverage of hate crime in *The New York Times* reflects official hate crime reporting in the United States. To this aim, we reviewed patterns of hate crime victimization based on the FBI's UCR Hate Crime Statistics and systematically collected and analyzed over 200 news articles published between 2001 and 2015 in *The New York Times*. Several key findings warrant further discussion.

One important finding of our research is that there are clear discrepancies between the reality of hate crime as presented in official reports and the extent to which hate crime is covered by prominent news media. As shown in Figure 10.2, there have been competing trend lines in the number of *The New York Times* hate crime articles published and the number of official hate crimes reported to the FBI since 2001.

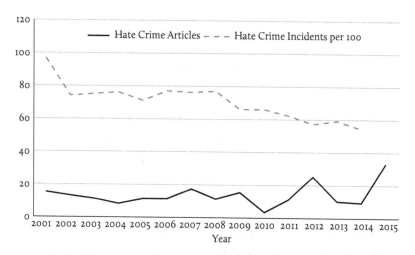

FIGURE 10.2   Line graph depicting the distribution of *The New York Times* hate crime articles published between 2001 and 2015 compared to official reporting of hate crime incidents between 2001 and 2015. UCR hate crime data were collected from the UCR Hate Crime Statistics. Each hate crime reflected in the graph above depicts one incident for every one hundred that were reported to the FBI.

For example, the line graph reveals an increase in the number of hate crime articles published between 2008 and 2009 and then another increase between 2010 and 2012. However, the number of official hate crimes reported during these time periods reflect declines in this type of crime.

In regard to who was most often targeted by hate crime, news media coverage in some ways paralleled FBI hate crime reporting. For example, most racial hate crime articles focused on common anti-Black crimes, and sexual orientation and gender identity hate crime articles centered on incidents targeting gay males. However, also emerging from our analysis were discrepancies between *The New York Times* coverage of hate crime victim groups and those victims most commonly represented in official hate crime data. For instance, while FBI hate crime statistics reveal that Asians represent the second largest minority group to be targets of racial hate crime in the United States (FBI, 2015d; see also Turpin-Petrosino, 2015), only a single article reported on hate crimes against Asians.

Another key finding of our study is that high-profile hate crimes that become sensationalized in the media misrepresent or distort the official reality of hate crime. One reason this may occur is because hate crimes are linked to other prominent issues like terrorism. Recall that a majority of the religious-based hate crimes in our study period were committed against Jews at approximately 65 percent, while hate crime incidents against Muslims represented about 13 percent. Nonetheless, only seven percent of articles published between 2001 and 2015 reported on discriminatory crimes against Jews. This disproportionate media focus on anti-Muslim crimes is likely due to an increase in high-profile attacks against persons perceived to be Muslims following 9/11 (Byers & Jones, 2007; Deloughery et al., 2012; Disha et al., 2011; King & Sutton, 2013; Swahn, et al., 2003).

Hate crimes may also receive more coverage because of their novelty. Again, 33 percent of religious hate crime articles in *The New York Times* addressed crimes committed against the Amish community. News coverage of anti-Amish crimes stemmed from a complicated case of beard-cutting in one Ohio community that was investigated by the FBI. Crimes involving more than one type of bias may also be viewed as novel and, in effect, especially newsworthy. For instance, according to UCR Hate Crime Statistics, during the study period only 111 of the 105,129 (0.1%) hate crimes reported involved multiple types of biases. However, multiple biases were reported in seven of the 203 (3%) hate crime articles.

Supporting previous studies of media and crime more generally, a final key finding of our research is that hate crimes against persons are more likely to be covered by news media than hate crimes against property. We found that 85 percent of the articles reported on the victimization of persons, while only 13 percent of the articles indicated that property had been targeted. In contrast, FBI statistics showed that only 58 percent of offenses were directed against persons and 42 percent of them targeted property. Again, this discrepancy is likely due in part to the news values of reporters and editors and how they assess the newsworthiness of crime stories and victims.

CONCLUSION

There are limitations to the current study that prevent us from making a concrete conclusion about the relationship between the media construction of hate crime and official hate crime statistics. One issue is that we were unable to directly link *The New York Times* coverage with specific hate crimes, thereby limiting our ability to investigate what makes certain hate crimes more newsworthy than others. A second limitation is our ability to generalize our findings to other time periods and media forms. Our study is based *The New York Times* hate crime articles published from 2001 to 2015 and the FBI hate crime statistics accompanying these years. Future research must learn more about how hate crime is portrayed in news media reports prior to 2001 and in other local and regional media outlets, including television and web-based news.

Despite these limitations, this study ultimately demonstrated that, while *The New York Times* coverage corresponds with hate crime data published annually by the FBI in some respects, news media generally present a qualitatively different picture of hate crime than the one portrayed in official hate crime statistics. Considering that the FBI's hate crime statistics suffer from their own serious biases, it seems imperative that we identify alternative avenues for systematically collecting data on hate crime that are neither solely dependent on official crime data nor a single news media outlet. In particular, it is possible that alternative case identification and data collection methodologies that simultaneously draw from multiple open sources could, in the future, enhance our ability to more accurately capture the reality of hate crime in the United States.

REFERENCES

Bell, J. (2002). *Policing hatred: Law enforcement, civil rights, and hate crime.* New York: NYU Press.

Berk, R. A., Boyd, E. A., & Hamner, K. M. (1994). Thinking more clearly about hate-motivated crimes. In G. M. Herek & K. T. Berrill (Eds.), *Hate crimes: Confronting violence against lesbians and gay men* (pp. 123–138). Newbury Park, CA: SAGE Publications, Inc.

Boyd, E. A., Berk, R. A., & Hamner, K. M. (1996). "Motivated by hatred or prejudice": Categorization of hate-motivated crimes in two police divisions. *Law and Society Review, 30*(4), 819–850.

Byers, B. D., & Jones, J. A. (2007). The impact of the terrorist attacks of 9/11 on anti-Islamic hate crime. *Journal of Ethnicity in Criminal Justice, 5*(1), 43–56.

Cohen, J. R. (2015, June 19). The FBI has no idea how many hate crimes happen in America each year. *The Washington Post*. Retrieved from https://www.washingtonpost.com/posteverything/wp/2015/06/19/there-are-260000-hate-crimes-in-america-each-year-why-does-the-fbi-think-there-are-only-6000

Deloughery, K., King, R. D., & Asal, V. (2012). Close cousins or distant relatives? The relationship between terrorism and hate crime. *Crime & Delinquency, 58*(5), 663–688. doi:10.1177/0011128712452956

Disha, I., Cavendish, J. C., & King, R. D. (2011). Historical events and spaces of hate: Hate crimes against Arabs and Muslims in post-9/11 America. *Social Problems, 58*(1), 21–46. doi:10.1525/sp.2011.58.1.21

Eckholm, E. (2012, August 26). Trial to begin for 16 members of Amish group charged in beard-cutting attacks. *The New York Times*, A16.

Emery, T. (2012, August 16). Policy group in Washington is shooting site. *The New York Times*, A15.

Entman, R. M. (1990). Modern racism and the images of Blacks in local television news. *Critical Studies in Media Communication, 7*(4), 332–345.

Entman, R. M. (1992). Blacks in the news: Television, modern racism and cultural change. *Journalism Quarterly, 69*(2), 341–361.

Federal Bureau of Investigation. (2015a). *Uniform Crime Report, Hate Crime Statistics, 2014: Hate crime by jurisdiction*. Retrieved from https://www.fbi.gov/about-us/cjis/ucr/hate-crime/2014/topic-pages/jurisdiction_final.pdf

Federal Bureau of Investigation. (2015b). *Uniform Crime Report, Hate Crime Statistics, 2014: Incidents and offenses*. Retrieved from https://ucr.fbi.gov/hate-crime/2014/topic-pages/incidentsandoffenses_final.pdf

Federal Bureau of Investigation. (2015c). *Uniform Crime Report, Hate Crime Statistics, 2014: Location type*. Retrieved from https://www.fbi.gov/about-us/cjis/ucr/hate-crime/2014/topic-pages/locationtype_final.pdf

Federal Bureau of Investigation. (2015d). *Uniform Crime Report, Hate Crime Statistics, 2014: Victims*. Retrieved from https://www.fbi.gov/about-us/cjis/ucr/hate-crime/2014/topic-pages/victims_final.pdf

Franklin, K. (2002). Good intentions: The enforcement of hate crime penalty-enhancement statutes. *American Behavioral Scientist, 46*(1), 154–172.

Gerstenfeld, P. B., Grant, D. R., & Chiang, C. P. (2003). Hate online: A content analysis of extremist Internet sites. *Analyses of Social Issues and Public Policy, 3*(1), 29–44.

Gilliam, F. D., Jr., & Iyengar, S. (2000). Prime suspects: The influence of local television news on the viewing public. *American Journal of Political Science, 44*(3), 560–573.

Gruenewald, J. (2012). Are anti-LGBT homicides in the United States unique? *Journal of Interpersonal Violence, 27*(18), 3601–3623.

Haider-Markel, D. P. (2002). Regulating hate: State and local influences on hate crime law enforcement. *State Politics & Policy Quarterly, 2*(2), 126–160.

Hall, R. E. (2014) *Historical analysis of skin color discrimination in America*. New York: Springer.

Hamm, M. (1998). Terrorism, hate crime, and antigovernment violence: A review of the research. In H. W. Kushner (Ed.), *The future of terrorism: Violence in the new millennium* (pp. 59–96). Thousand Oaks, CA: SAGE Publications, Inc

Harlow, C. W. (2005). *Hate crime reported by victims and police* (Report No. NCJ 209911). Washington, DC: Bureau of Justice Statistics. Retrieved from http://www.bjs.gov/content/pub/pdf/hcrvp.pdf

Horowitz, J., Corasaniti, N., & Southall, A. (2015, June 18). South Carolina police search for shooter at Black church. *The New York Times*, A15.

Janofsky, M. (2001, April 21). Family, culture and law meet in a Utah court case. *The New York Times*, A8.

Jenness, V., & Grattet, R. (2001). *Making hate a crime: From social movement to law enforcement.* New York: Russell Sage Foundation.

King, R. D., & Sutton, G. M. (2013). High times for hate crimes: Explaining the temporal clustering of hate-motivated offending. *Criminology, 51*(4), 871–894.

Levin, J., & McDevitt, J. (2002). *Hate crimes revisited: America's war against those who are different.* Boulder, CO: Westview Press.

Lundman, R. J. (2003, September). The newsworthiness and selection bias in news about murder: Comparative and relative effects of novelty and race and gender typifications on newspaper coverage of homicide. *Sociological Forum, 18*(3), pp. 357–386.

Martin, S. E. (1995). "A cross-burning is not just an arson": Police social construction of hate crimes in Baltimore County. *Criminology, 33*(3), 303–326.

Martin, S. E. (1996). Investigating hate crimes: Case characteristics and law enforcement responses. *Justice Quarterly, 13*(3), 455–480.

McDevitt, J., Balboni, J. M., & Bennett, S. (2000). Improving the quality and accuracy of hate crime reporting. final report. Washington, DC: Bureau of Justice Statistics.

Messner, S. F., McHugh, S., & Felson, R. B. (2004). Distinctive characteristics of assaults motivated by bias. *Criminology, 42*(3), 585–618.

Meuchel-Wilson, M. (2014). *Hate crime victimization, 2004-2012—Statistical tables* (Report No. NCJ 244409). Washington, DC: Bureau of Justice Statistics. Retrieved from http://www.bjs.gov/content/pub/pdf/hcv0412st.pdf

Nolan, J. J., & Akiyama, Y. (1999). An analysis of factors that affect law enforcement participation in hate crime reporting. *Journal of Contemporary Criminal Justice, 15*(1), 111–127.

Perry, B. (Ed.). (2003). *Hate and bias crime: A reader.* New York: Routledge.

Perry, B. (2001). *In the name of hate: Understanding hate crimes.* New York: Routledge.

Pritchard, D., & Hughes, K. D. (1997). Patterns of deviance in crime news. *Journal of Communication, 47*(3), 49–67.

Stewart, N., & Perez-Pena, R. (2015, June 20). 'I will never be able to hold her again. But I forgive you.' *The New York Times*, A1.

Sudnow, D. (1965). Normal crimes: Sociological features of the penal code in a public defender office. *Social problems, 12*(3), 255–276.

Swahn, M. H., Mahendra, R. R., Paulozzi, L. J., Winston, R. L., Shelley, G. A., Taliano, J., … Saul, J. R. (2003). Violent attacks on Middle Easterners in the United States during the month following the September 11, 2001 terrorist attacks. *Injury Prevention, 9*(2), 187.

Thornton, W. E., Voigt, L., & Harper, D. W. (2013). *Why violence? Leading questions regarding the conceptualizations and reality of violence in society.* Durham, NC: Carolina Academic Press.

Turpin-Petrosino, C. (2015). *Understanding hate crimes: Acts, motives, offenders, victims, and justice*. New York: Routledge.

Zaykowski, H. (2010). Racial disparities in hate crime reporting. *Violence & Victims, 25*(3), 378–394. doi:10.1891/0886-6708.25.3.378

KEY TERMS

- *Hate Crime:* "[A] criminal offense against a person or property motivated in whole or in part by an offender's bias against a race, religion, disability, sexual orientation, ethnicity, gender, or gender identity" (Source: https://www.fbi.gov/investigate/civil-rights/hate-crimes).

- *Underreporting:* May occur because victims anticipate police will minimize their victimization experiences or will be unwilling or unable to help them, to avoid police attention (Perry, 2003), others may have historically had issues with law enforcement being unsympathetic, unresponsive, or even hostile toward them.

- *Uniform Crime Reports Hate Crime Statistics:* Hate crime data collected since 1995 through the Federal Bureau of Investigation's Uniform Crime Reports. This data collection effort works with state and local law enforcement agencies to gather crime statistics at the national level. Importantly, it does not include crimes that are not reported to law enforcement.

THE NEW YORK TIMES ARTICLES

Eckholm, E. (2012). Trial to begin for 16 members of Amish group charged in beard-cutting attacks. *The New York Times*. Retrieved from https://www.nytimes.com/2012/08/26/us/trial-to-begin-for-16-members-of-amish-group.html

Emery, T. (2012). Shooting at family research council in Washington. *The New York Times*. Retrieved from https://www.nytimes.com/2012/08/16/us/shooting-at-family-research-council-in-washington.html

Horowitz, J., Corasaniti, N., & Southall, A. (2015). Nine killed in shooting at Black church in Charleston. *The New York Times*. Retrieved from https://www.nytimes.com/2015/06/18/us/church-attacked-in-charleston-south-carolina.html

Janofsky, M. (2001). Family, culture and law meet in a Utah court case. *The New York Times.* Retrieved from https://www.nytimes.com/2001/04/21/us/family-culture-and-law-meet-in-a-utah-court-case.html

Stewart, N., & Perez-Pena, R. (2015). The powerful words of forgiveness delivered to Dylan Roof by victims' relatives. *The New York Times.* Retrieved from https://www.washingtonpost.com/news/post-nation/wp/2015/06/19/hate-wont-win-the-powerful-words-delivered-to-dylann-roof-by-victims-relatives/

DISCUSSION QUESTIONS

1. What are obstacles to studying the extent and nature of hate crime in the United States?
2. Do you have concerns about learning of hate crime from the news media? If so, what are they?
3. Why might there be periodic spikes in hate crime coverage even when hate crime rates are declining?
4. Why do news media cover anti-Muslim crimes at a higher rate than much more common anti-Semitic crimes?
5. Why are hate crimes targeting people more likely to be covered by news media than hate crimes targeting property?

CHAPTER 11

Victims of Terrorism

Zachary S. Mitnik, John Jay College of Criminal Justice; Joshua D. Freilich,
John Jay College of Criminal Justice and the Graduate Center—City
University of New York; Steven M. Chermak, Michigan State University

INTRODUCTION

Scholarly research on terrorism faces a number of challenges that do not
affect research on more traditional forms of crime. Terrorism is highly
politicized, to the point that the very definition is in dispute (for a full
discussion of the challenges in defining terrorism see Schmid, 2004). As a
result, official records of terrorism incidents face considerable pressure to
include certain incidents while avoiding others, leaving them unsuitable
for scholarly research. Recent research has been fueled by the creation of
two open-source databases: the **Global Terrorism Database** (GTD) (LaFree
& Dugan, 2007) and the **United States Extremist Crime Database** (ECDB)
(Freilich, Chermak, Belli, Gruenewald, & Parkin, 2014). These databases
have allowed for a number of analyses of both terrorism incidents and perpetrators (Fahey, LaFree, Dugan, & Piquero, 2012; Klein & Allison, 2017).
However, dedicated analysis of victims remains limited.

A number of factors are involved in the underrepresentation of terrorism victims in scholarly research. To begin with, the relatively small
number of terrorism victims makes systematic analysis difficult, and many
terrorism databases, including the GTD, have limited measurements of
victim-level data. Additionally, there is an assumption in scholarly research
that terrorism victims are random, guiding research in other directions
(Parkin, 2016). This assumption remains pervasive despite evidence to the
contrary (Parkin, Freilich, & Chermak, 2015).

In this chapter we suggest that the lack of representation of victims
of terrorism is not limited to scholarly research, but indicative of a larger
problem in the overall narrative of terrorism. The same news reports of

terrorist incidents that make up a large percentage of the source material for existing terrorism databases also serve as the primary source of information on terrorist attacks for the general public. Any misrepresentation in coverage can therefore propagate through both spheres.

To explore this issue further, this chapter will analyze *The New York Times* coverage of terrorism incidents in the United States occurring between 2001 and 2015. Our analysis is guided by the question *how much focus do terrorism victims receive in media coverage, and how does this coverage reflect known patterns of terrorism victimization?* The chapter will first address the existing databases of terrorism and the patterns they suggest, contrasted with the media's coverage of terrorism. Next, we provide the results of the current analysis and conclude the chapter with a discussion of the implications of our findings on both future research and coverage.

PATTERNS OF TERRORISM IN THE UNITED STATES

Due to the increased availability of reliable data on terrorist incidents, it is now possible to discern event-level and perpetrator-level patterns. In its codebook, the GTD defines **terrorism** as "the threatened or actual use of illegal force and violence by a non-state actor to attain a political, economic, religious, or social goal through fear, coercion, or intimidation" (National Consortium for the Study of Terrorism and Responses to Terrorism [START], 2017). Additionally, the GTD requires that two of three additional criteria be met for an incident to be included: the goals of the incident were ideological in nature, the incident was intended to convey some message to a group beyond the immediate victims, or the incident went outside the bounds of generally accepted rules of war by targeting civilians or other noncombatants. Incidents in the GTD are classified based on which of these criteria they meet, with an additional variable indicating whether there is any uncertainty as to whether the incident meets the criteria for inclusion. This allows the GTD to err on the side of inclusion while still providing the tools for individual analyses to exclude edge cases and ambiguous incidents.

Under its broadest inclusion criteria, the GTD recorded 305 terrorist incidents in the United States from 2001 to 2015 (START, 2017). One hundred and twenty-four of these incidents occurred in western states, with 53 incidents in California alone. Attacks were more evenly distributed in other regions, with 83 incidents occurring in the South, 52 occurring in the Midwest, and 46 occurring in the Northeast. Fifty percent of these attacks are classified as facility/infrastructure attacks, where the primary intent is property damage. The next two most common types of attacks are bombings (23%) and armed assaults (16%).

With regard to perpetrators, only 115 incidents were associated with any recognized group (START, 2017). One hundred twenty-one were carried out by individuals with no known group affiliation, and 69 (23%) incidents had unknown perpetrators. Of the incidents with known affiliations, the majority were carried out by far-left groups (77%), primarily environmental and animal rights activists. A further 17 percent were carried out by far-right groups, while only 5 percent were carried out by Jihadi groups. These statistics alone are somewhat misleading, as of the incidents carried out by unaffiliated individuals, almost half showed signs of far-right motives (45%), while a further 15 percent were Jihadi.

Although less information is available on patterns of victimization, some patterns still emerge. To begin with, many terrorist attacks have no human victims at all: only 22 percent of incidents in the United States between 2001 and 2015 resulted in the death or injury of someone other than the perpetrator (START, 2017). Of the attacks that do have victims, the limited data available suggests that the targets are not chosen randomly. An analysis of far-right motivated homicides in the ECDB suggests that these attacks were likely to target their victims based on race, sexual orientation, or occupation, with distinct victimization patterns not only when compared to overall homicide rates, but within the far-right movement as well (Parkin et al., 2015). Even when victims appear random, there is data that suggests that routine activities may play a role, although much of this data comes from outside the United States (Behlendorf, LaFree, & Legault, 2012; Canetti-Nisim, Mesch, & Pedahzur, 2006).

TERRORISM IN THE MEDIA

Even though open-source terrorism databases draw much of their information from news sources, the patterns they present differ considerably, as media coverage tends to sensationalize a select few incidents while providing little to no coverage of other attacks (Chermak & Gruenewald, 2006; Mitnik, Freilich, & Chermak, 2018; Weimann & Brosius, 1991). Between January 1, 1980, and September 10, 2001, only 55 percent of terrorist incidents received any coverage in *The New York Times* (Chermak & Gruenewald, 2006), and after 9/11, only 28 percent of incidents were covered (Mitnik et al., 2018). In both time frames, the top 15 incidents accounted for roughly 80 percent of all coverage in *The New York Times*.

The incidents that are most likely to be covered are far from representative of the incidents that actually occur. Incidents with fatalities, armed assaults, far-right incidents, and Jihadi incidents were all more likely to be covered by *The New York Times*, and all but far-right incidents were the focus of a larger quantity of articles when they were covered (Mitnik et al., 2018). The more common forms of incidents received relatively little coverage. For instance, only 10 percent of facility/infrastructure attacks were covered, even though these incidents made up half of all incidents in the time frame.

METHODOLOGY & RESULTS

Despite this body of research, the role of victims in media coverage of terrorism remains unexplored. The following analysis explores this role and the extent to which victims are present in coverage at all. This analysis was conducted using *The New York Times* articles from an existing dataset (Mitnik et al., 2018) of articles on each of 222 distinct U.S. based incidents in the Global Terrorism Database for the years 2001–2015 (Mitnik et al., 2018). As the dataset was originally used for a study on post-9/11 coverage, it did not include incidents that occurred in 2001 prior to 9/11 in 2001. Since none of these incidents resulted in any injuries or deaths, there was no need to add these incidents for this analysis. The dataset was created by searching *The New York Times* archives for articles on each incident, excluding articles that only mention the incident as part of a discussion of another topic. For this analysis, only the 40 incidents that resulted in the death or injury of someone other than the perpetrator were included. Eight of these incidents received no coverage, leaving 597 articles across 32 incidents. This does not include 9/11 itself, nor does it include the 2001 anthrax letters. 9/11 was excluded as its large number of victims and political significance makes it an extreme outlier, while the anthrax letters were excluded as it involved an entirely different form of violence than what is seen in other incidents.

INCIDENTS & ARTICLES

The distribution of incidents and articles by date is displayed in Table 11.1. The coverage of terrorism incidents with homicide victims fluctuates

TABLE 11.1   Incidents and Articles by Year

YEAR	INCIDENTS	ARTICLES
2001	0	0
2002	2	14
2003	0	0
2004	0	0
2005	0	0
2006	1	9
2007	0	0
2008	2	5
2009	6	171
2010	1	3
2011	0	0
2012	2	14
2013	4	195
2014	5	39
2015	9	147

TABLE 11.2 Incidents and Articles by Target Group and Attack Severity

GROUP	INCIDENTS	ARTICLES	ARTICLES/INCIDENT
General Attack	8	293	36.6
Religion	6	40	6.7
Race/Ethnicity	5	57	11.4
Police	4	46	11.5
Military	3	119	39.7
Abortion Providers	2	35	17.5
Other	6	14	2.3
All Incidents	32	597	18.7
Fatal Incidents	25	526	21.0
Injured Only Incidents	7	71	10.1

considerably from year to year, as such incidents are relatively uncommon. Peaks in coverage are a result of high-profile attacks, such as the Fort Hood shootings in 2009, the Boston Marathon bombings in 2015, and the combination of both the Charleston massacre and the San Bernardino mass fatality shootings in 2015. Although coverage of many of these incidents even extends into the following year, articles were grouped by the year of the incident.

We also examined the severity of the attacks and what group, if any, was targeted. The results of this analysis are shown in Table 11.2. Attacks with fatalities received considerably more coverage than those with only injured victims. Of the target groups, only general attacks and military targets receive increased coverage compared to the baseline of 18.7 articles per incident. Attacks targeting the military receive the largest amount of coverage per incident, possibly because these attacks fit into the narrative that terrorism is an act of war. Attacks targeting the general public receive only slightly fewer articles per incident, and actually make up a larger percentage of overall coverage due to the relative frequency of such incidents. The attention given to these attacks may be because attacks are relevant to the largest percentage of *The New York Times* readership, while coverage of an attack with a narrower focus may not draw as much attention from readers who do not identify with the victims. This theory is further supported by the fact that all other target groups receive less coverage than average.

Average word count per incident, displayed in Table 11.3, follows a similar pattern as average number of articles per incident. Average words per article, on the other hand, follow a different pattern. Most target groups receive articles that are slightly longer than average, while articles on incidents targeting racial/ethnic groups are considerably shorter.

VICTIM CHARACTERISTICS

In general, *The New York Times* provides minimal demographic information on victims. In many cases, terrorism incidents have multiple victims from various racial and religious backgrounds, none of which has any bearing on the narrative. The exception is when victims are targeted specifically because of their race, ethnicity, or religion. At this point, demographics become an integral part of the narrative. Table 11.4 details

TABLE 11.3 Average Word Count and Words per Article by Target Group and Attack Severity

GROUP	WORD COUNT	WORDS/ARTICLE
General Attack	34,517	942.3
Religion	6,029	921.7
Race/Ethnicity	13,191	717.2
Police	10,450	874.5
Military	36,530	912.6
Abortion Providers	17,276	1,095.0
Other	2,287	714.8
All Incidents	17,917	873.1
Fatal Incidents	20,368	923.6
Injured Only Incidents	9,165	692.7

TABLE 11.4 Specific Group Targeted

GROUP		INCIDENTS	ARTICLES	ARTICLES/ INCIDENT
Race/Ethnicity (n = 57)	Black	3	46	15.3
	Hispanic/Latino	1	4	4.0
	Israeli	1	7	7.0
Religion (n = 40)	Jewish	3	18	6.0
	Muslim	2	18	9.0
	Christian	1	3	3.0

the specific groups that were targeted when the attack targeted race, ethnicity, or religion.

Although the data suggests that incidents with Black victims receive considerably more coverage per incident than other ethnic groups, 41 of these articles were actually about one incident, the Charleston church shooting. With regard to articles covering incidents on religious groups, articles are split evenly between attacks targeting Jews and Muslims. However, not all of the victims of these attacks were actually members of the targeted group: three of the articles on incidents targeting Jews were about an incident in which a security guard at a Holocaust memorial was shot, and six were on an incident in which bystanders outside a Jewish Community Center were shot. Similarly, eight of the articles on incidents targeting Muslims were about an incident in which the victims were actually Sikh, with evidence that the perpetrator was unaware of the difference.

Additionally, we examined how many articles actually identify victims by name, or even mention them at all. Table 11.5 displays the results of this analysis across severity of attack and target group. Identification of dead and injured victims was counted separately, even within the same article. An article was only counted as not mentioning victims within a given category if the incident it was covering had victims of that type. If an incident had multiple victims within the same category, the article was

TABLE 11.5 Identification of Victims by Severity of Attack and Target

		IDENTIFIED		MENTIONED		NOT MENTIONED		TOTAL	
		n	%	n	%	n	%	n	%
Attack severity	All victims	200	34	272	46	125	21	597	100
	Dead victims	176	33	255	48	95	18	526	100
	Injured victims	43	9	192	40	235	49	483	100
Target group	General attack	45	16	142	49	103	35	290	100
	Religion	22	56	14	36	3	8	39	100
	Race/ethnicity	31	54	24	42	2	4	57	100
	Police	29	63	13	28	4	9	46	100
	Military	36	31	69	59	11	9	116	100
	Abortion providers	31	89	3	8	1	3	35	100
	Other	6	42	7	50	1	7	14	100

classified based on its highest level of identification. For instance, an article was classified as identifying a dead victim as long as it gave the name of at least one of the deceased, even if the incident had additional casualties that were not identified.

Overall, victims are identified by name one third of the time and mentioned without identification half the time. Most articles that mention victims without identification do so when stating the number of people that were killed or injured in the attack, often in a quick summary of the incident to provide context for the main story. The remaining articles make no mention of victims at all. They refer to the incident in general terms, such as "the shooting," that arguably imply the existence of victims, but do not explicitly state that anyone was killed or injured.

The attack severity and target group has a strong influence on how many articles feature victims. Injured victims were less likely to be mentioned by name than dead victims, and more likely to not be mentioned at all. The target groups with the most coverage, general attacks and military, had the lowest proportion of articles that named victims. For all other target groups, victims were identified by name in at least half of the articles. Articles covering attacks on abortion providers identified the victim by name most often, although this is something of an outlier, as many of these articles were covering the same victim: Dr. George Tiller, an abortion provider who was in the national spotlight even before he was killed. Dr. Tiller was identified by name in each of the 24 articles written about his shooting.

Finally, we examined how many articles actually focused on the victims. An article was considered to be victim focused if more than 50 percent of the article was about victims, with additional consideration given to articles in which victims were the focus of the headline. In practice, making a distinction was not difficult, as when articles did focus on victims, they

TABLE 11.6 Victim focus by severity of attack and target

		YES		NO		TOTAL	
		n	%	n	%	n	%
Attack severity	All victims	52	9	545	91	597	100
	Dead victims	36	7	472	93	508	100
	Injured victims	15	4	345	96	483	100
Target group	General attack	17	6	273	94	290	100
	Religion	3	8	36	92	39	100
	Race/ethnicity	6	10	51	90	57	100
	Police	4	9	42	91	46	100
	Military	15	13	101	87	116	100
	Abortion providers	6	17	29	83	35	100
	Other	1	1	13	93	14	100

generally did so for the entire article. The results of this analysis are displayed in Table 11.6. The results are fairly consistent across both attack severity and target group. With the exception of articles covering attacks on the military, abortion providers, or racial/ethnic groups, less than 10 percent of articles on terrorist incidents are actually about the victims.

CONCLUSION

ANALYZING PATTERNS OF VICTIMS OF TERRORISM

This chapter set out to explore the role of victims of terrorism in *The New York Times* coverage by reviewing almost 600 articles reporting on 32 incidents that occurred between 2001 and 2015. The analysis produced a number of findings deserving of further discussion.

The most striking finding is that even though 80 percent of the articles mention the victims in some form, victims are the focus of only 9 percent of the sample articles. Even then, many of these articles are not particularly substantial. Many of the articles are about funerals or memorial services, while others discuss a large number of victims with limited information on each one. The six articles that focus on the victims of the Charleston church shooting, the largest number of victim-focused articles for a single incident, are relatively substantial, with longer than average word counts. Even then, the articles are less about the victims themselves and more about the families and communities of the victims coming together to mourn. The articles focusing on the 13 who died in the Fort Hood shooting are more typical of articles focusing on slain victims: one article listing all the victims, one article going into marginally more detail on a subset of the victims, and two short captions regarding burials. High-profile victims receive only marginally more attention, with Dr. George Tiller being the subject of four articles, which was the largest number of articles focusing on a single victim.

Articles focusing on injured victims are a different matter. In general, injured victims are considered less newsworthy and are rarely the focus of an article. However, injured victims can potentially become newsworthy at some point after the attack. The majority of the articles focusing on injured victims were articles covering either the Fort Hood shooting or the Boston Marathon bombings. Some of these articles were focused on the extent of the victims' injuries and recovery, with one article even following up a year later on two brothers who both lost a leg in the bombings. However, this kind of focus is atypical. When an injured victim becomes newsworthy, it is more often because of their involvement in the perpetrator's trial: both incidents had three articles each covering victim testimonies in court. The final case in which an injured victim was worthy of news focus was when the victim was injured while stopping the perpetrator: three articles were written on the officers who exchanged fire with the Fort Hood shooter, and one article focused on the passenger on Northwest Airlines Flight 253 who was injured while tackling the Underwear Bomber.

Dead or injured, victims are rarely the focus of articles. When they are, it is in the context of the attack, with only limited discussion of their lives outside of their victimization. In contrast, a considerable amount of focus is often placed on perpetrators, whose life stories are picked apart in an attempt to find a motive, especially if a link can be found to Jihadi extremism (Mitnik et al., 2018; Powell, 2011).

Of the articles that do not focus on victims, most fail to identify the victims by name, referring to them only by number if they mention them at all. The extent to which victims are identified or mentioned seems to be tied to how well they fit into the narrative. Victims are identified in a manner that emphasizes the brutality of attacks. Almost half of the articles on incidents with injured victims fail to mention them at all, while less than 20 percent of articles fail to mention fatalities. For instance, while 88 percent of the articles on the San Bernadino shooting mention the 14 killed in the attack, only 54 percent acknowledge the injured victims. However, this pattern can shift in cases where the injuries highlight the severity of the attack: 70 percent of the articles covering the Boston Marathon bombing and the resulting manhunt mentioned at least one of the 132 injured victims of the attack.

As for coverage by target groups, it appears that victims are more likely to be identified by name when they are targeted for a distinct characteristic, such as race, religion, or occupation. The Charleston church shooting victims were identified in 61 percent of articles, the two NYPD officers shot in 2014 were identified in 88 percent of articles, and Dr. George Tiller was identified in all 24 of the articles covering his shooting. Attacks targeting the military are an exception to this pattern: the victims of the Chattanooga military base shooting were identified in 50 percent of articles, while the Fort Hood victims were identified in only 21 percent of articles. This may be a result of the larger numbers of victims in these attacks, reducing the attention received by any individual victim. The two soldiers shot at the Little Rock recruitment center in 2009 were identified in 90 percent of articles, supporting this theory further.

Victims of general attacks are the least likely to be identified and most likely to be ignored entirely, possibly for the same reason they are overlooked in scholarly research: they are assumed to be random. Victims of general attacks were generally mentioned without identification, as was the case for 83 percent of articles on the San Bernardino shooting, 49 percent of articles on the Boston Marathon bombing, and 55 percent of articles on the shooting of guests at the Curtis Culwell Center's exhibition on Prophet Muhammad cartoons. In 45 percent of articles on the Curtis Culwell Center shooting, and 31 percent of articles on the Boston Marathon bombing, victims were not mentioned at all.

Notably, the patterns of victim identification do not match the patterns of total coverage: general attacks receive more coverage than most other attacks, but the articles on these attacks are the least likely to focus on or even identify victims. Although the indiscriminate nature of these attacks draws increased coverage—and some of this attention does go to the victims themselves—by raw numbers, there are more articles identifying victims of general attacks than there are identifying victims that belong specific groups. However, this increased attention is not proportional, and the bulk of the additional coverage is focused elsewhere. The victims make the attack as a whole more newsworthy, eclipsing any newsworthiness the individual victims might have.

Although these findings are largely descriptive, they are very much in line with prior research on terrorism coverage in *The New York Times*

(Chermak & Gruenewald, 2006; Mitnik et al., 2018). Coverage is largely sensationalist, prioritizing the incidents that draw in the most readers. Detailed coverage of victims does not fit into this model, especially if victims are assumed to be random. The fact that *The New York Times* appears to share this assumption with scholarly work does not suggest that it is the source of the assumption, as its biases in other aspects of terrorism coverage, such as perpetrators and tactics used, do not seem to be reflected in the various open-source databases that draw from media coverage. It does, however, support this chapter's assertion that the assumption goes beyond scholarly research and reflects something core to the public understanding of terrorism. Addressing this assumption is key to ensuring that we establish a clearer picture of terrorism in the United States.

REFERENCES

Behlendorf, B., LaFree, G., & Legault, R. (2012). Microcycles of violence: Evidence from terrorist attacks by ETA and the FMLN. *Journal of Quantitative Criminology, 28*(1), 49–75. Retrieved from https://doi.org/10.1007/s10940-011-9153-7

Canetti-Nisim, D., Mesch, G., & Pedahzur, A. (2006). Victimization from terrorist attacks: Randomness or routine activities? *Terrorism and Political Violence, 18*(4), 485–501. Retrieved from https://doi.org/10.1080/09546550600880237

Chermak, S. M., & Gruenewald, J. (2006). The media's coverage of domestic terrorism. *Justice Quarterly, 23*(4), 428–461. Retrieved from https://doi.org/10.1080/07418820600985305

Fahey, S., LaFree, G., Dugan, L., & Piquero, A. R. (2012). A situational model for distinguishing terrorist and non-terrorist aerial hijackings, 1948–2007. *Justice Quarterly, 29*(4), 573–595. Retrieved from https://doi.org/10.1080/07418825.2011.583265

Freilich, J. D., Chermak, S. M., Belli, R., Gruenewald, J., & Parkin, W. S. (2014). Introducing the United States Extremist Crime Database (ECDB). *Terrorism and Political Violence, 26*(2), 372–384. Retrieved from https://doi.org/10.1080/09546553.2012.713229

Klein, B. R., & Allison, K. (2017). Accomplishing difference: How do anti-race/ethnicity bias homicides compare to average homicides in the United States? *Justice Quarterly*, 1–27. Retrieved from https://doi.org/10.1080/07418825.2017.1351576

LaFree, G., & Dugan, L. (2007). Introducing the Global Terrorism Database. *Terrorism and Political Violence, 19*(2), 181–204. Retrieved from https://doi.org/10.1080/09546550701246817

Mitnik, Z. S., Freilich, J. D., & Chermak, S. M. (2018). Post-9/11 coverage of terrorism in *The New York Times*. *Justice Quarterly*. doi:10.1080/07418825.2018.1488985

National Consortium for the Study of Terrorism and Responses to Terrorism (START). (2017). Global Terrorism Database [Data file]. Retrieved from https://www.start.umd.edu/gtd

Parkin, W. S. (2016). Victimization theories and terrorism. In G. LaFree & J. D. Freilich (Eds.), *The handbook of the criminology of terrorism* (pp. 162–174). Hoboken, NJ: John Wiley & Sons, Inc. Retrieved from https://doi.org/10.1002/9781118923986.ch10

Parkin, W. S., Freilich, J. D., & Chermak, S. M. (2015). Ideological victimization: Homicides perpetrated by far-right extremists. *Homicide Studies, 19*(3), 211–236. Retrieved from https://doi.org/10.1177/1088767914529952

Powell, K. A. (2011). Framing Islam: An analysis of U.S. media coverage of terrorism since 9/11. *Communication Studies, 62*(1), 90–112. Retrieved from https://doi.org/10.1080/10510974.2011.533599

Schmid, A. (2004). Terrorism—The definitional problem. *Case Western Reserve Journal of International Law, 36*(2), 375–419.

Weimann, G., & Brosius, H.-B. (1991). The newsworthiness of international terrorism. *Communication Research, 18*(3), 333–354. Retrieved from https://doi.org/10.1177/009365091018003003

KEY TERMS

- *Extremist Crime Database (ECDB):* An open-source database that collects information on criminal events in the United States, both violent and financial, that are perpetrated by individuals who adhere to an extremist ideology (Freilich et al., 2014).

- *Global Terrorism Database (GTD):* An open-source database that collects information on terrorist and suspected terrorist incidents around the world (LaFree & Dugan, 2007).

- *Terrorism:* "The threatened or actual use of illegal force and violence by a non-state actor to attain a political, economic, religious, or social goal through fear, coercion, or intimidation" (START, 2017).

THE NEW YORK TIMES ARTICLES

Apuzzo, M., Schmidt, M. S., & Preston, J. (2015). U.S. visa process missed San Bernardino wife's online zealotry. *The New York Times.* Retrieved from https://www.nytimes.com/2015/12/13/us/san-bernardino-attacks-us-visa-process-tashfeen-maliks-remarks-on-social-media-about-jihad-were-missed.html

Barstow, D. (2009). An abortion battle, fought to the death. *The New York Times.* Retrieved from https://www.nytimes.com/2009/07/26/us/26tiller.html

Bidgood, J. (2013). A tribute to Boston bombing victims, a step at a time. *The New York Times.* Retrieved from https://www.nytimes.com/2013/05/16/us/a-tribute-to-boston-bombing-victims.html

Corasaniti, N., Perez-Pena, R., & Alvarez, L. (2015). Church massacre suspect held as Charleston grieves. *The New York Times.* Retrieved from https://www.nytimes.com/2015/06/19/us/charleston-church-shooting.html

McFadden, R. D. (2009). Army doctor held as Fort Hood rampage kills 12. *The New York Times.* Retrieved from https://www.nytimes.com/2009/11/06/us/06forthood.html

DISCUSSION QUESTIONS

1. How might the definitional issues surrounding the term terrorism impact what the media covers as terrorism and, therefore, how the public thinks about and discusses terrorism?

2. Many scholars, practitioners, and members of the public believe that victims of terrorism are random, in other words, terrorists do not target them as individuals. In what cases might this not be true? Also, how might terrorist targeting behavior of specific types of locations or organizations increase the victimization risk of individuals?

3. As with other types of crime, high-profile terrorist events drive the majority of coverage. How can this disproportional coverage impact the public's perspective of what they think they know about terrorism and victimization risk?

4. This study only looked at *The New York Times* coverage of domestic terrorism between 2001 and 2015. How could international terrorism events, which also were occurring, impact coverage of domestic terrorist events (and vice versa)?

CHAPTER 12

Victims of Human Trafficking

Stephanie Martinez, Seattle University; Rebecca Pfeffer, University of Houston-Downtown; Brittany Stinett, Seattle University

INTRODUCTION

Human trafficking is a form of modern day slavery that currently affects over 20.9 million people worldwide (International Labour Organization [ILO], 2012). It is the second largest international crime industry and is connected with other forms of international crime, such as illegal drug and arms trafficking (U.S. Department of Health & Human Services, 2012). Human trafficking has always been present domestically and internationally, and concern over the sex industry and sexual exploitation (a form of human trafficking) can be traced to feminist groups in the 1980s (Weitzer, 2007). However, human trafficking more recently became a highly politicized issue and drew national attention through its connection to immigration and national security concerns post-September 11, 2001 (Farrell & Fahy, 2009). Human trafficking then became a focal point for the U.S. government—enacting laws to protect and support trafficking victims in 2000 (Victims of Trafficking and Violence Protection Act (VTVPA), 2000). Prior to this federal legislation, human trafficking discourse shifted from being primarily linked to women's rights, human rights, and anti-prostitution campaigns to a criminal justice issue (Alvarez & Alessi, 2012; Farrell & Fahy, 2009; Leppanen, 2007). Today, human trafficking discourse is highly politicized and continues to draw national attention through its connection to immigration and national security concerns (Farrell & Fahy, 2009).

Although human trafficking has gained public and official attention, there continues to be a lack of accurate, statistical data about the size and scope of human trafficking. Studies currently estimate that there are at least 20.9 million individuals trafficked worldwide (ILO, 2012). Domestically, it has been estimated that at least 100,000 minors are victimized through prostitution each year (Smith, Healy Vardaman, & Snow, 2009). However, it is important to note that these numbers likely underestimate the actual scope of human trafficking and sexually exploited women, men, and children. This can be partly attributed to varying state definitions of human trafficking, varying state laws criminalizing human trafficking, and the recent classification of human trafficking as a crime in the national Uniform Crime Report, as of January 2013. Adding to this, currently, there is no national protocol to correctly identify human trafficking victims, and due to differing state laws and law enforcement focus, there is a discrepancy between who is defined as a victim and who is defined as an offender (Macy & Graham, 2012). Overall, the lack of protocols and standard policies to address human trafficking nationally has led to a lack of reporting and a lack of data (Dank et al., 2014).

The first notable effort to eliminate all forms of human trafficking through law came through the enactment of the federal Victims of Trafficking & Violence Protection Act (VTVPA) of 2000. According to the VTVPA (2000), human trafficking and "**severe forms of trafficking in persons**" is generally defined as the recruitment, harboring, transportation, provision, or obtaining of a person for labor or services, through the use of force, fraud, or **coercion** for the purpose of subjection to involuntary servitude, peonage, **debt bondage**, or slavery. It also defines a **commercial sex act** as any sex act on account of which anything of value is given to or received by any individual. It further states that **sex trafficking**, being a form of human trafficking, is the recruitment, harboring, or transportation of individuals for the purpose of commercial sex induced by force, fraud, or coercion (VTVPA, 2000). The VTVPA (2000) criminalizes human trafficking, but also focuses on eradicating human trafficking through prevention, protection, and prosecution. The VTVPA (2000) outlines legislative goals to protect and assist victims of trafficking, but these goals are often contradicted by a lack of national protocols and training to correctly identify trafficking victims—there is often a discrepancy between who is defined as a victim and who is defined as an offender (Farrell, 2014; Macy & Graham, 2012; Mir, 2013; U.S. Department of State, 2013).

The discrepancy inherent in human trafficking state laws has led to inconsistencies between who is considered an offender or a victim (Mir, 2013; U.S. Department of State, 2013). For example, since prostitution is a state crime, different state jurisdictions have different approaches in legally punishing prostituted people. For instance, some states recognize that the force, fraud, or coercion defined in sex trafficking is also involved in the crime of prostitution. This newer framework changes misperceptions that the majority of women willingly choose to work in the sex industry, as law enforcements agencies and courts choose to focus their prosecutorial efforts on the buyer and trafficker of sex (Kelemen & Johansson, 2013; Yen, 2008). The original approach of using the law to prosecute prostituted persons and potential victims of sex trafficking has been at the expense of the victimized individual. Unfortunately, a victim of sex trafficking may experience this dual victimization from their trafficker and the criminal justice system that is intended to protect and offer support to victims of crime (Dank et al., 2014; Farrell, 2014; Mir, 2013; U.S. Department of State, 2013).

Though proper identification of victims is a significant issue in human trafficking, once a victim is correctly identified, it is important to connect victims to supportive services because of the physical and psychological violence victims endure (Cecchet & Thoburn, 2014; Macy & Johns, 2011; Zaykowski, 2014). Although there is currently scant research addressing the psychological experiences of sexually exploited children and adults in the United States, research demonstrates that sexually exploited children and adults experience brutal physical abuse, sexual assault, and psychological abuse (Cecchet & Thoburn, 2014; Gajic-Veljanoski & Stewart, 2007; Raymond & Hughes, 2001; Zimmerman et al., 2003). Although the physical abuse is substantial, sex trafficking trauma is not limited to physical trauma and extends to mental and emotional trauma from the verbal and physical violence. This trauma can have long-term effects resulting in depression, post-traumatic stress disorder (PTSD), and anxiety (Williamson & Prior, 2009). The traumatic and painful experiences of sex trafficking survivors illustrate the need for training in the identification of potential victims and the provision of victim support services.

The growing, politicized concern of human trafficking and the afore-mentioned research about the experiences of survivors demonstrates the need for more research concerning how victims of human trafficking are often discussed in public discourse and in the media. Therefore, this chapter focuses on victims of human trafficking, including those involved in both sex and labor trafficking. A content analysis is provided below using *The New York Times* articles from 2001 to 2015 involving victims of human trafficking. Content and themes in these articles were analyzed to investigate how victims of human trafficking are portrayed in the media compared to empirical literature. The chapter concludes with a discussion about further areas of research of human trafficking and next steps in understanding the evolving public framing of human trafficking in the media.

LITERATURE REVIEW

HUMAN TRAFFICKING

The first notable effort to eliminate human trafficking in the United States came about with the enactment of the Victims of Trafficking and Violence Protection Act (2000). Again, the VTVPA's definition of human trafficking requires the use of force, fraud, or coercion to achieve a traf-ficker's goal of victim exploitation (U.S. Department of State, 2013). A common misconception about human trafficking is that the person(s) need to be transported to meet the legal definition of trafficking; how-ever, current legislation does not require physical transportation (Logan, Walker, & Hunt, 2009; U.S. Department of State, 2013). Although human trafficking is a global phenomenon, the focus in this chapter is human trafficking in the United States, as the content analysis uses only articles that focus on victimization reported from the National Desk at *The New York Times*.

Furthermore, it is important to understand the varying definitions of human trafficking because of its direct effect on understanding human trafficking in the United States and its implications for how trafficking is reported and discussed. For example, sex trafficking is often associated with prostitution, but consent and coercion are key to its distinction (U.S. Department of State, 2013). If an adult is coerced, forced, or maintained in prostitution (even after initially consenting), then the person is considered a trafficking victim (U.S. Department of State, 2013). Sex trafficking can also occur in debt bondage, which means victims are forced into it and continue in order to "pay" their "debt" through their transportation or "sale" (U.S. Department of State, 2013). It is also important to recognize that an individual's "initial consent to participate in prostitution is not legally determinative: if one is thereafter held in service through psychological manipulation or physical force, he or she is a trafficking victim" (U.S. Department of State, 2013, p. 29). All of these laws and definitional explanations illustrate the importance of the force, fraud, or coercion component of the TVPA to determine what is considered human trafficking, including sex trafficking.

In addition to understanding the human trafficking definitions, it is equally important to understand the several actors responsible for the growing criminal enterprise of the commercial sex industry. For example, a sex buyer is the person who is exchanging money, or something else of value, for sex. Prior research finds that sex buyers range in age, ethnicity, and marital status (Serughetti, 2012). Besides buyers and sellers, there is often a third-party individual involved in crimes of demand: a pimp or trafficker. They are similar in that both manage sex workers and make money from the sex work performed. Yet an important distinction is that not all pimps exhibit behavior that meet the legal definition of trafficking, which would include the use of force, fraud, or coercion to compel the victim to engage in the commercial sex acts (Marcus, Horning, Curtis, Sanson, & Thompson, 2014; Nichols, 2016). Like sex buyers, there is no standard profile of pimps. Pimps and traffickers range in gender, age, and ethnicity. In the sex industry, a pimp is defined as the individual who controls the actions of others and profits from the work of these persons (Dank et al., 2014). A pimp could even be the owner of a brothel or nightclub that requires a portion of money the sex worker receives (Raphael & Shapiro, 2004).

The definitions of pimping and trafficking are often blurred and difficult to properly define, as are the definitions of prostitution and sex trafficking. Legally, pimping is trafficking when there is a threat to use or actual use of force, fraud, or coercion, along with payments being made to the person in control (Dank et al., 2014; United Nations Trafficking Protocol, 2000). Contrary to common perceptions, pimps do not have to be connected with organized crime, nor are they in most cases (Meshkovska, Siegel, Stutterheim, & Bos, 2015). Human traffickers are not only individual pimps, they are sometimes small businesses or international organized networks. Like pimps, traffickers can also be male or female and foreign nationals or U.S. citizens (Meshkovska et al., 2015). Human trafficking is a high-profit and low-risk industry. Overall, trafficking humans is highly profitable because traffickers not only gain money or services via profits from a victim's labor, but also via fees or non-monetary services taken from the victim and the resale or reuse of the person in the trafficking trade (Logan et al., 2009).

Additionally, although labor exploitation is frequently thought disparate from sexual exploitation, it is important to recognize that they should not be considered mutually exclusive. Sexual exploitation through private enterprises or homes of individuals who demand sex work is categorized as labor exploitation (Logan et al., 2009). Labor exploitation is arguably an overlooked issue due to the focus on sex trafficking and prostitution through politicized debates (Alvarez & Alessi, 2012). However, trafficked men, women, and children are forced to work in a wide range of industries, including sex work, agriculture, hospitality, food processing, and food service (Alvarez & Alessi, 2012).

Though labor exploitation often does not encompass sexual exploitation, other unclear aspects of human trafficking are migration and smuggling (Logan et al., 2009; Rafferty, 2013). As mentioned, the VTVPA states that human trafficking may include transportation, but human trafficking can also occur without transportation of the victim (VTVPA, 2000; U.S. Department of State, 2013). Therefore, it is important to understand the definitional differences between migration, smuggling, and human trafficking. For some individuals, trafficking occurs through travel; upon arrival, they find out they were deceived about what was awaiting them (Rafferty, 2013). Others may experience trafficking through migration—people leave their homes, generally willingly, to find better opportunities elsewhere (Global Movement for Children, 2010; Rafferty, 2013). However, those who migrate are vulnerable to traffickers and their deceptive schemes (Rafferty, 2013).

Smuggling, on the other hand, requires crossing a national border illegally (Rafferty, 2013). Smuggling does not involve the key element of coercion that is explicitly outlined in the TVPA (Rafferty, 2013). **Human smuggling** is typically consensual, and the relationship between those smuggled and the transporter generally ends upon reaching the destination (Logan et al., 2009). However, in human trafficking, the transportation of the person(s) may be an initial step as a means to entrap individuals (Logan et al., 2009). Overall, the components outlined in the TVPA (2000) of coercion, force, fraud, and deception are important to understand how human trafficking is categorized separately from migration and smuggling.

SIZE AND SCOPE OF HUMAN TRAFFICKING

As mentioned, there are often varying definitions and a lack of standard protocols about how to appropriately identify victims of human trafficking; therefore, the scope of human trafficking, including sex and labor trafficking, is often underestimated (Dank et al., 2014). Studies have estimated that the global profit is approximately $32 billion a year (Belser, 2005; Dank et al., 2014). An estimated $28 billion of this $32 billion can be attributed to commercial sexual exploitation alone (Belser, 2005). The International Labour Organization (ILO, 2012) also estimates that there are at least 20.9 million victims of human trafficking worldwide, defined as cases in which victims are forced, coerced, and cannot leave. The ILO's (2012) estimate captures human trafficking as encompassing labor and sexual exploitation, and these estimates cover the years 2002 through 2011. Additionally, of the total 20.9 million forced laborers, 18.7 million are exploited in the private economy—by individuals or enterprises (ILO, 2012). Of this, 4.5 million are victims of sexual exploitation and 14.2 million are victims of forced labor (e.g., activities of domestic work, agriculture, and construction) (ILO, 2012). It is also important to note that women and girls represent 11.4 million of the 20.9 million victims forced into labor (ILO, 2012).

Since the figures mentioned represent global figures produced by a United Nations agency, it is important to note figures produced from a leading agency that offers direct client service on a national level—the Polaris Project (Polaris Project, 2015). In December 2007, the Polaris Project opened a National Human Trafficking Hotline Resource Center (NHTRC) to combat trafficking by providing resources for victims of human trafficking in the United States. The NHTRC is a central hub for information on human trafficking in the United States; their data are collected through phone calls, emails, or online tips. For example, in the 2015 Annual Report, there were 24,757 reports received by the NHTRC (Polaris Project, 2015). Each request is then evaluated for evidence of human trafficking, and 5,544 were identified as unique cases of potential of human trafficking. Overall, our current calculations for the rates of human trafficking are likely underestimated because of the lack of identification protocols, the misidentification of victims, and the lack of standards for how non-governmental and governmental agencies track this data (Belser, 2005; Dank et al., 2014; Mir, 2013; Polaris Project, 2013).

Despite legislative reforms to criminalize sex trafficking and encourage victim support services, there is currently a lack of mandated practices, trainings, and protocols to assist first responders, namely law enforcement, in the correct identification of sex trafficking victims (Department of State, 2013). Victim misidentification inhibits access to justice and recovery; victims are re-victimized through being mislabeled by the criminal justice system (U.S. Department of State, 2013). Examples of mislabeling include labeling domestic minor sex trafficking victims as runaways, homeless youth, juvenile delinquents, or prostitutes. For adult victims of commercial sexual exploitation, mislabeling includes a law enforcement focus on arrest for the crime of prostitution, instead of labeling these individuals as victims in need of victim support services. For example, according to the Bureau of Justice Statistics (BJS), there were 62,670 arrests for prostitution and commercialized vice between 1990 and 2010 (Snyder, 2012). In these cases, the sex worker was female 69 percent of the time (Synder, 2012). The BJS also reported that between 1990 and 2010, the arrest rate for prostitution and commercialized vice decreased dramatically by half (down 55%) (Synder, 2012). It can be argued that part of this decrease is because of a shift by law enforcement to address the buyer or demand for sex rather than the sex workers (Serughetti, 2012; Shively, Kliorys, Wheeler, & Hunt, 2012).

Additionally, there are patterns in victim demographics involved in different forms of human trafficking. In a report about federal human trafficking cases that occurred between 2008 and 2010, Banks and Kyckelhahn (2011) reported several differences between labor trafficking victims and sex trafficking victims of 389 incidents confirmed to be human trafficking. First, 62 percent of labor trafficking victims were aged 25 or older, compared to just 13 percent for sex trafficking cases. They also found that sex trafficking victims were more likely to be White or Black, while labor trafficking victims were more likely to be Hispanic or Asian (Banks & Kyckelhahn, 2011). Furthermore, 83 percent of sex trafficking incidents involved U.S. citizens, while most labor trafficking victims were identified as undocumented—67 percent of victims were deemed undocumented and 28 percent were legal U.S. residents without citizenship (Banks & Kyckelhahn, 2011). The demographic and statistical patterns provided through varying agencies and research are important tools that draw attention to the victims of human trafficking and highlight the complexity in addressing the varying needs of victims.

THE GROWING HUMAN TRAFFICKING CONCERN

It can be argued that the issue of human trafficking, especially sex trafficking, has been at the forefront of discussions in the United States and is highly politicized due to the social construction of sex trafficking (Weitzer, 2007). The social construction framework examines how social problems can be constructed through a complex process involving the public, media, and government officials. For example, sex workers were described as being trafficked against their will for prostitution for the first time in the

United States during the Progressive Era (1890–1920) (Bromfield, 2016). However, there was a distinction between "what type" of sex workers were in need of rescue and protection due to a popular White slave narrative developed during this time (Bromfield, 2016). The term "White slavery" was applied to White women only, and these women were depicted as victims who were most often forced into prostitution (Bromfield, 2016). However, women of color, and particularly African American women, were seen as uncivilized, immoral, and deviant; therefore, women of color were excluded from public discourse about being forced into prostitution (Bromfield, 2016). Although White slavery received wide attention during the Progressive Era, there was little evidence to support this claim, and the term continued to be used to understand sex work and draw national attention, eventually becoming the narrative used to explain prostitution.

Additionally, this popular White slavery discourse and moral panic led to laws regulating prostitution in 1910 (Bromfield, 2016). The Mann Act of 1910, known as the White Slave Traffic Act, prohibited the transportation of women for "immoral purposes" or prostitution whether across countries or state lines (Bromfield, 2016). Although this was the most widely accepted federal legislation during the early 1900s, it did not mandate any supportive services to victims and did not protect victims from being treated as criminals (Bromfield, 2016). The Mann Act of 1910 was mainly used to prosecute sex trafficking cases in the United States until the enactment of the Trafficking Victims Protection Act (2000).

Furthermore, beginning in 1979, the radical feminist and prohibitionist frameworks viewed trafficking as a human rights issue, as supported through the feminist exposition efforts of Kathleen Barry (Marinova & James, 2012). Barry believed that sexual exploitation, including prostitution, was a violation against the woman's body and called for a convention outlawing violations against women's rights. She advocated for an international document outlawing trafficking; this occurred with the passage of The Convention on the Elimination of All Forms of Discrimination Against Women in 1979 (Marinova & James, 2012). With regard to prostitution, Barry asserted that states legalizing prostitution only signaled to traffickers and others that the sex industry is a legitimate enterprise;

she argued that the state essentially became another "pimp" receiving the earnings from prostituted people (Marinova & James, 2012). Overall, the violence against women movements and the feminist perspective drew attention to sex trafficking as a form of violence against women and children.

By the mid-1990s, human trafficking was depicted in the media and drew national attention as a human rights issue (Farrell & Fahy, 2009). News articles were focused on the dangerous and horrid conditions faced by women forced into prostitution and associated trafficking issues with poverty and inequality (Farrell & Fahy, 2009). The media covered stories about White women trafficked from brothels and highlighted victims who looked like "the girl next door" (Farrell & Fahy, 2009). In the late 1990s, trafficking gained institutional attention as Hilary Clinton and others began an international campaign for women's human rights. The Presidential Interagency Council of Women was then established by the Clinton administration in the 1990s and further promoted the prioritization of sex trafficking as a women's issue, with international and national implications (Farrell & Fahy, 2009). There continued to be debate over consensual prostitution which reemerged internationally during the creation of the United Nations Protocol to Prevent, Suppress, and Punish Trafficking in Persons, Especially Women and Children, also known as the Palmero Protocol. The Palmero Protocol addressed the international sex trade and supports states in developing laws and anti-trafficking strategies (Farrell & Fahy, 2009; Rafferty, 2013). Although anti-trafficking groups argued over theoretical differences between prostitution and consensual sex work, there was a consensus around the view that human trafficking needed a criminal justice response (Farrell & Fahy, 2009). Hilary Clinton continued to call for a focus on national legislation criminalizing human trafficking, and with growing public acceptance, the Victims of Trafficking and Violence Protection Act of 2000 was enacted making human trafficking a crime.

Additionally, during this time, the "client" grew to be depicted as responsible for the growth of the sex industry and for the victimization and oppression of sex workers (Shively et al., 2012). Like the market for any commodity, the commercial sex market is driven by demand (Logan et al., 2009). Sweden played a critical role in this framing after the passage of the Sex Purchase Act of 1999 (Berger, 2012). In Sweden, prostitution is viewed as an important social issue because it is viewed as a catalyst for violence against women. It is argued that this form of violence causes harm to the individual and has negative implications for the entire welfare of society. Though it stems from a gender-based movement, research by Bucken-Knapp, Schaffer, and Stromback (2012) found that the Swedish model emerged from anti-trafficking measures that paired national security with gender equality concerns. They argue that securitization had the greatest influence for the enactment of anti-trafficking policies (Swedish police and prosecutors were given the tools to fight trafficking), whereas, gender equality ideas shaped how these policy issues were discussed and proposed to the public (Bucken-Knapp et al., 2012). Unlike the United States, where the framing focuses on stricter penalties, international efforts have approached this as a social issue where there is a national concern for equality (Bucken-Knapp et al., 2012).

Furthermore, by the 2000s in the United States, the reframing and association of human trafficking to anti-immigration campaigns made it an increasingly popular issue in the media, as international organized crime groups became the focus behind this growing criminal enterprise (Farrell & Fahy, 2009; Kraska & Brent, 2011; Spector & Kitsuse, 1973). The news media blamed Eastern European and Southeast Asian organized crime groups, as well as mafias in Germany (Farrell & Fahy, 2009). Human trafficking then became linked to illegal migration, in which the traffickers (organized crime groups) exploited and abused people during their movements across borders (Jahic & Finckenauer, 2005). It can be argued that this viewpoint resulted in merging definitions of human trafficking, immigration, and smuggling, though clearly defined separately (Jahic & Finckenauer, 2005). The addition of organized criminal groups as offenders resulted in framing the issue about concerns over organized crime and away from illegal migration (Jahic & Finckenauer, 2005). The profits gained by these organized crime groups from human trafficking also added to growing concern over threats to global stability and safety (Jahic & Finckenauer, 2005).

With the media's influence, victims became portrayed as foreign nationals even though the TVPA did not require victims to actually cross borders or be immigrants to be deemed victims of human trafficking (Farrell & Fahy, 2009). Policymakers and legislatures then used this inaccurate depiction of victims to reframe trafficking as a national security concern. After the tragedies of September 11, 2001, politicians began to define human trafficking as a national security threat in need of a criminal justice response (Farrell & Fahy, 2009). Though human trafficking affects people regardless of citizenship status, this association rooted human trafficking in the terrorism discussions post-9/11, as the federal government began prioritizing homeland security and connected human trafficking to the fight against terrorism (Farrell & Fahy, 2009). Farrell and Fahy (2009) analyzed text from U.S. newspaper articles about human trafficking from 1990 to 2006 and found that the adoption of policies focused on national security. This development has been deemed a "migration approach" because trafficking, whether for labor or commercial sex, is viewed as an immigration issue, which is inherently tied to the national security discourse (Marinova & James, 2012).

In 2003, President Bush in a White House Press Release issued a National Security Presidential Directive that included combating human trafficking through the implementation of the Department of State's Office to Monitor and Combat Trafficking in Persons (The White House, 2003). This task force was developed to fight human trafficking by training federal agencies in proper identification and responsibilities; encouraging cooperation between local and state law enforcement agencies to identify local traffickers; and ensuring integration of international programs for prevention and identification purposes (Farrell & Fahy, 2009; U.S. Department of State, 2003). However, reframing this issue as a concern over immigration and national security not only brings more awareness and raises societal concerns, but it can simultaneously re-victimize survivors of trafficking due to labeling victims as offenders (U.S. Department of State, 2013). Human trafficking linked to a national security threat can perpetuate the criminalization of survivors rather than the offering of support services. For example, victims of sex trafficking may be misidentified and labeled as illegal immigrants or prostitutes in need of criminal sanctions rather than victims in need of protection (Bernat & Zhilina, 2010; U.S. Department of Justice, 2013). Overall, the view of human trafficking using the migration approach disregards the problem of consent and coercion because of the focus on national security.

VICTIM EXPERIENCES

The history of and growing concern about human trafficking continues to shed light on the horrid conditions and abuse that victims endure. Although there have been shifts in public discourse about how human trafficking is framed, there is still agreement about the need to criminalize human trafficking due to the abuse victims experience. Human trafficking victimization sometimes begins as early as the initial recruitment, when traffickers acquire their victims through the use of force, fraud, and/or coercion. Initial fraud or coercion can take many forms such as promises of financial stability, stable employment, or a better life. The trafficker will then force the victim into sex acts (e.g., pornography or prostitution), forced labor, or both (Hodge, 2008).

Psychological coercion is also prevalent when maintaining control over victims. Traffickers may convince their victim that if they leave or seek help from law enforcement they will not be believed or will face legal punishment. Victims may also be forced to pay some type of debt, often a large sum of money that will require a lengthy time to pay back, while accruing new charges for items such as passports, travel, food, and housing (Hodge, 2008; U.S. Department of State, 2013). This is known as debt bondage (Hepburn & Simon, 2010; Hodge, 2008). Foreign national victims may be stripped of their legal documents, such as their passport or identification, as a way to threaten deportation and instill fear in victims to ensure they submit to demands (Hodge, 2008; Raymond & Hughes, 2001).

A correct understanding of victims of human trafficking as victims rather than offenders is imperative to properly identify victims and offer the supportive services they so desperately need to recover from the traumatic abuse they have experienced. The health effects of sex trafficking are complex and extensive due to the psychological, emotional, physical, and sexual abuse endured (Cecchet & Thoburn, 2014; Gajic-Veljanoski & Stewart, 2007; Miller, Decker, Silverman, & Raj, 2007; Rafferty, 2013; Zimmerman et al., 2003). Physical violence is commonly observed in cases of human trafficking in which traffickers seek to reassert power and control over the victim. Zimmerman et al. (2003) found extensive physical abuse experiences by victims of sexual exploitation, such as rape, sexual assault, broken bones, burns, and various forms of torture. Even if the victim is compliant, the trafficker may threaten and/or use physical and sexual violence to instill fear in victims to ensure continued compliance (Hepburn & Simon, 2010; Hodge, 2008). Research on the victimization of sex workers has found that they face increased risk of rape, robbery, and assault (Cobbina & Oselin, 2011).

Furthermore, a study comparing indoor and outdoor prostitution found violence was dependent on the type of sex work the individual engaged in, whether as an escort, exotic dancer, or street worker (Raphael & Shapiro, 2004). This study measured the prevalence of violence of 222 women that were in indoor and outdoor prostitution venues (Raphael & Shapiro, 2004). Raphael and Shapiro (2004) found that street-level prostitution has the greatest prevalence of violence, such as being slapped, punched, and threatened with a weapon. Although they found that prostitutes outdoors generally reported higher levels of physical violence, women in indoor venues also experienced violence. Being threatened with rape and being raped were highest among drug houses, and exotic dancers experience having something thrown at them (Raphael & Shapiro, 2004). Moreover, of their sample, 50 percent of women that were in escort services reported forced sex, and 51.2 percent of women working as exotic dancers were threatened with a weapon (Raphael & Shapiro, 2004). Overall, the frequency of violence experienced across types of prostitution and venues demonstrates the abuse and violence that frequently occurs and the need to appropriately identify victims in order to offer supportive services.

Although the physical abuse is substantial, sex trafficking is not limited to physical abuse; it extends to psychological abuse as well (George, 2012; Hodge 2008; Macy & Johns, 2011). It is important to highlight the mental health experiences of sex trafficked victims because the mental, psychological, and emotional abuses experienced by the victim are shown to be substantial even at initial contact with the abuser due to the manipulation, coercion, and deceit used by the traffickers. Research to date demonstrates that the trauma that accompanies sexual exploitation is associated with anxiety, PTSD, suicide, and depression (Hodge, 2008; Macy & Johns, 2011; Raymond & Hughes, 2001; Williamson & Prior, 2009). Other potential and existing mental health issues specifically faced by child victims of sex trafficking include attachment disorders, conduct disorders, developmental disorders, learning disorders, eating disorders, and mood disorders (Smith, et al., 2009).

The various types of mental health disorders experienced by victims of sex trafficking can also be accompanied by substance abuse. Sex workers may also be struggling with drug addiction, which can negatively affect psychological well-being. According to a study by Miller et al. (2007), subjects who were victims of sex trafficking reported that substance use began and subsequently escalated during their involvement in sex work. Other research finds that substance use remains an issue even after victims are removed from the trafficking situation. During recovery and thereafter, chemical dependency is found as a significant problem for victims of commercial sexual exploitation (Miller et al., 2007; Raymond & Hughes, 2001). Drugs and alcohol were also used during recovery as a mechanism to cope with the various traumas endured by the victim (Miller et al., 2007; Raymond & Hughes, 2001).

Due to the mislabeling of victims as offenders, varying state-level legislation, and a lack of standard identification protocol, it can be argued that human trafficking victims experience structural violence. Structural violence occurs when there is an unequal distribution of power among actors; this power, therefore, systematically disadvantages those who do not hold as much (Galtung, 1969). Galtung (1969) coined the term structural violence, and it can be applied to the experiences of victims of human trafficking in their encounters with law enforcement and when seeking assistance. For example, in their effort to identify challenges in the investigation and prosecution of human trafficking cases, Farrell et al. (2012) found that there were continued concerns in law enforcement and the justice system about victim cooperation, credibility, and testimony. Victims may recant their testimony out of fear of their trafficker or mistrust of law enforcement; and the interview process to secure case evidence and information can be re-traumatizing for victims (Farrell et al., 2012). Victims may feel or be coerced into providing information to law enforcement, a structure of power, in which they may believe their safety is dependent upon their cooperation with enforcement (Farrell et al., 2012). Moreover, the hidden nature of human trafficking, the isolation and intimidation employed by traffickers, and the lack of awareness among victims about their status and legal rights are all factors that contribute to the lack of victim identification (Gallagher & Holmes, 2008).

Although victims of trafficking may be unaware of their legal rights or protections, the TPVA (2000) is the federal legislation that not only defines human trafficking but also focuses on combative efforts through prevention of the crime, protection of victims, and prosecution of traffickers. It calls for prevention by increasing international economic opportunities for potential victims of trafficking and enhancing public awareness. It provides protection by affording foreign victims of trafficking with T-visas that allow for temporary U.S. residency. Lastly, it strengthens prosecution by enhancing punishment against all forms of human trafficking (TVPA, 2000). Since the enactment of the TVPA (2000), it has been reauthorized in 2003, 2005, 2008, and 2013 to include provisions for federal funding, provisions to allow trafficking victims to sue their traffickers, support programs to shelter survivors of human trafficking, and support for databases on human trafficking (Farrell & Fahy 2009). However, correctly identifying victims of trafficking in order to appropriately offer support and immediate help remains difficult (Gallagher & Holmes, 2008). The continued misidentification of victims as offenders further inhibits access to justice and recovery due to the re-victimization experienced in the criminal justice system during this mislabeling (U.S. Department of State, 2013).

Although federal law requires a criminal justice response and state obligations to support and protect trafficking victims, Farrell et al. (2012) also found that law enforcement are often unprepared to handle the amount of trauma experienced by victims; therefore, at times they used tactics such as arresting and detaining victims to secure their cooperation. Victims of trafficking play a critical role in the prosecution of traffickers, but this heavy reliance on victims as witnesses can lead to tactics that harm victims or coerce them into cooperating (Gallagher & Holmes, 2008).

The Farrell et al. (2012) investigation found that there were several institutional barriers to prosecuting and addressing human trafficking cases. For example, police and prosecutors lack the training and knowledge in prosecuting human trafficking cases as well as resources to provide adequate care for victims throughout the arrest and trial process (Farrell et al., 2012). There were also few specialized task forces trained in policing human trafficking, and the negative attitudes of prosecutors and police toward the victims may limit the cases they investigate (Farrell et al., 2012; Gallagher & Holmes, 2008). Overall, although current legislative goals aim to address human trafficking through prevention, protection, and prosecution, the mislabeling of victims as offenders or the mistreatment of victims by the criminal justice system impedes these goals and can re-traumatize victims.

As mentioned, the federal legislative goals to criminalize human trafficking and support victims was influenced by shifts in public framing and, ultimately, the public acceptance of human trafficking as an issue in need of a criminal justice response. The media often shapes public acceptance, awareness, and perception; therefore, a content analysis was conducted to explore how human trafficking is depicted in national media.

CONTENT ANALYSIS OF *THE NEW YORK TIMES* ARTICLES

This section seeks to explore (1) how victims of human trafficking are represented in the media and (2) the extent to which this representation aligns with what is known about these victims in scholarly literature.

To accomplish this, we reviewed *The New York Times* articles about human trafficking from 2001 to 2015 and analyzed various content areas in these articles. The keywords used to gather articles for this analysis included prostitution, sex workers, sex trafficking, call girls, escort service, and human trafficking (excluding drug trafficking). It is important to note these keywords because, as mentioned in previous literature, these definitions are often mixed or interchangeable in public discourse. For example, human trafficking encompasses sex trafficking and is often associated with prostitution (with consent versus coercion being key to its distinction) (U.S. Department of State, 2013). Victims of trafficking are forced into different forms of trafficking, with prostitution, escort services, and pornography representing venues where commercial sexual exploitation can take place (Dank et al., 2014). Therefore, it was important to be over-inclusive of articles when analyzing human trafficking in *The New York Times*. Part of the content analysis focuses on the language and words used to describe victims of human trafficking. Of the articles included in this analysis, information about several variables was collected for each piece, including the gender of victim(s), gender of perpetrator(s), placement within the newspaper, year of publication, word count, whether the article was victim focused, use of the word smuggling, and the language used to describe trafficking victims (e.g., labor trafficking, sex trafficking, prostitution, etc.).

The initial search query pulled 1,046 articles that had the specific search terms in the articles or tags. The articles were reduced to a sample size of 139. The 139 articles included in this content analysis focused on victims or incidents related to human trafficking, including labor trafficking, sex trafficking, prostitution, and escort services. The types of violence that the articles discussed included homicide, assault, and individuals injured. Some articles were excluded from the sample because they did not meet the specific inclusion criteria mentioned above. For example, some of the articles that were unrelated to victimization and only pertained to legal policy, such as human trafficking legislation, were omitted.

A word count variable was included to examine how much media coverage was allotted to articles relating to victims of human trafficking. The amount of coverage of specific events speaks to the event's newsworthiness. The average number of words per article was 820. In addition, the location of the article in *The New York Times* was examined. This variable looked at whether the article was featured on the front page. A total of 15 articles (11%) included in the sample were featured on the front page of *The New York Times*. These articles were about homicides of prostitutes, sexual assault, and labor trafficking. Next, we coded the type of victimization that was featured in the article. Similar to the Uniform Crime Report's hierarchy rule, if the article featured several types of victimization, the most severe crime was counted (U.S. Department of Justice, 2014). For example, if an article described sexual assault and homicide, the article was coded as homicide, not sexual assault. The categories of crime types included prostitution, trafficking, smuggling, and sexual assault. The most frequent crime type mentioned in the sample was prostitution, with 62 percent (n = 86) of articles discussing prostitution in some form. More specifically, of those articles discussing prostitution, 53 percent (n = 46) were about homicides of prostitutes and five percent (n = 4) discussed sexual assault of prostitutes. Of the articles discussing prostitution, 24 percent (n = 21) were about prostitution of a minor. Prostitution of a minor was not coded automatically as sex trafficking in this analysis because the criminalizing of child prostitutes still varies across states nationwide (i.e., Safe Harbor Laws). Safe Harbor Laws provide legal protections to sexually exploited minors by reclassifying them as victims, providing legal immunity, and diverting them to programs rather than charging them with prostitution (Polaris Project, 2013). We argue, as the Safe Harbor Laws do, and as defined by the TVPA (2000), that minors cannot consent and therefore are forced to prostitute. Moreover, of the articles that focused on prostitution, words such as forced or coerced were only used to describe the victims in 17 percent (n = 15) of these articles, and interestingly, all of these articles were about prostitution of minors. It was important to determine and look at whether or not words such as forced or coerced were used to describe prostitution because, again, force, fraud, and coercion are essential in the TPVA (2000) to determine whether human trafficking or sex trafficking occurred. Furthermore, of the 139 articles sampled, nine percent (n = 13) mentioned sex trafficking, and of those sex trafficking articles, the majority (62%) were about the prostitution of minors.

Additionally, smuggling was the second most frequent crime type, with 23 percent (n = 32) of the articles mentioning it. Although there are fundamental differences between smuggling and human trafficking and the word "smuggling" was not part of the search query, 16 percent of articles (n = 5) from this sample used the words human trafficking interchangeably with smuggling. Interestingly, there was also a pattern where smuggling was the main crime type, but the article focused on the killings, murder, and/or deaths resulting from smuggling. More specifically, of the sample of smuggling articles, 66 percent (n = 21) were about deaths resulting from smuggling.

Furthermore, trafficking was the third most frequent crime type mentioned with 11.5 percent (n = 16) of the sample discussing trafficking in some form. More specifically, of the trafficking sample, 81 percent of the trafficking themed articles (n = 13) discussed labor trafficking. They were labeled as labor trafficking when stories described debt bondage, workers being forced to work, workers experiencing violence in the workplace, and/or threats or lies being used to force people to work. Interestingly, all but one of the articles focused on labor trafficking were explicitly linked to illegal migration concerns. Moreover, two of the trafficking articles mentioned prostitution, but they were not coded as prostitution because words like forced or coerced were used in the story when discussing prostitution. Therefore, these two articles were labeled as trafficking since a form of sex trafficking is prostitution when force, fraud, or coercion is evident. Interestingly, both explicitly labeled the crime as sex trafficking instead of prostitution and used the words "forced prostitution" in the article. However, this does not mean that those articles labeled with the crime type of prostitution did not involve force or coercion; it just means that these articles did not explicitly use those words to describe the prostitution and, therefore, were not coded as trafficking. Of the trafficking sample, only three articles discussed sex trafficking (19%); a larger percentage of articles actually discussed labor trafficking (81%).

Articles were also coded according to whether they focused on the victim, meaning that at least 50 percent of the article focused on the victim and their victimization. Only about 21 percent of the articles in the sample met the criteria of focusing on the victim(s). Approximately 80 percent of the articles in the sample focused on the offender or other events that were irrelevant to the victim's perspective or victimization.

Demographic characteristics of the victim and the offender were all recorded. Beginning with the gender of victims, approximately 19 percent of the articles featured both females and males. More specifically, the majority (75%) of crimes associated with the articles featuring both female and male victims were about smuggling. Moreover, female victims were represented in 52 percent of the articles. The articles featuring females as victims ranged across varying crime types—trafficking, prostitution, and sexual assault. However, of the female-featured articles, the majority (90%) were about prostitution. Interestingly, the majority (60%) of the articles about prostitution of female victims were also about the homicide of prostitutes. Additionally, male victims were identified in approximately 10 percent of the articles. The articles featuring males as victims also ranged across all varying crime types about trafficking, prostitution, and sexual assault. However, 57 percent of these articles were prostitution focused (e.g., a case regarding a 4-year-old boy trafficked into the United States with individuals who had the intention of prostituting him). Lastly, 19 percent of the articles did not specify the gender of the victim. Interestingly, 44 percent of the articles where the gender was unknown were about labor trafficking victims.

The gender of the perpetrator was also recorded for each article when the gender was specified. Approximately 54 percent (n = 75) of articles identified one male or multiple males as perpetrators, whereas only four percent (n = 6) of articles featured females as the sole perpetrators of victimization. Of the articles identifying males as the perpetrators, the majority (73%) involved male perpetrators of prostitution victimization, and 65 percent involved male perpetrators murdering/killing prostitutes. Lastly, six percent (n = 8) of the articles identified both female and male

TABLE 12.1 The Type of Crime On Which
Each Article Focused (N = 139)

	n	%
Prostitution	86	61.9
Smuggling	32	23.0
Trafficking	16	11.5
Other	5	3.6

perpetrators, and 36 percent (n = 50) of the articles did not explicitly specify the gender of the perpetrator.

There were several specific cases/events/trials that were the focus of multiple articles in *The New York Times*. The frequencies of these types of cases were coded and analyzed. The case that featured the most articles (n = 15) was a story about 19 people who were killed during a human smuggling transport. A total of 74 people were harmed during the transport. Twenty percent of these articles focused on a 4-year-old Thai boy who was trafficked into the United States for purposes related to prostitution. Finally, 15 percent covered the Tyson Farms smuggling scandal in which employees were charged for conspiring to smuggle workers for cheap labor and helping them to gain counterfeit work papers at more than a dozen Tyson plants. Additionally, of the 139 articles, 14 percent focused on high-profile cases regarding offenders and the trial process for the cases.

DISCUSSION

This chapter providing a literature review of victims of human trafficking and the sequential content analysis explored (1) how victims of human trafficking are represented in the media and (2) the extent to which this representation aligned with what is known about victims in the literature. First, this chapter provided a literature review exploring definitions related to human trafficking, historical context about the criminalization of human trafficking and the growing human trafficking concern via public framing, and an overview of victims' experiences. Through this literature review, the importance in understanding the varying definitions related to human trafficking and how human trafficking is defined and criminalized in the United States was evident because of the frequent mislabeling of victims as offenders (Farrell & Fahy, 2009; U.S. Department of State, 2013). Therefore, the content analysis included an examination of how language was used to depict victims of human trafficking. Finally, as mentioned, articles that were excluded in this analysis were those dealing with legal policy and legislation pertaining to human trafficking.

It is important to note and reiterate that there was an over-inclusion of articles of prostitution and sex work, in general, to capture more articles regarding human trafficking and sex trafficking specifically. The initial search query included prostitution, sex workers, sex trafficking, call girls, escort service, and human trafficking (excluding drug trafficking). As mentioned in the analysis, although trafficking was the third most frequent crime type of the articles, it was important to discuss the other crime types of prostitution and smuggling because these crime types.

VICTIMS OF HUMAN TRAFFICKING REPRESENTED IN THE MEDIA

First, this content analysis was conducted to explore how victims of human trafficking were portrayed and represented in *The New York Times*. As noted in the literature, some acts that law enforcement criminalizes that relate to the sex industry include adult and minor prostitution, and the sex trafficking of adults (Dank et al., 2014). However, due to varying state laws, there is often a discrepancy between who is labeled as a victim or an offender, as some states recognize that force, fraud, or coercion defined in sex trafficking is also involved in prostitution (Mir, 2012; U.S. Department of State, 2013). Therefore, in this content analysis, crime types of prostitution, trafficking, smuggling, and sexual assault were differentiated and coded appropriately. Although these were not predetermined in terms of search categories, it was evident in *The New York Times* articles that coding crimes accordingly would make for a more meaningful analysis.

Also, prostitution was the most frequent crime type mentioned in the 139-article sample (62%). More specifically, 54 percent of the articles discussing prostitution were about the homicide of victims. These articles more frequently discussed the offender, the trial, and the charges against the perpetrator rather than a more victim-focused article about the victim's experiences. For example more articles were about killers' families, murder convictions, and guilty pleas. As in the criminal justice system, in the media the victim is often largely ignored or mislabeled as an offender rather than as a victim. As noted in the literature, victims are often considered offenders in need of punishment rather than supportive services; therefore, law enforcement agencies focus on prosecutorial efforts against the victims of trafficking rather than the buyer or trafficker of sex (Kelemen & Johansson, 2013; Mir, 2012; U.S. Department of State, 2013; Yen, 2008).

Similarly, of the articles that focused on prostitution, words such as forced or coerced were only used in 17 percent of the articles, and all of these articles were about the prostitution of minors. This is in alignment with federal law, which states that force, fraud, or coercion does not need to be explicitly found to determine that a prostituted minor is a victim of sex trafficking; sexual exploitation of a minor is automatically coercive (TVPA, 2000). However, it can be argued that this finding highlights common perceptions of choice (entering prostitution through coercion) are disregarded for adults and it is more widely accepted as being coercive for minors (Mir, 2013). Indeed, we found that of the 139-article sample, 13 percent described the crime as sex trafficking, and of this subset of sex-trafficking articles, the majority (62%) were about the prostitution of minors. Overall, we argue again that this highlights that perceptions of choice in prostitution and the labeling of sex trafficked individuals as victims, rather than offenders, may be easier to do for minors than for adults. Additionally, the placement of the article and the victim and offender demographics were analyzed, which contributed to understanding how victims are represented in the media. In total, 11 percent of articles included in the analysis were featured on the front page of *The New York Times*. However, these articles focused on the offender and the crime rather than the experiences of victims.

In all, it was also found that only 21 percent of sample of articles met the criteria for focusing on the victim. Moreover, female victims were represented in the majority of articles (52%) and 90 percent of these articles were about prostitution. More specifically, of these prostitution female-featured articles, 60 percent were about homicides of prostitutes. However, these articles were again offender-focused, featuring information about the trials, charges, and the perpetrator of the murder, rather than the victims themselves. Additionally, we found that 65 percent of articles discussed male(s) as perpetrators of prostitution-homicide related crimes; overall, of the 139-article sample, the majority (54%) identified male(s) as the perpetrator. In conclusion, we argue that these findings highlight that although potential sex trafficking victims, in the form of victimization of prostitutes, make up the majority of articles in this study sample, the victims and their experiences are largely left absent from the discussion.

HUMAN TRAFFICKING DEFINED & REPRESENTED IN THE MEDIA

As noted in the literature, more recently, human trafficking has become a legitimate concern because of its connection to immigration and national security (Farrell & Fahy, 2009; Kraska & Brent, 2011; Spector & Kitsuse, 1973). Therefore, it is important to understand not only how victims are depicted in the media, but also how human trafficking is defined in the media. Interestingly, we found that smuggling was the second most frequent crime type mentioned in the sample, with 23 percent of articles focused on the smuggling of individuals. As mentioned, smuggling was coded as a separate variable from trafficking because of the fundamental differences (i.e., not involving the key element of coercion and consensual intention of being transported to the destination) (Logan et al., 2009; Rafferty, 2013). It is also interesting that smuggling was found as a second crime type because the search query did not include smuggling, explicitly, yet these articles entered the sample because they utilized other keywords or terms. However, despite being different phenomena, the terms of smuggling and human trafficking were interchangeable in the articles. These findings align with the literature, in which human trafficking became linked to illegal migration, with traffickers exploiting people during movement across borders in the 2000s (Jahic & Finckenauer, 2005). Although human trafficking affects both U.S. national and foreign citizens, the association of human trafficking to U.S. homeland security and anti-terrorism campaigns was rooted in the 9/11 attacks, after which, trafficking was linked to the national discourse on immigration (Farrell & Fahy, 2009). Overall, this post-9/11 pattern is evident in the articles that linked smuggling to human trafficking, with smuggling being the second most frequent crime type coded in the sample.

As mentioned in the content analysis, we found that the vast majority of articles in the sample were labeled as labor trafficking because stories described workers being forced to work in some way. The interesting finding is that all but one of the labor trafficking articles focused on labor trafficking and illegal migration concerns. For example, some articles were about corporations exploiting immigrants, arranging for transportation of immigrants across borders to false promises, forced work, and/ or low pay. Therefore, we argue that the finding that labor trafficking is linked to immigration in all but one article is in alignment with literature showing that the public framing of human trafficking has shifted towards linking human trafficking to concerns about national security and illegal immigration (Farrell & Fahy, 2009; Kraska & Brent, 2011; Spector & Kitsuse, 1973).

On a similar note, and counter to literature, we found that only 19 percent of the subset of trafficking articles were explicitly focused on sex trafficking. It has been noted in the literature that sex trafficking is often more recognized in public discussion over labor trafficking because of highly politicized debates over sex trafficking and prostitution; however, it is notable that labor trafficking was discussed more frequently (Alvarez & Alessi, 2012; Logan et al., 2009). Although sex trafficking was discussed less in the trafficking articles, one could argue that this finding also reinforces the notion that labor trafficking, as it is linked to the discourse on national security and immigration, takes precedence during discussions regarding human trafficking. It also could be evidence that the discourse surrounding sex trafficking, which recognizes the high likelihood that individuals in the sex industry are potential victims of trafficking, has not yet been incorporated into the national discourse used by the media.

Although we did conduct an analysis of publication years and crime types, there were no significant patterns in which varying language was used or highlighted during specific years. Interestingly, however, it should be noted that human trafficking was not used explicitly to describe trafficking as a crime in the media until 2005. This 2005 article discussed a Korean sex trafficking ring and included the use of words like forced prostitution and sex trafficking to describe human trafficking. Although the TVPA defined and criminalized human trafficking in the United States in 2000, our data indicate a lag in adoption of the TVPA language by the news media and that widespread adoption of TVPA language was likely impacted by the changing sentiment surrounding immigration and national security concerns post-9/11.

LIMITATIONS

The findings here provide insight into how victims of human trafficking are represented in the media, specifically *The New York Times*, and how these depictions compare to the scholarly literature. There are, however, some limitations that should be noted. As stated, legislation and policy pertaining to human trafficking was excluded from the query of articles for this sample. As noted in the literature, prior to the 2000s, there was a shift in framing in which human trafficking became a growing concern and developed from a human rights issue to an immigration issue (Farrell & Fahy, 2009; Kraska & Brent, 2011; Spector & Kitsuse, 1973). Therefore, this may have excluded articles written earlier that discussed human trafficking in different terms, which might have proven useful in describing the evolution of human trafficking discourse.

Human trafficking is both a national and international phenomena; however, in this analysis the articles included were from the National Desk only. We excluded articles from the International Desk, which could impact how or whether victims are discussed in the media and the sample articles. A common misperception is that human trafficking victims are foreign; the TVPA (2000) does not require victims to actually cross borders or be immigrants (Farrell & Fahy, 2009). Associated with this, immigration and smuggling were not included specifically in this search, which may have limited the types of articles received. As mentioned, human trafficking has been linked to national security and immigration in the media and public starting in the 2000s; therefore, not specifically including words like immigration and smuggling in the search could impact the articles included in the sample and underrepresent the amount of trafficking-related articles during the time frame from 2001 to 2015.

There has also been a more recent focus on the demand or buyers of sex. The keywords used to search for articles did not explicitly include buyers or pimps. This could have limited the trafficking-specific articles included in the sample. As mentioned, there has been a shift in law enforcement and public discourse about the buyers of sex being responsible for the oppression of sex workers and driving commercial sexual exploitation (Shively et al., 2012). Therefore, the exclusion of these words in the article search could underrepresent the number of offender-oriented trafficking articles. Lastly, it was found that 14 percent of articles in the sample focused on high-profile cases pertaining to offenders and their trial process, which could impact how many articles focused on the offender and the type of crimes coded in the sample. In conclusion, the search terms and inclusion criterion likely impacted the patterns noticed in how victims and human trafficking were defined and portrayed in the media during the time period from 2001 to 2015.

NEXT STEPS/FUTURE RESEARCH

Overall, the findings and limitations highlight the importance of future analysis in to understand how victims of human trafficking are represented in the media. As mentioned, it is important to understand the shift in public discourse and framing about the definition of human trafficking, not only because it represents how human trafficking is deemed a concern for that specific time but also because of its influence on how the public and person(s) of law enforcement agencies may identify human trafficking victims. It is important to have a proper criminal justice response, but in order to do so, it is equally important to appropriately identify a victim as a victim and an offender as an offender (Gallagher & Holmes, 2008). Victims of trafficking are too often criminalized and traffickers or buyers of sex are only recently being thought of as responsible for the victimization (Gallagher & Holmes 2008; Shively et al., 2012). It can be argued that with the media's influence, and the continued public framing of linking national security concerns with human trafficking, the identification of victims may continue to encompass common misperceptions (e.g., foreign victims, choice in sex trafficking, etc.). Therefore, it would be critical for research to continue to analyze the shifts in public framing going forward as the media has an influence not only on public perception but also on policy, as public acceptance continues to be influenced by the media.

This analysis did not include articles that focused primarily on human trafficking legislation and policy; however, human trafficking was only more recently criminalized. Therefore, it would be important for researchers to analyze the systematic or institutional violence that can be re-traumatizing for victims. For example, the mislabeling of victims as offenders and varying state laws that criminalize minors of prostitution miss the mark on validating victims' experiences and providing needed supportive services. As states continue to criminalize human trafficking, and law enforcement agencies shift focus on the demand/buyers of sex, it would be interesting to analyze how this is discussed in the media and how this impacts the way victims are depicted. Overall, the media does have an influence on public perceptions, and therefore it is important to analyze how victims of human trafficking are represented in order to understand how legislation and policy move forward with growing public acceptance.

REFERENCES

Alvarez, M. B., & Alessi, E. J. (2012). Human trafficking is more than sex trafficking and prostitution: Implications for social work. *Affilia: Journal of Women and Social Work, 27*(2), 142–152. doi:10.1177/0886109912443763

Banks, D., & Kyckelhahn, T. (2011). *Characteristics of suspected human trafficking incidents: 2008–2010.* Washington, DC: Office of Justice Programs.

Belser, P. (2005). Forced labour and human trafficking: Estimating the profits. *Working Paper, 42*. Geneva: International Labour Office.

Berger, S. M. (2012). No end in sight: Why the "end demand" movement is the wrong focus for efforts to eliminate human trafficking. *Harvard Journal of Law & Gender, 35,* 523–570.

Bernat, F. P., & Zhilina, T. (2010). Human sex trafficking: The local becomes global. *Women and Criminal Justice, 20,* 2–9. doi:10.1080/08974451003641289

Bromfield, N. F. (2016). Sex slavery and sex trafficking of women in the United States: Historical and contemporary parallels, policies, and perspective in social work. *Affilia: Journal of Social Work, 21*(1), 129–139.

Bucken-Knapp, G., Schaffer, J. K., Stromback, K. P. (2012). Security, equality, and the clash of ideas: Sweden's evolving anti-trafficking policy. *Human Rights Review, 13,* 167–185. doi:10.1007/s12142-011-0214-y

Cecchet, S. J., & Thoburn, J. (2014). The psychological experience of child and adolescent sex trafficking in the United States: Trauma and resilience in survivors. *Psychological Trauma: Theory, Research, Practice, and Policy, 6*(5), 482–493. doi:10.1037/a0035763

Cobbina, J. E., & Oselin, S. S. (2011). It's not only for the money: An analysis of adolescent versus adult entry into street prostitution. *Sociological Inquiry, 81*(3), 310–332.

Dank, M., Khan, B., Downey, P. M., Kotonias, C., Mayer, D., Owens, C., ... Yu, L. (2014). *Estimating the size and structure of the underground commercial sex economy in eight major US cities.* Washington, DC: Urban Institute.

Farrell, A. (2014). Environmental and institutional influences on police agency responses to human trafficking. *Police Quarterly, 17*(1), 3–29.

Farrell, A., & Fahy, S. (2009). The problem of human trafficking in the U.S.: Public frames and policy responses. *Journal of Criminal Justice, 37,* 617–626. doi:10.1016/j.jcrimjus.2009.09.010

Farrell, A., McDevitt, J., Preffer, R., Fahy, S., Owens, C., Dank, M., & Adams, W. (2012). *Identifying challenges to improve the investigation and prosecution of state and local human trafficking cases.* Washington, D.C.: National Institute of Justice.

Gajic-Veljanoski, O., & Stewart, D. E. (2007). Women trafficked into prostitution: Determinants, human rights and health needs. *Transcultural Psychiatry, 44*(3), 338–358.

Gallagher, A., & Holmes, P. (2008). Developing an effective criminal justice response to human trafficking: Lessons from the front line. *International Criminal Justice Review, 18*(3), 318–343. doi:10.117/1057567708320746

Galtung, J. (1969). Violence, peace, and peace research. *Journal of Peace Research, 6*(3), 167–191.

George, S. (2012). The strong arm of the law is weak: How the Trafficking Victims Protection Act fails to assist effectively victims of the sex trade. *Creighton Law Review, 45,* 563–580.

Global Movement for Children. (2010). *Leaving home: Voices of children on the move.* Barcelona, Spain. Retrieved from http://www.gmfc.org/images/pdf/leavinghome.pdf

Hepburn, S., & Simon, R. J. (2010). Hidden in plain sight: Human trafficking in the United States. *Gender Issues, 27*(1), 1–26.

Hodge, D. R. (2008). Sexual trafficking in the United States: A domestic problem with transnational dimensions. *Social Work, 5*(2), 143–152.

Human Smuggling and Trafficking Center, The. (2006). *Fact sheet: Distinctions between human smuggling and human trafficking.* Retrieved from https://www.state.gov/documents/organization/90541.pdf

International Labour Organization. (2012). *A global alliance against forced labour and trafficking in persons.* Geneva, Switzerland: International Labour Organization.

Jahic, G., & Finckenauer, J. O. (2005). Representations and misrepresentations of human trafficking. *Trends in Organized Crime, 8*(3), 24–40.

Kelemen, K., & Johansson, M. C. (2013). Still neglecting the demand that fuels human trafficking: A study comparing the criminal laws and practice of five European states on human trafficking, purchasing sex from trafficked adults and from minors. *European Journal of Crime, Criminal Law, and Criminal Justice, 21,* 247–289. doi:10.1163/15718174-21042030

Kraska, P. B., & Brent, J. J. (2011). *Theorizing criminal justice.* Long Grove, IL: Waveland Press, Inc.

Leppanen, K. (2007). Movement of women: Trafficking in the interwar era. *Women's Studies International Forum, 30,* 523–533. doi:10.1016/j.wsif.2007.09.007

Logan, T. K., Walker, R., & Hunt, G. (2009). Understanding human trafficking in the United States. *Trauma, Violence, & Abuse, 10*(3), 3–30. doi:10.1177/1524838008808327262

Macy, R. J., & Graham, L. M. (2012). Identifying domestic and international sex-trafficking victims during human service provision. *Trauma, Violence, & Abuse, 13*(2), 59–76. doi:10.1177/1524838012440340

Macy, R. J., & Johns, N. (2011). Aftercare services for international sex trafficking survivors: Informing U.S. service and program development in an emerging practice area. *Trauma, Violence, & Abuse, 12*(2), 87–98. doi:10.1177/1524838010390709

Marcus, A., Horning, A., Curtis, R., Sanson, J., & Thompson, E. (2014). Conflict and agency among sex workers and pimps: A closer look at domestic minor sex trafficking. *Annals of the American Academy of Political and Social Science, 653*(1), 225–246.

Marinova, N. K., & James, P. (2012). The tragedy of human trafficking: Competing theories and European evidence. *Foreign Policy Analysis, 8,* 231–253. doi:10.1111/j.1743-8594.2011.00162x

Meshkovska, B., Siegel, M., Stutterheim, S. E., & Bos, A. E. R. (2015). Female sex trafficking: Conceptual issues, current debates, and future directions. *Journal of Sex Research, 52*(4), 380–395. doi:10.1080/00224499.2014.1002126

Miller, E., Decker, M. R., Silverman, J. G., & Raj, A. (2007). Migration, sexual exploitation, and women's health. *Violence Against Women, 13*(5), 456–497. doi:10.1177/1077801207301614

Mir, T. (2013). Trick or treat: Why minors engaged in prostitution should be treated as victims, not criminals. *Family Court Review, 51*(1), 163–177. doi:10.1111/fcre.12016

Nichols, A. (2016). *Sex trafficking in the United States: Theory, research, policy, and practice.* New York: Columbia University Press.

Polaris Project. (2013). Human trafficking trends in the United States: National Human Trafficking Resource Center, 2007–2012, *10*(2), 126–139.

Polaris Project. (2015). National Trafficking Resource Center (NHTRC) data breakdown: United States Report 1/1/2015–12/31/2015. Retrieved from https://polarisproject.org/resources/2015-hotline-statistics

Rafferty, Y. (2013). Child trafficking and commercial sexual exploitation: A review of promising prevention policies and programs. *American Journal of Orthopsychiatry, 83*(4), 559–575. doi:10.1111/ajop.12056

Raphael, J., & Shapiro, D. L. (2004). Violence in indoor and outdoor prostitution venues. *Violence Against Women, 10*(2), 126–139. doi:10.1177/1077801203260529

Raymond, J. G., & Hughes, D. M. (2001). *Sex trafficking of women in the United States: International and domestic trends*. U.S. Department of Justice. Retrieved from http://www.ncjrs.gov/pdffiles1/nij/grants/187774.pdf

Serughetti, G. (2012). Prostitution and clients' responsibility. *Men and Masculinities, 16*(1), 35–48.

Shively, M., Kliorys, K., Wheeler, K., & Hunt, D. (2012). *A national overview of prostitution and sex trafficking demand reduction efforts, final report*. Washington, DC: U.S. Department of Justice.

Smith, L. A., Healy Vardaman, S., & Snow, M. A. (2009). *The national report on domestic minor sex trafficking: America's prostituted children*. Vancouver, WA: Shared Hope International.

Snyder, H. (2012). *Patterns & trends: Arrests in the United States, 1990–2010*. Washington, DC: U.S. Department of Justice.

Spector, M., & Kitsuse, J. I. (1973). Social problems: A re-formulation. *Social Problems, 21*(2), 145–159.

The White House. (2003). *Trafficking in persons national security directive*. Office of the Press Secretary.

United Nations Trafficking Protocol. (2000). *United Nations protocol to prevent, suppress and punish trafficking in persons, especially women and children, Supplementing the United Nations Convention Against Transnational Organized Crime*. Retrieved from www.unodc.org

U.S. Department of Health & Human Services. (2012). *Fact sheet: Human trafficking*. Retrieved from http://www.acf.hhs.gov/programs/orr/resource/fact-sheet-human-trafficking

U.S. Department of Justice. (2014). *Crime in the United States. Federal crime data, 2014*.

U.S. Department of State. (2013). *Trafficking in persons report*. Retrieved from http://www.state.gov/j/tip/rls/tiprpt/2013/

Victims of Trafficking and Violence Protection Act (VTVPA) of 2000, Pub. L. 106-386. 114 Stat. 1464, codified as amended at 22 U.S.C. § 7101.

Weitzer, R. (2007). The social construction of sex trafficking: Ideology and institutionalization of a moral crusade. *Politics & Society, 35*(3), 447–475. doi:10.1177/0032329207304319

Williamson, C., & Prior, M. (2009). Domestic minor sex trafficking: A network of underground players in the Midwest. *Journal of Child & Adolescent Trauma, 2*, 46–61. doi:10.1080/19361520802702191

Yen, I. (2008). Of vice and men: A new approach to eradicating sex trafficking by reducing male demand through educational programs and abolitionist legislation. *The Journal of Criminal Law & Criminology, 98*(2), 653–686.

Zaykowski, H. (2014). Mobilizing victim services: The role of reporting to the police. *Journal of Traumatic Stress, 27*, 365–369. doi:10.1002/jts.21913

Zimmerman, C., Yun, K., Watts, C., Shvab, I., Trappolin, L., Treppete, M., ... Regan, L. (2003). *The health risks and consequences of trafficking in women and adolescents: Findings from a European study.* London: London School of Hygiene & Tropical Medicine.

KEY TERMS

- *Coercion:*

  - Threats of serious harm to or physical restraint against any person;

  - Any scheme, plan, or pattern intended to cause a person to believe that failure to perform an act would result in serious harm to or physical restraint against any person; or

  - The abuse or threatened abuse of the legal process (VTVPA, 2000).

- *Commercial Sex Act:* Any sex act on account of which anything of value is given to or received by any person (VTVPA, 2000).

- *Debt Bondage:* Status or condition of a debtor arising from a pledge by the debtor of his or her personal services or of those of a person under his or her control as a security for debt, if the value of those services as reasonably assessed is not applied toward the liquidation of the debt or the length and nature of those services are not respectively limited and defined (VTVPA, 2000).

- *Human Smuggling:* The facilitation, transportation, attempted transportation, or illegal entry of a person(s) across an international border, in violation of one or more countries' laws, either clandestinely or through deception, such as the use of fraudulent documents (Human Smuggling and Trafficking Center, 2006).

- *Severe Forms of Trafficking In Persons:*

  - Sex trafficking in which a commercial sex act is induced by force, fraud, or coercion, or in which the person induced to perform such act has not attained 18 years of age; or

- The recruitment, harboring, transportation, provision, or obtaining of a person for labor or services, through the use of force, fraud, or coercion for the purpose of subjection to involuntary servitude, peonage, debt bondage, or slavery (VTVPA, 2000).

- *Sex Trafficking:* Recruitment, harboring, transportation, provision, or obtaining of a person for the purpose of commercial sex (VTVPA, 2000).

THE NEW YORK TIMES ARTICLES

Associated Press. (2011). Farms charged with human trafficking. *The New York Times.* Retrieved from https://www.nytimes.com/2011/04/21/us/21brfs-Washington.html

Cave, D., & Almanzar, Y. (2008). Tactics used in U.S. raids draw claims of brutality. *The New York Times.* Retrieved from https://www.nytimes.com/2008/12/10/us/10florida.html

Georgia: Dozens arrested over sex-trafficking. (2015). *The New York Times.* Retrieved from https://www.nytimes.com/2015/10/31/us/georgia-dozens-arrested-over-sex-trafficking.html

Marshall, C. (2005). Agents said to dismantle a Korean sex ring. *The New York Times.* Retrieved from https://www.nytimes.com/2005/07/02/us/agents-said-to-dismantle-a-korean-sex-ring.html

Teenage prostitution ring broken in Detroit. (2003). *The New York Times.* Retrieved from: https://www.nytimes.com/2003/01/16/us/teenage-prostitution-ring-broken-in-detroit.html

DISCUSSION QUESTIONS

1. Media has an influence on public perception and discourse regarding criminal justice issues. Specifically, this section discussed the historical public framing of human trafficking. Discuss how human trafficking is discussed in the media today. As described, do you think it is still linked to concerns about immigration and national security?

2. Sex trafficking, a form of human trafficking, is discussed more often as a pressing issue in need of a criminal justice response in comparison to labor trafficking. Do you think this is true today? Where do you find examples in the media today?

3. The historical shifts of public framing of human trafficking discussed in this section went from trafficking being a human rights

issue to a reframing of trafficking by linking it to immigration and national security. Do you think the media and public perception will shift back to human trafficking being a human rights issue? Discuss what is happening today that makes you believe it would or would not shift back to a discussion around human rights rather than immigration.

About the Authors

Leana Bouffard, Ph.D., is Professor and Chair in the Department of Sociology at Iowa State University. Her research interests include violence against women, including criminal justice response to domestic violence and sexual assault, consequences of victimization, and sexual aggression among college students. She also conducts research on life course and developmental approaches to understanding offending, including the impact of various life events (e.g., military service and parenting/parenthood) on offending patterns. Her work has been published in *Criminology*, *Justice Quarterly*, and *Criminal Justice and Behavior*, among others.

John Brent, Ph.D., is an Assistant Professor in the School of Justice Studies at Eastern Kentucky University. He holds a Ph.D. in Criminology from the University of Delaware. His interests focus on the cultural and structural dynamics of crime and crime control, how institutions create and perpetuate inequalities, building a theoretical foundation for criminal justice theory, and how individuals are disciplined and punished. Among other projects, his recent work includes a series of publications examining the intersections of institutional discipline and punishment, cultural dispositions, and inequality.

Carol Burciaga-Kirchner was born and raised in Albuquerque, New Mexico, where she also completed her undergraduate degree at The University of New Mexico with a Bachelor's Degree in Criminology with a minor in Sociology. After working in public and private substance abuse and rehabilitation centers as a Substance Abuse Technician, she wanted to continue her education. She graduated from Seattle University in 2017 with a Master's Degree in Criminal Justice with a specialization in

Investigative Criminology. In her free time, she enjoys travel and reading books of all genres.

Steven M. Chermak, Ph.D., is a Professor in the School of Criminal Justice at Michigan State University. He studies domestic terrorism, media coverage of crime and justice issues, and the effectiveness of specific policing strategies. Recent publications have appeared in *Terrorism & Political Violence* and *Journal of Quantitative Criminology.*

Peter A. Collins, Ph.D., is an Associate Professor in the Criminal Justice Department at Seattle University. He earned his Ph.D. in Criminal Justice from Washington State University in 2011 with a focus on corrections, cost-benefit and evaluation research, and criminal justice organizations. His research interests include issues surrounding the death penalty, the intersection of criminal law and criminal justice policy, public policy analysis, and criminology within the context of popular culture. His work has been published in *The Journal of Criminal Justice, The Journal of Offender Rehabilitation, Criminal Justice Studies, Western Criminology Review, Police Quarterly, The Prison Journal, Criminal Justice Policy Review, The Journal of Crime and Justice, The Seattle Journal for Social Justice,* Routledge Press, Carolina Academic Press, LFB Scholarly Publishing, Oxford University Press, and Cognella Academic Publishing, among other outlets.

David Patrick Connor, Ph.D., is an independent criminologist. For three years, Dr. Connor served as an Assistant Professor of Criminal Justice at Seattle University in Seattle, Washington. Primarily recognized as an expert on sex offender legislation, Dr. Connor is regularly consulted by correctional agencies and interviewed by media outlets about such laws. His other work often focuses on the experiences of individuals involved in the criminal justice system, including justice system professionals, justice-involved people, and survivors and their families.

Devan M. Duenas is a researcher at the Treuman Katz Center for Pediatric Bioethics at Seattle Children's Hospital and Research Institute.

His current work is in research ethics, human challenge trials, informed consent, decision-making, and stakeholder engagement. Mr. Duenas earned his Master's Degree in Criminal Justice at Seattle University with a specialization in Investigative Criminology where he researched hate crime victimization. Prior to his graduate education, Mr. Duenas earned his Bachelor's in Criminology, Law & Society and Psychology & Social Behavior where he researched false memory, susceptibility, and eyewitness misidentification.

Joshua D. Freilich, Ph.D., is a member of the Criminal Justice Department at John Jay College/The Graduate Center, CUNY. He is a creator and co-director of the Extremist Crime Database (ECDB), a creator and co-director of the School Shooting Database (SSDB) and the Chair (2017–2019) of the American Society of Criminology's Division on Terrorism and Bias Crimes. Freilich's research has been funded by the U.S. Department of Homeland Security and the U.S. National Institute of Justice.

Andrea Giuffre, is a doctoral student in the Criminology and Criminal Justice Department at the University of Missouri—St. Louis (UMSL). Giuffre currently works with Dr. Beth Huebner on the Arnold Foundation Multi-State Study of Monetary Sanctions. Prior to arriving at UMSL, Giuffre earned her Master of Arts in Criminal Justice with a specialization in Victimology from Seattle University. Her research interests include sexual assault prevention, sex offender treatment and rehabilitation, restorative justice, procedural justice, and punishment policy.

Jeff Gruenewald, Ph.D., is an Associate Professor in the School of Public and Environmental Affairs at Indiana University Purdue University, Indianapolis (IUPUI). His research interests include violence, terrorism and homeland security policy, hate crime, and media coverage of crime and justice issues. His research has been funded by the National Consortium for the Study of Terrorism and Responses to Terrorism (START Center), a Department of Homeland Security Center of Excellence, and the National Institute of Justice. Some of his recent published work has appeared in journals such as *Justice Quarterly, Journal of Quantitative Criminology, Criminology and Public Policy, Terrorism & Political Violence*, and *Crime & Delinquency*.

Caitlin M. Healing is an embedded Intelligence Analyst with a Fortune 500 company based out of Silicon Valley. She obtained her Master of Arts in Criminal Justice with an emphasis in Investigative Criminology from Seattle University and a Bachelor of Science in Psychology with an emphasis in Personality from Saint Mary's College of California. Her research interests include hate groups, social media, and physical security threats. A native of California, she spent time in Seattle working as a researcher for U.S. Probation and Pretrial Services and currently resides in Austin, Texas, with her dog, Wally.

Jacqueline B. Helfgott, Ph.D., is Professor and Director of the Seattle University Department of Criminal Justice Crime and Justice Research Center. She has a Ph.D. and Master's Degree in Administration of Justice with a graduate minor in Psychology from Pennsylvania State University and a Bachelor's Degree from the University of Washington in Psychology and Society & Justice. Her research interests include criminal behavior, psychopathy, copycat crime, corrections, offender reentry, and community and restorative justice. She is author of *No Remorse: Psychopathy and Criminal Justice* (Praeger, 2019), *Criminal Behavior: Theories, Typologies, and Criminal Justice* (SAGE Publications, 2008), editor of *Criminal Psychology*, Volumes 1–4 (Praeger, 2013), and coauthor of *Offender Reentry: Beyond Crime and Punishment* (Lynne Rienner Publishers, 2013) and *Women Leading Justice: Experiences and Insights* (Routledge, 2019). She is currently working on a book entitled *Copycat Crime: How Mass Media and Digital Culture Influence Criminal Behavior* (Praeger). Her work has been published in journals including *Aggression and Violent Behavior; International Journal of Law & Psychiatry; Criminal Justice & Behavior; International Journal of Offender Therapy and Comparative Criminology; Journal of Forensic Psychology Practice; Journal of Police and Criminal Psychology; International Review of Victimology; Crime Victim's Report; Federal*

Probation; Criminal Justice Policy Review; Corrections: Policy, Practice, and Research; Journal of Community Corrections, the Journal of Theoretical and Philosophical Criminology; and *Journal of Qualitative Criminal Justice & Criminology.*

Matthew J. Hickman, Ph.D., is Associate Professor and Chair of the Department of Criminal Justice at Seattle University. In addition to conducting research in the general areas of police behavior and quantitative research methods, he teaches a variety of courses including statistics, research methods, ethics, and crime mapping. He was previously employed as a statistician at the Bureau of Justice Statistics (BJS), the statistical research arm of the U.S. Department of Justice. Hickman is a past President of the Western Society of Criminology, and he also served on the inaugural board of the American Society of Criminology Division of Policing.

Sarah 'Maurya' Hiden currently works for the Washington State Department of Corrections Graduated Reentry Program as a Community Corrections Officer. In 2017, she completed her Master of Arts in Criminal Justice with a focus in investigative criminology at Seattle University. She previously completed a Bachelor of Arts in Criminal Justice and Psychology at the University of Washington. Her research interests include prison reform, offender reentry, social injustice, sex offender treatment and rehabilitation, and juvenile rehabilitation.

Gloria Lara is currently a Senior Analyst for Data-Driven Policing at the Seattle Police Department. As a Senior Analyst, she is responsible for administrative and strategic analysis and assists with the department's crime and accountability meeting, SeaStat. Ms. Lara earned a Master of Arts in Criminal Justice with a specialization in Investigative Criminology from Seattle University and a Bachelor of Arts in Criminal Justice from California State University, Fullerton. Her research interests include evidence-based policing practices, police/community collaboration, and crime and intelligence analysis.

Stephanie Martinez is currently a Research Coordinator for Michigan State University, in which she manages a statewide longitudinal evaluation about domestic violence and housing in California. Stephanie is passionate about the intersectionality between housing stability, homelessness, and survivors of crime. She earned her Master's Degree in Criminal Justice with a specialization in Victimology from Seattle University. Stephanie calls the Pacific Northwest home and enjoys mountain biking and hiking with her dog, Koa.

Zachary S. Mitnik is a Ph.D. candidate in the Criminal Justice Department at John Jay College. He is a Research Assistant for the United States School Shooting Database, an open-source relational database of gun violence incidents on school grounds in the United States. His research focuses on how our narratives and definitions of terrorism shape our responses and policies.

William S. Parkin, Ph.D., is an Associate Professor in the Department of Criminal Justice at Seattle University. His research interests include ideological violence, violent victimization, and the relationship between the media and the criminal justice system. His work has been published in the *Journal of Quantitative Criminology, Homicide Studies, PLos ONE, Crime & Delinquency, Journal of Interpersonal Violence, Economic Letters, International Criminal Justice Review, Terrorism & Political Violence, Perspectives on Terrorism and Studies in Conflict & Terrorism* and *Sociological Spectrum.*

Rebecca Pfeffer, Ph.D., is an Assistant Professor of Criminal Justice at the University of Houston—Downtown. Her research focuses generally on the victimization of vulnerable populations, including victims with special needs and victims of human trafficking. Her current research focuses on public policies addressing prostitution, both in terms of the buying and selling of sex, and specifically investigates effective law enforcement response to the problem of prostitution.

Karmen Schuur currently resides in Seattle where she works as a Data-Driven Analyst with the Seattle Police Department, providing strategic assistance and information to command staff. She holds a Master's Degree in Criminal Justice from Seattle University and a Bachelor's in Psychology from the University of Washington. Her other written work includes a Master's thesis on the impacts of the federal oversight on the Seattle Police Department. When not reading with a cat loafed upon her chest, she enjoys hiking, running, and cooking with her husband.

Amy Shlosberg, Ph.D., is an Associate Professor of Criminology at Fairleigh Dickinson University where she teaches a variety of courses, including Wrongful Convictions, Offender Reentry and Reintegration, Race and Crime, Penology, Comparative Justice Systems, Data Analysis, and Research Methods. Her primary research focuses on the negative implications of incarceration and issues surrounding reentry, with an emphasis on policy and procedural reform. Her works in this area have been accepted for publication in several academic journals, including the *Albany Law Review, Journal of Criminal Law and Criminology*, and *Deviant Behavior*.

Brittany Stinett currently works as a Residential Counselor for Juvenile Rehabilitation in the State of Washington. She completed her Master of Arts in Criminal Justice at Seattle University in 2017 and previously received her Bachelor of Arts in Criminal Justice with a minor in Human Rights at The University of Washington-Tacoma. She is an active participant in giving back to the community with current volunteer positions at The Pierce County Juvenile Court and The IF Project in Seattle.

Mary K. Stohr, Ph.D., is a professor in the Department of Criminal Justice and Criminology at Washington State University. She has published over 90 academic works, including seven books and over 60 journal articles, primarily in the area of corrections. Her current research concerns the effects of solitary confinement and marijuana law implementation. She served as Executive Director of the Academy of Criminal Justice Sciences for five years, and received the Founder's Award from ACJS in 2009 and the Fellow's Award in 2018. Many moons ago she worked as a correctional officer and then as a counselor in an adult male prison.

Kelly Szabo is married, with three kids and one dog. She holds a Certificate in Crime Analysis and a Master of Arts in Criminal Justice (with a specialization in Investigative Criminology), both from Seattle University. Kelly has worked in various positions in the criminal justice field, including personal recognizance and administrative. She is currently employed with the King County Sheriff's Office, Patrol Operations Division, and enjoys running, practicing Spanish, and hunting for agates. Kelly resides with her family in King County, Washington.

Chelsea Toby was born and raised in California, but has lived in the Seattle area since moving to attend the University of Washington. After receiving her Bachelor of Arts in Law, Societies, and Justice, she attended Seattle University and received her Master of Arts in Criminal Justice. She is currently working as a Background Investigator and hopes to eventually work in the field of juvenile justice or offender reentry.

Elisabeth Walls. After transitioning from a career in journalism and marketing, Elisabeth Walls now employs her research, analysis, and writing skills in the criminal justice and national security field. Elisabeth earned her Master's Degree in criminal justice from Seattle University where she focused her research on the intersection of traditional, new, and social media with crime and criminal justice. Her specific research interests include examining the use of social media by law enforcement and the impact of traditional and online media on criminal behavior, criminal justice policy, and public opinion of criminal justice issues.

Kevin Wright, Ph.D., is an Associate Professor in the School of Criminology and Criminal Justice and Director of the Center for Correctional Solutions at Arizona State University. His work focuses on enhancing the lives of those living and working in the correctional system through research, education, and community engagement. His published research on these topics has appeared in *Justice Quarterly, Criminology & Public Policy,* and *Journal of Offender Rehabilitation,* and he is the co-editor of *Criminology & Public Policy: Putting Theory to Work* (2nd ed., Temple University Press).

Index

intimidation, 243
isolation. *See* social isolation

J

Jewish, 308
Jihadi, 327
Johnson, Micah, 8
justifiable homicide, 101, 128
juvenile, 101, 128. *See also* victim-offender relationships
age of, 101
as victims, 86

K

killed in the line of duty, 11, 13, 27
King, Rodney, 3
Klebold, Dylan, 243

L

labor exploitation, 346
law enforcement agencies, 5–6
law enforcement families, intimate
partner violence, 137–139
Law Enforcement Killed in the Line of
Duty (LEOKA), 11
law enforcement officers, 11–13
legal/procedural innocence, 30
LGBTQ youth, 136
lifestyle/opportunity theory, 63, 94–95
Lindsay, R. C., 35
liquor sales, high-risk occupations,
223
Loftus, E. F., 35
The Los Angeles Times, 25

M

MacCrate report, 42
males. *See* homosexual males
Mann Act of 1910, 350
manslaughter. *See* non-negligent
manslaughter
marginalization, 245
masculine attitude, 165

masculinity, 245
mass shooting
in school violence, 252–256
in workplace violence, 206, 210
media-mediated crimes, 281
media potrayals of
of hate crime, 308–309
human trafficking, 364–366
sexual violence, 167–168
victimization, 84–88
medical neglect, victimization, 75
Mejia, P., 167
#MeToo movement, 163
middle schools, 245
minorities, 5, 9–10. *See also* racial
minorities
moral panic, 167, 195, 239
murder and non-negligent
manslaughter, 100–101
Muslims, 308

N

National Center for Education
Statistics (NCES), 241
National Crime Victimization Survey
(NCVS), 132, 158, 305
National Electronic Injury
Surveillance System occupational
injury supplement (NEISS-Work),
70–71
National Human Trafficking Hotline
Resource Center (NHTRC),
348
National Instant Criminal
Background Check (NICS)
Improvement Amendment, 240
National Institute of Justice, 240
National Intimate Partner and Sexual
Violence Survey, 132, 158–159
National Prisoner Survey (NIS), 68
national security, 353–354. *See
also* human trafficking
National Security Presidential
Directive, 353

National Sexual Violence Resource Center, 161–162
National Survey of Children's Exposure to Violence II (NatSCEV), 247–248
National Survey of Children's Exposure to Violence (NatSCEV) Series, 242
National Survey of Youth in Custody (NSYC), 68
negative stimuli, 208
negligent manslaughter, 101
newsworthiness, 182–185
    in school violence, 256–261
    of victims of youth homicide offenders, 120–123
The New York Times, 3, 15, 23, 31, 111
    attributes of hate crime articles in, 309–311
    human trafficking, articles analysis, 358–363
    intimate partner violence, reporting in, 144–148
nonconsensual sex acts, 62
non-Hispanics, 135
non-lethal physical violence, 140
non-negligent manslaughter, 101
no rehab, victimization, 75
normal crime, 308
Nuefeld, Peter, 42

O

occupation
    of offenders, 179–182
    of victims, 175–177
occupation, of victims, 175–177
Oedipus, 99
offender, 165–166. *See also* youth homicide offenders
    age groups, 108–109, 113–115
    organized criminal groups as, 352
offense, 166–167
Office of Justice Programs, 240

Office of Juvenile Justice and Delinquency Prevention, 102
officer-on-prisoner assault, 62
officers. *See* police officers
Office to Monitor and Combat Trafficking in Persons, 353
oil rig explosion, 213, 224
Oregon Killer Described as Man of Few Words, Except on Topic of Guns, 230
Orestes, 99
othering, 168
other rights violation, victimization, 75
overt harassment, 208–209

P

Pacific Islanders, 307
Packer, Herbert, 31
Palmero Protocol, 351
partner. *See* intimate partners
patriarchal terrorism. *See* coercive controlling violence
perception. *See* police perception
personal/domestic relation-on-employee, 210
personal relationships, 136, 205
physical abuse, 356
physical assault, victimization, 75
physical fitness, high-risk occupations, 223
physical victimization, 65
physical violence, 131, 158
pimping, 346
pimps, 245–246
police officers, 3–4, 8, 10–12, 137–138
    family members of, 12
police perception, 5, 13–14
police use of deadly force, 3, 27
policing
    biased, 10
    community-oriented, 6, 27
    overview, 3–8
    political era of, 4
    reform era of, 5

severe forms of trafficking in persons, 342, 374–375

sex
intimate partner violence, 132–134
offenders, 177–179
of victims, 173–175
of youth homicide offenders, 103–104

sex act. *See* commercial sex act

Sex Purchase Act of 1999, 352

sex trafficking, 342, 345, 375
child victims of, 356
mental health disorders in, 356

sexual assault. *See* sexual violence

sexual assault perpetration, 165, 189

sexual beliefs. *See* aggressive sexual beliefs

sexual harass, victimization, 75

sexual orientation, intimate partner violence, 136–137

sexual victimization, 65

sexual violence, 131, 159, 161–232
analysis of, 186–189
literature review, 164–168
location of, 170–171
media depictions of, 167–168
overview, 161–164

sex work. *See* sex trafficking

shooting. *See* ambush shootings; school shootings

shoving, 131

situational couple violence, 133, 159

slavery. *See* debt bondage

smuggling. *See* human smuggling

social isolation, 244

social learning theory, 280, 297

social movement, 55

social service workers, workplace violence, 202

social work, high-risk occupations, 223

socioeconomic status, 205–206

solitary confinement, victimization, 75

Sparks, R., 14

speaking. *See* public speaking

spill over, 138

SSV. *See* Survey of Sexual Victimization (SSV)

staff-on-prisoner assault, 65

stalking, 131, 159. *See also* cyberstalking

state violence, 29–34

status. *See* generational status

stereotypes of sex offenders, 167

Sterling, Alton, 7

stimuli
negative, 208
positive, 208

strain theory. *See* general strain theory

stranger-on-employee workplace violence. *See* type 1 workplace violence

students. *See* deaf students

substance abuse, 136, 161. *See also* intimate partner violence

suburban communities, 242

suicide, 64–65, 67, 206

Supplementary Homicide Report, 102–103, 108–111

Survey of Sexual Victimization (SSV), 67–68

T

taxi driver, workplace violence, 202–203

teachers. *See* school teachers

teasing, 248

terrorism, 325–339
defined, 326
in the media, 328–335
in United States, 326–327

Time's Up, 163

traffickers, 345

transphobia, 137

trauma, 248. *See also* vicarious trauma

tunnel vision, 36–37

type 1 workplace violence, 198–199, 236

type 2 workplace violence, 199, 201, 236

type 3 workplace violence, 199, 201, 204–205, 236
type 4 workplace violence, 199, 237

U

underreporting, 305, 322
Uniform Crime Reports Hate Crime Statistics, 303, 322
Upper Big Branch Mine, 223–224
urban communities, 242

V

vandalism, 248
Vanderbilt Rape Trial Didn't Stir Vanderbilt, 179
verbal abuse, 202
verbal bullying, 247. *See also* bullying
vicarious trauma, 162
victim blaming, 82, 95
victimization, 4–5
    characteristics of, 75–78
    within correctional facilities, 62–71
    of correctional officers, 70–71
    limitations/implications for future research, 88–90
    media portrayals of, 84–88
    motives for, 82
    of older prisoners, 69
    responsibility for, 82
    in school violence, 257–259
    types, 8–24
victim/offender overlap, 63, 95
victim-offender relationships, 107–108, 128, 171–172
victims. *See also* sexual violence; wrongful conviction
    age of, 80, 173
    analysis in wrongful conviction, 52–56
    communities, 14–15
    of cyberbullying, 271–272
    of cyberstalking, 277
    demographics, 50–52
    disadvantaged groups, 6, 9–10

ethnic groups as, 5
focus by severity of attack and target, 334–335
of hate crimes, 311–316
identification by severity of attack and target, 332
of incarceration, 72–75
incarceration of, 72–75, 78–81
incident-level newsworthiness measures for, 120–123
law enforcement officers, 11–13
minorities, 5, 9–10
portrayal of, 78–82
race/ethnicity, 80–81
of sexual violence, 164–165
of terrorism, 331–335
types, 8–24
of workplace violence, 221–228
victims of terrorism, analyzing patterns of, 335–338
Victims of Trafficking & Violence Protection Act (VTVPA), 342
violence
    coercive controlling, 133
    intimate partner, 131–153
    physical, 131
    school, 239–264, 266
    sexual. *See* sexual violence
    situational couple, 133, 159
    state, 29–34
    type 2. *See* type 2 workplace violence
    type 3. *See* type 3 workplace violence
    types of, 150
    type 1 workplace, 198–199, 236
    type 4 workplace, 199, 237
    workplace. *See* workplace violence
Virginia Tech shooting, 213
virtual violence, 269–293, 298
    analysis of victims of, 287–291
    criminological theories, 279–280. *See also* specific theory
    overview, 260–270

vision. *See* tunnel vision
VTVPA. *See* Victims of Trafficking &
    Violence Protection Act (VTVPA)

W

The Washington Post, 22
weapons used by, youth homicide
    offenders, 105
wedding cake theory, 53–54
Wells, G. L., 35
White Slave Traffic Act. *See* Mann Act
    of 1910
witnesses, 34
workplace violence, 197–232, 237
    gender differences, 205–206
    mass shooting, 206
    overview, 197
    policy implications for, 210
    prevalence of, 199–200
    statistics on, 203–204
    theories, 207–209
    types of, 198–199, 224–225
World Prison Brief, 61

wrongful conviction, 29–56
    cause of, 50
    content analysis in, 46–52
    cost of, 40–41
    innocents in, 34–40
    state violence, 29–34
    victims, analysis of, 52–56

Y

Yoshioka, M. R., 135
youth homicide offenders, 99–126
    age of, 101–103
    analyzing victims of, 124–125
    newsworthiness of victims of,
        120–123
    overview, 99–101
    race of, 104–105
    sex of, 103–104
    weapons used by, 105–107

Z

Zanni, G., 35
zero-tolerance policies, 239

CPSIA information can be obtained
at www.ICGtesting.com
Printed in the USA
LVHW080154240421
685374LV00010B/16